A GUIDE TO
EZRA POUND'S
PERSONÆ
(1926)

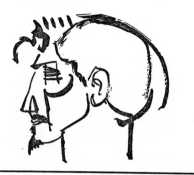

A GUIDE TO
EZRA POUND'S
PERSONÆ
(1926)

K. K. RUTHVEN

UNIVERSITY OF CALIFORNIA PRESS
BERKELEY AND LOS ANGELES 1969

University of California Press
Berkeley and Los Angeles, California
University of California Press, Ltd.
London, England

PREFACE

Early in 1925 there appeared a limited edition of *A Draft of XVI. Cantos,* described on the title page as "The Beginning of a Poem of some Length." It was the result of a decade of experimentation, a demonstration that Pound had at last discovered an epic form into which all his poetic energies might be channeled. He was in his fortieth year and it seemed an appropriate time to collect the best of his earlier poems in a volume that might be seen, retrospectively, as prentice work. The canonical volume was published by Boni and Liveright in 1926 as *Personæ: The Collected Shorter Poems of Ezra Pound,* and served its purpose for almost a quarter of a century, if not longer, for recently augmented editions by New Directions (1949) and Faber and Faber (1968) make very few alterations to the original canon. To students of modernism, *Personæ* (1926) is a landmark in the period, and in supplying an imaginary newcomer to this volume with a set of annotations I have collected what I feel to be the important discoveries made about these poems, and added comments on aspects that have been overlooked. Memories of my own undergraduate days, and experience of teaching undergraduates, convince me that one can take very little for granted, and so I have made a practice of overannotating. The notes are grouped under the title of the poem to which they refer, and the titles then arranged alphabetically so that the book can be consulted in dictionary fashion. Original texts are supplied in the case of poems translated from the French, Provençal, German, Italian, Latin, and Greek, but not from the Chinese, for Pound's Chinese translations are based on English versions by various sinologists, notably Fenollosa. In addition, I have tried to identify allusions, trace the origin and recurrence of common themes in Pound's work, and relate them to similar preoccupations in contemporary writing. Important stages in the printing history of the poems in *Personæ* (1926) are recorded in a Chronological List. A full collation yields several hundred variants, the bulk of which testify only to Pound's carelessness as a proofreader; they will have to be recorded eventually, but this is not the place for them. Instead, I have selected what seem to be the few significant textual divergencies from the

1926 text published by Boni and Liveright (conveniently offset-reprinted in 1949 by New Directions), and have incorporated these among the annotations. Since British readers will use the Faber and Faber reprint of 1968, I have also noted important errors, corrections, and omissions in the Faber and Faber text.

Information about the printing history of each poem is enclosed in square brackets immediately after the title. PORTRAIT D'UNE FEMME, for example, is followed by "[NO. 62. PRINTINGS: 15, 42, 43, 53, 55]." This means that PORTRAIT D'UNE FEMME is the sixty-second poem recorded in the Chronological List (pp. 23–30) and was printed in the books classified there by the italic numbers 15 (*Ripostes*, 1912), 42 (*Lustra*, 1917, unabridged), 43 (*Lustra*, 1917, *abridged*), 53 (*Umbra*, 1920), and 55 (*Personæ*, 1926). The fourth line of this poem begins with the word "Ideas" in all texts except the one printed in *Umbra*, where "Ideas" becomes "Ideals." The textual discrepancy is noted thus: "[4. Ideas   *15–43, 55; Ideals   53*]." In line seventeen, on the other hand, it is the *Personæ* text which introduces a new reading by substituting "a tale or two" for "a tale for two"; hence: "[17. tale for   *15–53;*   tale or   *55*]." If the change had occurred as early as *Lustra*, it would have been recorded as "[17. tale for   *15;*   tale or   *42+*]." Alterations to titles, subtitles, epigraphs, and footnotes are listed in exactly the same way.

To avoid cluttering the book with material of secondary importance, I have not acknowledged the source of every specific item taken from the corpus of Pound scholarship. All the books and articles that have contributed annotations are listed in the bibliography, and my indebtedness to them will be obvious to those who know about Pound.

K. K. R.

University of Canterbury
New Zealand

ACKNOWLEDGMENTS

To the University Grants Committee of New Zealand, for a research grant; and to Amy L. Jamieson and Catherine Swift, for providing the necessary books, articles, and microfilms.

To John D. Jump, Hugh Kenner, Frank Kermode, and an unidentified publishers' reader, all of whom contributed helpful advice and numerous points of information.

To the representatives of Faber and Faber and New Directions, who kindly answered my queries about the publishing history of Pound's poems; and to my publishers, for invaluable assistance with copyright and editorial problems.

To the University of Chicago Library and the Lockwood Memorial Library, for supplying microfilms of Pound's unpublished correspondence; and to the Committee for Ezra Pound for permission to quote from this unpublished material.

To New Directions Publishing Corporation for permission to reprint selections from the following books:
(a) copyright by Ezra Pound: *Personæ*, © 1926, 1954; *Cavalcanti Poems*, © 1966; *Pavannes and Divagations*, © 1958; *The Cantos*, copyright 1934, 1937, 1940, 1948, © 1956, 1959.
(b) all rights reserved by New Directions Publishing Corporation: *ABC of Reading, The Spirit of Romance, Gaudier-Brzeska, The Literary Essays, Guide to Kulchur.*
(c) copyright by Ezra Pound and New Directions Publishing Corporation: *A Lume Spento and Other Early Poems*, © 1965.

To New Directions Publishing Corporation, agents for Dorothy Pound, for permission to reprint selections from *Jefferson and/or Mussolini*, copyright 1935, 1936 by Ezra Pound.

To Harvard University Press for quotations from the following volumes in the Loeb Classical Library (copyright by the President and Fellows of Harvard College): *Catullus, Tibullus and Pervigilium Veneris; The Greek Anthology; Greek Bucolic Poets; Horace: Odes and Epodes; Homer: Iliad and Odyssey; Lyra Graeca; Ovid: Metamorphoses; Pindar: Odes; Scriptores Historiae Augustae; Propertius.*

And finally to my wife, to whom a more original book would have been dedicated.

CONTENTS

INTRODUCTION, 1

CHRONOLOGICAL LIST OF THE POEMS IN *Personæ* (1926), 23

NOTES ON THE POEMS IN *Personæ* (1926), 31

Appendixes:

   (*a*) ADDITIONAL POEMS IN *Personæ* (1949), 248
   (*b*) ILLUSTRATIONS, EPIGRAPHS, DEDICATIONS, ETC., 261
   (*c*) ADDITIONAL POEMS IN *Collected Shorter Poems*
      (1968), 265

BIBLIOGRAPHY, 269

INTRODUCTION

I

Our gradual emancipation from Romantic aesthetics is making us more tolerant of artifice in poetry. The true voice of feeling, we discover, has more often than not been schooled in the art of expressing feeling, and in literature spontaneity is always the result of art. We are no longer suspicious of poetry that needs to be annotated, and yet to compare an edition of Milton with the annotations assembled in this *Guide* is to be made aware of the fact that there are different ways of being allusive, and that Pound differs from Milton in the sort of material to which he alludes. Whereas Milton's classicizing was a way of enriching his readers' experience by bringing to bear on his theme a body of knowledge that was by no means unfamiliar to an educated contemporary, Pound's allusiveness is often so idiosyncratic that the ideal reader of the *Cantos* is not any one man but a committee of specialists in classics, Romance languages, history, economics, English and American literature, and Oriental studies. Writing at a time when there is no longer a body of knowledge common to all educated men, Pound has created a poetry that draws on his private reading in a variety of literatures. Lacking a common tradition, he created a tradition of his own; he tried to be a learned poet at a time when the conditions that foster learned poetry had ceased to exist.

The origins of Pound's allusive method are not hard to find. At university Pound specialized in Romance languages and was trained in the methods of comparative literature. *The Spirit of Romance* (1910) reveals what sort of books he was reading in these years and the manner in which he read them. It proves that his interest in Provençal poetry, Dante, Villon, and so on was primarily critical: he studied them not for linguistic reasons or as material for *Stoffgeschichte* but with a view to evolving a scale of comparative literary values that would enable him to "weigh Theocritus and Mr. Yeats with one balance." [1] *The Spirit of Romance* is the history of a search for standards of excellence in literature, a search based largely

[1] *The Spirit of Romance* (London, 1910), p. vi.

on the literatures of southern Europe. At the same time as he was trying to weigh Theocritus and Yeats with one balance, however, Pound was also trying to become a poet. The two disciplines were complementary: Pound brought a poet's insight to the academic study of literature, and he also carried the methods of comparative literary studies into the art of poetry. For underlying all Pound's statements about criticism or poetry is the assumption that literature is basically a matter of technical discoveries, a record of the methods by which literature has managed to cope with the varieties of human experience. But the findings of scholarship are felt to impose certain responsibilities on the practicing poet. If literature is technique then the writing of literature is a craft, a craft that has to be learned by the novitiate poet. In his apprenticeship to the craft of letters the young poet "should master all known forms and systems of metric" [2] and imitate the work of the great, for "one finds that all the old masters of painting recommend to their pupils that they begin by copying masterwork, and proceed to their own composition." [3] Several of Pound's early poems might well be called "A Poem in the Manner of Villon," or Rossetti, or Bertran de Born, or any of a dozen other writers. By pastiche the beginner learns how the most characteristic effects of the great poets have been achieved in terms of purely verbal arrangements. As a result of these carefully planned exercises his own technical resources will be increased so that when the time comes for him to write original work he will not be handicapped by technical inadequacy.

In becoming a voluntary apprentice to dead masters the young poet learns a good deal about subject matter as well as about poetic technique. A careful reading of literature from Homer to Yeats makes it difficult for him to have a Romantic respect for the uniqueness of subjective experience; certain themes and attitudes have already been repeated too often to make it worthwhile repeating them anymore. Pound listed some of these commonplaces in 1908:

1. Spring is a pleasant season. The flowers, etc. etc. sprout bloom etc. etc.
2. Young man's fancy. Lightly, heavily, gaily etc. etc.
3. Love, a delightsome tickling. Indefinable etc.
   A) By day, etc. etc. etc. B) By night, etc. etc. etc.
4. Trees, hills etc. are by a provident nature arranged diversely, in diverse places.
5. Winds, clouds, rains, etc. flop thru and over 'em.
6. Men love women. . . .

[2] "Prolegomena," *Poetry Review*, I, 2 (Feb. 1912), 73.
[3] *Ibid.*, p. 74.

7. Men fight battles, etc. etc.
8. Men go on voyages.[4]

The inference was obvious: "Why write what I can translate out of Renaissance Latin or crib from the sainted dead?" [5] For many poets this attitude would impose the most crippling limitations, but Pound seems not to have minded spending several years writing poems that are little more than pastiches. Consequently, the marketing of commonplaces in the guise of originality has always struck him as being fraudulent and unpardonable.

> If a certain thing was said once for all in Atlantis or Arcadia, in 450 Before Christ or in 1290 after, it is not for us moderns to go saying it over, or to go obscuring the memory of the dead by saying the same thing with less skill and less conviction.[6]

The poets referred to in "Fratres Minores" are criticized for precisely these reasons: semieducated in their craft, they

> Still sigh over established and natural fact
> Long since fully discussed by Ovid.[7]

Robert Frost, on the other hand, is admired for "not using themes that anybody could have cribbed out of Ovid." [8]

From observations like this one can see a further reason why Pound came to develop an allusive style. Allusiveness is a way of acknowledging antecedents, of admitting that others have been here before us; if a poet finds himself compelled to say something that has already been said before, the least he can do is to refer directly to the earlier writer or quote him in whatever language he happens to have written. Here again we see the habits of an academic discipline shaping Pound's attitude toward his creative work. The more you read, the more antecedents you become aware of, and this is why allusion seems to overwhelm originality as Pound gets older; paradoxically, the originality of the later *Cantos* lies in the organization of heterogeneous allusions.

A reader who bears in mind that Pound uses allusion as a mode of imitation and also as an acknowledgment of indebtedness to earlier writers is not likely to make the mistake of thinking that the allusions are there simply to show us how widely read the author is. The surface is often macaronic to the point of garishness, and it is easy to regard the allusive-

---

[4] *The Letters of Ezra Pound, 1907–1941,* ed. D. D. Paige (London, 1951), pp. 37–38.

[5] *Ibid.,* p. 37.

[6] "Prolegomena," pp. 74–75.

[7] *Personæ* (New York, 1926), p. 148.

[8] "Modern Georgics [review of Robert Frost's *North of Boston*]," *Poetry,* V, 3 (Dec. 1914), 127.

ness as an elaborate game. But familiarity with the origins of the method and a knowledge of the sources of Pound's quotations make one reluctant to reject his poems for being fundamentally perverse in conception. In Pound as in Eliot the allusions are often deliberately and ironically inappropriate. To take a familiar example:

> O bright Apollo,
> τίν' ἀνδρα, τίν' ἤρωα, τίνα θεὸν,
> What god, man, or hero
> Shall I place a tin wreath upon! [9]

The point of this passage is not to show us that Pound has read Pindar, nor to see whether we can identify the third line as a translation from the Greek. The point is to establish a sense of the grandeur and the dignity of man by quoting from Pindar a particularly magniloquent line; and having done so, to demolish the idea by introducing that devaluative image of the tin wreath. In such instances the quotation is inappropriate in a meaningful way: the confrontation of gods and tin wreaths, the contrast between the powerfully rhythmic and the flatly prosaic, persuade us that heroic action and heroic literature are equally anachronistic in our time. This point could scarcely have been made with such economy without a quotation from the classics. Here we have the ultimate sophistication of a device that originated in the academic habit of providing references for one's quotations.

II

As one might expect, a poet who believes that literature is a craft to be learned from earlier writers will produce translations as well as pastiches in the course of his apprenticeship. *The Spirit of Romance* is full of translations that Pound considered "merely exegetic," [10] and his early volumes of verse contain more ambitious translations from the Greek, Latin, Old English, Provençal, French, Italian, and German. These are selected invariably because they illustrate some perception about the technical development of the art of poetry: they are the documentary evidence presented by Pound-as-poet in support of the judgments of Pound-as-critic. While admitting that there is a "national chemical" [11] in every literature which makes it unique, Pound was sufficiently committed to his studies in comparative literature to believe that excellence in literature is transferable from one language to another. The

[9] *Personæ* (1926), p. 189.
[10] *The Spirit of Romance*, p. 93.
[11] "Patria Mia [XI]," *New Age*, XII, 2 (Nov. 14, 1912), 33.

art of the lyric could be traced from Provence to England via Italy and France; the techniques of satire, from the *Greek Anthology* to Jules Laforgue, with Martial, Heine, and others at various intermediary stages. A reader of Pound's early poems, encountering translations from various literatures and various periods in time, is in fact being supplied with standards of excellence by which to assess Pound's less derivative poems (and also, incidentally, with crucial documents in the history of European poetry). The quality and nature of these translations vary considerably, ranging from literal renderings of Heine to facetious improvisations on Propertius. John Dryden conveniently separated three major sorts of translation when he distinguished *metaphrase* ("turning an author word by word, and line by line, from one language into another") from *paraphrase* (where the "words are not so strictly followed as [the] sense") and *imitation* (where the poet takes "the liberty . . . to forsake [words and sense] as he sees occasion").[12] Pound's best work is in his imitations, as is usually the case when a poet turns his hand to translation. Dryden grasped the inherent virtues and limitations of the mode when he observed that "imitation . . . is the most advantageous way for a translator to shew himself, but the greatest wrong which can be done to the memory and reputation of the dead."[13] "Homage to Sextus Propertius" is a controversial poem for this very reason: Pound shows himself to advantage at the same time as he does a disservice to the reputation of Propertius (though Pound complicates matters by insisting that his Propertius is the *real* Propertius). By the time Pound was writing, imitation in this technical sense had become obsolete, with the result that poems like "The Seafarer" and "Homage to Sextus Propertius" were misjudged even by scholars who should have known better.[14]

Part of the trouble has been our not unreasonable demand for consistency in translation, our immediate assumption that a translation must be either literal or free. In actual fact it is rare to find a translation by Pound which is a pure example of *metaphrase,* or *paraphrase,* or *imitation.* As often as not the different modes coexist: some parts will be stiffly literal, syntactically fettered by translators' jargon; elsewhere Pound will sacrifice the letter to the spirit with magnificent results, and in other places whimsically make nonsense of the original.

[12] Preface to *Ovid's Epistles* (1680). Reprinted in John Dryden, *Of Dramatic Poesy and Other Critical Essays,* ed. G. Watson (London and New York, 1962), I, 268.

[13] *Ibid.,* p. 271.

[14] See, for example, W. G. Hale, "Pegasus Impounded [on "Homage to Sextus Propertius"]," *Poetry,* XIV, 1 (April 1919), 52–55; and Kenneth Sisam, "Mr. Pound and 'The Seafarer,'" *Times Literary Supplement,* no. 2734 (June 25, 1954), 409.

Somewhere in the process Pound's academic respect for the literal sense of a poem is overwhelmed by his poetic interest in what he can make of it by treating it as the starting point for something else. Just as Pound's views on "tradition" are highly idiosyncratic, so his interpretation of the poems which make up the tradition is equally idiosyncratic. When academic *metaphrase* yields to poetic *imitation*, we begin to feel that the pedagogic function of these translations as milestones in the history of European poetry is far less important than their place as prentice pieces in the development of Pound's poetic art. Consequently, we note Pound's views on tradition for what they tell us about his poetry; we do not read his translations for insights into literary history.

Pound's methods as a translator have been attacked and defended in terms of specific poems but never in terms of his translations as a whole. Having tried and failed to systemize his methods I leave the reader with notes on the various translations and the general warning that Pound never hesitated to be literal, free, or fanciful whenever he felt so inclined. The most misunderstood aspect of these imitations has been their use of the creative mistranslation—most famously in "Homage to Sextus Propertius," of course, but more systematically in "The Seafarer." Creative mistranslation is not acknowledged as a literary device because it is often identical with schoolboy howlers and makes frequent use of the bilingual pun. Sufficient examples have now been uncovered to establish the creative mistranslation as a literary mode: Surrey has been caught translating the Italian *scorge* ("points the way") as "whipp," [15] Marlowe read Latin *cānis* ("hoary") as *canis* ("dog"),[16] and W. M. Rossetti was disturbed to find his brother translating the Italian *amo* ("hook") as though it were Latin ("I love").[17] In the same spirit Pound turned to Latin and rendered *orgia* ("mysteries") as "orgies," *minas* ("threats") as "mines," *vela* ("sails") as "veil"; [18] Old English yielded "blade" for *blæd* ("glory"), "twain" for *tweon* ("to doubt"), "reckon" for *wrecan* ("to compose"), and many other examples.[19] These transpositions are made so consistently that there is no point in trying to ridicule them as juvenile mistranslations. Pound certainly made mistakes in translation: he failed to dis-

---

[15] H. A. Mason, *Humanism and Poetry in the Tudor Period* (London, 1955), pp. 238–239.

[16] *Marlowe's Poems*, ed. L. C. Martin (London, 1931), p. 161.

[17] *The Works of Dante Gabriel Rossetti*, ed. W. M. Rossetti (London, 1911), pp. 677–678.

[18] "Homage to Sextus Propertius," I, 4; V, 48; VIII, 26 (*Personæ* [1926], pp. 207, 217, 222).

[19] "The Seafarer," ll. 90, 70, 1 (*Personæ* [1926], pp. 66, 64). For a more detailed account of creative mistranslation in this poem, see the note to THE SEAFARER.

tinguish between the German *Leid* ("sorrow") and *Lied* ("song"),[20] Old English *þurh* ("through") and *þruh* ("coffin"); [21] but his mistakes are usually distinguishable from his transpositions. Out of context a creative mistranslation looks ludicrous; in context the surface is unruffled:

> And how ten sins can corrupt young maidens;
>   Kids for a bribe and pressed udders,
> Happy selling poor loves for cheap apples.[22]

Rhythmically these lines are so assured that the sequence of ideas is undisturbed by the presence of a mistranslation, and it is only by checking Pound's lines against Propertius' text that we find he has read *mālum* ("apple") as *malum* ("evil") so as to get the image of "ten sins." In such instances all we need demand is that the predominant tone of a passage should not be disturbed by the presence of isolated mistranslations. And as a general rule we can learn to distrust Pound whenever he tries to justify his mistranslations as part of " 'the new method' in literary scholarship." [23]

III

To write in the manner of a great poet involves learning to speak with his voice, and so to imitate many poets is to learn to speak with many voices. Before finding a poetic voice of his own, Pound saw himself as a mimic of other men's voices and thought of his prentice pieces as masks or personæ by means of which, for the duration of the poem, he would pretend to speak with the voice of Peire Vidal, François Villon, or some other poet. This proliferation of personæ he considered essential for a young writer who had not found a poetic voice of his own. "In the 'search for oneself,' " Pound wrote in 1914,

> in the search for "sincere self-expression," one gropes, one finds some seeming verity. One says "I am" this, that, or the other, and with the words scarcely uttered one ceases to be that thing.
>   I began this search for the real in a book called *Personæ* [1909], casting off, as it were, complete masks of the self

[20] "Translations and Adaptations from Heine," II, 5, 7 (*Personæ* [1926], p. 44).

[21] "The Seafarer," l. 90 (*Personæ* [1926], p. 66).

[22] *Ibid.*, p. 229.

[23] "The Seafarer" was advertised in these terms in *New Age*, X, 5 (Nov. 30, 1911), 107. Pound made similar claims for his imitation of Propertius.

in each poem. I continued in a long series of translations, which were but more elaborate masks.[24]

Lacking a poetic personality, the poet experiments with personæ until he eventually discovers the "sincere self-expression" that gives an individual quality to his verse. In practice Pound's personæ turn out to be somewhat Browningesque, although this was perhaps inevitable. Occasionally we are led to believe that he valued his personæ as something more than mere five-finger exercises: he writes in "In Durance," [25] for example, as though the imitation of past writers compensated for his loneliness; and in an uncollected poem called "Histrion" he associates the creation of personæ with the sort of metempsychosis described in Yeats's essay on "Magic":

No man hath dared to write this thing as yet,
And yet I know, how that the souls of all men great
At times pass through us,
And we are melted into them, and are not
Save reflexions of their souls.
Thus am I Dante for a space and am
One François Villon, ballad-lord and thief
Or am such holy ones I may not write,
Lest blasphemy be writ against my name;
This for an instant and the flame is gone.[26]

The creation of personæ, in fact, is not so impersonal a device after all, and certainly is not without its quasi-mystical implications.

Pound's early concern with personæ had a decisive influence on his mature work. By pastiche and translation he was able to experience a sense of contemporaneity with the great writers of the past, creating literary dialects by means of which he could converse with Heine or Villon. But when he developed a poetic style of his own the process was reversed: instead of trying to write like a contemporary of Propertius, he made Propertius sound like a contemporary of Pound, achieving in this way the effect that Coleridge was pleased to find in Chapman's Homer. As soon as this happened his translations acquired the importance of original poems and his prentice days were over.

His early preoccupation with the literary tradition from Homer to Yeats has also affected his awareness of time and shaped the temporal structure of the *Cantos*. A poet who can feel himself a contemporary of Homer or Villon, or feel Homer and Villon contemporaries of himself, is unlikely to experience

[24] "Vorticism," *Fortnightly Review,* XCVI, 573 (Sept. 1, 1914), 463–464.
[25] *Personæ* (1926), pp. 20–21.
[26] *Exultations* (London, 1909), p. 38.

historical time in a conventional manner. In the *Cantos* all time is contemporaneous, the point of focus being the consciousness of the writer whose mind ranges backward and forward over many hundreds of years. What has become a literary method in the *Cantos* is already implied in Pound's attitude toward major writers in the European tradition, and is made explicit in the opening pages of *The Spirit of Romance:*

> It is dawn at Jerusalem while midnight hovers above the pillars of Hercules. All ages are contemporaneous. It is B.C., let us say, in Morocco. The Middle Ages are in Russia. . . . This is especially true of literature, where the real time is independent of the apparent, and where many dead men are our grandchildren's contemporaries. . . .[27]

Having a conventionally historical sense of time we feel exasperated when, leafing through the first eight pages of *Personæ* (1926), we encounter random allusions to Ovid, Arthurian legend, Yeats, Cino da Pistoia, Browning, Bertran de Born, and François Villon. All these exist, however, not in historical or "apparent" time but in what Pound calls "real" time; they coexist because they are contemporaneous in the mind of the poet, for whom they have a significance that transcends the claims of historical time.

Ultimately, the creation of personæ is a way of imposing order on the chaos of history and serves much the same function as myth in *The Waste Land* or *Ulysses*. The rise and fall of national cultures in the last three thousand years is made meaningful when simplified in terms of national achievements: every culture perfects some mode of literature as represented in a few masterpieces; convert the masterpieces into personæ, and you have salvaged the high points of artistic development from the ruins of time (and also, incidentally, you have collected touchstones of excellence for the guidance of young writers). By means of personæ, therefore, the poet learns the techniques of his trade; and in assembling personæ he gives a shape and significance to the literary tradition whose techniques he is learning.

IV

Pound did not publish anything like a formal *ars poetica* until 1913.[28] To get an idea of what he had discovered about poetry before 1910 we need only turn to *The Spirit of Romance*, a work which is still marvelously fertile when read for its criti-

---

[27] *The Spirit of Romance*, p. vi.
[28] "A Few Don'ts by an Imagiste," *Poetry*, I, 6 (March 1913), 200–206.

cal ideas and not for its tedious synopses. The book is based on lectures given in 1909 and, even at that early date, contains many characteristic pronouncements. Here we learn, among other things, that poetry should have the virtues of good prose ("Ovid . . . writes . . . in a polished verse, with the clarity of French scientific prose" [29]); that adjectives are stylistically a weakness ("The true poet is most easily distinguished from the false, when . . . he writes without adjectives" [30]); that imagery may be visual but never pictorial ("The poet must never infringe upon the painter's function" [31]); that literature should aspire to the precision of science ("Poetry is a sort of inspired mathematics, which gives us equations . . . for the human emotions" [32]). A couple of years later he had worked out the relationship between functional rhythms and the *mot juste:*

> I believe in an ultimate and absolute rhythm as I believe in an absolute symbol or metaphor. The perception of the intellect is given in the word, that of the emotions in the cadence. It is only, then, in perfect rhythm joined to the perfect word that the twofold vision can be recorded. . . . The rhythm of any poetic line corresponds to a particular emotion.[33]

And on the theory of form: ". . . some poems may have form as a tree has form, some as water poured into a vase." [34]

These principles were far ahead of Pound's poetic capabilities, as the bulk of *Ripostes* (1912) testifies. But by 1913 the poems were abreast of the theories and Pound had the satisfaction of practicing what he preached. In April of that year he condensed his discoveries to produce the three points of the first imagist manifesto:

1. Direct treatment of the "thing," whether subjective or objective.
2. To use absolutely no word that [does] not contribute to the presentation.
3. As regarding rhythm: to compose in sequence of the musical phrase, not in sequence of a metronome.[35]

[29] *The Spirit of Romance*, p. 6. Flaubert, who was to become Pound's "true Penelope" in stylistic matters, insisted that prose should be as well written as verse: "une bonne phrase doit être comme un bon vers, *inchangeable*, aussi rhythmée, aussi sonore" (*Correspondance*, 2me ser., 1847–52 [Paris, 1926], p. 469).

[30] *Ibid.*, p. 219. [31] *Ibid.*, p. 65. [32] *Ibid.*, p. 5.

[33] *The Sonnets and Ballate of Guido Cavalcanti* (London, 1912), pp. 11, 12.

[34] "Prolegomena," p. 73.

[35] "Imagisme," *Poetry*, I, 6 (March 1913), 199. The article is signed by F. S. Flint but was written by Pound. Flint told Wallace D. Martin that "his own part in it was confined to correcting a few stylistic idiosyncrasies for which he could not, with a clear conscience, take the

Clustered around each of these axioms were various recommendations and taboos that collectively made up a fairly extensive aesthetic. To believe in the importance of "direct treatment" was to learn to distrust abstract words, pictorial descriptions, discursive opinion, and synaesthesia; to fear the superfluous led one to rate the single image very highly and agree with Flint that the long poem is a thing of the past;[36] and to respect the musical phrase involved a thorough study of the nature of sound values in poetry.[37] Of these three requirements, however, only the first is new in Poundian criticism; the second derives from earlier views on superfluous adjectives and the need for a mathematical accuracy of language; the third is simply a restatement of Pound's 1912 views on functional rhythms. What was true for imagism, however, had to be true for poetry in general, and Pound continued to revise his ideas until he had evolved a more comprehensive theory of poetry. Before very long he had discarded the tripartite division of the original imagist manifesto: the first two items were combined and labeled "imagism"; the third was also retained but renamed *melopœia*. By 1918 he had a new triad: *melopœia* ("poetry which moves by its music"), *imagism* ("poetry wherein the feelings of painting and sculpture are predominant"), and *logopœia* ("poetry which is a dance of the intelligence among words").[38] A few years later he changed the word *imagism* to *phanopœia*,[39] and in doing so produced his final statement on the major elements in the art of poetry. The categories of his latest formulation resemble those that Coleridge used when comparing the fine arts with different kinds of poetry. In an essay "On the Principles of Genial Criticism," Coleridge distinguishes "poetry of language" (Pound's *logopœia*) from "poetry of the ear" (*melopœia*) and "poetry of the eye" (*phanopœia*).[40] What Pound meant by *logopœia* is never clearly defined. He seems to have used the word to describe various kinds of verbalism: puns, portman-

---

responsibility" ("The Literary Significance of *The New Age* under the Editorship of A. R. Orage, 1907–1922" [doctoral dissertation, London, 1961], p. 262). See also Christopher Middleton, "Documents on Imagism from the Papers of F. S. Flint," *Review*, no. 15 (April 1965), 31–51 (with photostats); and Le Roy C. Breunig, "F. S. Flint, Imagisme's 'Maître d'École,'" *Comparative Literature*, IV, 2 (Spring 1952), 118–136.

[36] Reviewing "Recent Verse," F. S. Flint said that "the day of the lengthy poem is over—at least for this troubled age" (*New Age*, III, 11 [July 11, 1908], 213).

[37] All these prescriptions are taken from "A Few Don'ts by an Imagiste."

[38] "A List of Books," *Little Review*, IV, 11 (March 1918), 57.

[39] "On Criticism in General," *Criterion*, I, 2 (Jan. 1923), 152.

[40] S. T. Coleridge, *Biographia Literaria*, ed. J. Shawcross (Oxford, 1954), II, 220–221. See also the note on IN DURANCE.

teau words, nonce words, and so on—almost any phenomenon, in fact, which involves an element of wordplay. He may
have thought *logopœia* essentially undefinable; if so, this
would explain why he leaves us, as Eliot so often does, with a
metaphor in place of a definition: "a dance of the intelligence
among words."

This skeletal account of the evolution and shaping of
Pound's critical theories omits many of those insights into
poetic style which make his literary essays an essential vade
mecum for the young critic. It does, however, suggest that
Pound's detailed observations on the merely technical aspects
of writing are entirely his own and are based on a method
of studying literature which a later generation was to know
as practical criticism. I doubt whether Pound had much to
learn from his contemporaries on the technical aspects of
verse writing. On matters of general aesthetics, however, and
particularly on the "doctrine of the Image," Pound seems to
have owed a good deal to his contemporaries, particularly to
T. E. Hulme. Similarities in the writings of Hulme and Pound
are striking: both of them disapprove of conceptual language
and both make high claims for the image as the essence of
poetry and the medium for extrarational experience. Both of
them studied French writers who boosted the image at the ex-
pense of the concept. Hulme found in Bergson that abstract
concepts are insufficiently flexible to cope with the subtleties
of experience, and that vital knowledge is communicated in-
tuitively by means of images. And Pound absorbed a similar
lesson from Remy de Gourmont: concepts are merely desic-
cated images; language is revivified by poets who coin fresh
visual images, redeeming dead metaphors and restoring life
to the language. Given this knowledge, it is only to be expected
that Hulme and Pound should have written in a similar way
about the relative values of image and concept and the function of images in poetry. Strangely enough, neither of them
seems to have had much time for the other's sources: Pound
mocked Hulme for wasting his time on "crap like Bergson," [41]
and we have no proof that Hulme ever studied *Le Problème
du Style*. In fact, the similarities between Hulme and Pound
might be explained solely in terms of the similarities between
Bergson and Gourmont were it not for the evidence of one
illuminating remark made by Pound in 1914: "The point of
Imagisme is that it does not use images *as ornaments*. The
image is itself the speech. The image is the word beyond formulated language." [42] In other words, as Hulme had written

[41] "This Hulme Business," *Townsman*, II, 5 (Jan. 1939), 15.
[42] "Vorticism," p. 466.

(paraphrasing Bergson), "Images in verse are not mere decoration, but the very essence of an intuitive language." [43]

Who can doubt that here we have the kernel of imagist aesthetics—the mysterious "doctrine of the Image" which Pound and Flint refused to discuss in their imagist manifesto of 1913 because "it did not concern the public, and would provoke useless discussion"? And here Gourmont is altogether out of the running; Pound follows Hulme or Bergson in justifying the poet's preoccupation with images. This is why the place of Hulme and Pound in the development of imagism might be redefined as follows: Pound brought his great technical skills to the development of a mode of poetry that derived its *raison d'être* from Hulme. Put this way, it can now be seen why Pound has consistently played down the importance of Hulme. Pound considered himself a better craftsman than Hulme and set a higher value on poetic technique than on aesthetic theory; as a practicing poet Hulme simply did not exist, having given up verse for the consolation of philosophy. In the process of ignoring Hulme, Pound has tried to raise the reputation of Ford Madox Ford and establish him as a seminal influence on imagist poetry: "The critical LIGHT during the years immediately pre-war in London shone not from Hulme but from Ford." [44] Ford, however, seems to have been incapable of talking analytically about poetry, which he regarded as an "uncontrollable process" and very different from a "conscious and workable medium" like prose. [45] If the critical light fell on poetry from Ford, it did so only because Pound was intelligent enough to take what Ford had to say about the conscious and workable art of prose and apply it to the uncontrollable process of poetry; and he could do this because he

[43] T. E. Hulme, "Searchers After Reality, II. Haldane," *New Age*, V, 17 (Aug. 19, 1909), 315; reprinted in *Speculations*, ed. Herbert Read (London, 1924), pp. 135–136. The case for Hulme's originality in these matters is argued by Alun R. Jones in *The Life and Opinions of T. E. Hulme* (London, 1960). On the imagist movement in general, see Stanley R. Coffman, Jr., *Imagism: A Chapter for the History of Modern Poetry* (Norman, Okla., 1951). The Romantic and symbolist origins of imagism are traced by Frank Kermode in *Romantic Image* (London, 1957).

[44] "This Hulme Business," p. 15. As early as 1913 Pound was saying he "would rather talk about poetry with Ford . . . than with any man in London," largely because Ford's views on poetry were "in diametric contrast to those of Mr. Yeats" (see "Status Rerum," *Poetry*, I, 4 [Jan. 1913], 123–127). Ford's influence is assessed by Alun R. Jones in "Notes toward a History of Imagism: An Examination of Literary Sources," *South Atlantic Quarterly*, IX, 2 (Summer 1961), 262–285; and by K. L. Goodwin in *The Influence of Ezra Pound* (London, 1966), pp. 7–8.

[45] F. M. Hueffer [Ford], "The Poet's Eye [I–II]," *New Freewoman*, I, 6 (Sept. 1, 1913), 107.

had already discovered for himself that Ovid's verse is good insofar as it has the clarity of French scientific prose.

V

The theories of Gourmont and Hulme were confirmed unexpectedly when Pound came into contact with the writings of Ernest Fenollosa, a sinologist who had discovered in Chinese precisely those qualities that imagist poets were trying to create in English. What Fenollosa has to say about the pictorial qualities of Chinese is very similar to what Hulme and Gourmont were writing about the visual element in poetic imagery. According to Gourmont, language originates in *mots-images* (the verbal equivalent of sensation) and degenerates via *mots-idées* into *mots-sentiments:* [46] ". . . une idée n'est qu'une sensation défraîchie." [47] Hulme agreed. "Every word in the language originates as a live metaphor," he wrote, "but gradually of course all visual meaning goes out of them and they become a kind of counters." [48] If so, the poet is truly the redeemer of language, for he checks the natural devaluation of language by reconverting counters into live metaphors, replacing *mots-idées* by *mots-images;* and these *mots-images*, Hulme reminds us, "have the power of conveying an actually felt visual sensation," [49] a power that makes poetry into "a compromise for a language of intuition which would hand over sensations bodily." [50] Pound too admired poetry in which "the phrases correspond to definite sensations undergone," [51] and he was very much taken with what Fenollosa had to say about the visual element in Chinese. Fenollosa aligns himself with Gourmont and Hulme in preferring language at an imagistic stage before it is refined into concepts and thus devitalized. He shows the same contempt for mere "mental counters" [52] as Hulme does for the "abstract counters" of prose,[53] and by treating the ideogram as a pictogram he is able to observe that "Chinese notation is something much more than arbitrary symbols. It is based upon a vivid shorthand picture of the operations of nature." [54] In his account the Chinese language is composed of

[46] Remy de Gourmont, *Le Problème du Style* (Paris, 1902), p. 81.
[47] *Ibid.*, p. 69.
[48] Hulme, *Speculations*, p. 152.
[49] *Ibid.*, p. 164.   [50] *Ibid.*, p. 135.
[51] "Donna Mi Prega," *Dial*, LXXXV, 1 (July 1928), 8.
[52] "The Chinese Written Character as a Medium for Poetry [II]," *Little Review*, VI, 6 (Oct. 1919), 58.
[53] Hulme, *Speculations*, p. 135.
[54] "The Chinese Written Character as a Medium for Poetry [II]," p. 57.

visual images and is therefore superior to an analytic language
like English: Chinese is already imagistic; the language does
not need to be revivified by imagist poets. Without believing in
the visual qualities of written Chinese (modern sinologists
don't),[55] one can nevertheless appreciate how extraordinarily
relevant Fenollosa's work must have seemed to Pound in 1913.
Coming from his intensive reading of Gourmont, and with
Hulme's doctrine of the image still on his mind, Pound's sudden discovery of Fenollosa must have appeared little short of
miraculous. For here was a man who presented him with the
key to a language that seemed to fulfill quite spontaneously
all that Gourmont and Hulme had expected of poetry. The
Chinese language, in Fenollosa's account, is inherently visual
and therefore, to an imagist poet, unavoidably poetic.

Pound has emphasized the seminal importance of "The
Chinese Written Character as a Medium for Poetry" so often
that nobody is likely to underestimate its influence on his own
writings. Some of Fenollosa's remarks on style are excellent,
particularly his recommendation of transitive verbs and his
opposition to passive constructions and the verb *to be*.[56] Others
are more dubious but nonetheless influential on Pound. Fenollosa's notes on the structure of ideograms, for example, on how
the word *red* is defined by the components "rose—cherry—iron
rust—flamingo,"[57] inspired the ideogrammic method in the
early *Cantos,* where Pound presents hundreds of facts and
observations that are intended to accumulate and so define the
truth of his poem. Similarly, Pound's indifference to syntax is
Fenollosan in origin. For if "the primary pigment of poetry is
the IMAGE,"[58] a poem is simply a cluster of images and syntax
is superfluous; the significance of a poem is transmitted from
image to image in a series of semantic explosions.[59] Before
grappling with Fenollosa, Pound talked of the image as if it
were a static phenomenon ("an emotional and intellectual
complex in an instant of time"[60]); afterwards, it was the dynamic element that counted: the image was renamed "vor-

[55] See George Kennedy, "Fenollosa, Pound, and the Chinese Character," *Yale Literary Magazine,* no. 126 (Dec. 1958), 24–36.

[56] Fenollosa's assumptions about the verb *to be* and transitive and intransitive verbs are questioned by Christine Brooke-Rose in *A Grammar
of Metaphor* (London, 1958). His comments on the verb *to be* could
be illustrated from the way in which Wordsworth revised *The Prelude*
(e.g., in IV, 330–334).

[57] *ABC of Reading* (London, 1934), p. 6; "The Chinese Written Character as a Medium for Poetry [III]," *Little Review,* VI, 7 (Nov. 1919), 60.

[58] "Vortex," *Blast,* no. 1 (June 20, 1914), 154.

[59] Donald Davie examines the effects of Fenollosan views on the
syntax of English poetry in *Articulate Energy* (London, 1955).

[60] "A Few Don'ts by an Imagiste," p. 200.

tex" [61] and defined as "a radiant node or cluster," [62] Pound
clearly remembering Fenollosa's recommendation of words
that are "charged with intense meaning at the center, like a
nucleus, and then radiating out toward infinity, like a great
nebula." [63] It is no exaggeration to say that the reading of
Fenollosa's essay was a liberating experience for Pound.
Trapped by imagist aesthetics (with its concentration on "the
STATIONARY image" [64]), Pound discovered in what Fenollosa
had to say about the structure of the ideogram a way of evolving a new dynamism in poetry. By conceiving of the ideogrammic method as a structural device for poems, he made it
possible for images to be grouped in such a way as to have a
dynamic relationship with one another. And at the same time
he made it possible for a man to write long poems without entirely abandoning imagist theory.

VI

In retrospect one has the illusion that certain writers have been
exceptionally fortunate in living when they did; and, without
in any way minimizing Pound's early struggle to get his work
recognized, one feels that he too has been fortunate insofar as
his self-imposed apprenticeship to the craft of verse coincided
with a fresh wave of optimism in the arts following upon the
coronation of George V in 1910. Initially such optimism was a
belated *nouveau siècle* phenomenon, and specifically English:
with the death of Edward VII the Victorian era was finally
over, it was felt, and England was about to experience a new
vigor that would manifest itself in an efflorescence of the arts.
There was not much to point to in 1912 by way of evidence for
this supposition, but many people speculated about an appropriate name for the new age. Lascelles Abercrombie found a

[61] The shift from imagism to vorticism involved a change in name
only, as everybody has suspected. Proof comes from an unpublished
letter to Harriet Monroe, dated August 7, 1914: "my article on Imagisme
has been stoked into the *Fortnightly Review*, under an altered title.
VORTICISM being the generic term now used on all branches of the
new art, sculpture, painting, poetry" (Chicago MSS). See n. 24 and
U. Weisstein's "Vorticism: Expressionism English Style," *Yearbook of
Comparative and General Literature*, no. 13 (1964), 28–40. In an essay
on "Vorticism and the Career of Ezra Pound" (*Modern Philology*, LXV,
3 [Feb. 1968], 214–227), H. N. Schneidau traces Pound's growing fasci-
nation with the *vortex* as "a dynamic whirling ideogram" (p. 222).

[62] "Vorticism," p. 469.

[63] Ernest Fenollosa, "The Nature of Fine Art [I]," *Lotos*, no. 9 (April
1896), 756. Quoted from Lawrence W. Chisolm, *Fenollosa: The Far
East and American Culture* (New Haven and London, 1963), pp. 216,
225.

[64] *ABC of Reading*, p. 36.

suitable analogue in pre-Socratic Greece; Galsworthy thought we were in for a third renaissance; Binyon anticipated Edward Marsh's proclamation that a new Georgian period was about to begin.[65] In March 1913 D. H. Lawrence pooled the two most common suggestions and wrote enthusiastically of a "Georgian Renaissance," while a couple of months later Pound had appropriated these purely English sentiments and declared his belief in "the imminence of an American Renaissance." [66] By the autumn of that year he had acquired the Fenollosa manuscripts and was suggesting that Chinese might very well be the Greek of this new renaissance, with Fenollosa its Chrysoloras.[67] The list of subsequent annunciations could be extended, but one may as well stop with the "New Renaissance" advertised by Wyndham Lewis in the first issue of *Tyro* (April 1921). The whole phenomenon is more in the nature of a *renascence* than a *renaissance,* to borrow Panofsky's distinction. Surprisingly, the 1912 prophecies turned out to be accurate, although the eventual heroes of the renascence were rather different from the contenders favored at the time (Alice Meynell, Francis Thompson, Rupert Brooke, etc.). Ignored by the prophets, Pound was nevertheless able to share the excitement of living in that dawn when to be young (Pound was twenty-five in 1910) was very heaven.

Reading through the little magazines published between 1910 and 1920 one realizes that the period was teeming with ideas (the notion of an imminent renascence is among the most engaging of these). But poems are made with words and not ideas, Mallarmé told Degas; [68] and Pound has left abundant evidence of the difficulty he experienced in inventing a style and vocabulary capable of dealing honestly with the conditions of modern life. Among the concluding poems in *Personæ* (1909) is one that bravely advocates a "Revolt / Against the Crepuscular Spirit in Modern Poetry" (pp. 53–54), but turns

[65] Abercrombie, in *Poetry Review,* I (1912), 169; Galsworthy, *The Inn of Tranquillity* (London, 1912), p. 260; Binyon, in *Rhythm,* I (1912), 1–2; Marsh, preface to *Georgian Poetry, 1911–12* (London, 1912), p. [iii]. See chapter 8 of Wallace Martin's *"The New Age" under Orage* (Manchester, 1967), and Robert H. Ross, *The Georgian Revolt* (London, 1967).

[66] Lawrence, in *Rhythm,* II (1913), 17–20; Pound, "America: Chances and Remedies [I]," *New Age,* XIII, 5 (May 1, 1913), 9.

[67] "The Renaissance [I]," *Poetry,* V, 5 (Feb. 1915), 233. In the sixth of his "Affirmations" ("Analysis of This Decade") Pound said that "Fenollosa's finds . . . are no less potent than Crisolora's manuscripts" (*New Age,* XVI, 15 [Feb. 11, 1915], 411). See also the introductory note to SONG OF THE BOWMEN OF SHU and HUGH SELWYN MAUBERLEY (ll. 2–3n).

[68] "Ce n'est point avec des idées, mon cher Degas, que l'on fait des vers. C'est avec des *mots*" (Paul Valéry, *Œuvres,* ed. Jean Hytier [Paris, 1957], I, 1324).

out on inspection to be an equally crepuscular protest against "the lethargy of this our time." The bugbear in Pound's case was Rossetti. Even in 1912 he was aware that Rossetti had been his "father and mother" [69] when it came to translating Cavalcanti. Years later his diagnosis was more incisive: "I was obfuscated by the victorian language . . . the crust of dead english, the sediment present in my own available vocabulary. . . . Rossetti made his own language. I hadn't in 1910 made a language, I don't mean a language to use, but even a language to think in." [70] To use Rossetti's language meant seeing the world through Rossetti's eyes and made it impossible to record a personal response to reality. On one page of the 1926 *Personæ* we read:

> If I have merged my soul, or utterly
> Am solved and bound in, through aught here on earth,
> There canst thou find me, O thou anxious thou,
> Who call'st about my gates for some lost me. . . .

Over the page we find this:

> I suppose there are a few dozen verities
> That no shift of mood can shake from us. . . .[71]

The difference is immense. "Au Salon" (from which the last two lines are quoted) is Pound's first really modern poem. Here we find the conversational rhythms of his best work, the ironic tone of voice, and preference for the Latinate word (think of the difference if "verities" had been merely "truths"). Here at last is poetry that has the virtues of good prose. Yet it was still a year or more before Pound set about developing the techniques he had discovered in "Au Salon." Why did the process of modernization take so long? One reason seems to have been that Pound saw himself as a professional poet but a mere amateur at prose. "My prose is bad," he wrote in March 1913, "but on ne peut pas pontifier and have style simultaneously." [72] The truth is that his prose at the time was *not* bad: it had a vigor and a directness that made his critical perceptions seem unusually pertinent and authoritative. If his prose had had "style" it would have been as stiff-fingered as his early verse. The modernization of poetry, the business of laying the ghost of Rossetti, was ultimately a matter of introducing into his verse the difficult art of calling a spade a spade—an art that he developed more or less unconsciously in his prose because

---

[69] *The Sonnets and Ballate of Guido Cavalcanti*, p. 6.
[70] "Guido's Relations," *Dial*, LXXXVI, 6 (July 1929), 561.
[71] *Personæ* (1926), pp. 51, 52.
[72] *Letters*, p. 50.

he believed that prose was not really his *métier*. The obvious parallel here is with D. H. Lawrence, a writer who acknowledged prose as his medium and yet managed to write convincing poems in dialect at a time when his prose style was still quite mannered.

It was the aim of all the modernists, as of earlier revolutionaries in English poetry, to make the language of poetry coincide with the language of everyday speech. "We would write nothing that we might not say actually in life—under emotion," Pound observed in 1915.[73] Using language such as men do use, the revolutionary hopes to increase the audience for poetry by narrowing the gap between the spoken language and the language of poetry, "to write 'poetry' that a grown man could read without groans of ennui."[74] In trying to get rid of archaisms and similar impediments to modernist ambitions Pound was no doubt assisted by Ford Madox Ford, who advocated using a contemporary spoken language for literary purposes, aiming "to register [his] own times in terms of [his] own time."[75] Pound later acknowledged Ford's insistence on "a contemporary spoken or at least speakable language" as one of the four most useful things he had learned in his London years.[76] Rejected along with the vocabulary of Rossetti was what is called *rhetoric* in the criticism of the period (i.e., "verbiage").[77] "The revolution of the word"[78] was an immediate necessity if language was ever to be purged of the "opalescent word"[79] that Pound identified as the unwanted legacy of Victorianism. Also engaged in "the cleaning up of the WORD"[80] was W. B. Yeats, who had been warring against *rhetoric* for many years, but who never talked about it in specifically Poundian terms until after 1911. Listening to Ford on prose and Yeats on poetry Pound went ahead with his own experiments and by the autumn of 1912 had published his first modern volume of poems (*Ripostes*). His days as a translator and pasticheur were by no means over, but he had at last found a style of his own—a style flexible enough to mingle

[73] *Poetical Works of Lionel Johnson* (London, 1915), p. vi.
[74] *Letters*, p. 156. Such ideas may have evolved as a result of a renewed interest in public readings of verse, especially after about 1912 (see Joy Grant, *Harold Monro and the Poetry Bookshop* [London, 1967], p. 69).
[75] F. M. Hueffer [Ford], "The Poet's Eye [I–II]," p. 108.
[76] "On Criticism in General," pp. 144–145. Pound's other acknowledged debts were to Bridges ("caution against homophones"), Yeats ("NO compromise with the public"), and Hardy ("interest in 'subject' as opposed to 'treatment'"). Cf. *Letters*, p. 245.
[77] In Verlaine's poem, "Art Poétique," *éloquence* and *littérature* are used in a similarly derogatory sense.
[78] *Polite Essays* (London, 1937), p. 50.
[79] "The Prose Tradition in Verse," *Poetry*, IV, 3 (June 1914), 112.
[80] *Polite Essays*, p. 50.

pretty lyricism with ironic comments on *mœurs contempo-raines*. Odd bedfellows indeed; but the prettiness and the irony were to stay with him for the rest of his life.

VII

Pound's brilliance as a verse craftsman is self-evident, but his importance as a poet is by no means established. Technique alone is not enough; too many readers have felt that Pound has really nothing to say for the criticism to be totally irrelevant. Wyndham Lewis put his finger on the inherent weakness of the craftsman's approach to literature when he complained that Pound "would teach *anybody* how to be Dante, *technically.*" [81]

What we miss in the bulk of *Personæ* (1926) is a sense of involvement, a feeling that the translations and pastiches are there for any other reason than that Pound happened to admire the writers he imitated. A suspicion that there is no man behind the masks has led to the damaging criticism that Pound is a sensibility without a mind.[82] In every great writer there is a center from which the total work is organized, some insight into the human condition which shapes the course of individual works. This is one of the reasons why Pound is not a great writer. At the center of his work is the belief that people should take an active interest in the continuity of the arts and have a critical respect for the achievements of the past. His paramount concern is the quality and availability of cultural sustenance; his values, in fact, are those of a pedagogue. As an academic he has used poetry to remind us of what we miss by dissociating English literature from the European literary tradition. Similarly he has used prose as propaganda on behalf of living writers we have ignored and dead writers we would do well to remember. Poems and essays have accumulated voluminously, but it is only at rare moments, when Pound has confessed to a failure in his didactic ambitions, that his work has acquired an urgency that makes it memorable. His two finest works, "Hugh Selwyn Mauberley" (1920) and *The Pisan Cantos* (1948), are compelling because they present a narrator in the toils of overwhelming circumstances. The usual technical characteristics recur in these poems—allusion, juxtaposition, irony, translation, and so on; but the work derives its strength from another and more compelling source: we no longer feel obliged to admire Pound's technical virtuosity because we are caught up in the actual subject matter of these

[81] *Men without Art* (London, 1938), p. 67.
[82] Yvor Winters, *In Defense of Reason* (Denver, 1947), p. 496.

works. Instead of admiring the brilliance with which Pound relates something he has read about, we are drawn to these works by the manifest anguish of the narrator, less so in "Hugh Selwyn Mauberley" (which chronicles a man's failure to be a great poet) than in *The Pisan Cantos* (which deal with the possibility that a man's whole life has been flawed). In works like these, technique is reduced to its proper status, not as something that draws attention to itself, but as something that articulates a deeply moving experience, simply and unobtrusively.

Pound was mistaken in believing that if you take care of the technique the content will take care of itself. Too often his poems are about nothing in particular. He wanted to write poems but he had few poems inside him which demanded to be written. Consequently he paid more attention to literature than to life, being more interested in how other men write poems than in how other men live. Allusiveness need not, of course, be a weakness, provided it remains a method of enrichment and does not become an end in itself. The allusions of a Spenser or a Milton are a means of enrichment in this sense, for both Spenser and Milton have something unique to say which would survive the peeling off of their allusions. But with Pound there is often no subject, no center, nothing around which the allusions can be organized. Unlocalized and impersonal, his poems strive toward a cosmopolitan lucidity of style and run the risk of becoming a mere "broken bundle of mirrors." [83]

There are many reasons why we should not be put off Pound's verse by its superficial difficulties. Poems that have earned the respect of writers so different as Yeats and Eliot are clearly worth reading for their technical skills; written by the noisiest defender of modernism in literature, they have earned a place in the history of twentieth-century poetry; drawing so extensively on European literature, they encourage us to look or look again at the poems of Sappho, Villon, Heine, and so on; and for the reader who likes poetry in the form of cryptograms they yield complex delights. We may read Pound's poems for any or all of these reasons, provided we remember that the business of evaluating them is another matter altogether: that the technical, historical, pedagogic, and enigmatic qualities of these poems are no criterion whatsoever of their ultimate value as literature. The Pound who wrote the *Cantos* is a person we are not yet competent to assess, but the Pound who wrote *Personæ* (1926) is in my opinion a good minor poet and nothing more. The reader who makes up his own mind on this matter will, I hope, have found this *Guide* useful.

[83] *Personæ* (1926), p. 157.

CHRONOLOGICAL LIST
OF THE POEMS IN
PERSONÆ (1926)

Based on Gallup's *Bibliography,* this list records the first appearance in print, whether in book or periodical, of all poems collected subsequently in *Personæ* (1926). All titles are those of the 1926 collection. Original titles which differ from those in the collected volume are noted in square brackets (e.g., "De Ægypto [Ægupton]"); and in cases where a poem first appeared as part of a sequence, the original title of the sequence and relevant subsections are also recorded (e.g., "Les Millwin [*Lustra,* II]"). No account is taken of poems reprinted in periodicals after publication in book form, or of the contents of reissued volumes of verse.

1 *A Lume Spento* (Venice, June 1908).

   1. Cino
   2. De Ægypto [Ægupton]
   3. Eyes, The [The Cry of the Eyes]
   4. Famam Librosque Cano
   5. For E. McC
   6. La Fraisne
   7. Mesmerism
   8. Na Audiart
   9. On His Own Face in a Glass
   10. Praise of Ysolt [Vana]
   11. Threnos
   12. Tree, The
   13. Villonaud: Ballad of the Gibbet, A
   14. Villonaud for This Yule

2 *A Quinzaine for This Yule* (London, December 1908).

   15. Night Litany

3 *Personæ of Ezra Pound* (London, April 1909).

   Reprints 1, 4–8, 10, 13, 14. New poems:
   16. And Thus in Nineveh
   17. In Durance
   18. Marvoil
   19. White Stag, The

4 *English Review,* II, 3 (June 1909), 419–420.

  20. Sestina: Altaforte

5 *English Review,* III, 3 (October 1909), 382–383.

  21. Ballad of the Goodly Fere

6 *Exultations of Ezra Pound* (London, October 25, 1909).

Reprints 3, 9, 15, 20, 21. New poems:
22. Francesca
23. Guido Invites You Thus
25. Planh for the Young English King

7 *The Book of the Poets' Club* (London, December 1909), p. 53.

  26. Paracelsus in Excelsis

8 *Provença* (Boston, November 22, 1910).

Reprints 1, 3–8, 12–16, 18–21, 25, 26.

9 *Canzoni of Ezra Pound* (London, July 1911).

Reprints 2, 11, 12, 26. New poems:
27. Altar, The [Und Drang, X]
28. Au Jardin [Und Drang, XII]
29. Au Salon [Und Drang, XI]
30. Ballatetta
31. "Blandula, Tenulla, Vagula"
32. Erat Hora
33. Flame, The [Und Drang, VIII]
34. Her Monument, the Image Cut Thereon
35. Horæ Beatæ Inscriptio [Und Drang, IX]
36. House of Splendour, The [Und Drang, VII]
37. Mr. Housman's Message [Song in the Manner of Housman]
38. Prayer for His Lady's Life
39. Rome
40. Satiemus [Victorian Eclogues, II]
41. Speech for Psyche in the Golden Book of Apuleius
42. Translations and Adaptations from Heine, I–VII

10 *New Age,* X, 5 (November 30, 1911), 107.

  43. Seafarer, The

11 *North American Review,* CXCV, 674 (January 1912), 75.

  44. Cloak, The [Echos, II: Two Cloaks]

12 *Poetry Review,* I, 2 (February 1912), 77–81.

  45. Dieu! Qu'il La Fait
  46. Δώρια
  47. Sub Mare

48. Translations and Adaptations from Heine, VIII [Oboes, II]

13 *Smart Set,* XXXVII, 1 (May 1912), 122.

49. Silet

14 *English Review,* XI, 3 (June 1912), 343–344.

50. Apparuit
51. Return, The

15 *The Ripostes of Ezra Pound* (London, October 1912).

Reprints 43, 44 [Echoes, II], 45–47, 49–51. New Poems:
52. Girl, A
53. In Exitum Cuiusdam
54. Needle, The
55. N.Y.
56. Object, An
57. Of Jacopo del Sellaio
58. Pan Is Dead
59. "Phasellus Ille"
60. Picture, The
61. Plunge, The [Plunge]
62. Portrait d'une Femme
63. Quies
64. Tomb at Akr Çaar, The
65. Virginal, A

16 *Poetry,* II, 1 (April 1913), 1–12.

66. Commission
67. Condolence, The
68. Dance Figure
69. Garden, The
70. Garret, The
71. In a Station of the Metro
72. Ortus
73. Pact, A
74. Salutation
75. Salutation the Second
76. Tenzone

17 *New Freewoman,* I, 5 (August 15, 1913), 87–88.

Reprints 68–71, 74–76.

18 *Poetry,* III, 2 (November 1913), 53–60.

77. Ancora
78. April
79. Dum Capitolium Scandet [*Xenia,* VII]
80. Further Instructions [*Lustra,* III]
81. Gentildonna
82. Ité [*Xenia,* VI]
83. Les Millwin [*Lustra,* II]

84. Rest, The [*Lustra,* I]
85. Song of the Degrees, A [I–III] [*Xenia,* III–V]
86. Surgit Fama

19   *New Freewoman,* I, 12 (December 1, 1913), 228.

Reprints 77, 78, 80, 81, 83, 84, 85 [Convictions], 86.

20   *Smart Set,* XLI, 4 (December 1913), 47–48.

87. Alba [Zenia, II]
88. Arides [Zenia, VIII]
89. Bath Tub, The [Zenia, VII]
90. Causa [Zenia, VI]
91. Encounter, The [Zenia, IX]
92. Epitaph [Zenia, III]
93. Simulacra [Zenia, X]
94. Tame Cat [Zenia, XI]
95. To Dives [Zenia, I]

21   *Glebe,* I, 5 (February 1914), 41–46.

Reprints 46, 51. New poems:
96. After Ch'u Yuan
97. Fan-Piece for Her Imperial Lord
98. Liu Ch'e
99. Ts'ai Chi'h

22   *Poetry and Drama,* II, 1 (March 1914), 20–24.

100. Albatre
101. Coitus
102. "Dompna Pois De Me No'us Cal" [A Translation from the Provençal of En Bertrans de Born]
103. Faun, The
104. Heather
105. Society
106. Tempora
107. To Formianus' Young Lady Friend

23   *Blast,* no. 1 (June 20, 1914), 45–50.

108. Before Sleep
109. Come My Cantilations
110. Epitaphs
111. Fratres Minores
112. L'Art, 1910 [L'Art]
113. Meditatio
114. Monumentum Ære, Etc.
115. New Cake of Soap, The
116. Post Mortem Conspectu [His Vision of a Certain Lady Post Mortem]
117. Salutation the Third
118. Women before a Shop

24   *Poetry,* IV, 5 (August 1914), 169–177.

119. Amities
120. Bellaires, The

121. Ladies
122. Salvationists
123. Seeing Eye, The
124. Study in Æsthetics, The
125. To Καλόν

25 *Poetry and Drama*, II, 4 (December 1914), 353.

126. "Ione, Dead the Long Year" [Dead Iönè]

26 *Poetry*, V, 6 (March 1915), 251–261.

127. Coming of War: Actæon, The
128. Exile's Letter
129. Game of Chess, The [Dogmatic Statement Concerning
    the Game of Chess]
130. Gypsy, The
131. Image from D'Orleans
132. Provincia Deserta
133. Spring, The

27 *Cathay* (London, April 6, 1915).

Reprints 43, 128. New poems:
134. Beautiful Toilet, The
135. Four Poems of Departure [From Rihaku Four Poems
    of Departure]
        (i)   Separation on the River Kiang
        (ii) Taking Leave of a Friend
        (iii) Leave-Taking near Shoku
        (iv) The City of Choan
136. Jewel Stairs' Grievance, The
137. Lament of the Frontier Guard
138. Poem by the Bridge at Ten-shin
139. River-Merchant's Wife: a Letter, The
140. River Song, The
141. Song of the Bowmen of Shu
142. South-Folk in Cold Country

28 *Blast*, no. 2 (July 1915), 19–22.

Reprints 129. New poems:
143. Ancient Music
144. Ancient Wisdom, Rather Cosmic
145. Our Contemporaries
146. Social Order, The

29 *Smart Set*, XLVI, 4 (August 1915), 130.

Reprints 100.

30 *Smart Set*, XLVII, 2 (October 1915), 134.

147. Black Slippers: Bellotti [Her Little Black Slippers]

31 *Others*, I, 5 (November 1915), 84–85.

148. Coda
149. Patterns, The

150. Phyllidula [Phylidula]
151. Shop Girl
152. Tea Shop, The

32 *Catholic Anthology: 1914–1915* (London, November 1915), pp. 86–92.

Reprints 69–71, 80, 100, 104, 124, 129, 130.

33 *Poetry*, VII, 3 (December 1915), 111–121.

153. Near Perigord
154. Villanelle: the Psychological Hour

34 *Poetry*, VII, 3 (December 1915), 143–145.

Reprints 102 [The Canzon]

35 *Others, An Anthology of the New Verse,* ed. Alfred Kreymborg (New York, March 25, 1916), pp. 83–84.

Reprints 148–152.

36 *New Age*, XIX, 8 (June 22, 1916), 186–187.

155. Ballad of the Mulberry Road, A
156. Old Idea of Choan by Rosoriu
157. Sennin Poem by Kakuhaku
158. To-Em-Mei's "The Unmoving Cloud"

37 *Others*, III, 1 (July 1916), 31–32.

Reprints 158.

38 *Poetry*, VIII, 6 (September 1916), 275–282.

159. Dans un Omnibus de Londres
160. Fish and the Shadow [The Fish and the Shadow]
161. Homage to Quintus Septimius Florentis Christianus
162. 'Ιμέρρω [O Atthis]
163. Impressions of François-Marie Arouet (de Voltaire)
164. Lake Isle, The
165. Pagani's, November 8 [Pagani's]
166. Three Poets, The

39 *Lustra of Ezra Pound* (London, September 1916) [unabridged].

Reprints 66–107, 110, 112, 113, 115, 118–142, 144–162.
166. New poems:
167. Epilogue
168. Papyrus
169. To a Friend Writing on Cabaret Dancers

40 *Lustra of Ezra Pound* (London, October 1916) [abridged].

As 39, but lacking 66, 75, 92, 113, 115, 123, 149, 150, 162.

41 *To-Day*, I, 5 (July 1917), 185–186.

Reprints 163.

42 *Lustra of Ezra Pound with Earlier Poems* (New York, September 19, 1917) [unabridged].

As *39*, but with additional reprints: 17, 24, 27–29, 31–36, 37 [Housman's Message to Mankind], 38, 39, 42–48, 49 [*untitled*], 50–65, 143, 163–165. New poem:
170. The Temperaments

43 *Lustra of Ezra Pound with Earlier Poems* (New York, October 16, 1917) [abridged].

As 42, but lacking 170.

44 *Little Review*, IV, 11 (March 1918), 35.

171. Cantico del Sole

45 *Little Review*, V, 1 (May 1918), 19–31.

172. Langue d'Oc [Homage a la Langue d'Or]
173. Mœurs Contemporaines

46 *New Age*, XXIII, 9 (June 27, 1918), 137–138.

Reprints 172 [Homage a la Langue d'Oc]

47 *Little Review*, V, 7 (November 1918), 1–6.

174. Cantus Planus
175. Phanopœia [Φανοποεια]

48 "Poems from the Propertius Series [I–IV]," *Poetry*, XIII, 6 (March 1919), 291–299. [Sections I–III and VI of 176 below].

49 "Homage to Sextus Propertius" [Sections I, III–VI, and VIII of 176 below], *New Age*, XXV,

8 (June 19, 1919), 132–133: I.
10 (July 3, 1919), 170: II [now IV].
12 (July 17, 1919), 200: III.
14 (July 31, 1919), 231: IV [now VIII].
16 (August 14, 1919), 264: V.
18 (August 28, 1919), 292: VI.

50 *Quia Pauper Amavi* (London, October 1919).

Reprints 172, 173. New poem:
176. Homage to Sextus Propertius, I–XII [incorporates 48 and 49]

51 *Instigations of Ezra Pound* (New York, April 25, 1920).

Reprints 171.

52 *Hugh Selwyn Mauberley* (London, June 1920).

177. Hugh Selwyn Mauberley

53 *Umbra* (London, June 1920).

Reprints 1, 3–10, 12–25, 28, 43–65, 174, 175. New poem: 178. Alchemist, The

54 *Poems 1918–21* (New York, December 8, 1921).

Reprints 172, 173, 176, 177.

55 *Personæ. The Collected Poems of Ezra Pound* (New York, December 22, 1926).

Reprints 1–178.

56 *Diptych Rome-London* (London, New York and Verona, October 24, 1958).

Reprints 174, 176, 177.

Personæ (1926) was published by Boni and Liveright and is now available from New Directions, who brought out an offset reprint of the original text in May 1949. Pages 1–231 of the New Directions *Personæ* differ from the Boni and Liveright edition only in the number and placing of illustrations.

Diptych Rome-London is included in this list because it is the first volume since 1926 to incorporate Pound's own revisions to poems printed in the Boni and Liveright *Personæ* (but see also p. 265 below).

NOTES
ON THE POEMS IN
PERSONÆ (1926)

AFTER CH'U YUAN
[NO. 96. PRINTINGS: *21, 39, 40, 42, 43, 55*]

Ch'ü Yüan (332–295 B.C.), who is mentioned in THE RIVER SONG (l. 9*n*), was a minister under Huai-wang, ruler of the Chu state. AFTER CH'U YUAN was inspired not by the original Chinese (*Ch'u-tz'u*, II, 2.26*a*) but by the version in H. A. Giles's *A History of Chinese Literature* (1901, pp. 52–53). A comparison shows that Pound ignored Ch'ü Yüan's theme (the grief of exile) but borrowed a few of his images: Giles supplied a deity "clad in wistaria . . . riding on the red pard," a dark grove and tangled vine; Pound added the silver blue flood, ivory car, and maidens.

LIU CH'E and FAN-PIECE, FOR HER IMPERIAL LORD are also based on translations by Giles. Evidently, Pound was making poems out of Chinese materials even before he acquired the Fenollosa papers.

6. *grapes for the leopards:* The Dionysus episode in Canto 2 contains the phrase "feeding grapes to my leopards." The association of a Chinese deity with Bacchus testifies to Pound's interest in pagan Greek cults (see in this respect the note to SURGIT FAMA).

[9. out of   *21–43;*   out from   *55*]

10. *procession:* Processions are a recurrent motif in the *Lustra* poems (see COITUS and THE COMING OF WAR: ACTAEON). The word itself was a cachet of modernity. Ford Madox Ford observed ironically that a modern poet "could not use the word Procession in an English poem. It would not be literary" (*New Freewoman* [Sept. 1, 1913], 108). Pound used the word frequently, and in this way advertised his break with poetic convention.

ALBA
[NO. 87. PRINTINGS: *20, 39, 40, 42, 43, 55*]

[TITLE: *[untitled section II of "Zenia"]*   *20;*   *Alba   39+*]

This is merely a fragment of an unwritten *alba* or "dawn poem," a genre examined in *Eos* (ed. Hatto, 1965) and well represented in LANGUE D'OC. Pound seems to have been attracted to the form very early for his first published poem is called "Belangal Alba" (*Hamilton Literary Magazine* [May 1905], 324). In content, however, ALBA is a typical imagist fragment.

ALBATRE

[NO. 100. PRINTINGS: 22, 29, 32, 39, 40, 42, 43, 55]

[3. little white dog   22, 32+;   little dog   29]

3–4. *delicate . . . delicate:* See Richard Aldington's parody of THE GARDEN, reproduced in the notes to that poem. "Delicate" (used ironically here) is a favorite word of the *Lustra* period, recurring in THE CONDOLENCE and ΙΜΕΡΡΩ.

5. *Gautier:* Seeing that Pound admired the poetry of Swinburne and felt a spiritual kinship with Whistler, it is not surprising that he should have been attracted to the poetry of Théophile Gautier (1811–1872), whose "Symphonie en Blanc Majeur" inspired Whistler's "Symphonies in White" and Swinburne's "Before the Mirror."

As Holbrook Jackson noted in his book on *The Eighteen Nineties* (1913), "white" was a nineties color (pp. 140–142); and Pound, with his Whistlerian sensibility, was still in many ways a nineties poet when he wrote ALBATRE. Perhaps this is why he never parodied Gautier in the way that he parodied other poets who influenced his style. Certainly, there is nothing among Pound's published work comparable to Heine's "Der Weisse Elephant."

Among other poems showing the influence of Gautier are TO A FRIEND WRITING ON CABARET DANCERS and HUGH SELWYN MAUBERLEY.

ALCHEMIST, THE

[NO. 178. PRINTINGS: 53, 55]

With the exception of Saîl de Claustra, who was a twelfth-century Provençal poetess, all the women's names in this poem occur fictitiously in the literatures of southern Europe. Some of them (Alcmena, Briseis, Alcyon) belong to Greek mythology; others (Aelis, Tibors, Audiarda) are found in Provençal literature and also in NA AUDIART and NEAR PERIGORD; others can be traced to French and Italian sources. Because

Pound is using these names merely for their beautiful sounds (as Henley does in his "Villanelle: of Ladies' Names"), there is no point in identifying them.

Rimbaud's "Alchimie du Verbe" established alchemy as a common metaphor for the poetic process, and the theme of Pound's poem is that sequences of beautiful names, when chanted, will have the magical powers of the elusive Philosophers' Stone. Pound's interest in the esoteric significance of what he called the "love chivalric" was stimulated by J. A. Péladan's *Le Secret des Troubadours,* published in 1906 and reviewed by Pound for the *Book News Monthly* in September of that year. He observed in *The Spirit of Romance* (1910) that "feminine names were used as charms or equations in alchemy" (pp. 92–93). These equations "were apt to be written as women's names, and the women so named endowed with the magical powers of the compounds" (*Sonnets . . . of . . . Cavalcanti* [1912], p. 3). A few months later, in commenting on the fifth ballata in his selection from Cavalcanti, he developed the idea further and produced what might be regarded as the genesis of THE ALCHEMIST: "For effect upon the air, upon the soul, etc., the 'lady' in Tuscan poetry has taken on all the properties of the Alchemist's stone" (*Quest* [Oct. 1912], 41).

3. *under the larches of Paradise:* The phrase is repeated in Canto 94. *Section: Rock-Drill* (Cantos 85–95) contains so many echoes of poems in *Personæ* (1926) as to suggest that at one stage Pound entertained the idea of a circular form for the *Cantos:* he would end where he began, establishing the unity of his life's work by echoing some of his earliest poems in the last few pages of his epic. Allusions to Canto 1 in *The Pisan Cantos* show that Pound was capable of reading his own earlier writings typologically, and some of the images in the early poems seem to be uncannily proleptic—notably the prophecy in the uncollected "Scriptor Ignotus":

> I see my greater soul-self bending
> Sibylwise with that great forty-year epic.

Personæ (1909), p. 25. For examples of other allusions to early poems in *Section: Rock-Drill,* see AMITIES (I, 5), DUM CAPITOLIUM SCANDET, HEATHER, NEAR PERIGORD (1. 38), PHANOPŒIA (III, 22f), and TAME CAT.

12. *Audiarda:* A lost *sirventes* by Dante (mentioned in the *Vita Nuova,* VI) named the sixty most beautiful women in Florence, of whom the ninth was Beatrice. Audiarda is numerically and alphabetically the ninth of the thirty-five names in THE ALCHEMIST (cf. NA AUDIART).

15. *silver rustling of the wheat:* This image is repeated in A SONG OF THE DEGREES.

25. Provençal *midonz,* "lady."

25–26. *gold . . . silver:* Perfection was represented alchemically as a combination of the solar and lunar principles, of gold and silver.

33. *Alodetta:* Spelled Allodetta in line 61 (in all printings).

40. *Ysaut, Ydone:* These names are paired again in Canto 93.

43. *Queen of Cypress:* Cyparissus was male according to Ovid (*Metamorphoses,* X, 106–142).

44. *Erebus:* The darkness between the earth and Hades. The phrase "out of Erebus" recurs in Canto 90.

51. Latin *manes,* "the spirits of the dead."

58. *Latona:* The mother of Apollo and Artemis, the sun and moon: hence her place in the alchemical scheme of the poem.

ALTAR, THE
[NO. 27. PRINTINGS: 9, 42, 43, 55]

See the note to THE HOUSE OF SPLENDOUR. The image of an "altar fire" of love is repeated from an earlier poem, GUIDO INVITES YOU THUS.

AMITIES
[NO. 119. PRINTINGS: 24, 39, 40, 42, 43, 55]

The epigraph comes from W. B. Yeats's poem "The Lover Pleads with His Friend for Old Friends":

> Though you are in your shining days,
> Voices among the crowd
> And new friends busy with your praise,
> Be not unkind or proud,
> But think about *old friends the most:*
> *Time's bitter flood* will rise,
> Your beauty perish and be lost
> For all eyes but those eyes.

The second of the italicized phrases is quoted as the opening words of IN EXITUM CUIUSDAM, a poem published some two years before AMITIES. Pound evidently took issue with the point of view expressed in Yeats's poem and went on to write these four epigrams on old friends who were best forgotten. A truly Yeatsian nostalgia for old friends permeates *The Pisan Cantos* (1948).

AMITIES is one of several Poundian examples of what Renaissance poets called "answers," in the sense that Donne's "The Bait" is an answer to Marlowe's "The Passionate Shepherd to His Love." Yeats's "Reconciliation" is answered by "The Fault of It" (*Forum* [July 1911], 107) and "The Cap and Bells" by AU JARDIN; "Canzon: the Yearly Slain" (*Canzoni* [1911], pp. 1–3) answers Frederick Manning's "Koré"; "Fifine Answers" (*Personæ* [1909], pp. 17–18) originates from Browning's "Fifine at the Fair" (vii, 5); and in *A Lume Spento* (1908) the poem called "In Tempore Senectus" (corrected in later printings to "In Tempore Senectutis") is offered as an "anti-stave" to Dowson, who printed a poem with this title in his *Verses* (1896). GUIDO INVITES YOU THUS is an answer to an answer.

For parodies of Yeats, see HOMAGE TO SEXTUS PROPERTIUS (IV, 23n).

I, 5. *Te voilà, mon Bourrienne:* The phrase is used also in Canto 103 (cf. THE ALCHEMIST, l. 3n). L. A. F. de Bourrienne (1769–1834) was private secretary to Napoleon from 1797 to 1802 and later published his reminiscences.

II, 6. *discipleship:* For an example, see TRANSLATIONS AND ADAPTATIONS FROM HEINE (VI).

III, 1. Provençal *bos amic,* "good friend." According to Aldington (quoted by Grant, p. 44), the friend is Harold Monro (1879–1932), editor of *Poetry and Drama* and owner of The Poetry Bookshop in Great Russell Street, London. Pound later published an obituary essay on Monro in the *Criterion* ([July 1932], 581–592).

    4. *chop-house:* Bellotti's, according to Aldington (see BLACK SLIPPERS: BELLOTTI).

[III, 2. For to you   24+;   For you   *Faber and Faber*]

IV. Written by Pound in dog Latin to the rhythms of the *Dies Irae:* "This one was an uncultivated fellow, / God be praised that he is buried, / May the worms eat his face / A-a-a-a—A-men. / I, however, like Jove / Shall rejoice as a partner / Of his delightful wife."

[6. Gaudebo in contubernalis   24; Gaudero contubernalis   39+]

6. The earlier reading *gaudebo* is grammatically correct.

ANCIENT MUSIC
[NO. 143. PRINTINGS: 28, 42, 43, 55]

A parody of the Middle English lyric which begins: "Sumer is icumen in, / Llude sing cuccu!" Frank Sidgwick's parody, published the same year as Pound's, opens with the words: "Wynter ys i-cumen in; / Lhoudly syng *tish-ù!*" (*Some Verse* [1915], p. 25). The London winter forms part of the scene in THE PLUNGE.

[*Footnote:* is found 28; is to be found 42+; *the Faber and Faber text lacks the whole footnote*]

"Dr. Ker" is W. P. Ker (1855–1923), whose discovery, Pound was pleased to note, "put an end to much babble about folk song" (*Poetry* [Jan. 1914], 139; cf. *Letters*, p. 185). Believing that poetry is produced only by craftsmen, Pound was unsympathetic toward Romantic notions about spontaneous folk poetry ("das Volk dichtet," etc.).

ANCIENT WISDOM, RATHER COSMIC
[NO. 144. PRINTINGS: 28, 39, 40, 42, 43, 55]

On the origin of Pound's translations from the Chinese, see the note to SONG OF THE BOWMEN OF SHU. ANCIENT WISDOM, RATHER COSMIC is based on a poem by Li Po that H. A. Giles translated in *A History of Chinese Literature* (1901, p. 63).

1. *So-shu:* Japanese *So-shu* from Chinese *Chuang Chou* (Fang), Giles's *Chuang Tzŭ*.

2. *a bird, a bee:* Li Po's Chuang Chou merely dreams that he is a butterfly.

3. *uncertain:* "Now I do not know whether I was then a man dreaming I was a butterfly, or whether I am now a butterfly dreaming I am a man" (Giles's version).

ANCORA
[NO. 77. PRINTINGS: 18, 19, 39, 40, 42, 43, 55]

The Italian word *ancora* means "again." Pound wrote ANCORA because Harriet Monroe objected to some poems of his, notably COMMISSION, which she published in *Poetry* in April 1913 (*Letters*, pp. 53–54). Seven months later Pound had a group of equally *risqué* poems printed in the same magazine. The first of these was ANCORA, obviously written in protest against editorial prudery.

1. *risqué:* Pound wrote to Harriet Monroe in March 1913: "Again to your note: 'Risqué'. Now really!!! Do you apply that term to all nude statuary? . . . Surely you don't regard the Elizabethans as 'risqué'? It's a charming word but I don't feel that I've quite qualified" (*Letters*, p. 54). Fur-

ther examples of her censorship of his poems are noted in TO A FRIEND WRITING ON CABARET DANCERS (l. 36n).

2. Italian *canzonetti*, "little songs."

3–4. A fellow imagist, Richard Aldington, commented: "[imagists] convey an emotion by presenting the object and circumstance of that emotion without comment. . . . Thus, Mr. Pound does not say 'His Muse was wanton, though his life was chaste,' but he says that he and his songs went out into the 4 A.M. of the world composing albas" (*Egoist* [June 1, 1914], 202). The comparison Aldington has in mind seems to be with Herrick's epigram: "To his Book's end this last line he'd have plac't, / *Jocond his Muse was; but his Life was chast.*"

   alba: See the note to ALBA.

6. *Artemis:* We glimpse the moon goddess in the Actæon passage of Canto 4, and her "Compleynt . . . Against Pity" is heard at the beginning of Canto 30. On the theme of the survival of the pagan gods, see the note to SURGIT FAMA.

10. *granite Helicon:* Ironically recast in HOMAGE TO SEXTUS PROPERTIUS as "cushioned Helicon" (II, 1).

13. *knee-joints:* To speak of "knees and ankles" (SALUTATION THE SECOND) was part of the modernist program for shocking the bourgeois.

15. *Castalian:* Castalia was a spring on Mt. Parnassus, sacred to Apollo and the Muses.

AND THUS IN NINEVEH
[NO. 16. PRINTINGS: 3, 8, 53, 55]

A fanciful reconstruction of the obsequies accorded to poets in ancient Nineveh, where the royal residence of Assyria was located.

13. *subtle-souled:* The adjective is Shelley's, who applied it to Coleridge in "Peter Bell the Third" (V, ii, 2).

15. The movement of the whole line is Swinburnian.

16–19. An antistrophe to lines 1–4.

[20. Raama 3; Raana 8+]

20. Rana is goddess of the sea in Norse mythology. The earlier form "Raama" suggests the biblical "Raamah" (Genesis 10:7).

22. *drink of life:* A favorite expression in these early poems which recurs in THE FLAME and APPARUIT.

APPARUIT
[NO. 50. PRINTINGS: *14, 15, 42, 43, 53, 55*]

The title alludes to Dante's description in the *Vita Nuova* of his first sight of Beatrice. In Rossetti's version it reads (p. 311):

> At that moment the animate spirit, which dwelleth in the lofty chamber whither all the senses carry their perceptions, was filled with wonder, and speaking more especially unto the spirits of the eyes, said these words: *Apparuit jam beatitudo vestra* [Your beatitude hath now been made manifest unto you]. . . . I say that, from that time forward, Love quite governed my soul. . . .

Pound comments: "That the 'Vita Nuova' is the idealization of a real woman can be doubted by no one who . . . has known in any degree the passion whereof it treats" (*The Spirit of Romance* [1910], p. 115).

APPARUIT describes the effect of seeing the transfiguration of a young girl who is usually "a slight thing." The poem is an attempt at Sapphics, a difficult form that Pound was later to refer to as "the age-old bogie" (*Egoist* [Sept. 1917], 121).

It was partly as a result of Edward Marsh's criticism of this poem that Pound avoided becoming involved with the Georgian group in its early days. In *A Number of People* (1939) Marsh has recorded the incident which implanted in him "a lasting suspicion" of Pound's "artistic seriousness" (pp. 328–329):

> In the middle of dinner [Pound] asked me if I was up in the new system of quantitative verse; and as I had studied William Stone's paper on the subject and been further indoctrinated by Robert Bridges, I admitted that I was. Thereupon he produced a version of Sappho's ode to Aphrodite, and begged me to tell him if he had made any mistakes. He had; and when I pointed them out, he put the paper back in his pocket, blushing murkily, and muttering that it was only a first attempt. "Judge of my surprise" when some weeks later the piece appeared in the Poetry Review without a single amendment.

APPARUIT is not "a version of Sappho's ode to Aphrodite," but this inaccuracy does not invalidate Marsh's anecdote. See also the notes to BALLAD OF THE GOODLY FERE.

APPARUIT was set to music in 1913 by the concert pianist Katherine Ruth Heyman, to whom Pound dedicated the uncollected poem "Scriptor Ignotus" (*A Lume Spento* [1908], pp. 26–28).

1. *Golden . . . house:* In a Sapphic fragment (CXXIX) the muses are said to inhabit a golden house.

5. *roses bend:* Pound had already used this image in the uncollected "Sonnet: Chi è Questa?":

> Who is she coming, that the roses bend
> Their shameless heads to do her passing honour?

Provença (1910), p. 75.

7. *drinkst . . . life:* Repeated from the closing lines of AND THUS IN NINEVEH.

10. *steely:* The metaphor is proleptic: as the girl walks she cuts the air like a knife (an image used later in GENTILDONNA).

15. *oriel:* The entrance hall, now visible as she moves away from the portal and comes toward the poet.

18–19. *loveli- / est:* There is precedent for this breaking of a word at the end of a line in Sappho (LXXXVI).

[23. though in *14;* thou in *15+*]

23. *slight thing:* The girl in A VIRGINAL has "slight arms."

cunning: Her posture and skillful manner of dressing.

APRIL
[NO. 78. PRINTINGS: *18, 19, 39, 40, 42, 43, 55*]

[*Epigraph:* [*lacking*] *18, 19;* Nympharum membra disjecta *39+*]

The Latin epigraph ("the scattered limbs of the nymphs") is adapted from Ovid's description of the dismembering of Pentheus (*Metamorphoses*, III, 723–724).

1. *three spirits:* There are "three souls" in THE TOMB AT AKR ÇAAR and "three white forms" in an uncollected poem called "An Idyll for Glaucus" (*Personæ* [1909], p. 38). Enigmatic accounts of *tres puellae* are an ancient commonplace which Pound may have come upon in Dante's poem about *tre donne,* only one of whom is actually named (*Odes*, XIX).

4–5. In the first printing of APRIL there is a strophe division between the penultimate and final lines of the poem, which has the effect of isolating and focusing attention on the image which is to embody or "present" the experience that Pound is trying to communicate (as in GENTILDONNA and LIU CH'E). According to F. S. Flint, the device of separating the last line from the rest of the poem is borrowed from Verlaine (*New Age* [Dec. 9, 1909], 138).

Richard Aldington's parody, "Elevators," reads:

> Let us soar up higher than the eighteenth floor
> And consider the delicate delectable monocles
> Of the musical virgins of Parnassus:
> Pale slaughter beneath purple skies.

See FURTHER INSTRUCTION (1. 1*n*).

ARIDES

[NO. 88. PRINTINGS: 20, 39, 40, 42, 43, 55]

[TITLE: [*untitled section VIII of "Zenia"*]   20;   Arides   39+]

The motif of an ugly wife recurs in PHYLLIDULA.

AU JARDIN

[NO. 28. PRINTINGS: 9, 42, 43, 53, 55]

[*Epigraph:* [*lacking*]   9–43, 55;   From *Canzoni*   53]

See the note to THE HOUSE OF SPLENDOUR. AU JARDIN answers W. B. Yeats's poem "The Cap and Bells" by presenting a Pierrot who is unwilling to die for his love. See the note to AMITIES for other answers to Yeats.

3. *lattices:* The lady in Yeats's poem is at her window when she turns down the jester's offer of his love.

6. This is the opening line of "The Cap and Bells."

8–9. In Yeats's poem the lady sings her love song only after the jester is dead.

10. Yeats's jester gave the lady his cap and bells before he died.

AU SALON

[NO. 29. PRINTINGS: 9, 42, 43, 55]

See the note to THE HOUSE OF SPLENDOUR. AU SALON is the first of Pound's original poems to succeed in combining the rhythms of conversation with an ironic tone of voice, a formula that was to produce one of the most characteristic effects of Pound's later work.

10. *tea:* In an earlier section of "Und Drang" Pound represents the triviality of life by the image of people passing "between their teas and their teas" (*Canzoni* [1911], p. 47). Later, however, discussing the conventional habits of poets, he admitted wryly that at certain hours of the

day "tea is more palatable than mead and mare's milk" (*Poetry Review* [Feb. 1912], 72). Aldington noted in Pound and other American expatriate writers "an almost insane relish for afternoon tea" (cf. THE TEA SHOP), with the result that the birth of imagism took place in a Kensington tea shop (*Life for Life's Sake* [1941], p. 134).

15. *Sir Roger de Coverley:* Created by Joseph Addison in the *Spectator* as a representative of the squirearchy in Queen Anne's reign.

17. Pound's Latin ("thus the glory of the world increases") reverses the more familiar adage, *sic transit gloria mundi.*

18. *some circle:* See the note on CAUSA. Pound's disillusionment with such a circle is recorded in IN EXITUM CUIUSDAM.

21. *aegrum vulgus:* In *The Spirit of Romance* (1910) Pound mentions the work of an Italian neo-Latin writer of the Renaissance, Giovanni Aurelio Augurello (1440–1524), and observes that this man's " '*aegrum vulgus*,' 'diseased rabble,' is one degree more contemptuous than the *'profanum vulgus'* of Horace" (pp. 250–251; *Carmina Illustrium Poetarum Italorum* [1719], vol. 1, p. 408). Like the other "Men of 1914" (as Wyndham Lewis called them) Pound saw himself as one of the intellectual Samurai whose task was to uphold the finest standards in the arts and keep at bay "the aegrum and tiercely accursed groveling vulgus" (*Letters*, p. 54).

25. The Latin phrase means "dear household and family deities."

BALLAD OF THE GOODLY FERE
[NO. 21. PRINTINGS: 5, 6, 8, 53, 55]

[*The text of 5 was printed so badly that when the poem was reprinted in 6 it bore this note: "The Publisher desires to state that the 'Ballad of the Goodly Fere'—by the wish of the Author—is reproduced exactly as it appeared in the 'English Review.' " According to Pound, it was the publisher (Mathews) who "insisted on that funny little note" (Chicago MSS, May 4, 1916).*]

Pound once said that he wrote BALLAD OF THE GOODLY FERE as a result of having "been made very angry by a certain sort of cheap irreverence" (*T. P.'s Weekly* [June 6, 1913], 707). "For the first time in my life," he went on, "I had written something that 'everyone could understand,' and I wanted it to go to the people." He told Malcolm Cowley in 1923 that the poem

was "the first of the masculine ballads in the genre that Masefield would afterward exploit" (*Exile's Return* [1951], p. 121).
In actual fact, Pound's temporary interest in ballads was anticipated by John Masefield, who saw that the ballad might
be revived as a means of popularizing poetry. Pound was later
to reject the ballad as an obsolescent form (*Criterion* [July
1932], 587–588); and in any case, the idea of simply repeating the ballad formula was anathema, as he explained to Cowley (*ibid.*): " 'Having written this ballad about Christ,' he said,
'I had only to write similar ballads about James, Matthew,
Mark, Luke and John and my fortune was made.' "

Among the more famous early admirers of this poem was
Edward Marsh, who wanted Pound to submit two poems to
the first Georgian anthology which he and Rupert Brooke were
hoping to bring out in December 1912. In the September of
that year he asked Pound's permission to print BALLAD OF THE
GOODLY FERE and one other poem (probably PORTRAIT D'UNE
FEMME) which was due to appear in *Ripostes* that autumn.
Pound refused, and wrote to Marsh: "I'm sorry I can't let you
have *that* poem as I'm bringing it out in a volume of my own.
Is there anything in the earlier books that you like? (not *The
Goodly Fere* as it doesn't illustrate any modern tendency). . . .
Canzoni is the only one that comes within your two years'
radius" (quoted by Christopher Hassall in *Edward Marsh*
[1959], p. 193). Marsh was not impressed by any of the poems
in *Canzoni* (1911) and so Pound's work was not represented
in *Georgian Poetry, 1911–1912*. Later volumes were devoted
exclusively to British writers with the result that Pound's
work never appeared in them—an accident that saved him
from having to make what would have been an embarrassed
secession from the Georgian group a year or two later. See the
note to APPARUIT.

The epigraph's Simon Zelotes (sometimes called Simon the
Canaanite) was an apostle of Christ.

2. *gallows tree:* Medieval poets sometimes speak of the gallows
   rather than the cross because hanging was a more familiar
   capital punishment than crucifixion. Pound used the word
   earlier in A VILLONAUD: BALLAD OF THE GIBBET.

3. *lover . . . of brawny men:* Pound's Christ is the Victorian
   activists' Christ, the advocate of muscular Christianity.

7. *let these go:* Cf. John 18:8.

11. *Why took ye not me:* Cf. Luke 22:53.

[13. drank   5–8;   drunk   53+]

13. *we drunk:* Cf. Matthew 26:27.

18. *bundle o' cords:* Cf. Matthew 21:12–13.

39. *hounds:* An allusion to Francis Thompson's poem, "The Hound of Heaven."

44. *eyes . . . grey:* This feature recurs in CINO and VILLO-NAUD FOR THIS YULE.

45–48. Alludes to Mark 6:47–51. This episode had already provided Pound with a simile in an uncollected poem called "Partenza di Venezia":

> As once the twelve storm-tossed on Galilee
> Put off their fear yet came not nigh
> Unto the holier mystery. . . .

A Quinzaine for This Yule (1908), p. 15.

47. *Genseret:* Gennesaret (Mark 6:53).

BALLAD OF THE MULBERRY ROAD, A
[NO. 155. PRINTINGS: *36, 39, 40, 42, 43, 55*]

On the origin of Pound's translations from the Chinese see the introductory note to SONG OF THE BOWMEN OF SHU. A BALLAD OF THE MULBERRY ROAD is a translation of the first fourteen lines of an anonymous poem of fifty-three lines in *Yo-fu shih-chi*, VII, 28.5a (Fang).

2. *Shin:* Japanese *Shin* from Chinese *Ch'in*, the name of a state (Fang).

3. *Rafu:* Japanese *Rafu* from Chinese *Lo-Fu* (Fang).

5. *"Gauze Veil":* Lee and Murray note that this is not the meaning of Rafu.

10. *Katsura:* Unidentified.

12–16. Another example of imagist "presentation" (see AN-CORA, ll. 3–4*n*). The emotions of the men on seeing Rafu are implied but not stated.

BALLATETTA
[NO. 30. PRINTINGS: *9, 55*]

The Italian *ballatetta* means "a little ballade."

3. *light doth melt us into song:* See HOMAGE TO SEXTUS PROPERTIUS (V, 28*n*).

4. *healm:* Helmet. There is a similar image in THE HOUSE OF SPLENDOUR.

5. *jurisdiction:* A borrowing from Guido Cavalcanti, a "metaphysical" poet who used technical and scholastic terminol-

ogy in love poems. Pound's text and translation of Cavalcanti's fourth *ballata* read:

> Vedette, ch'io son un, che vo piangendo,
> E dimonstrando il giudizio d'Amore. . . .

> Weeping ye see me, in Grief's company,
> One showing forth Love's jurisdiction.

Sonnets . . . of . . . Cavalcanti (1912), pp. 96–97.

BATH TUB, THE
[NO. 89. PRINTINGS: 20, 39, 40, 42, 43, 55]

[TITLE: [*untitled section VII of "Zenia"*] 20; The Bath
Tub 39+]

A mock-heroic simile. In a covering note to Harriet Monroe,
Pound wrote (Chicago MSS, Dec. 3, 1912):

> The "Bath Tub" is intended to diagnose the sensation of
> two people who never having loved each other save in the
> Tennysonian manner have come upon a well-meaning sa-
> tiety. . . . No "spiritual gravity" or "quodlibet." 2 bodies re-
> duced to their chemical components. . . .
> It is the job of this art of ours to hale a man naked into
> the presence of his God (or whatever equivalent). . . .

An earlier title for this poem was "Courtesy" (Chicago MSS).

BEAUTIFUL TOILET, THE
[NO. 134. PRINTINGS: 27, 39, 40, 42, 43, 55]

See the introductory note to SONG OF THE BOWMEN OF SHU.
THE BEAUTIFUL TOILET is translated from *Wen-Hsüan*, XV,
29.1b–2a (Fang), the title being taken from the fifth line of
the original. There are versions of the same poem in H. A.
Giles's *A History of Chinese Literature* (1901, pp. 97–98; cf.
Letters, p. 154); Arthur Waley's *A Hundred and Seventy Chinese Poems* (1918, p. 40); and R. E. Teele's *Through a Glass
Darkly* (1949, pp. 29–31). Fenollosa's crib is printed by Stock
in *Perspectives* (p. 178).

1. *Blue:* "Green" (Teele). In Chinese the two words are inter-
   changeable, blue and green being regarded as shades of
   the same color. Fenollosa usually supplied *blue* where more
   recent, naturalistic translations have *green:* hence the exotic, willow-pattern element in *Cathay*. "Blue" also carries
   appropriate connotations of sadness.

4. "Bright, bright, (she sits) at the window; / Graceful, graceful, and adorned with red powder" (Teele).

6. *courtezan:* "singing girl" (Teele); similarly EXILE'S LETTER (l. 53*n*).

BEFORE SLEEP
[NO. 108. PRINTINGS: 23, 55]

Lapsing from consciousness at the moment of falling asleep, the speaker is suddenly aware of being in contact with the pagan deities in Hades (cf. FISH AND THE SHADOW). On the origins of this theme in Pound's poetry, see the note to SURGIT FAMA.

5. *She:* Presumably Pallas.

[6. Annuis 23; Annubis 55]

6. *Annubis:* Anubis was the Egyptian ruler of the dead.

[7. To these 23; These 55]

[9. Undulent 23+; Undulant *Faber and Faber, 1968*]

12. *Pallas:* Pallas Athene, goddess of wisdom.

BELLAIRES, THE
[NO. 120. PRINTINGS: 24, 39, 40, 42, 43, 55]

The epigraph is taken from Heine's *Lyrisches Intermezzo,* XXXVI ("Out of my great sorrows I make little songs"). On Heine see the note to TRANSLATIONS AND ADAPTATIONS FROM HEINE.

5. The numerical technique derives from Martial and is used more spectacularly in THE TEMPERAMENTS.

7–8. The monotonous rhymes are used for ironic effect throughout the poem, the sound -*air* occurring some seventeen times.

13. *attainder:* Forfeiture.

20. *Charles:* King of France, 1322–1328.

22. *Henry:* King of England, 1399–1413.

27. *Replevin:* A writ enabling a man to reclaim goods which have been seized to pay off his debts, and keep them until a court has decided whether or not he should surrender them.

estoppel: A statement that cannot legally be denied.

espavin: A facetious addition to legal jargon. "Spavin" (Old French *espavain*) is a disease in horses.

35–40. These towns are all in the south of France, in the departments of Aude (Carcassonne), Gard (Alais and Beaucaire [cf. THE GYPSY]), and Hérault (Agde and Beziers). "Pui" is perhaps Le Puy, in the department of Haute Loire. PROVINCIA DESERTA is a more ambitious exploration of the poetry of names.

BLACK SLIPPERS: BELLOTTI
[NO. 147. PRINTINGS: 30, 39, 40, 42, 43, 55]

[TITLE: Her Little Black Slippers 30; Black Slippers: Bellotti 39+]

Between 1910 and 1920 Pound and his friends used to dine at Bellotti's Ristorante Italiano, 12 Old Compton Street, London (*Letters,* p. 149). This is apparently the "moderate chophouse" of AMITIES (III, 4).

[2. little black slippers 30; little suède slippers 39+]

[3. her little white- 30; her white- 39+]

6. *Ostende:* A deliberate deflation. Ostende is easily accessible by Channel ferry and is not the place one associates with the exotic south, Italian ladies, *La Celestina,* etc.

[7–11. *In* 30 *only, the text reads as follows:*

The gurgling Italian lady on the other side of the restaurant
Attempts to recall her Pekinese,
. . . Fruitlessly . . .
For the sombre male customer caresses it
. . . Effusively . . .
The gurgling Italian lady on the other side of the restaurant
Glares, grunts, and replies monosyllabicly
To the remarks of the first, possibly Spanish, French product,
    And I wait.
I converse with my *vis-à-vis.*
I wait with patience.
To see how she will climb back into her black suède
Bright-buckled slippers.
    She re-enters them with a groan.]

"BLANDULA, TENULLA, VAGULA"
[NO. 31. PRINTINGS: 9, 42, 43, 55]

The title alludes to the lines quoted by Ælius Spartianus as the Emperor Hadrian's dying address to his soul:

Animula vagula blandula
hospes comesque corporis,
quae nunc abibis in loca

pallidula rigida nudula?
nec ut soles dabis iocos!

("O blithe little soul, thou, flitting away, / Guest and comrade of this my clay, / Whither now goest thou, to what place / Bare and ghastly and without grace? / Nor, as thy wont was, joke and play"—Loeb.) Unlike Hadrian, whose tone is speculative and uncertain, Pound conceives of immortality in terms of an earthly paradise.

"Tenulla" is a misquotation (a nonce word?) which Pound has never altered, and one that occurs elsewhere in his writings, as for example in his obituary note on Remy de Gourmont: "M. de Gourmont has gone—Blandula, tenulla, vagula —almost with a jest on his lips . . ." (*Poetry* [Jan. 1916], 202). The Latin poem was imitated by Pope and translated by Byron before the first four lines came to stand at the head of chapter eight in Pater's *Marius the Epicurean,* which accounts for its reappearance in Arthur Symons' *Cities* (1903) and Dowson's story "The Dying of Francis Donne" (1896): other Paterian motifs appear in SPEECH FOR PSYCHE IN THE GOLDEN BOOK OF APULEIUS and COITUS. Pound quotes in the original French Fontenelle's translation of Hadrian's lines as a postscript to "Twelve Dialogues of Fontenelle" (*Pavannes and Divagations* [1918], p. 142).

5. *Sirmio:* Pound alludes to Catullus, XXXI. *Sirmio* is the Latin name for what is now the town of Sirmione, which is mentioned in THE STUDY IN AESTHETICS.

7. *headland:* The promontory on which Sirmione stands is on the south shore of the Lago di Garda, which is alluded to in THE FLAME.

15. *Riva:* A town near the northernmost tip of the Lago di Garda, backed by the lower Alps. In a mock pastoral written a few months after this poem Pound speaks of the delights of being able to "lie on what is left of Catullus' parlour floor and speculate the azure beneath it and the hills off to Salo and Riva with their forgotten gods moving unhindered amongst them . . ." (*Poetry Review* [Feb. 1912], 72–73).

CANTICO DEL SOLE
[NO. 171. PRINTINGS: *44, 51, 55*]

[*Epigraph:* [*lacking*]   *44, 51;*   (From "Instigations")   *55*]

In the *Fioretti di San Francesco,* a fourteenth-century account of St. Francis of Assisi (d. 1226), there is a "Canticle of the Sun" by St. Francis which Pound translated in *The Spirit of Romance* (1910, pp. 88–89).

9. The Vulgate's *nunc dimittis* is translated in the Authorized Version as "now lettest thou depart" (Luke 2:29). Pound here poses as a latter-day Simeon who perceives that the "light to lighten the Gentiles" will never shine on an America which has closed its eyes to the classics.

The poem was written as a protest against Comstockery in America. The October 1917 issue of the *Little Review* was banned by the United States postal authorities because it contained Wyndham Lewis' short story, "Cantelman's Spring-Mate." The editress, Margaret Anderson, took the matter to court and succeeded in winning her case; but the whole action infuriated Pound. He quoted the judge who handled the case as saying:

> I have little doubt that numerous really great writings would come under the ban if tests that are frequently current were applied, and these approved publications doubtless at times escape only because they come within the term "classics," which means, for the purpose of the application of the statute, that they are ordinarily immune from interference, because they have the sanction of age and fame and USUALLY APPEAL TO A COMPARATIVELY LIMITED NUMBER OF READERS.

Commenting on the phrase which he printed in block capitals, Pound wrote:

> The gentle reader will picture to himself the state of America IF the classics were widely read; IF these books which in the beginning lifted mankind from savagery, and which from A.D. 1400 onward have gradually redeemed us from the darkness of medievalism, should be read by the millions who now consume Mr. Hearst and the *Lady's Home Journal!!!!!!* . . . No more damning indictment of American civilization has been written than that contained in Judge Hand's "opinion."

Little Review (March 1918), 34; CANTICO DEL SOLE follows on page 35.

[17*a.* [*lacking*]   44, 55;   *Oravimus*   51]

CANTUS PLANUS
[NO. 174. PRINTINGS: 47, 53, 55, 56]

The title is Medieval Latin for "plainsong." It is in keeping with Pound's views on the survival of the pagan gods (cf. SURGIT FAMA) that he should associate Christian plainsong with an invocation to Bacchus.

CANTUS PLANUS was reprinted in *Diptych: Rome–London*

(1957), partly because the publishers were short of copy and partly because the copy text used for this edition consisted of pages torn out of *Personae* (1926), in which CANTUS PLANUS follows HOMAGE TO SEXTUS PROPERTIUS as the last poem in the book.

3. The Latin *evoe* was the cry of the Bacchanals.

4. *Zagreus:* Dionysus, Bacchus.

5. There is a "black panther" in HEATHER (l. 1*n*).

6. Adapted from Catullus, LXII: "Vesper adest" ("The evening is come"—Loeb). Hesperus (the Evening Star) is invoked by Catullus later in the same poem.

CAUSA
[NO. 90. PRINTINGS: 20, *39, 40, 42, 43, 55*]

[TITLE: [*untitled section VI of "Zenia"*] 20; Causa 39+]

Causa is Latin for "reason" (in the sense of "the reason why").

1. *four people:* In AU SALON the élite was to consist of "not more than three." Such an attitude encouraged the use of semiprivate references in literature and resulted in obscurantism and *poésie à clefs.*

[3. World 20; O world 39+]

[4. know the 20; know these 39+]

CINO
[NO. 1. PRINTINGS: *1, 3, 8, 53, 55*]

An exercise in Browningesque monologue. From the location and date given in the epigraph it is evident that the Cino of this poem is the Italian poet Cino da Pistoia, who went into exile in 1307 (but see, however, NEAR PERIGORD, line 2*n*). It is likely that CINO was intended to be a companion piece to other imaginative sketches of earlier poets such as MARVOIL and PIERE VIDAL OLD. Pound's dissatisfaction with CINO—and with most of the poems in *A Lume Spento* (1908)—comes out in the letter he wrote to W. C. Williams in October 1908: " 'Cino'—the thing is banal. He might be anyone. Besides he is catalogued in his epitaph" (*Letters,* p. 39).

The epigraph seems to allude to Walt Whitman's "Song of the Open Road."

1. "I have had enough of women, and enough of love," says the wanderer in Arthur Symons' "Wanderer's Song" (*Im-*

ages of Good and Evil [1899], p. 178). Like Cino, he is attracted by the open road ("a long white road"), especially when "the sun shines and the road shines." But although the theme of CINO has been suggested by Symons, the expression is Browningesque, especially in this forthright opening which echoes the first words of "Soliloquy of the Spanish Cloister": "Gr-r-r- there go, my heart's abhorrence!" Pound uses the same device at the beginning of SESTINA: ALTAFORTE, and the debt is openly acknowledged in Canto 2:

> Hang it all, Robert Browning,
> there can be but the one "Sordello."

As Pound wrote to Iris Barry in 1916: "The hell is that one catches Browning's manner and mannerisms. At least I've suffered the disease" (*Letters*, p. 141). MESMERISM is another acknowledgment of Browning's influence.

25. *Polnesi:* The Italian word *Polinesi* means "Polynesia," but seeing that Cino lived for a time in Bologna Pound's "Polnesi" probably represents a dialectal pronunciation of *Bolognese* ("Bolognan").

34. *And:* If.

36. Pound seems to be using the Italian word *sinistro* ("ominous") in the heraldic sense of a "bend sinister," an indication of bastardy. Cino knows that the lord he is addressing in his thoughts is illegitimate and that if the secret ("all I knew") were out the lord would lose his inherited estates. The pun recurs in HOMAGE TO SEXTUS PROPERTIUS (II, 11*n*).

37–38. *women . . . all one:* When Dante took Cino to task for his inconstancy in love, Cino replied with a sonnet (LXXXVII) which ends:

> Un piacer sempre mi lega, e dissolve,
> Nel qual convien, ch'a simil di biltate
> Con molte donne sparte mi diletti.

Rossetti translates (p. 353):

> One pleasure ever binds and looses me;
> That so, by one same Beauty lured, I still
> Delight in many women here and there.

40. *grey eyes:* This motif recurs in VILLONAUD FOR THIS YULE and BALLAD OF THE GOODLY FERE.

42. *'Pollo Phoibee:* Phoebus Apollo, the sun. Nagy calls this part of the poem "a kind of facetious 'Cantico del Sole'" (p. 119).

47. German *Wanderlied*, "roving song."

47, 49. An early example of the kind of bilingual rhyming Pound was later to use in HUGH SELWYN MAUBERLEY.

50. *rast-way:* Path. In Canto 15 Pound describes his escape from Hell along a "narrow rast."

CLOAK, THE
[NO. 44. PRINTINGS: *11, 15, 42, 43, 53, 55*]

[TITLE: "Two Cloaks" [*section II of "Echos"*] *11;* [*untitled section II of "Echoes"*] *15;* The Cloak *42+*]

In its original 1912 printings THE CLOAK is paired with an uncollected poem called "Guido Orlando, Singing" under the inclusive and Henleyan title of "Echoes." THE CLOAK is a poem on the *carpe diem* theme and is based on a couple of epigrams from the *Greek Anthology* (V, 85 and VII, 32). Other translations from the same source are collected in HOMAGE TO QUINTUS SEPTIMIUS FLORENTIS CHRISTIANUS.

1–6. A paraphrase of an epigram by Asclepiades (3rd century B.C.):

> Φείδη παρθενίης· καὶ τί πλέον; οὐ γὰρ ἐς" Ἅδην
> ἐλθοῦσ' εὑρήσεις τὸν φιλέοντα, κόρη.
> ἐν ζωοῖσι τὰ τερπνὰ τὰ Κύπριδος· ἐν δ' Ἀχέροντι
> ὀστέα καὶ σποδιή, παρθένε, κεισόμεθα.

("Thou grudgest thy maidenhead? What avails it? When thou goest to Hades thou shalt find none to love thee there. The joys of Love are in the land of the living, but in Acheron, dear virgin, we shall lie dust and ashes"— Loeb.)

7. *cloak of dust:* Adapted from Julianus (4th century B.C.):

> "Πίνετε, πρὶν ταύτην ἀμφιβάλησθε κόνιν."

("'Drink ere ye put on this garment of the dust'"—Loeb.)

CODA
[NO. 148. PRINTINGS: *31, 35, 39, 40, 42, 43, 55*]

The synaesthetic word "coda" is properly a musical term for a passage of more or less independent character introduced after the completion of the essential parts of a movement, so as to form a more definite and satisfactory conclusion (*O. E. D.*).

CODA was written specially for *Lustra* (1916) and planned as a tailpiece to LADIES, PHYLLIDULA, and THE PATTERNS. The English publisher (Mathews) was reluctant to publish the latter two poems, which is why in the trade edition of *Lustra* (1916) CODA appears immediately after LADIES; in all other printings, however, CODA is placed correctly after THE PATTERNS.

COITUS
[NO. 101. PRINTINGS: 22, 39, 40, 42, 43, 55]

[TITLE: Coitus   22, 40+;   Pervigilium   39]

Coitus is Latin for "coition." Mathews protested against the inclusion of this poem in *Lustra*, whereupon Pound changed the title temporarily to evoke more explicitly the erotic *Pervigilium Veneris* which is the source of his poem. See SIMULACRA (l. 5n) for another example of Mathews' censorship: nine poems in all had to be omitted from the 1916 trade edition of *Lustra* (for details see the Chronological List, item 40). Censorship was a blight throughout this period, as Joyce and Lawrence knew only too well. Even Rupert Brooke had to be watched: Sidgwick agreed to publish his *Poems* (1911) only after Brooke had changed offensive titles like "Lust" and "Seasick Lover" into "Libido" and "Channel Passage."

1. *phaloi:* Greek φάλοι, "phalluses." The imagery in COITUS is reminiscent of what Pound had already criticised as the "middling-sensual erotic verses" of D. H. Lawrence (*Poetry* [July 1913], 149). There are other examples of erotic floral symbolism in MŒURS CONTEMPORAINES (V, 20) and HUGH SELWYN MAUBERLEY (l. 293n).

3. *naught of dead gods:* On the survival of the gods, see the note to SURGIT FAMA.

4. *procession:* See AFTER CH'U YUAN (l. 10n).

[5. Julio   22;   Giulio   39+]

5. Giulio Romano (1499–1546) is mentioned perhaps because he painted mythological scenes as though they were something he had experienced and not merely read about: in his art the pagan gods live on.

7–8. *Dione . . . nights . . . dew:* Dione, the mother of Aphrodite, is the presiding goddess in the *Pervigilium Veneris*, part of which Pound may here be paraphrasing:

ipsa roris lucidi,
noctis aura quem relinquit, spargit umentes aquas.

("It is she [Dione] who scatters the damp of the gleaming dew, which the night wind leaves behind him"—*The Spirit of Romance* [1910], p. 11.) Pound's interest in the *Pervigilium Veneris*, like Dowson's, was stimulated probably by Pater's use of the poem in *Marius the Epicurean*. Other Paterian motifs appear in "BLANDULA, TENULLA, VAGULA" and SPEECH FOR PSYCHE IN THE GOLDEN BOOK OF APULEIUS.

COME MY CANTILATIONS
[NO. 109. PRINTINGS: 23, 55]

A cantillation is a musical recitation of the sort Florence Farr used to make to the accompaniment of the psalter.

Between lines 2 and 3 Pound originally had the following six lines which he canceled before publication (Chicago MSS):

> They are a small and pungent lot,
> Their objects are scarce worth the mention,
> Let us have out with them,
> Let us cast them forth and be gone,
> There is too much else in the wood
> To be bored to name them further.

3, 12. The Mediterranean climate symbolizes for Pound the qualities of mind he admires in Mediterranean culture.

4. *pavements:* For an earlier rejection of urban surroundings, see THE PLUNGE.

5. *printers:* An allusion to Pound's numerous clashes with Mrs. Grundy, some of which are listed in TO A FRIEND WRITING ON CABARET DANCERS (1. 36*n*).

[12. And of   23;   Of   55]

COMING OF WAR: ACTÆON, THE
[NO. 127. PRINTINGS: 26, 39, 40, 42, 43, 55]

If the war mentioned in the title is the First World War, which had been in progress for nine months when this poem was published, then Pound's attitude toward it is extremely anachronistic. As an evocation of classical myth, however, THE COMING OF WAR: ACTÆON has affinities with SURGIT FAMA and similar poems about the pagan gods. It is also akin stylistically to the sequence of impressionistic phrases in the Actæon passage in Canto 4.

Ovid describes in the *Metamorphoses* (III, 143–252) how Actæon was punished for having seen Diana naked. There is possibly a submerged comparison between Actæon (metamorphosed into a stag and then killed) and the men who are meta-morphosed into soldiers.

5–8. Pound had used similar imagery in ΔΏΡΙΑ.

15. *Actæon of golden greaves:* An imitation of Homeric for-mulae, as in the *Iliad* (VI, 359): κορυθαίολος ῞Εκτωρ ("Hector of the flashing helm"—Loeb). There is a similar usage in THE RETURN. Greaves was the name for armor that pro-tected the lower parts of a man's legs.

[19. Host   26;   Hosts   39+]

20. *cortège:* See AFTER CH'U YUAN (l. 10*n*).

COMMISSION
[NO. 66. PRINTINGS: *16, 40, 42, 43, 55*]

This attack on sacrosanct institutions is in the tradition of Shavian Ibsenism. Pound's awareness of the importance of individual freedom was sharpened by his reading of Henry James, in whom he saw one of the great campaigners for per-sonal liberties. What James fights, he once wrote, "is 'influ-ence,' the impinging of family pressure, the impinging of one personality on another; all of them in the highest degree damn'd, loathsome and detestable" (*Little Review* [Aug. 1918], 7). Earlier he had quoted with approval a remark he attributed to William Blake: "The only evils are cruelties and repres-sions" (*New Age* [Oct. 31, 1912], 635).

[2. nerve-wracked   16+;   nerve-racked   *Faber and Faber*]

9. *dying of her ennuis:* The lady in THE GARDEN is "dying of . . . emotional anæmia."

14. *bought wife:* The theme of SOCIETY.

16–17. *delicate . . . delicate:* See ALBATRE (ll. 3–4*n*). When defending these lines, which Harriet Monroe found objectionable, Pound wrote: "The tragedy as I see it is the tragedy of finer desire drawn, merely by being de-sire at all, into the grasp of the grosser animalities" (*Letters*, pp. 53–54).

21. *algæ:* On this image see SUB MARE (l. 6*n*).

28–30. In defending these lines, Pound told Harriet Monroe: "We've had too much of this patriarchal sentimental-ity. Family affection is occasionally beautiful. Only people are much too much in the habit of taking it for granted that it is always so" (*Letters*, p. 54). In Canto 35 Pound protests in a similar vein against the intramural, the almost intravaginal warmth of hebrew affections, in the family, and nearly everything else. . . .

[34–35. *In 16 only, the poem ends:*

Speak for the kinship of the mind and spirit.
Go, against all forms of oppression.]

The two lines subsequently canceled seem to have been published as the result of an oversight on the part of Harriet Monroe. In March 1913 Pound wrote to her: "Note re / Commission . . . delete last two lines and use the line // 'Be against all sorts of mort-main.' "

35. *mortmain:* The legal sense seems to be less dominant than the etymological one ("dead hand").

CONDOLENCE, THE
[NO. 67. PRINTINGS: *16*, *39*, *40*, *42*, *43*, *55*]

Before abandoning the academic world in 1908 Pound had intended to write a doctoral dissertation on the Spanish drama-tist Lope de Vega (1526–1635). In the epigraph to THE CON-DOLENCE he quotes the opening lines of a poem by Lope called "La Doreata," which in 1910 he had translated in support of his theory that the "true poet is most easily distinguished from the false, when he trusts himself to the simplest expression, and when he writes without adjectives."

To my solitudes I go,
From my solitudes return I,
Sith for companions on the journey,
Mine own thoughts (do well) suffice me.

The Spirit of Romance, p. 219. The second line of the Spanish is echoed in Canto 80.

3. *Red Bloods:* Pound once diagnosed the diseases of American letters as being primarily "dry rot" and "magazitis," and among minor ailments he listed "the 'school of virility,' or 'red blood'; it seems to imagine that man is differentiated from the lower animals by possession of the phallus. Their work reads like a Sandow booklet" (*New Age* [Sept. 26, 1912], 516). See also FRATRES MINORES and L'HOMME MO-YEN SENSUEL (l. 67). Pound later changed his ideas on this subject, probably after reading Remy de Gourmont: see HOMAGE TO SEXTUS PROPERTIUS (V, 28*n*).

10. *fantastikon:* The Greek word φανταστικός means "receptive of images." Pound had earlier supplied an explanation of

this term when he wrote that "the consciousness of some seems to rest, or to have its centre more properly, in what the Greek psychologists called the *phantastikon*. Their minds are, that is, circumvolved about them and are like soap-bubbles reflecting sundry patches of the macrocosmos" (*Quest* [Oct. 1912], 44–45). However, in a covering note to Harriet Monroe he defined the word as signifying "what Imagination really meant before the term was debased—presumably by the Miltonists, tho' probably before them. It has to do with the seeing of visions" (Chicago MSS, March 1913).

DANCE FIGURE
[NO. 68. PRINTINGS: *16, 17, 39, 40, 42, 43, 55*]

The epigraph alludes to John 2:1: "And the third day there was a marriage in Cana of Galilee."

Swinburne and the Authorized Version of the Bible influenced the writing of this poem which evokes its subject matter by an almost incantatory use of rhythm. Hurwitz traces the exoticism to Rabindranath Tagore.

"There is vers libre with accent heavily marked as a drumbeat (as par example my 'Dance Figure')," Pound wrote in *Pavannes and Divisions* (1918, p. 108); but in a more critical mood he admitted that the poem "has little but its rhythm to recommend it" (*Letters*, p. 45). Originally DANCE FIGURE had a subtitle ("A Thoroughly Sensuous Image") but this was canceled before the poem was published (Chicago MSS, Dec. 3, 1912). The poem was set to music in 1932 by John J. Becker.

4. In "Aholibah" Swinburne writes: "There was none like thee in the land." This construction is used frequently in the Bible.

13. *almonds . . . husk:* When Lovelace watches Lucasta take a bath he is reminded of an almond blanched from its crust, but Pound's source is more likely to have been Swinburne's "At Eleusis," which is closer to the biblical tones of DANCE FIGURE:

> Also at night, unwinding cloth from cloth
> As who unhusks an almond to the white
> And pastures curiously the purer taste,
> I bared the gracious limbs and the soft feet. . . .

Pound had already written a poem in praise of Swinburne called "Salve Pontifex" (*Poetry Review* [Feb. 1912], 78–80).

18. *Nathat-Ikanaie:* Unidentified. It looks like a scrambled version of Ikhnaton.

20. *frosted stream:* An un-Galilean detail reminiscent of the *chinoiserie* elsewhere in Pound's writings.

DANS UN OMNIBUS DE LONDRES
[NO. 159. PRINTINGS: *38, 39, 40, 42, 43, 55*]

Pound evidently tried and failed to translate this poem into English before telling Harriet Monroe that she would "have to take it in the original" (Chicago MSS). The title indicates the sort of subject matter modernists feel they ought to write about. The need to create a new "poetry of the city" (cf. the note to N.Y.) is recognized in the titles of various books of verse published in London in the 1890s, such as Henley's *London Voluntaries* (1893), Davidson's *Fleet Street Eclogues* (1893 and 1896), Binyon's *London Visions* (1895), and Symons' *London Nights* (1895). "Omnibus" seems to have been a fascinatingly unusable word to poets ambitious of modernizing their diction (in Wilde's "Symphony in Yellow," for instance, an omnibus gets into the opening line, only to be compared disastrously to a butterfly). DANS UN OMNIBUS DE LONDRES evades the challenge that its title seems to imply, and shows that Pound had not yet acquired Auden's skill at writing poems about shunting engines and overshot waterwheels: certainly, the romantically "wandering busses" of VILLANELLE: THE PSYCHOLOGICAL HOUR are far less plausible than the skidding bus (which "sloppeth us") in ANCIENT MUSIC.

[1. morte aimée *38–43;* morte *55*]

1–2. A translation of the opening lines of THE PICTURE.

12. *colonnes . . . en "toc":* The scene is recalled in Canto 7:

> Another day, between walls of a sham Mycenian,
> "Toc" sphinxes, sham-Memphis columns. . . .

13. *Parc Monceau:* The scene of the remembered episode is Paris.

DE ÆGYPTO
[NO. 2. PRINTINGS: *1, 9, 55*]

[TITLE: Ægupton *1;* De Ægypto *9+*]

This poem "concerning Ægyptus" testifies (like THE HOUSE OF SPLENDOUR or PRAISE OF ISOLT) to the influence of Rossetti. Ægyptus inherited Arabia from his father Belus and conquered the land which is called Egypt after him.

1. *I even I, am he:* Rossetti uses this construction in "The Choice" (*The House of Life*, LXXIII):

Man clomb until he touched the truth; and I,
Even I, am he whom it was destined for.

The mannerism is of course biblical (I Kings 18:22) and recurs also in Dowson's poem "Vain Hope."

5. In Rossetti's story, "The Hand and Soul," the young painter Chiaro dell'Erma sees his own soul appear before him in the shape of a woman. Her outward resemblance to Pound's "Lady of Life" is unmistakable: "A woman was present in his room, clad to the hands and feet with a green and grey raiment . . ." (*Works* [1911], p. 553).

9. The Latin phrase means "my hand painted my soul." At the end of "The Hand and Soul" the narrator describes Chiaro's most impressive painting: "The picture I speak of is a small one, and represents merely the figure of a woman, clad to the hands and feet with a green and grey raiment, chaste and early in its fashion, but exceedingly simple. . . . On examining it closely, I perceived in one corner of the canvas the words *Manus Animam pinxit*, and the date 1239" (Rossetti, *Works* [1911], pp. 555–556). Francis Thompson has a poem called " 'Manus Animam Pinxit.' "

[12. chaunt *1;* chant 9+]

14. *Lotus of Kumi:* Probably an invented name, though Nagy calls it "the symbol of Egypt" (p. 103). Egyptology was to inspire THE TOMB AT AKR ÇAAR and Pound's later volume, *Love Poems of Ancient Egypt* (1962).

[18. I, that *1;* I, who 9+]

[20. my kiss *1;* my lips 9+]

[24. Of the sky *1;* Through the sky 9+]

[*In* 1, *four additional lines complete the poem:*

I will return unto the halls of the flowing
Of the truth of the children of Ashu.

I—even I—am he who knoweth the roads
Of the sky and the wind thereof is my body.

With minor variations, these lines reappear in 9, *but nowhere else.*]

DIEU! QU'IL LA FAIT
[NO. 45. PRINTINGS: 12, 15, 42, 43, 53, 55]

[*Epigraph:* From Charles D'Orleans / For Music 12–53;
————D'Orleans 55]

A translation of a song [VI] by Charles d'Orléans (1394–1465):

> DIEU, qu'il la fait bon regarder
> La gracieuse, bonne et belle!
> Pour les grans biens qui sont en elle,
> Chascun est prest de la louer.
>
> Qui se pourroit d'elle lasser?
> Tousjours sa beauté renouvelle.
> Dieu, qu'i[l la fait bon regarder,]
> La gra[cieuse, bonne et belle!]
>
> Par deça ne dela la mer,
> Ne sçay dame, ne damoiselle
> Qui soit en tous biens parfais telle;
> C'est un songe que d'y penser.
> Dieu, qu'i[l la fait bon regarder!]

In 1909 Claude Debussy's setting for d'Orléans' poem had been performed in Europe as the first of *Trois Chansons de Charles d'Orléans*. Pound had already done English versions of poems by Verlaine with Debussy's settings (*Miss Florence Schmidt . . . Book of Words*, 1910), and it is probable that he wrote DIEU! QU'IL LA FAIT with Debussy's music in mind. Some years later he expressed the opinion that "Debussy's settings of Charles d'Orléans" are among "the great songs one remembers" (*Dial* [July 1928], 18). IMAGE FROM D'ORLEANS is another translation.

1. The rendering of *regarder* by "regard her" recalls the method of translation used in THE SEAFARER. The French seems to mean "God, how good it is to look at her."

[4. folk   12–53;   folks   55]

"DOMPNA POIS DE ME NO'US CAL"
[NO. 102. PRINTINGS: 22, 34, 39, 40, 42, 43, 55]

[TITLE: A Translation from the Provençal of En Bertrans de
    Born   22, 39, 40;   The Canzon   34;   "Dompna Pois
    De Me No'us Cal"   42+]

[*Epigraph:* Original Composed about 1185 A.D.   22;   From
    the Provençal of En Bertrans de Born—Original————
    34;   "Dompna Pois De Me No'us Cal"   39, 40;   A
    Translation from the Provençal of En Bertrans de Born
    42, 43;   From the————55]

In the epigraph, the Provençal *en* means "lord." This is the poem referred to in the epigraph to NA AUDIART. Bertran de Born was a twelfth-century Provençal poet whose work inspired a number of Pound's early poems, notably NA AUDIART, NEAR PERIGORD, PLANH FOR THE YOUNG ENGLISH KING, and SESTINA: ALTAFORTE. According to legend, Bertran sang the praises of Maent de Montagnac with faithful consistency except for a short time when he turned his attention to Guischarda de Beaujeu. Maent is said to have discovered this minor infidelity and accordingly dismissed Bertran from her service, whereupon he wrote this poem in the hope of regaining her favor (see Boutière and Schutz, *Biographies des Troubadours* [1950], pp. 39–40). In this as in other stories relating to the troubadours there is a discrepancy between the romantic fiction invented by thirteenth-century Provençal biographers and the historical facts discovered by modern scholars such as Stanislaw Stroński, whose investigations are exactly contemporary with Pound's mythopœic evocations (*La Légende Amoureuse de Bertran de Born*, 1914).

In *The Spirit of Romance* (1910) Pound says that Bertran's poem is unique in Provençal literature (p. 41). It was, however, imitated by Elias de Barjols (I), and may be related to better-known "composite mistresses," some of which I have described in *Aumla* (Nov. 1966), 198–214.

The text of Bertran's poem reads as follows in Thomas' edition (1888):

Domna, pois de mi nous chal
E partit m'avetz de vos
Senes totas ochaisos,
No sai on m'enquiera,
Que jamais
Non er per mi tan rics jais
Cobratz, e si del semblan
No trob domna a mon talan
Que valha vos qu'ai perduda
Jamais non volh aver druda.

Pois nous posc trobar egal,
Que fos tan bela ni pros,
Ni sos rics corps tan joios,
De tan bela tiera
Ni tan gais,
Ni sos rics pretz tan verais,
Irai per tot achaptan
De chascuna un bel semblan
Per far domna soiseubuda,
Tro vos me siatz renduda.

Frescha color natural
Pren, bels Cembelis, de vos
El douz esgart amoros,
E fatz gran sobriera
Quar rei lais,

Qu'anc res de be nous sofrais.
Mi donz n'Aelis deman
Son adreit parlar gaban:
Quem do a mi donz ajuda,
Pois non er fada ni muda.

De Chalés la vescomtal
Volh quem done ad estros
La gola els mas amdos.
Pois tenc ma chariera,
Nom biais,
Ves Rochachoart m'eslais
Als pels n'Anhès quem daran,
Qu' Iseutz, la domna Tristan,
Qu'en fo per tot mentauguda,
Nols ac tan bels a saubuda.

N'Audiartz, sibem vol mal,
Volh quem do de sas faissos,
Quelh estai gen liazos,
E quar es entiera,
Qu'anc nos frais
S'amors nis vols en biais.
A mon Melhz-de-bé deman
Son adreit, nou corps prezan,
De que par a la veguda
La fassa bo tener nuda.

De na Faidida autretal	Bels-Senher, eu nous quier al
Volh sas belas dens en dos,	Mas que fos tan cobeitos
L'acolhir el gen respos	D'aquesta com sui de vos,
Dont es presentiera	Qu'una lechadiera
Dinz son ais.	Amors nais,
Mos Bels-Miralhz volh quem lais	Don mos cors es tan lechais,
	Mais volh de vos lo deman
Sa gaieza a son bel gran,	Que autra tener baisan.
E quar sap son benestan	Doncs mi donz per quem refuda,
Far, dont es reconoguda,	
E no s'en chamja nis muda.	Pois sap que tan l'ai volguda?

There is an alternative English version of all but the fifth stanza in Ida Farnell's *Lives of the Troubadours* (1896, pp. 114–117). Both Farnell and Pound omit the *envoi* which completes Bertran's poem, but the essence of this concluding quatrain is worked into NEAR PERIGORD (ll. 69–70, 115–116).

1. *lady:* Maent de Montagnac. Modern editors transcribe the Provençal word as *Maeuz* (French *Maeut,* "Maud"), but earlier editors like Stimming read it as *Maenz*—hence the form *Maent* in Farnell and Pound. Stroński argues that the story of Bertran's relationship with Maent was fabricated by Provençal biographers.

21. *Bels Cembelins:* The pseudonym of some unknown lady of Limousin.

28. *Midons Aelis:* Hélis de Montfort, the wife of Bernard de Casnac, was allegedly Maent's sister.

30. *phantom:* His imaginary lady.

31. *Viscountess:* Tibors de Montausier, the wife of Olivier de Chalais, is said to have reconciled Maent with Bertran (Boutière and Schutz, *Biographies,* pp. 43–44). She appears earlier in MARVOIL (l. 18n), and her real name was Guiborc (Stroński, pp. 87–88).

37. *Anhes:* Agnès was the wife of the Vicomte de Rochechouart.

40. *Audiart:* Reputedly Audiart de Malemort, but her real identity is unknown (Stroński, p. 96). Pound wrote a poem about her called NA AUDIART.

47. *Miels-de-ben:* In French *Mieux-que-bien.* It was the pseudonym of Guischarda de Beaujeu (the wife of the Vicomte de Comborn) and is mentioned in NA AUDIART.

51. *Faidita:* Stroński says that Faidida was probably a relative of an important baron called Peire Faidit (p. 96).

56. *Bels Mirals:* "Fair Mirror," pseudonym of an unknown lady.

61. *Bels Senher:* Maent's pseudonym, "Fair Sir."

65. *flame-lap:* The expression "lapped by flame" occurs in Canto 78.

ΔΩΡΙΑ
[NO. 46. PRINTINGS: *12, 15, 21, 42, 43, 53, 55*]

The title is ambiguous. If Pound's Δώρια is the Greek δωρεα (or δωρεια), meaning "a gift," then the gift is "me" (l. 5); but the word is probably an approximation to Δωρεια (or Δώρεια), i.e., "Doria," "the Dorian manner"—meaning by this that the firm and unspectacular love he offers will be of a quality more Dorian than (say) Mycenaean. Charles Norman suggests in his biography (p. 80) that Δώρια is Dorothy (Dorothy Shakespear) whom Pound met in 1909 and married in 1914.

Pound here rejects the transient attractions of romantic love in favor of something that is closer to harsh reality and therefore more likely to be durable.

1. *eternal moods:* The same phrase is used in Canto 80: "Actæon / of the eternal moods has fallen away." The term is Yeatsian. By "moods" Yeats meant states of mind which (like the psychic residue in Jung's "collective unconscious") are common to all men at all times—hence "eternal." See also Pound's commentary on LA FRAISNE, quoted on page 158 below.

6–7. The image recurs in THE COMING OF WAR: ACTÆON.

10. *Orcus:* The infernal regions.

DUM CAPITOLIUM SCANDET
[NO. 79. PRINTINGS: *18, 39, 40, 42, 43, 55*]

See the notes to A SONG OF THE DEGREES and MONUMENTUM AERE, ETC. Pound takes his title from Horace (*Odes*, III, xxx, 8–14):

> dum Capitolium
> scandet cum tacita virgine pontifex,
> dicar, qua violens obstrepit Aufidus
> et qua pauper aquae Daunus agrestium
> regnavit populorum, ex humili potens
> princeps Aeolium carmen ad Italos
> deduxisse modos.

("So long as the Pontiff climbs the Capitol with the silent Vestal, I, risen high from low estate, where wild Aufidus thunders and where Daunus in a parched land once ruled o'er a peasant folk, shall be famed for having been the first to adapt

Aeolian song to Italian verse"—Loeb.) The phrase *dum capi-tolium scandet* reappears in Canto 77 and is altered in Canto 88 to "Dum ad Ambrosiam scandet" (cf. THE ALCHEMIST, l. 3*n*).

5 ff. The apostrophe is reminiscent of Whitman.

6. *children:* Literary protégés (cf. TEMPORA). Pound was already beginning to attract poetasters who were content, as A. R. Orage noted, to "make their verses in his imagism" (*New Age* [Nov. 19, 1914], 69).

ENCOUNTER, THE
[NO. 91. PRINTINGS: 20, 39, 40, 42, 43, 55]

[TITLE: [*untitled section IX of "Zenia"*] 20; The Encounter 39+]

[1. while that they 20; while they 39+]

1. *new morality:* Sigmund Freud's books began to appear in English translations as early as 1910 with *Three Contributions to a Theory of Sex,* and the first translation of *The Interpretation of Dreams* (1913) was published privately only a few months before THE ENCOUNTER. Pound, however, has never taken a creative interest in Freudian theories (although he may, as Martin believes, have used the word *complex* in a Freudian sense when defining poetry as "an emotional and intellectual complex"); consequently, he was able to boast later of having "escaped the germy epoch of Freud" (*Letters,* p. 347; *Jefferson and/or Mussolini* [1935], p. 100).

EPILOGUE
[NO. 167. PRINTINGS: 39, 40, 42, 43, 55]

This poem is different from one of the same title described in Pound's *Letters* (pp. 45–46). See page 266 below.

4. *Chicago:* Many of the poems collected in *Lustra* were first published in *Poetry* (Chicago). Harriet Monroe, who edited *Poetry* at that time, has recorded in *A Poet's Life* (1938) the public reaction to the poems she printed (pp. 302–315).

7. *calash:* A woman's hood made of silk, supported with whalebone or cane hoops, and projecting beyond the face (*O. E. D.*).

9. *Only emotion remains:* Another "perfectly plain statement": see TO A FRIEND WRITING ON CABARET DANCERS

(ll. 24–25*n*). The epilogue to Pound's essay "A Retrospect" is subtitled "Only Emotion Endures" (*Pavannes and Divisions* [1918]); cf. "And the passion endures" (Canto 7).

10–11. *emotions . . . of a maître-de-café:* These are described in some detail in T. S. Eliot's poem, "Dans le Restaurant."

EPITAPHS
[NO. 110. PRINTINGS: 23, 39, 40, 42, 43, 55]

[I] A translation from Fu I (A.D. 554–639). There is another version of this poem (*Chiu T'ang-shu,* 79/3338b [Fang]) in H. A. Giles's *A History of Chinese Literature* (1901, p. 135).

[1. loved the green hills and the white clouds, 23; loved the high cloud and the hill, 39+]

[2. of drink 23; of alcohol 39+]

[*Footnote:* Fu I was born in A.D. 554 and died in 639. This is his epitaph very much as he wrote it. 23; [*lacking*] 39+]

[II] Pound translated twelve poems by Li Po (A.D. 701–762) in *Cathay.* Here he follows Giles's account of how Li Po died "from leaning one night too far over the edge of a boat in a drunken effort to embrace the moon" (*A History of Chinese Literature,* p. 153).

ERAT HORA
[NO. 32. PRINTINGS: 9, 42, 43, 55]

The Latin title means "it was an hour," one of those hours of total satisfaction when the ideal coincides with the actual and which are valuable as potential memories (HORÆ BEATÆ INSCRIPTIO). The Romantic notion that significant experience occurs in isolated moments of great intensity contributed to the stylistic devices of fragmentation and juxtaposition that Pound uses in the *Cantos.*

The use of a Latin title in a poem describing some transient experience of love recalls the practice of Lionel Johnson and Ernest Dowson.

EXILE'S LETTER
[NO. 128. PRINTINGS: 26, 27, 39, 40, 42, 43, 55]

[*Epigraph:* From the Chinese of Rihaku (Li Po), usually considered the greatest poet of China: written by him

while in exile about 760 A.D., to the Hereditary War-
Councillor of Sho, "recollecting former companion-
ship." 26; [*lacking*] 27+]

See the introductory note to SONG OF THE BOWMEN OF SHU.
EXILE'S LETTER is translated from *Li T'ai-po*, VI, 13.7*b*–9*b*
(Fang). Other versions are available in books on Li Po by
Obata (1923: pp. 89–92) and Waley (1950: pp. 12–15). In
1920 Pound selected EXILE'S LETTER, THE SEAFARER, and
HOMAGE TO SEXTUS PROPERTIUS as examples of his "major
personæ" (*Umbra*, p. 128).

1. *To So-Kin:* Japanese *Tō So-Kiu* from Chinese *Tung Tsao-*
   ch'iu (Fang). "To" is therefore not the English preposition
   but part of the man's name (the association with "to soak
   in" is unfortunate).

   Rakuyo: Japanese *Rakuyō* from Chinese *Lo-yang* (Fang).

   Gen: Japanese *Gen* from Chinese *Yüan*, i.e., Chancellor
   Yüan (Fang).

3. *Ten-Shin:* Japanese *Ten-shin* from Chinese *T'ien-chin*
   (Fang).

[5. month after   26;   month on   27+]

11. *regret:* "hesitation" (Obata); "they held nothing back"
    (Waley).

[12. And then   26+;   And when   *Faber and Faber*]

12. *Wei:* Japanese *Wai* from Chinese *Huai-nan* (Fang).

14. *Raku-hoku:* Unidentified. "Lo" (Obata, Waley).

[15. memories between us   26;   memories in common
    27+]

[16. And when   26;   And then, when   27+]

[17. travelled together into   26;   travelled into   27+]

17. *Sen-Go:* Japanese *Sen-jō* from Chinese *hsien-ch'eng*, "city
    of the genii" (Fang). Name of a mountain near Han-tung
    (Waley).

[19. of a thousand   26;   of the thousand   27+]

[21. And on into   26;   And into   27+]

[22. With   26;   And with   27+]

[22*a.* prostrating themselves on the ground   26;   [*lacking*]
    27+]

[23. came   26, 55;   come   27–43]

23. *East of Kan:* "Han-tung" (Obata, Waley). "Kan" becomes "Kan Chu" at line 28: Japanese *Kan-chū* from Chinese *Han-chung* (Fang), a state south of the river Han.

foreman: "Governor" (Obata, Waley). Pound repeats his odd translation at line 28. For all his attention to the *mot juste* Pound often seems unaware of idiomatic usage. An uncollected poem called "Nicotine," first printed in *A Lume Spento* (1908), is subtitled "A Hymn to the Dope" (p. 66); and his writing paper in the 1930s was stamped with an inscription used in copies of *Exile: "res publica, the public convenience."*

24. *True man:* "Taoist initiates" (Obata), "Holy Man" (Waley).

Shi-yo: Japanese *Shi-yō* from Chinese *Tzu-yang* (Fang). The Taoist Hu Tzu-yang (died *c.* 742), for whose grave Li Po composed an inscription (Waley).

25. *mouth-organ:* "bamboo pipes" (Obata), "reed pipe" (Waley).

26. *San-Ko:* Japanese *San-ka* from Chinese *Ts'ang-hsia* (Fang); "the Tower of Mist-feasting" (Obata), "the tower that he had built" (Waley).

Sennin: Pound's addition: see THE RIVER SONG (l. 6*n*).

[28. And the 26; The 27+]

31. *brocade:* An embroidered coat which the governor brought him.

[32. high that it 26; high it 27+]

34. *So:* Japanese *So* from Chinese *Ch'u* (Fang). A state to the north of Hankow.

35. *river-bridge:* "the bridge over the Wei" (Waley).

36. *leopard:* "leopard and tiger" (Obata); omitted by Waley.

37. *Hei Shu:* Japanese *Hei shu* from Chinese *Ping-chou* (Fang). A town in central Shansi.

42. *late . . . year:* The phrase is used again in IMPRESSIONS OF FRANÇOIS-MARIE AROUET (DE VOLTAIRE), III, 4.

[46. Then what 26; And what 27+]

47. *blue:* "green" (Obata, Waley). See THE BEAUTIFUL TOILET (l. 1*n*).

49. *castle:* "city" (Obata, Waley).

50. *blue:* "emerald" (Obata), "grey" (Waley).

51. *mouth-organs:* "pipes" (Obata), "flageolet" (Waley).

53. *courtezans:* "singing girls" (Obata), "girls" (Waley). See THE BEAUTIFUL TOILET (l. 6*n*).

[56. waters 26; water 27+]

60. *transparent brocade:* "robes of thin silk" (Obata), "gauze dresses" (Waley).

[66. Choyu 26; Choyo 27+]

66. *Layu:* Japanese *Yō Yū* from Chinese *Yang Hsiung* (53 B.C.–A.D. 18), "author of the rhymeprose on the Ch'ang Palace which does not mean 'the Ode of the Long Willows' as Obata would have it" (Fang). Waley translates: "my ballad of Tall Willows."

Choyo: Japanese *Chōyō* from Chinese *Ch'ang-yang* (Fang).

67. *no promotion:* High-ranking civil service posts went to men of literary ability (cf. the introductory note to FOUR POEMS OF DEPARTURE).

[70. again we met, later, at 26; again, later, we met at 27+]

71. *San palace:* Chinese *Ts'an-t'ai*, "Ts'an terrace" (Fang). Waley renders this as "the Terrace of Tso" and identifies it as the modern Pochow.

[78–79. knees to write and seal 26; knees here / To seal 27+]

[80. And I send 26; And send 27+]

[*Footnote:* Translated by Ezra Pound from the notes of the late Ernest Fenollosa, and the decipherings of the Professors Mori and Araga 26; By Rihaku 27+]

The original footnote to EXILE'S LETTER became the prefatory note to *Cathay* (1915). On Fenollosa, Mori, and Ariga, see page 263 below; Rihaku is Japanese for Li Po.

EYES, THE
[NO. 3. PRINTINGS: *1, 6, 8, 53, 55*]

[TITLE: The Cry of the Eyes *1*; The Eyes *6+*]

16–17. In Shakespeare's *Love's Labour's Lost* (I, i, 72–93) book learning is contrasted with the knowledge to be gained from contemplating the eyes of a lady.

FAMAM LIBROSQUE CANO
[NO. 4. PRINTINGS: *1, 3, 8, 53, 55*]

The Latin title ("I sing of fame and books") parodies the opening line of Virgil's *Aeneid:* "Arma virumque cano" ("Arms

I sing and the man"—Loeb), a phrase given fresh currency after the production of G. B. Shaw's *Arms and the Man* (1894).

[7. time *1–53, Faber and Faber;* times 55]

7. *what times:* A Latinism in the Miltonic manner ("quo tempore").

[8. Her *1+;* Here *Faber and Faber*
    then the *1;* the *3+*]

18. *book: A Lume Spento* (1908), in which the present poem was first published.

26. *age-lasting:* The adjective occurs also in an uncollected poem called "Sandalphon" (*A Quinzaine for This Yule* [1908], p. 18).

32. *Mammon:* See also TO DIVES. Pound's later preoccupation with his "usury axis" (*Letters,* p. 427) enabled him to deal more strikingly with the corruption of wealth.

[36. Shows *1,* 53+; Show *3, 8;* Show's *Faber and Faber*]

38 ff. Like Austin Dobson (in his poem " 'Sat Est Scripsisse' "), Pound here imagines his book having a fate similar to that of Edward Fitzgerald's *The Rubáiyát of Omar Khayyám,* which was consigned within a few months to the bargain box of a bookseller and "lay there till Rossetti found it remaindered / at about two pence" (Canto 80). See also HUGH SELWYN MAUBERLEY (l. 110*n*); *ABC of Reading* (1934, p. 64).

41. The Latin *loquitur* means "he speaks."

FAN-PIECE, FOR HER IMPERIAL LORD
[NO. 97. PRINTINGS: 21, 39, 40, 42, 43, 55]

This poem, which is one of Pound's pre-Fenollosan adaptations from the Chinese (like LIU CH'E and AFTER CH'U YUAN), has been condensed from H. A. Giles's account of an episode in the life of Pan Chieh-yü, a poetess of the first century B.C. When the Emperor took a younger mistress than "Lady Pan" (as Giles calls her) she sent him a silk screen inscribed with these lines (*Wen-hsüan,* XIV, 27.22*a–b* [Fang]):

> O fair white silk, fresh from the weaver's loom,
> Clear as the frost, bright as the winter snow—
> See! friendship fashions out of thee a fan,
> Round as the round moon shines in heaven above,
> At home, abroad, a close companion thou,

Stirring at every move the grateful gale.
And yet I fear, ah me! that autumn chills,
Cooling the dying summer's torrid rage,
Will see thee laid neglected on the shelf,
All thought of bygone days, like them bygone.

A History of Chinese Literature (1901), p. 101.

FAN-PIECE, FOR HER IMPERIAL LORD shows Pound's willingness to impose imagist principles on Chinese poems that are not manifestly imagist in method: the central image is isolated, "et tout le reste est littérature." The technique of THE JEWEL STAIRS' GRIEVANCE seems to have suited him better.

FAUN, THE
[NO. 103. PRINTINGS: 22, 39, 40, 42, 43, 55]

4. *capriped:* The word is used again in Canto 23 (Latin *capripes*, "goat-footed, a satyr").

5. *Auster:* The south wind.

Apeliota: Apheliotes, the east wind. These names occur together in a short poem by Catullus (XXVI), the last line of which Pound was later to use as the title of an uncollected poem called "The Draughty House (*'ventus horribilem'*)" (*Furioso* [New Year, 1940], 5).

FISH AND THE SHADOW
[NO. 160. PRINTINGS: 38, 39, 40, 42, 43, 55]

[TITLE: The Fish and the Shadow 38; Fish —— 39+]

The "shadow" is possibly the memory of an earlier life, a memory stirred only in dreams. In her sleep the girl has experienced an incident which took place in medieval Provence (cf. BEFORE SLEEP). Similar imagery is used in ORTUS.

16–17. The Provençal phrase means, "that I am handsome, I know." A Provençal biographer tells us that Arnaut de Mareuil (Pound's MARVOIL) was "avinenz hom de la persona" (Boutière and Schutz, *Biographies des Troubadours* [1950], p. 18); and in one of his poems Arnaut describes himself as "avinens" (III).

FLAME, THE
[NO. 33. PRINTINGS: 9, 42, 43, 55]

See the introductory note to THE HOUSE OF SPLENDOUR. Although the young Pound regarded poetry as primarily a literary craft, he wrote occasionally as though it were also a mystique, an indefinable something that gives the privileged poet access to arcane and quasi-mystical experiences. THE FLAME is a product of his preimagist ideas on the nature of poetry. The "flame" is an image for the elusive and transcendent qualities of an art that enables man to " 'pass through' " routine existence and taste "immortal moments."

2. *Provence:* Pound's views on the mystical aspects of Provençal love poetry are presented in an essay in *Quest* (Oct. 1912); see also the notes to THE ALCHEMIST.

[9. tales they ever writ of Oisin / Say   9–43;   tales of Oisin say   55]

9. *Oisin:* The "Ossian" of the Romantic poets. Pound would have read about this legendary Gaelic warrior in Yeats's poems.

12. *Ever-living:* The gods of Irish mythology.

[14a–b. *Additional lines in* 9:

> Barters of passion, and that tenderness
> That's but a sort of cunning! O my Love,

Reprinted with a slight change in punctuation in 42, 43]

18. *days and nights:* Arthur Symons had observed that since the true subject of art is "man with trouble born to death," the poet's "song is less of Days than Nights" (*Days and Nights* [1889], p. 4).

23. *gods . . . we have seen:* See the note to SURGIT FAMA.

[25. chrysophrase   9, 55;   chrysoprase   42, 43, *Faber and Faber*]

25. *chrysophrase:* On Pound's use of exotic precious stones (a pre-Raphaelite and nineties preoccupation) see Nagy's book on the preimagist phase (p. 84).

26. *Benacus:* The Latin name for the Lago di Garda, which is described in "BLANDULA, TENULLA, VAGULA."

40 ff. Keats's "chamelion poet" creates personæ without ever being a "person."

FOR E. McC
[NO. 5. PRINTINGS: *1, 3, 8, 53, 55*]

Eugene McCartney was a fellow student of Pound's at the University of Pennsylvania, where Leonardo Terrone was the fencing coach.

19. *Toledos:* The Spanish town of Toledo was once famous for the manufacture of sword blades.

FOUR POEMS OF DEPARTURE
[NO. 135. PRINTINGS: 27, 39, 40, 42, 43, 55]

The origin of Pound's translations from the Chinese is discussed in the introductory note to SONG OF THE BOWMEN OF SHU. There is a detailed study of FOUR POEMS OF DEPARTURE in *Literature East and West* ([Sept. 1966], 292–301) by R. P. Benton, who also reprints Chinese texts of the poems Pound translated and describes the milieu in which poems of departure originally came to be written. Civil service posts were awarded to men of literary talent (cf. EXILE'S LETTER, ll. 65–68) who were then sent to remote areas in order to avoid the possibility of political corruption in their native provinces. Of the poems selected by Pound as examples of this genre, only "The City of Choan" is not a true poem of departure.

Epigraph: The verse epigraph (*Wang Yu-ch'eng*, 5.5b [Fang]) is translated also in Soame Jenyns' *Selections from Chinese Verse* (1899, p. 39). According to Benton, the title of the original is "Seeing Envoy Yüan Erh Off to Anshi" (Anshi being to the west of Ch'ang-an, the capital of the empire).

1. *Light rain:* "Morning rain" (Benton; Lee and Murray).

6. *Go:* Japanese *Yō* from Chinese *Yang*, the Yang Pass (Fang), in the province of Kansu.

7. *Omakitsu:* The Japanese form of *Wang Mo-chieh*, i.e., Wang Wei (Fang). He died in A.D. 759 and was regarded by Pound as an "eighth century Jules Laforgue Chinois" (*Letters*, pp. 144, 154). In early printings Pound attributed the poem to Rihaku (Li Po) only.

[I] *"Separation on the River Kiang."* There are versions of this poem (*Li T'ai-po*, VI, 15–17a [Fang]) in H. A. Giles's *Chinese Poetry in English Verse* (1898, p. 66) and Obata's *Works of Li Po* (1923, p. 68). Benton's title is "At the Yellow Crane House, Taking Leave of Meng Hao-jan on His Departure to Kuang Ling." Lee and Murray point out that Pound's title is tautological because *kiang* (*chiang*) means "river" (the same error appears in THE RIVER-MERCHANT'S WIFE: A LETTER, l. 26).

1. *Ko-jin:* Chinese *ku-jên*, rendered as "friends" in the verse epigraph and "old acquaintances" in "Taking Leave of a Friend" below (Fang). The friend is Meng Hao-jan (A.D. 689–740), poet and recluse (Benton).

west: So Benton, but Fang has the friend sail eastward.

Ko-kaku-ro: The Japanese form of *Hang-hao-lou* (Fang), the Yellow Crane House at Wuchang, Hupeh (Benton).

2. *smoke-flowers:* "flower-scented mist" (Benton), "misty day of blooming flowers" (Lee and Murray).

5. *Kiang: Ch'ang chiang* ("long river") is a common euphemism for the Yangtze (Benton), which the Yellow Crane House overlooked.

[II] *"Taking Leave of a Friend."* There are versions of this poem (*Li T'ai-po,* VII, 18.2a [Fang]) in Giles's *Chinese Poetry in English Verse* (p. 70) and Obata's *Works of Li Po* (p. 94).

2. "Clear water winding around east of the city" (Benton).

4. *thousand:* "ten thousand" (Obata). There is the same discrepancy in THE RIVER SONG (l. 31*n*). Benton has "untold miles."

7. *clasped hands:* "waving our hands" (Obata; similarly Benton).

[III] *"Leave-Taking Near Shoku."* Obata prints a version of this poem (*Li T'ai-po,* VII, 18.3a [Fang]) in his *Works of Li Po* (p. 36). The original title is "Seeing Friends Off for Shu" (Benton).

Shoku: Japanese *Sho-ku* from Chinese *Shu,* the modern state of Ssuchuan.

Sanso: Japanese for *Ts'an-ts'ung,* first king of Shu. Fang also notes that Pound derived his epigraph from a commentary on the poem and later repeated the line as "So Shu, king of Soku, built roads" (*Jefferson and/or Mussolini* [1935], p. 100).

6. *Shin:* Japanese for *Ch'in* (Fang), the modern province of Shensi (Benton).

7. *burst through the paving:* "Fragrant trees encompass the plank highway of Ch'in" (Benton).

10. *diviners:* The fortune teller is Chün P'ing in the original (Benton). Pound's substitution of the general for the particular is a justifiable concession to Anglo-American readers, but quite untypical.

[IV] *"The City of Choan."* Obata translates this poem (*Li T'ai-po,* VIII, 21.9a [Fang]) in his *Works of Li Po* (p. 114). Pound's title is derived erroneously from the last line of Li Po's poem, according to Fang. Obata's title is "The Phoenix Bird Tower," Benton's "The Phoenix Tower of Nanking."

Choan: Japanese *Chōan* from *Ch'ang-an* (Fang), now Hsian-fu in Shensi and formerly capital of the empire (Benton).

1. *terrace:* "Tower" (Obata).

5. *Go:* Japanese for *Wu* (Fang), a third-century dynasty (Benton).

6. *Shin:* The Ch'in Dynasty lasted A.D. 25–419 (Benton). Cf. "Leave-Taking Near Shoku" (l. 6*n*).

7. *Three Mountains:* Twenty miles southwest of Nanking (Benton).

8. *Mountains fall:* "peaks hang aloft as though half-dropt from the sky" (Obata).

FRANCESCA
[NO. 22. PRINTINGS: 6, 53, 55]

Another of those many pre-Raphaelite beauties who derive ultimately from Dante's Francesca.

FRATRES MINORES
[NO. 111. PRINTINGS: 23, 55]

The term *fratres minores* usually signifies the Franciscan order of friars, but Pound is obviously referring here to the "lesser brethren" among his fellow poets.

[1, 6, 7. [*canceled with printers' ink*] 23]

2. *poets:* See THE CONDOLENCE (l. 3*n*).

4–5. *fact . . . discussed by Ovid:* Notably in the *Ars Amatoria.* See also page 3 above.

6, 7. Wyndham Lewis, who thought this poem a pleasant change from Pound's customary *passéisme,* wrote in 1949 explaining how the concluding lines came to be censored: "John Lane, the publisher of *Blast,* asked me to come and see him, and I was obliged to allow him to black out these two lines. Happily the black bars laid across them by the printer were transparent. This helped the sales" (*The Letters of Wyndham Lewis* [1963], p. 492). Iris Barry includes a facsimile reproduction of the *Blast* printing in her memoir of Pound (*Bookman* [Oct. 1931], 163).

FURTHER INSTRUCTIONS
[NO. 80. PRINTINGS: *18, 19, 32, 39, 40, 42, 43, 55*]

1. *Come, my songs:* Direct address to the "song" (as in an *envoi*) is a device used in various poems in *Lustra* such as ANCORA, CODA, COMMISSION, EPILOGUE, ITÉ, SALVATIONISTS, and SALUTATION THE SECOND. Richard Aldington no doubt felt that Pound had overworked this mannerism, for the first of his parodies of Pound's *Lustra* phase is called "Tenzone Alla Gentildonna" and reads quite simply: "Come, my songs" (*Egoist* [Jan. 15, 1914], 36). In this sequence Aldington included parodies of APRIL, THE GARDEN, IN A STATION OF THE METRO, and A SONG OF THE DEGREES, which are reproduced here in the notes to the appropriate poems because Pound himself once recommended critics to read "the very excellent parodies made by Mr. Richard Aldington" before composing their own (*Poetry* [June 1915], 158; see also the note to MR. HOUSMAN'S MESSAGE).

[2. envy for *18–32;* envy of *39+*]

3. *idle:* Cf. SALUTATION THE SECOND (l. 36).

[5. about the *18–32;* about in the *39+*]

[8. nobility *18–32;* nobilities *39+*]

14. *devoid of clothing:* Cf. SALUTATION THE SECOND (l. 16n).

17–18. *China . . . dragons:* Together with the opening of A SONG OF THE DEGREES these lines are among the earliest examples of *chinoiserie* in Pound's poetry. Both poems were published shortly after Mrs. Fenollosa sent Pound her husband's transcripts of Chinese poetry.

[20. Christ at *18–43;* Christ in *55*]

20. *Santa Maria Novella:* A Dominican convent in Florence.

GAME OF CHESS, THE
[NO. 129. PRINTINGS: *26, 28, 32, 39, 40, 42, 43, 55*]

[TITLE: Dogmatic Statement Concerning the Game of Chess: Theme for a Series of Pictures *26, 32;* — — — Statement on the Game and Play of Chess *28;* The Game of Chess *39+*]

[*Subtitle:* [*lacking*] *26, 32;* (Theme for a Series of Pictures) *28;* Dogmatic Statement Concerning the Game of Chess: Theme for a Series of Pictures *39+*]

When this poem was first published Pound was already an enthusiastic supporter of a new movement in the visual arts which he himself had named "Vorticism" and which brought together the diverse talents of such people as Wyndham Lewis, Jacob Epstein, and Henri Gaudier-Brzeska. In trying to define what the new art meant to a writer, Pound described the "Vortex" as being something "from which, and through which, and into which, ideas are constantly rushing" (*Fortnightly Review* [Sept. 1, 1914], 469). THE GAME OF CHESS is in these terms a vorticist poem, using a string of present participles to create an effect of flux and turmoil.

Harriet Monroe evidently thought that Pound had here written a futurist poem, but he corrected her by pointing out that the

> pictures proposed in the verse are pure vorticism. . . . The two movements are not synonymous.
> Admitted there is a shade of dynamism in the proposition, to treat the pieces as light potentialities, still the concept arrangement is vorticist.

Chicago MSS (April 10, 1915); cf. *Letters* (p. 101), and above, page 16.

The title of the *Blast* printing (28) recollects William Caxton's *The Game and Playe of the Chesse* (1475).

[4. lines in   26, 32+;   lines of   28]

12. *vortex:* The function of modern art, according to the Futurist Manifesto of 1910, is "to express the vortex of modern life." Pound had little time for the futurists (cf. LES MILLWIN, l. 9n) but he probably owed to them his conception of vorticism. He first used the word *vortex,* however, in an uncollected poem called "Plotinus" (*A Lume Spento* [1908], p. 44).

[14. light   26, 32;   lights   28, 39+
        Renewing   26–32;   Renewal   39+]

GARDEN, THE
[NO. 69. PRINTINGS: *16, 17, 32, 39, 40, 42, 43, 55*]

The epigraph derives from the prefatory poem in Albert Samain's *Au Jardin de l'Infante* (1893), which begins: "Mon âme est une infante en robe de parade." Pound comments favorably on this poem in the *Little Review* ([Jan. 1918], 6). Samain (1858–1900) represented for Pound the sort of poet who was "soft" in comparison with a "hard" poet like Théophile Gautier—more a poet of evocation than definition (*Poetry* [Feb. 1918], 264–271).

The woman in Pound's poem bears a slight resemblance to the Infanta of Samain's, and there are a few verbal parallels; but Pound seems to be interested mainly in the relation of aesthetics to social realities. THE GARDEN is an ironic modernization of seventeenth-century poems on the theme of "his mistress walking," like Suckling's "Upon My Lady Carliles Walking in Hampton-Court Garden." In such "promenade" poems, the lady is usually surrounded by flowers, not street urchins. Pound's parody of the convention was in turn parodied by Richard Aldington in "Convicted":

Like an armful of greasy engineer's-cotton
Flung by a typhoon against a broken crate of ducks' eggs
She stands by the rail of the Old Bailey dock.
Her intoxication is exquisite and excessive,
And delicate her delicate sterility.
Her delicacy is so delicate that she would feel affronted
If I remarked nonchalantly, "Saay, stranger, ain't you dandy."

Egoist (Jan. 15, 1914), 36; cf. FURTHER INSTRUCTIONS (l. 1*n*). The latter half of "Convicted" parodies ALBATRE.

[1. railing   *16, 17, 39*+;   railings   *32*]

1. *blown:* Cf. SHOP GIRL (l. 2).

> *dying of . . . emotional anæmia:* COMMISSION is directed in part toward "the bourgeoise who is dying of her ennuis."

7. *inherit the earth:* An ironic allusion to Matthew (5:5): "Blessed are the meek: for they shall inherit the earth." The list of beatitudes and comminations from the parallel passage in Luke (chap. 6) is probably one of the sources of the "blast" and "bless" sections in *Blast* (another being the *merde* and *rose* of Apollinaire's *L'Antitradition Futuriste* [1913]).

8. *end of breeding:* The relationship between aesthetic refinement and sexual sterility is one of the themes in HUGH SELWYN MAUBERLEY.

GARRET, THE
[NO. 70. PRINTINGS: *16, 17, 32, 39, 40, 42, 43, 55*]

Amorous episodes in attic studios, with intermittent sniping at bourgeois conventionality, are the stock-in-trade of literary bohemianism as popularized in Henry Mürger's *Scènes de la Bohème* (1851). Pound thought THE GARRET was "about the best" of the poems published as "Contemporania" in the April 1913 issue of *Poetry* (Chicago MSS, April 1913). In 1922 the poem was set to music by J. C. Holbrooke, who had been blasted in *Blast* (1914).

6–7. The image derives from Sappho (XIX), who speaks of the χρυσοπέδιλλος αὔως ("golden-slippered Dawn"—Loeb). In "The Critic as Artist" Wilde describes Beauty as having "slim gilded feet" (*Intentions*, 1891).

7. *Pavlova:* The Russian ballerina Anna Pavlova (1885–1931) first danced in England in 1910 and was afterwards celebrated in A. T. Cull's *Poems to Pavlova* (1912). Pound later described Pavlova as "that image of whom no one was privileged to speak who could not compass blank verse. . . . A decade ago . . . it was her own delicate and very personal comment of emotion upon the choreographic lines of Fokine which won her the myriad hearts . . ." (*Athenæum* [April 23, 1920], 553). The Russian ballet is mentioned less favorably in LES MILLWIN.

GENTILDONNA
[NO. 81. PRINTINGS: *18, 19, 39, 40, 42, 43, 55*]

The Italian *gentildonna* means "a gentlewoman."

2–3. *clinging / in the air:* This image occurs in an earlier uncollected poem called "Canzone: Of Angels," where Pound describes

> one round whom a graciousness is cast
> Which clingeth in the air where she hath past.

Provença (1910), p. 74.

3. *air . . . severed:* Cf. the image in APPARUIT (ll. 10–12).

4–5. On the use of the strophe division, see APRIL (ll. 4–5n).

GIRL, A
[NO. 52. PRINTINGS: *15, 42, 43, 53, 55*]

Like THE TREE, this poem is a study in Ovidian metamorphosis and is therefore related to the metamorphic sections of the *Cantos* which M. B. Quinn has studied. Daphne (also mentioned in THE TREE) extends her leafy hands toward E. P. in HUGH SELWYN MAUBERLEY (l. 195).

GUIDO INVITES YOU THUS
[NO. 23. PRINTINGS: *6, 53, 55*]

"Guido" is the Italian poet Guido Cavalcanti (1250–1300), whose poems Pound translated in *The Sonnets and Ballate of Guido Cavalcanti* (1912). GUIDO INVITES YOU THUS is an "answer to an answer" and rather more complicated than the "answers" listed in the note to AMITIES. Dante wrote a sonnet (XXXII) describing how he, Guido, Lapo Gianni, and their three ladies might embark together on an idyllic voyage of love. Guido replied with a sonnet (translated in *Sonnets . . . of . . . Cavalcanti,* p. 63) in which he declared that he was no longer in love with the same woman and therefore unworthy to accompany Dante and Lapo. Pound, however, liked to believe that Guido was happily married (*ibid.,* p. 10), and suggests here that Guido rejected Dante's offer simply because he was too much in love with his own wife to want to share her company with others.

Rossetti translated the relevant sonnets by Dante and Guido (*Works* [1911], pp. 361–362).

2. *thee:* Guido's wife.

GYPSY, THE
[NO. 130. PRINTINGS: 26, 32, 39, 40, 42, 43, 55]

6, 10. *Clermont . . . Arles . . . Biaucaire:* Towns in the south of France, in the departments of Hérault (Clermont), Bouches du Rhône (Arles), and Gard (Beaucaire: cf. THE BELLAIRES, ll. 35–40n). Pound walked extensively in this area before writing PROVINCIA DESERTA.

HEATHER
[NO. 104. PRINTINGS: 22, 32, 39, 40, 42, 43, 55]

Pound's comments on IN A STATION OF THE METRO are of more use to the reader of this poem than his evasive remark that HEATHER "represents a state of consciousness, or 'implies,' or 'implicates' it" (*Fortnightly Review* [Sept. 1, 1914], 464). Perhaps he meant that the technique of HEATHER is symbolist: see the note to PHANOPŒIA.

1. *black panther:* In CANTUS PLANUS and Canto 93 "the black panther lies under his rose tree." On the significance of such repetitions see THE ALCHEMIST (l. 3n).

HER MONUMENT, THE IMAGE CUT THEREON
[NO. 34. PRINTINGS: 9, 42, 43, 55]

[*Epigraph:* From the Italian of Leopardi / (Written 1831–3 circa) 9–43; From ——— Leopardi 55]

Pound has never formulated a critical attitude toward the poetry of Giacomo Leopardi (1798–1837). "In Leopardi," he once wrote, untypically, "there is such sincerity, such fire of sombre pessimism, that one can not carp or much question his manner" (*Poetry* [Feb. 1915], 232). "Sopra il Ritratto di Una Bella Donna" has had less influence on Pound's work than the famous ode "All'Italia," the opening lines of which Pound quoted in the *New Age* ([Sept. 16, 1915], 471) and which gave him the title ("Patria Mia") for a series of articles on "the state of America" that he published in the *New Age* in 1912. He seems to have been interested more in the content of Leopardi's poetry than in its verse technique, and particularly admired Leopardi's use of the past in assessing the values of modernity.

HER MONUMENT, THE IMAGE CUT THEREON is among the most literal of Pound's translations, although it contains the usual omissions, transpositions, alterations, and misunderstandings. Pound seems to have lost track of the Italian syntax at lines 10–12, 26–31, and 41–45, and he alters the tone of the original in a couple of places. In lines 18–21, for example, he seems to have gone out of his way to avoid Leopardi's insistence on the physical decay of the body after death. He renders the precise phrase, "fango / Ed ossa" ("filth and bones"), by the genteel circumlocution "Shameful"—thus losing the counterpoint with "l'ossa e il fango" in the second line of the Italian; and later, at line 52, he ignores Leopardi's "polve ed ombra" ("dust and shade"). Another notable omission occurs at the point where Pound excises lines 15–16 of Leopardi's poem, and in doing so betrays an unexpected coyness. The censored lines read:

> E il seno, onde la gente
> Visibilmente di pallor si tinse ...

("The breast which visibly / Made men turn pale"—Origo and Heath-Stubbs). For the rest, it is worth noting that this translation is rather more adjectival than the original and as such is censurable on strictly Poundian terms, for words like "rusted," "speeding," and "swift" are mere padding. In places Pound has tried to duplicate Leopardi's use of medial rhymes, but his successes were intermittent: "dusted / rusted," "Mounts / fount" are evidence of such an attempt, and he also draws attention to what would have been medial rhymes by breaking long lines in half—"thou / now," "fates / state," "art / part," and "thought / wrought." The Italian text reads as follows (ed. Origo and Heath-Stubbs, 1966):

> Tal fosti: or qui sotterra
> Polve e scheletro sei. Su l'ossa e il fango
> Immobilmente collocato invano,
> Muto, mirando dell'etadi il volo,
> Sta, di memoria solo
> E di dolor custode, il simulacro
> Della scorsa beltà. Quel dolce sguardo,

Che tremar fe, se, come or sembra, immoto
In altrui s'affisò; quel labbro, ond'alto
Par, come d'urna piena,
Traboccare il piacer; quel collo, cinto
Già di desio; quell'amorosa mano,
Che spesso, ove fu porta,
Sentì gelida far la man che strinse;

. . . .
Furo alcun tempo: or fango
Ed ossa sei: la vista
Vituperosa e trista un sasso asconde.

   Così riduce il fato
Qual sembianza fra noi parve più viva
Immagine del ciel. Misterio eterno
Dell'esser nostro. Oggi d'eccelsi, immensi
Pensieri e sensi inenarrabil fonte,
Beltà grandeggia, e pare,
Quale splendor vibrato
Da natura immortal su queste arene,
Di sovrumani fati,
Di fortunati regni e d'aurei mondi
Segno e sicura spene
Dare al mortale stato:
Diman, per lieve forza,
Sozzo a vedere, abominoso, abbietto
Divien quel che fu dianzi
Quasi angelico aspetto,
E dalle menti insieme
Quel che da lui moveva
Ammirabil concetto, si dilegua.

   Desiderii infiniti
E visioni altere
Crea nel vago pensiere,
Per natural virtù, dotto concento;
Onde per mar delizioso, arcano
Erra lo spirto umano,
Quasi come a diporto
Ardito notator per l'Oceano:
Ma se un discorde accento
Fere l'orecchio, in nulla
Torna quel paradiso in un momento.

   Natura umana, or come,
Se frale in tutto e vile,
Se polve ed ombra sei, tant'alto senti?
Se in parte anco gentile,
Come i più degni tuoi moti e pensieri
Son così di leggeri
Da sì basse cagioni e desti e spenti?

29. *quivering splendour cast:* Italian *splendor vibrato.* Pound works into his translation the two senses of *vibrare*, "to hurl" and "to quiver."

[42. thought 9+; thoughts *Faber and Faber*]

45. *pilot:* Italian *notator*, "swimmer." Did Pound confuse *notator* with *nauta* ("navigator")?

46. *tympanum:* Italian *orecchio*, "ear." Pound's word is anatomically exact and also develops the musical sense of "concord" three lines earlier.

HOMAGE TO QUINTUS SEPTIMIUS FLORENTIS CHRISTIANUS
[NO. 161. PRINTINGS: 38, 39, 40, 42, 43, 55]

This selection of epigrams translated from the *Greek Anthology* is dedicated to Florent Chrétien (1540–1596), who latinized his name (in the manner of Tertullian) as Quintus Septimius Florens Christianus when publishing a volume of *Epigrammata ex Libris Graecae Anthologiae* (1608). In a canceled footnote to this sequence of poems Pound wrote: "I am quite well aware that certain lines above have no particular relation to the words or meaning of the original" (Chicago MSS). These poems show how the epigrammatic tradition was transmitted from pagan Greece to Christendom.

There are echoes of two other poems from the *Greek Anthology* in THE CLOAK; see also the note to PHYLLIDULA. In earlier printings [38–43] the Latin phrase *ex libris Graecae* ("from the Grecian books") is an epigraph to the whole sequence, as it is in the Faber and Faber text of 1968.

[I] A translation from Simonides (c. 556–468 B.C.), a writer of lyric and elegiac poems (*Greek Anthology*, X, 105):

> Χαίρει τις Θεόδωρος, ἐπεὶ θάνον· ἄλλος ἐπ' αὐτῷ
> χαιρήσει. θανάτῳ πάντες ὀφειλόμεθα.

("A certain Theodorus rejoices because I am dead. Another shall rejoice at his death. We are all owed to death"—Loeb.)

[*Footnote: Incerti Auctoris 38; [lacking] 39+*]

[II] From Anyte (fl. 290 B.C.), an Arcadian poetess (*Greek Anthology*, IX, 144):

> Κύπριδος οὗτος ὁ χῶρος, ἐπεὶ φίλον ἔπλετο τήνᾳ
> αἰὲν ἀπ' ἠπείρου λαμπρὸν ὁρῆν πέλαγος,
> ὄφρα φίλον ναύτῃσι τελῇ πλόον· ἀμφὶ δὲ πόντος
> δειμαίνει, λιπαρὸν δερκόμενος ξόανον.

("This is the place of Cypris, for it is sweet to her to look ever from the land on the bright deep, that she may make the voyages of sailors happy; and around the sea trembles, looking on her polished image"—Loeb.) Richard Aldington's version of this poem (*Egoist* [Sept. 1, 1915], 139) preceded Pound's by a year.

1. *Cyprian:* Venus was worshiped in Cyprus.

[III] From Palladas of Alexandria (fl. A.D. 400), a school-master (*Greek Anthology*, X, 59):

Προσδοκίη θανάτου πολυώδυνός ἐστιν ἀνίη·
τοῦτο δὲ κερδαίνει θνητὸς ἀπολλύμενος.
μὴ τοίνυν κλαύσῃς τὸν ἀπερχόμενον βιότοιο·
οὐδὲν γάρ θανάτου δεύτερόν ἐστι πάθος.

("The expectation of death is a trouble full of pain, and a mortal, when he dies, gains freedom from this. Weep not then for him who departs from life, for there is no suffering beyond death"—Loeb.) A few weeks before this poem was published Pound wrote to Iris Barry telling her that poetry relies on stylistic concision and the presentation of images, but that in addition "one can make simple emotional statements of fact, such as 'I am tired,' or simple credos like 'After death there comes no other calamity' " (*Letters*, p. 141). Parts of TAME CAT and TO A FRIEND WRITING ON CABARET DANCERS (ll. 24–25*n*) have been shaped by the same idea. "The charm of Palladas' impartial pessimism" is commended in Pound's essay on Horace (*Criterion* [Jan. 1930], 218).

2. *inane expenses of the funeral:* A facetious rendering of Chrétien's Latin, "lucri funus inane," where *funus* means "the dead man."

[IV] From Agathias Scholasticus (A.D. 536–582), who com-piled one of the first collections of Greek epigrams (*Greek Anthology*, IX, 153):

'Ω πόλι, πῇ σέο κεῖνα τὰ τείχεα, πῇ πολύολβοι
νηοί; πῇ δὲ βοῶν κράατα τεμνομένων;
πῇ Παφίης ἀλάβαστρα, καὶ ἡ πάγχρυσος ἐφεστρίς;
πῇ δὲ Τριτογενοῦς δείκελον ἐνδαπίης;
πάντα μόθος χρονίη τε χύσις καὶ Μοῖρα κραταιὴ
ἥρπασεν, ἀλλοίην ἀμφιβαλοῦσα τύχην.
καί σε τόσον νίκησε βαρὺς φθόνος· ἀλλ' ἄρα μοῦνον
οὔνομα σὸν κρύψαι καὶ κλέος οὐ δύναται.

("Where are those walls of thine, O city, where thy temples full of treasure, where the heads of the oxen thou wast wont to slay? Where are Aphrodite's caskets of ointment and her mantle all of gold? Where is the image of thy own Athena?

Thou hast been robbed of all by war and the decay of ages, and the strong hand of Fate, which reversed thy fortunes. So far did bitter Envy subdue thee; but thy name and glory alone she cannot hide"—Loeb.) There are *ubi sunt* passages in *The Pisan Cantos*, such as the one beginning: "Nancy where art thou?" (Canto 80).

1. *profits:* Pound read Chrétien's translation *moenia* ("walls") as *moenera* ("gifts").

[4. perfume   38;   perfumes   39+]

[5. are the works   38;   is the work   39+]

6. *tooth:* The expression recurs in HOMAGE TO SEXTUS PROPERTIUS (IX, 19).

8. *douth:* Pound defended this archaism in a footnote that was canceled before publication (Chicago MSS): "The word 'douth' exists in English but it has been mislaid by the pedants. Ang-sax: duguth (as yuguth which becomes youth). 'Doughtiness' from the derivative adjective is a doubly insipid form."

[*Footnote:* Agathias   38, *Faber and Faber*, 1968;   Agathas   39+]

[V] From Palladas (*Greek Anthology*, XI, 381):

Πᾶσα γυνὴ χόλος ἐστίν· ἔχει δ' ἀγαθὰς δύω ὥρας,
τὴν μίαν ἐν θαλάμῳ, τὴν μίαν ἐν θανάπῳ.

("Every woman is a source of annoyance, but she has two good seasons, the one in her bridal chamber and the other when she is dead"—Loeb.)

[VI] Attributed by the Loeb editor to a practically unknown poet called Callicter, and by Chrétien to Nicarchus of Alexandria (1st century A.D.):

Οὔτ' ἔκλυσεν Φείδων μ', οὔθ' ἥψατο· ἀλλὰ πυρέξας
ἐμνήσθην αὐτοῦ τοὔνομα, κἀπέθανον.

("Phidon did not purge me with a clyster or even feel me, but feeling feverish I remembered his name and died"—Loeb.)

[*Title:* Nicharcus   38+; Nicarchus *Faber and Faber*, 1968]

HOMAGE TO SEXTUS PROPERTIUS

[NO. 176. PRINTINGS: 48 [I–III, VI *only*], 49 [I, III–VI, VIII *only*], 50, 54, 55, 56]

HOMAGE TO SEXTUS PROPERTIUS is one of Pound's "major personæ" (*Umbra* [1920], p. 128) and is made up of a series of adaptations from the *Elegies* of Sextus Propertius, a Roman poet who lived and wrote during the last fifty years of the first century A.D. Propertius' liaison with "Cynthia" provided material for his first book of *Elegies*, after the publication of which he became acquainted with Gaius Cilnius Maecenas, who was at that time a powerful political figure as well as patron of the literary circle that included Virgil and Horace. In the second book of *Elegies* we discover that Propertius was asked to write fewer love poems and begin writing patriotic and political verses. Required to produce what was in effect government propaganda, he contrived (by a series of evasions and occasional compromises) to go on writing the sort of poetry for which he knew he was best fitted.

Propertius' struggle to maintain what would now be called his artistic integrity in conditions that constantly demanded a compromise of his talents was something that appealed to Pound for obvious reasons. Propertius, he felt, in resisting the solicitations of Maecenas, was almost a symbolic figure, representing "the spirit of the young man of the Augustan Age, hating rhetoric and undeceived by imperial hog-wash" (*Letters*, p. 212). In the first part of HUGH SELWYN MAUBERLEY Pound was to present himself as similarly struggling against the Maecenases of the modern world (*Letters*, p. 321); and his sense of identity was further strengthened by the fact that both he and Propertius were writing in time of war and in countries committed to imperialistic policies: the situation was a "repeat in history" (*Letters*, p. 285) of the sort explored in the *Cantos*. Pound put the matter succinctly when, in 1931, he said that his poem "presents certain emotions as vital to me in 1917, faced with the infinite and ineffable imbecility of the British Empire, as they were to Propertius some centuries earlier, when faced with the infinite and ineffable imbecility of the Roman Empire" (*Letters*, p. 310).

HOMAGE TO SEXTUS PROPERTIUS is based on selected passages from the second and third books of the *Elegies* (Loeb numbering). Pound often follows the original quite closely, occasionally barely alludes to it, and sometimes apparently mistranslates it. The apparent mistranslations have brought a good deal of ridicule on the poem. Pound, on the other hand, protests that he never intended to produce a literal translation. "There was never any question of translation, let alone literal translation," he wrote in 1919. "My job was to bring a dead man to life, to present a living figure" (*Letters*, p. 211). And again: "The thing is no more a translation than my 'Altaforte' is a translation, or than Fitzgerald's Omar is a translation" (Chicago MSS, April 14, 1919). As he pointed out, if he had wanted to do a literal rendering he could have produced an accurate one by using a "Bohn crib" (*Letters*, p. 245). Readers who find such remarks plausible sometimes propose treating the poem as an *imitation,* in the neoclassical sense. This is the gist of a persuasive defense of the HOMAGE by J. P. Sullivan, who regards it as the only recent poem comparable to *The Vanity of Human Wishes* or *The Rubáiyát of Omar Khayyám.* Yet one's experience in reading this poem of Pound's is not exactly what it ought to be if Sullivan is right, for HOMAGE TO SEXTUS PROPERTIUS is not so obviously an imitation of Propertius as *The Vanity of Human Wishes* is an imitation of Juvenal's tenth satire. Its frame of reference is insufficiently English, and there are not enough anachronisms: one cannot feel that the poem is conditioned by wartime London, nor imagine Propertius as a contemporary of Eliot and a contributor to the *Little Review;* the references to Yeats, Kandinsky, and the rest are far too subtle to be effective. If it is an imitation then it is not a very satisfactory one, but I find it hard to believe that Pound wanted simply to make Propertius relevant to our own times (which is what writers of imitations usually aim at doing). HOMAGE TO SEXTUS PROPERTIUS is essentially the work of a scholar *manqué* convinced that he has finally uncovered the "real" Propertius whose qualities have been overlooked by orthodox scholars who spend their time obscuring the texts with philology (Canto 14). Propertius was to be redeemed from scholarly bondage as a result of Pound's brilliant but problematic notion that Propertius had evolved a complex form of verbal irony, using the vocabulary of Virgil and Horace but at the same time parodying it by various forms of wordplay. Academics, of course, had been blind to these subtleties (*Letters,* pp. 245–246):

> Mac[k]ail (accepted as "right" opinion on the Latin poets) hasn't, apparently, *any* inkling of the *way* in which Propertius is using Latin. Doesn't see that S. P. is tying blue ribbon in the tails of Virgil and Horace, or that sometime after his first "book" S. P. ceased to be the dupe of magniloquence and began to touch words somewhat as Laforgue did.

The confident tone is so very typical, so very Poundian, for bright ideas tend to have the status of facts when a man believes that in one day's reading he can discover the key to ancient and residual problems (Canto 74). This is why I believe that HOMAGE TO SEXTUS PROPERTIUS was designed as a light to lighten all those academic Gentiles who had never noticed that Propertius is really a proto-Laforgue, superbly proficient in the art of *logopœia.*

Half a century later, even a sympathetic classicist like Sullivan feels that Propertius was not quite what Pound made him out to be. We must still distinguish the historical figure from the persona and not confuse Propertius with Propoundius. In

July 1916 Pound suggested to Iris Barry that he might "rig up" translations of Propertius and Catullus if she found the existing ones unsatisfactory (*Letters*, p. 142). Rereading the *Elegies* later that year he discovered Propoundius by using an elegy commonly admitted to be ironical (IV, viii) as a key to the rest: on the evidence of a single elegy (which he did not incorporate into his HOMAGE) he convinced himself that Propertius was a highly sophisticated ironist. As Sullivan shows, Propoundius has a sense of humor that makes him more like Ovid than Propertius; he expresses anti-imperialistic sentiments of a sort that would have brought exile or death to the Roman poet; he is unpatriotic where Propertius was quite the reverse (for example in IV, vi, which Pound omits from his HOMAGE); he is less respectful of Virgil, less tolerant of mythological poetry, and has no interest whatsoever in Propertius' idealization of Cynthia. On the other hand, Propoundius is far more of an artist than Propertius used to be considered in the days when biographical speculation passed for literary criticism; and there are reasons for supposing that, when all reservations are made, Pound has succeeded in the years since 1919 in making academics change their minds about Propertius. He can claim justifiably with Fitzgerald to have made "some things readable which others have hitherto left unreadable" (*Works*, p. 597), and since neither "translation" nor "imitation" adequately describes Pound's rewriting of Propertius, we could do worse than borrow the term Fitzgerald coined for his *Agamemnon* and speak of HOMAGE TO SEXTUS PROPERTIUS as a "per-version" (*Works*, p. 386).

There are qualities in this poem that more than compensate for the desecration of the *Elegies*. Even the most outrageous mistranslations are convincingly Propoundian, such that differences between Propertius and Propoundius seem relatively unimportant. Every distortion heightens and in some sense reasserts those qualities of mind that Pound admired in Propertius: unswerving loyalty to one's poetic talent, faith in the value of the private life of the individual, antipathy toward the grandiose gestures of public life, mockery of imperial warmongering, and a wide-ranging sense of irony. One ought therefore, perhaps, to regard Propertius' *Elegies* as a source for HOMAGE TO SEXTUS PROPERTIUS only in the sense that one regards Plutarch and North as sources for certain parts of *Antony and Cleopatra*.

Pound read Propertius in the Teubner edition, and in the notes that follow, the Teubner text (rearranged so as to correspond section by section with Pound's poem) is given together with the Loeb translation. Variations between the two texts are noted only when they have influenced Pound's rendering of the Latin (in general, the differences are very

slight). Sullivan prints a text of HOMAGE TO SEXTUS PROPER-
TIUS which incorporates various changes authorized by Pound,
all of which are noted below. It is essentially an eclectic text.
The first fifteen lines of the poem, for example, have been put
together from separate printings: lines 1, 7, and 11 come from
the March 1919 issue of *Poetry* (Chicago); lines 2, 3, and 13–
15 are from the text as it appears in *Quia Pauper Amavi* (October 1919); and line 10 is from *Personæ* (1926). The accompanying textual notes are misleading because in several
places Sullivan fails to reveal the presence of variants. In the
third line of the poem he prints "font" (50–55) without indi-
cating that he prefers this reading to "font," (48, 49) and
"fount" (56: a printing that also embodies "authorized" corrections); and there are similar omissions of substantial variants (all noted below) at I, 31; II, 7, 24, 31, 37; IV, 19; V, 47;
VI, 33; VII, 36; and IX, 19.

Title: Thomas Hardy was sufficiently aware of the Browningesque pedigree of this poem to suggest in 1921 that "Propertius Soliloquizes" would have been a better title for it. Pound
explained that by *homage* he means what Debussy had meant
in writing his "Hommage à Rameau" (*Images*, 1905), i.e., "a
piece of music recalling Rameau's manner" (Hutchinson,
Southern Review [Jan. 1968], 99).

Epigraphs: The date "(1917)" refers presumably to the date of
composition (cf. *Letters*, p. 310). As in the case of L'HOMME
MOYEN SENSUEL, Pound had difficulty in placing this poem
with a publisher, and only reluctantly did he agree to let
Harriet Monroe "print the left foot, knee, thigh and right ear
of [his] portrait of Propertius" (Chicago MSS, Dec. 1918).

Orfeo is the Middle English spelling of Orpheus and appears
on the dedicatory page to *Quia Pauper Amavi* (1919), in which
HOMAGE TO SEXTUS PROPERTIUS was first published in its entirety. The title of this volume is taken from Ovid's *Ars Amatoria* (II, 165): "Pauperibus vates ego sum, quia pauper
amavi" ("I am the poet of the poor, because I was poor when
I loved"—Loeb). There is a pun on Propertius and *paupertas*
("poverty").

Section I.

[IV, i] Callimachi Manes et Coi sacra Philetae,
    In vestrum, quaeso, me sinite ire nemus.
  Primus ego ingredior puro de fonte sacerdos
    Itala per Graios orgia ferre choros.
5 Dicite, quo pariter carmen tenuastis in antro?
    Quove pede ingressi? quamve bibistis aquam?
  A valeat, Phoebum quicumque moratur in armis!
    Exactus tenui pumice versus eat,
  Quo me Fama levat terra sublimis, et a me

10   Nata coronatis Musa triumphat equis,
      Et mecum in curru parvi vectantur Amores,

      Non datur ad Musas currere lata via.
15 Multi, Roma, tuas laudes annalibus addent,
      Qui finem imperii Bactra futura canent.
      Sed, quod pace legas, opus hoc de monte sororum
      Detulit intacta pagina nostra via.

20   Non faciet capiti dura corona meo.
      At mihi quod vivo detraxerit invida turba,
      Post obitum duplici fenore reddet Honos.
      Omnia post obitum fingit maiora vetustas,

25 Nam quis equo pulsas abiegno nosceret arces,
      Fluminaque Haemonio cominus isse viro,
      Idaeum Simoenta Iovis cum prole Scamandro,
      Hectora per campos ter maculasse rotas?
      Deiphobumque Helenumque et Polydamanta et in armis
30   Qualemcumque Parin vix sua nosset humus.
      Exiguo sermone fores nunc, Ilion, et tu
      Troia bis Oetaei numine capta dei.

35 Meque inter seros laudabit Roma nepotes:
      Illum post cineres auguror ipse diem.
      Ne mea contempto lapis indicet ossa sepulcro,
      Provisumst Lycio vota probante deo.
      Carminis interea nostri redeamus in orbem,
40   Gaudeat in solito tacta puella sono.
      Orphea delenisse feras et concita dicunt
      Flumina Threicia sustinuisse lyra:
      Saxa Cithaeronis Thebas agitata per artem
      Sponte sua in muri membra coisse ferunt:
45 Quin etiam, Polypheme, fera Galatea sub Aetna
      Ad tua rorantes carmina flexit equos:
      Miremur, nobis et Baccho et Apolline dextro,
      Turba puellarum si mea verba colit?
      Quod non Taenariis domus est mihi fulta columnis,
50   Nec camera auratas inter eburna trabes,
      Nec mea Phaeacas aequant pomaria silvas,
      Non operosa rigat Marcius antra liquor;
      At Musae comites et carmina cara legenti,
      Et defessa choris Calliopea meis.
55 Fortunata, meo siqua es celebrata libello!
      Carmina erunt formae tot monimenta tuae.
      Nam neque pyramidum sumptus ad sidera ducti,
      Nec Iovis Elei caelum imitata domus,
      Nec Mausolei dives fortuna sepulchri
60   Mortis ab extrema condicione vacant.
      Aut illis flamma aut imber subducet honores,
      Annorum aut ictu pondera victa ruent.
      At non ingenio quaesitum nomen ab aevo
      Excidet: ingenio stat sine morte decus.

([III, i] "Shade of Callimachus and sacred rites of Philetas, suffer me, I pray, to enter your grove. I am the first with priestly service from an unsullied spring to carry Italian mysteries among the dances of Greece. Tell me, in what grotto did ye weave your songs together? With what step did ye enter? What sacred fountain did ye drink? Away with the man who keeps Phoebus tarrying among the weapons of war! Let verse run smoothly, polished with fine pumice. 'Tis by such verse as this that Fame lifts me aloft from the earth, and the Muse, my daughter, triumphs with garlanded steeds, and tiny Loves ride with me in my chariot. . . . Narrow is the path that leadeth to the Muses. Many, O Rome, shall add fresh glories to thine annals, singing that Bactra shall be thine empire's bound; but this work of mine my pages have brought down from the Muses' mount by an untrodden way, that thou mayest read it in the midst of peace. . . . no hard crown will suit my brow. But that whereof the envious throng have robbed me in life, Glory after death shall repay with double interest. After death lapse of years makes all things seem greater. . . . Else who would know aught of the citadel shattered by the horse of fir-wood, or how rivers strove in mortal conflict with Haemonia's hero? Who would know aught of Idaean Simois and Scamander sprung from Jove, or that the chariot-wheel thrice dragged Hector foully o'er the plain? Scarce would their own land know Deiphobus, Helenus, and Pulydamas, and Paris that sorry warrior. Little talk now would there be of thee, Ilion, and of thee, Troy, twice captured by the power of Oeta's god. . . . Me too shall Rome praise in the voices of late-born generations; myself I foresee that day beyond the fatal pyre. No man shall spurn the grave where the headstone marks my bones! So ordaineth Lycia's god, for he hath approved my vows. [III, ii] Meanwhile let us return to our wonted round of song; let the heart of my mistress be moved with joy at the old familiar music. They say that Orpheus with his Thracian lyre tamed wild beasts and stayed rushing rivers, and that Cithaeron's rocks were driven to Thebes by the minstrel's art and of their own will gathered to frame a wall. Nay, Galatea too beneath wild Etna turned her steeds that dripped with brine to the sound of thy songs, Polyphemus. What marvel, when Bacchus and Apollo smile on me, that a host of maidens should adore my words? My house is not stayed on Taenarian columns; I have no ivory chamber with gilded beams; no orchards have I to vie with Phaeacia's trees, nor hath art built me grottoes watered by the Marcian fount. But the Muses are my comrades, and my songs are dear to them that read, nor ever is Calliope aweary with my dancing. Happy she that book of mine hath praised! My songs shall be so many memorials of thy beauty. For neither the Pyramids built skyward at such cost, nor the house of Jove at Elis that matches heaven, nor the wealth of Mausolus' tomb are exempt from the end imposed by death. Their glory is stolen away by fire or rain, or the strokes of time whelm them to ruin crushed by their own weight. But the fame that my wit hath won shall never perish: for wit renown endureth deathless"—Loeb.)

I. The difficulty of trying to continue the Greek lyric tradition in an age that prefers poems about military exploits.

1. *Callimachus:* Cyrenaic poet and critic (b. 310 B.C.).

   Philetas: Philetos of Cos, Greek poet and grammarian (c. 300 B.C.) whose love poems influenced Ovid and Propertius. Cos is an island in the Aegean.

[3. font *48–55;* fount *56*]

4. *orgies:* Pound's rendering implies that the *orgia* ("mysteries") have degenerated into "orgies" in the modern sense. Similar bilingual puns are noted at I, 38; I, 56; II, 11; II, 30; V, 48; VIII, 26; IX, 6; XII, 43; and XII, 59. The distortion of Latin for ironic purposes was first attempted in TO FORMIANUS' YOUNG LADY FRIEND (l. 7*n*).

10. *Martian generalities:* Platitudes about war. For Pound, this signifies the Virgilian as against the Propertian modes of writing.

14. *ascends . . . æther:* There is a similar phrase in PHANO-PŒIA (I, 5).

15. *no high-road:* Pound wrote to Mary Barnard in 1934: "You hate translation??? What of it?? Expect to be carried up Mt. Helicon in an easy chair?" (*Letters,* p. 337).

17. *celebrities:* Public officials from Bactra, which came under Roman control in 20 B.C. In creating lines like this, Pound deliberately ignored the fact that Propertius' words have a grammatical relationship with one another. Instead, he treated them as if they were purely separate elements capable of meaning whatever one wants them to mean. Pound's method approximates to the cubist technique of *collage,* as Richardson notes (p. 23). Sullivan relates these "*collages* of sense" to the methods of Apollinaire's poetry.

18. *distentions:* Irony through *logopœia*—the "extensions" are distentions because the empire is already too big.

20. *forked hill:* This is Cleveland's rendering of *Parnassus biceps* ("The Author to His Hermaphrodite") and recurs in

Pope's "Epistle to Dr. Arbuthnot" (l. 231). In Canto 8
Pound writes of "the forked rocks of Penna and Billi."

21. *wreath . . . crush:* After reading T. S. Eliot's review of
Quia Pauper Amavi in the *Athenæum* ([Oct. 31, 1919],
1132), Pound remarked: "Eliot has done a dull but, I
think, valuable puff in the *Athenæum;* granite wreaths,
leaden laurels, no sign of exhilaration . . ." (*Letters,*
p. 213).

27. *deal-wood horse:* The wooden horse by means of which
Troy was destroyed (*Odyssey,* IV, VIII, XI).

28. *Achilles . . . Simois:* An allusion to Achilles' battle with
the rivers of Troy, Simois and Scamander (*Iliad,* XXI).

29. *spattering:* I.e., with his own blood. Hector's dead body
was dragged behind Achilles' chariot (*Iliad,* XXII).

[30. Polydamas ——— Deiphobus *48, 49;* Polydmantus
——— Deiphoibos *50+*]

30. Polydamas was one of the Trojan leaders. Pound rejected
Sullivan's suggestion (p. 97) that the earlier and correct
spelling should be restored. Helenus and Deiphobus were
sons of Priam, the king of Troy.

[31. door-yard *48;* door-yards *49+*]

32. *Ilion . . . Troad:* Troy. *Ilion* was the citadel, *Troia*
(Pound's "Troad") the town.

[33. Oetaean *48, 49;* Oetian *50+*]

33. In Propertius "Oeta's god" is Hercules, so called because
he died on Mt. Oeta. Pound's rendering was probably intended to sound vaguely "classical" and no more (as in I,
44*n* and XII, 19*n*). He told Sullivan that to correct "gods"
to "god" would "bitch the movement of the verse" (p. 97).

38. *vote:* Latin *votum* ("wish, vow"). Other examples of bilingual punning are listed at I, 4*n*.

Phoebus . . . Lycia . . . Patara: Patara was a town in
Lycia, a province on the southwest coast of what is now
Turkey. Pound is here glossing Propertius' "Lycian god,"
i.e., Phoebus Apollo. Similar glosses occur at I, 51 and
XII, 18.

40. *devirginated young ladies:* A famous crux (like II, 50*n*).
The Latin reads "Gaudeat in solito tacta puella sono" ("Let
the heart of my mistress be moved with joy at the old familiar music"—Loeb). W. G. Hale, who thought that
Pound was "incredibly ignorant of Latin," considered
Pound's rendering of this passage to be "peculiarly un-
pleasant." He complained that "there is no trace of the

decadent meaning which Mr. Pound read into the passage by misunderstanding *tacta,* and taking the preposition *in* as if it were a negativing part of the adjective *insolito"* (*Poetry* [April 1919], 52, 54, 55). Some time in April 1919 Pound wrote a critique of Hale's critique, the following sections of which are relevant here (*Letters,* pp. 212, 213):

As for "trace of decadent meaning."...
    Does the Drive to Lanuvium [IV, viii] contain trace of gentle raillery to be found in my "distortion" of the "tacta puella"?

Precisely what I do not do is to translate the *in* as if it negatived the *solito.* IF I was translating, I [would] have translated the *solito* (accustomed) by a commentary, giving "when they have got over the strangeness" as an equivalent, or rather emphasis of "accustomed." Absolutely the contrary of taking my phrase, as the ass Hale does, for the equivalent of *unaccustomed.* He can't read English. . . . I note that my translation "Devirginated young ladies" etc. is as literal, or rather more so than his. I admit to making the puella (singular) into plural "young ladies." It is a possible figure of speech as even the ass admits. Hale, however, not only makes the "girl" into "my lady," but he has to supply *something for her to be "touched* BY." Instead of allowing her to be simply *tacta* (as opposed to *virgo intacta*), he has to say that she is touched (not, oh my god, no not by the — — — — of the poet, but by "my words").

Pound's rendering rests on the assumption that *tactus* can mean "unchaste" or "devirginated," a nuance not recorded by Lewis and Short but nevertheless proposed by Sullivan in connection with a phrase in Catullus (LXII, 45). Innuendo of this sort may surprise readers of Propertius but not readers of Propoundius, with whom this kind of *double entendre* is habitual (see the notes to I, 56; X, 11; XII, 55).

43. *Threician:* Thracian.

44. *Citharaon:* All printings have this spelling, which Sullivan corrects to "Cithaeron" (the name of a mountain near Thebes). Propertius alludes to the story of how Amphion played his harp so skillfully that the stones left the mountains and arranged themselves in the form of city walls. It is not clear whether Pound is deliberately blurring the classical reference (as he appears to do at I, 33) or interpreting the myth in terms of a natural phenomenon such as an earthquake.

46. *Polyphemus . . . Galatea:* Polyphemus was a Cyclops who fell in love with the sea nymph Galatea.

47. *Aetna:* Mt. Etna, Sicily.

50. *palaver:* Propertius has simply *verba* ("words").

51. *Taenarian columns:* Columns made from the black marble quarried at Taenarus, Sparta. The remainder of this long line is Pound's interpolation, on which Hale comments: "These three Baedekeresque explanations seem to have been gathered, with a modicum of labor, from Harper's *Latin Lexicon*, under the word *Taenarus*" (*Poetry* [April 1919], 52). However, given the satiric nature of the whole poem and Pound's dissatisfaction with the academic way of reading the classics, it is possible that he included this gloss with the intention of burlesquing academic annotations (cf. I, 38n; XII, 18n).

   Laconia: Sparta.

[54. Phaeacia   *48, 49;*   Phaeacia   *50+*]

54. Sullivan restores the correct reading "Phaeacia." Propertius' orchard is inferior to that of Alcinous (*Odyssey*, VII) who was king of the Phaeacians.

55. *Ionian:* Ionia was the central province on the west coast of what is now Turkey. Pound confuses the mythical island of Phaeacia with the Ionian town of Phocaea.

56–57. *Marcian . . . Numa Pompilius:* Hale comments:

   The Marcian aqueduct was Rome's best water supply, recently renovated by Agrippa. Mr. Pound seems to have taken *liquor* as spirituous. He must then have thought of age as appropriate, and so interpreted *Marcius* as referring to the legendary King Ancus Marcius; after which it was easy to add another legendary king, Numa Pompilius. The result is three lines, all wrong, and the last two are pure padding.

   Poetry ([April 1919], 54). This was the only criticism of Hale's that Pound accepted (*Letters,* pp. 212, 309). The pun on *liquor* is in the same category as the pun on *orgia* (I, 4n).

[59. *[lacking]*   *48–54;*   Nor is it equipped with a frigidaire patent;   *55+*]

67. *Jove . . . East Elis:* The temple of Zeus was at Olympia in Elis, a state in the northwest of the Greek Peloponnese.

68. The body of Mausolus (d. 353 B.C.) was housed in the Mausoleum at Halicarnassus.

73. *a name not to be worn out with the years:* A line in Swinburne's *Atalanta in Calydon* reads: "A name to be washed out with all men's tears."

Section II.

[IV, ii] Visus eram molli recubans Heliconis in umbra,
   Bellorophontei qua fluit umor equi,
  Reges, Alba, tuos et regum facta tuorum,
   Tantum operis, nervis hiscere posse meis,
5 Parvaque tam magnis admoram fontibus ora,
   Vnde pater sitiens Ennius ante bibit,
  Et cecini Curios fratres et Horatia pila,
   Regiaque Aemilia vecta tropaea rate,
  Victricesque moras Fabii pugnamque sinistram
10 Cannensem et versos ad pia vota deos,
  Hannibalemque Lares Romana sede fugantes,
   Anseris et tutum voce fuisse Iovem;
  Cum me Castalia speculans ex arbore Phoebus
   Sic ait aurata nixus ad antra lyra:
15 'Quid tibi cum tali, demens, est flumine? quis te
   Carminis heroi tangere iussit opus?
  Non hinc ulla tibi sperandast fama, Properti:
   Mollia sunt parvis prata terenda rotis,
  Vt tuus in scamno iactetur saepe libellus,
20 Quem legat expectans sola puella virum.
  Cur tua praescripto sevectast pagina gyro?
   Non est ingenii cymba gravanda tui.
  Alter remus aquas, alter tibi radat harenas:
   Tutus eris: medio maxima turba marist.'
25 Dixerat, et plectro sedem mihi monstrat eburno.

  Orgia mustarum et Sileni patris imago
30 Fictilis et calami, Pan Tegeaee, tui,
  Et Veneris dominae volucres, mea turba, columbae
   Tingunt Gorgonio Punica rostra lacu,
  Diversaeque novem sortitae rura puellae
   Exercent teneras in sua dona manus.
35 Haec hederas legit in thyrsos, haec carmina nervis
   Aptat, at illa manu texit utraque rosam.
  E quarum numero me contigit una dearum:
   Vt reor a facie, Calliopea fuit:
  'Contentus niveis semper vectabere cygnis,
40 Nec te fortis equi ducet ad arma sonus.
  Nil tibi sit rauco praeconia classica cornu
   Flare nec Aonium tinguere Marte nemus,

   et Teutonicas Roma refringat opes,
 45 Barbarus aut Suevo perfusus sanguine Rhenus
   Saucia maerenti corpora vectet aqua.
  Quippe coronatos alienum ad limen amantes
   Nocturnaeque canes ebria signa fugae,
  Vt per te clausas sciat excantare puellas,
50 Qui volet austeros arte ferire viros.'
  Talia Calliope, lymphisque a fonte petitis
   Ora Philetaea nostra rigavit aqua.

([III, iii] "Methought I lay in the soft shades of Helicon, where
flows the fountain of Bellerophon's steed, and deemed I had

the power with sinews such as mine to sing of thy kings, O Alba, and the deeds of thy kings, a mighty task. Already I had set my puny lips to those mighty fountains, whence father Ennius once slaked his thirst and sang of the Curian brothers and the javelins of the Horatii and the royal trophies borne in Aemilius' bark, of the victorious delays of Fabius, the fatal fight of Cannae and the gods that turned to answer pious prayers, of the Lares frighting Hannibal from their Roman home, and of Jove saved by the cackling goose. But of a sudden Phoebus espied me from his Castalian grove and spake thus, leaning on his golden lyre nigh to a cavern: 'Madman, what hast thou to do with such a stream? Who bade thee essay the task of heroic song? Not hence, Propertius, mayest thou hope for fame! Soft are the meads o'er which thy little wheels must roll, that oft thy book may be read by some lonely girl, that waits her absent lover, and oft be cast upon the stool at her feet. Why has thy page swerved from the ring prescribed for it? The shallop of thy wit can bear no heavy cargo! Let one oar skim the water, the other the sand; so shalt thou be safe: mighty is the turmoil in mid-sea.' He spake, and with his ivory quill showed me a dwelling. . . . the mystic instruments of the Muses and the clay image of father Silenus, and thy reeds, O Pan of Tegea; and doves, birds of my lady Venus, the birds I love, dipped their red bills in the Gorgon's fount, while here and there the Maidens nine, to each of whom the lot hath given her several realm, busied their soft hands about their diverse gifts. One gathered ivy for the thyrsus-wand, another tuned her song to the music of the lyre, a third with either hand wove wreaths of roses. Then one of the number of these goddesses laid her hand upon me—'twas Calliope, as I deem by her face: 'Thou shalt alway be content to be drawn by snowy swans, nor shall the tramp of the war-horse lead thee to battle. Care not thou with hoarse trumpet-blast to blare forth martial advertisement nor to stain Aonia's grove with war. . . . and Rome beats back the Teuton's power, nor where the wild Rhine, steeped with the Swabian's blood, bears mangled bodies down its sorrowing waves. For thou shalt sing of garlanded lovers watching before another's threshold, and the tokens of drunken flight through the dark, that he who would cheat stern husbands by his cunning may through thee have power to charm forth his imprisoned love.' So spake Calliope, and, drawing water from the fount, sprinkled my lips with the draught Philetas loved"— Loeb.)

II. Propertius is assured by Phoebus and Calliope that his genius is for love poetry and not for Virgilian epic.

1–16. There a detailed analysis of this passage by T. Drew-Bear in *American Literature* ([May 1965], 204–210).

1. *Helicon:* See ANCORA (l. 10*n*).

2. *Bellerophon's horse:* Pegasus, on which Bellerophon rode when killing the Chimaera. Propertius' line alludes to the legend that when Pegasus stamped on Mount Helicon the waters of the Hippocrene began to flow (cf. II, 330).

[7. Whereof 48; Wherefore 50; Wherefrom 54+]

7. The translators' jargon is used ironically.

8. *Curian . . . Horatian:* The struggle between Rome and Alba was decided allegedly by single combat between three Roman brothers (the Horatii) and three Albanian brothers (the Curiatii).

9. *Flaccus:* Propertius and Horace (Quintus Horatius Flaccus) were both under the patronage of Maecenas and are supposed to have disliked one another: hence the disparaging reference to Q. H. Flap Eared. Needless to say, this is Pound's interpolation (like the one at V, 55*n*). An alleged pun on the word "Horatian" (l. 8) was probably the source of this facetiousness.

10–13. An ironic survey of suitable subjects for "Martian generalities."

10. *Aemilia:* A pejorative reference to the victory procession of Aemilius Paulus (hence the feminine form of the name?). Hale comments: "As for 'royal Aemilia,' had there ever been such a lady, Propertius could not have meant her, since the two Latin words are in different cases" (*Poetry* [April 1919], 53–54).

11. *Fabius:* Q. Maximus Fabius, whose delaying tactics checked Hannibal's advance on Rome.

   Cannae: Here the Romans were heavily defeated by Hannibal. Pound puns on the literal and metaphorical senses of *sinister* ("on the left hand," "unfavorable, adverse"). See I, 4*n* and CINO (l. 36*n*).

12. *lares fleeing:* It was thought that Hannibal's retreat from Rome was due to the power of the Lares, the spirits which guard the city. Pound, on the other hand, sees the Lares themselves deserting Rome because life had become intolerable there. Hale admits no irony in the original and says that Pound simply confused *fugantes* with *fugientes* (*Poetry* [April 1919], 53).

16. *Jove . . . geese:* The cackling of the sacred geese saved Rome from being captured by the Gauls in 387 B.C.

17. The Castalian spring was on Mt. Parnassus.

[24. her man   *48;*   her lover   *50+*]

[30. earthen   *48, 50;*   earthern   *54+*]

30. *Orgies of vintages:* See I, 4*n.* Teubner *Orgia mustarum,* Loeb *Orgia Musarum.*

   Silenus: A satyr, companion of Dionysus.

[31. Tegean   *48;*   Tegaean   *50+*]

31. Tegea was in Arcadia, hence its association with Pan.

[32. Cytherean   *48;*   Cytharean   *50+*]

32. Sullivan restores the correct spelling "Cytherean." The birds referred to are the doves of Venus.

33. *Punic faces:* Hale comments: "Where Propertius speaks of the 'purple beaks' (*punica rostra*) of the doves of Venus, Mr. Pound renders by the nonsensical phrase 'their Punic faces'—as if one were to translate 'crockery' by 'China'" (*Poetry* [April 1919], 53). Pound defended his version by pointing out that Hale "ignores English":

   [This is] one of my best lines. Punic (*Punicus*) used for dark red, purple red by Ovid and Horace as well as Propertius. Audience familiar with Tyrian for purple in English. To say nothing of augmented effect on imagination by using Punic (whether in translation or not) instead of "red." . . . It may instruct Hale to tell him that the Teubner text (printed 1898) uses Punica with a cap. P, especially emphasizing the Latin usage of proper name in place of a colour adjective. I.e., the Teubner editor is emphasizing a Latinism which I have brought over. He is not allowing the connection of the proper name with a particular dark red to drift into an uncapitalized adjective.

   Letters, pp. 211, 212.

   Gorgon's lake: The Hippocrene was created by Pegasus, the winged horse that sprang from the blood of the Gorgon Medusa (cf. II, 2*n*).

[37. songs   *48;*   song   *50+*]

40. Calliope is the muse of epic poetry.

45. *Aeonium:* Corrected by Sullivan to "Aeonia," the name of a part of Greece that includes Mt. Helicon (and therefore a place remote from the concerns of war).

47–48. *Rhine . . . Suevi:* The Suebi crossed the Rhine in 29 B.C. and were defeated in battle there.

50. *Night dogs:* Another crux (cf. I, 40*n*). Hale comments: "Mr. Pound mistakes the verb *canes,* 'thou shalt sing,' for

the noun *canes* (in the nominative plural masculine) and translates by 'dogs.' Looking around then for something to tack this to, he fixes upon *nocturnae* (genitive singular feminine) and gives us 'night dogs'! (*Poetry* [April 1919], 53; Pound made no comment on this). Sullivan, who is sympathetic toward Pound's attempts at uncovering *logopœia* in the Latin, says that "by no stretch of the imagination could Propertius have worked for this connotation" (p. 100). Perhaps one ought to remember that the meaning of *canes* and similar words has been a source of pedagogic mirth for hundreds of years. Varro associates *canis* with *canere* (*De Lingua Latina*, V, 99; VII, 32); in Christopher Marlowe's version of Ovid's *Amores* (I, viii, 56) *cānis* ("hoary") is confused with *canis* ("dog"); and in some medieval manuscripts Dominican friars are depicted as dogs because they are *domini canes*.

56. *Philetas:* Cf. I, 1n.

Section III.

[IV, xv] Nox media, et dominae mihi venit epistula nostrae:
      Tibure me missa iussit adesse mora,
      Candida qua geminas ostendunt culmina turres,
      Et cadit in patulos lympha Aniena lacus.
5 Quid faciam? obductis committam mene tenebris,
      Vt timeam audaces in mea membra manus?
      At si distulero haec nostro mandata timore,
      Nocturno fletus saevior hoste mihi.
      Peccaram semel, et totum sum pulsus in annum:
10 In me mansuetas non habet illa manus.
      Nec tamen est quisquam, sacros qui laedat amantes:
      Scironis media sic licet ire via.
      Quisquis amator erit, Scythicis licet ambulet oris:
      Nemo adeo, ut noceat, barbarus esse volet.
15 Luna ministrat iter, demonstrant astra salebras,
      Ipse Amor accensas percutit ante faces,
      Saeva canum rabies morsus avertit hiantes:
      Huic generi quovis tempore tuta viast.
      Sanguine tam puro quis enim spargatur amantis
20 Inprobus? ecce, suis fit comes ipsa Venus.
      Quod si certa meos sequerentur funera casus,
      Talis mors pretio vel sit emenda mihi.
      Adferet haec unguenta mihi sertisque sepulchrum
      Ornabit custos ad mea busta sedens.
25 Di faciant, mea ne terra locet ossa frequenti,
      Qua facit adsiduo tramite volgus iter.
      Post mortem tumuli sic infamantur amantum:
      Me tegat arborea devia terra coma,
      Aut humer ignotae cumulis vallatus harenae:
30 Non iuvat in media nomen havere via.

([III, xvi] " 'Twas midnight when a letter came to me from my
mistress bidding me come without delay to Tibur, where the
white hills heave up their towers to right and left and Anio's
waters plunge into spreading pools. What should I do? Trust
myself to the dark that shrouded all and tremble lest my limbs
should be gripped by ruffian hands? Yet if I should put off
obedience out of fear, her tears would be more terrible than
any midnight foe. Once had I sinned, and was rejected for a
whole year long. Against me her hands are merciless. Yet
there is none would hurt a lover: lovers are sacred: lovers
might travel Sciron's road unscathed. A lover, though he walk
on Scythia's shores, will find none so savage as to have heart
to harm him. The moon lights his path; the stars show forth
the rough places, and Love himself waves the flaming torch
before him; the fierce watchdog turns aside his gaping fangs.
For such as him the road is safe at any hour. Who is so cruel
as to embrue his hands in a lover's worthless blood, above all
when Venus herself bears him company? But did I know that
if I perished I should surely receive due rites of burial, death
would be worth the purchase at such price. She will bring unguents to my pyre and adorn my tomb with wreaths, she will
sit beside my grave and keep watch there. God grant she place
not my bones in some crowded spot, where the rabble journeys
on the busy highway. Thus after death are lovers' tombs dis-
honoured. Let me be shadowed by leafy trees in some field far
from the roadside; else let me be buried walled in by heaps of
nameless sand. I would not that my name should be recorded
amid the bustle of the street"—Loeb.)

III. Late at night Propertius receives a message from Cynthia
     inviting him to visit her, and out of cowardice he declines
     her offer.

2. *Tibur:* Now Tivoli, a few miles northeast of Rome.

4–5. Propertius becomes momentarily an imagist poet (as at
     XII, 52).

4. *Bright tips:* The same phrase is used in THE SPRING (l. 5).

5. *Anienan:* The river Anio is a tributary of the Tiber.

11. *lamentations:* Cynthia's complaints are listed in IX, 10 ff.

14. *me-ward:* A poeticism first used in IN DURANCE (l. 22*n*).

16. *Via Sciro:* Sciron's road. Sciron was a legendary robber
     who used to murder his victims by pushing them over a
     cliff along the road from Athens to Megara.

18. *Scythian:* Scythia was the name of the country to the north
     of the Black Sea.

[21. the stars *48+*; and the stars *Faber and Faber*]

26. *pure gore:* Teubner *sanguine . . . puro*, Loeb *sanguine . . . parvo*.

27. *Cypris:* The Cyprian, Venus.

37. *uncatalogued:* The irony is Pound's addition.

Section IV.

[IV, v] Dic mihi de nostra, quae sentis, vera puella:
    Sic tibi sint dominae, Lygdame, dempta iuga.
    Num me laetitia tumefactum fallis inani,
    Haec referens, quae me credere velle putas?
5 Omnis enim debet sine vano nuntius esse,
    Maioremque timens servus habere fidem.

22 Aequalem multa dicere habere domo!
    Nunc mihi, siqua tenes, ab origine dicere prima
    Incipe: suspensis auribus ista bibam.
    Sicine eam incomptis vidisti flere capillis?
10 Illius ex oculis multa cadebat aqua?
    Nec speculum strato vidisti, Lygdame, lecto?
    Ornabat niveas nullane gemma manus?
    At maestam teneris vestem pendere lacertis,
    Scriniaque ad lecti clausa iacere pedes?
15 Tristis erat domus, et tristes sua pensa ministrae
    Carpebant, medio nebat et ipsa loco,
    Vmidaque inpressa siccabat lumina lana,
    Rettulit et querulo iurgia nostra sono?
    'Haec te teste mihi promissast, Lygdame, merces?

22 Aequalem multa dicere habere domo!

25 Non me moribus illa, sed herbis inproba vicit:
    Staminea rhombi ducitur ille rota.
    Illum turgentis ranae portenta rubetae
    Et lecta exectis anguibus ossa trahunt.
    Et strigis inventae per busta iacentia plumae,
30 Cinctaque funesto lanea vitta toro.

33 Putris et in vacuo texetur aranea lecto:
    Noctibus illorum dormiet ipsa Venus.'

32 Poena erit ante meos sera, sed ampla, pedes,

23 Gaudet me vacuo solam tabescere lecto.
    Si placet, insultet, Lygdame, morte mea.

([III, vi] "Tell me truly what thou thinkest of my love: so, Lygdamus, be the yoke of thy mistress taken from thy neck. Dost thou cheat me and make me swell with baseless joy, telling me such news as thou thinkst I would fain believe? Every messenger should be blameless of lying, and a slave should be all the truer by reason of his fear. . . . 'and keep in his house one such as I would not name?' . . . Now set forth thy tale to me from the first beginning, if thou rememberest aught; I will listen with eager ears. Did her tears rain even so when thou beheldest her weep with hair dishevelled? Didst thou see no mirror, Lygdamus, on her couch? Did no jewelled ring adorn her snowy hands? Didst thou see a sad-hued robe hang from her soft arms, and did her toilet caskets lie closed at the bed's foot? Was the house sad, and sad her handmaids as they plied their tasks, and was she knitting in their midst? Did she press the wool to her eyes to dry their moisture, and repeat my chidings with plaintive tone? 'Is this the reward he promised me in thy hearing, Lygdamus? . . . and keep in his house one such as I would not name? . . . 'Twas by no winning ways, but by magic herbs, that she, the wretch, hath conquered me: he is led captive by the magic wheel whirled on its string. He is drawn to her by the monstrous charms of the swelling bramble-toad and by the bones she has gathered from dried serpents, by the owl-feathers found on low-lying tombs, and the woollen fillet bound about the doomed man. . . . The spider shall weave her mouldering threads about his empty couch, and Venus herself shall slumber on the night of their embrace. . . . he shall yield me vengeance, late, yet ample, as he grovels at my feet. . . . He rejoices that I pine forlorn in my empty bed. If it please him, Lygdamus, let him mock me even in death"—Loeb.)

IV. Talking to his slave Lygdamus, who carries messages between the lovers, Propertius speculates as to how Cynthia will have responded to his rejection of her offer.

[*Subtitle:* Difference of Opinion 49; — — — Opinion with Lygdamus 50+]

1. *our . . . lady:* Pound has drawn attention to "Propertius' delicate use of 'nostra,' meaning 'my' as well as 'our,' but in a stylist how delicately graduated against 'mihi' by Propertius. Heine's poem ending, 'Madame, ich liebe Sie' is clumsy in comparison" (*Letters*, p. 212). The implication is that Propertius, by using *nostra* instead of *mihi*, was admitting that Cynthia had already been unfaithful to him with Lygdamus: hence the irony of "our *constant* young lady." Cynthia's subsequent infidelities with Lynceus are recorded in section XII.

3. *bought . . . mistress:* Cynthia was a prostitute. This and the following line are Pound's addition.

10. A variation on this line appears at line 29.
[19. orfeverie 49; orfevrerie 50+]

19. The word *orfèvrerie* is borrowed from the poem by Voltaire which Pound translated as the first of his IMPRESSIONS OF FRANÇOIS-MARIE AROUET (DE VOLTAIRE). Pound must have been reminded of the clutter of objects surrounding Phyllidula, and used Voltaire's term to point up the analogy.

23. *desolated because she had told them her dreams:* In March 1922 Pound asked Harriet Monroe: "Has your local prof. [Hale] yet discovered that my introduction of Words-worth's name, and my parody of Yeats were not produced (in my Propertius) in an endeavor to give a verbatim rendering of the Latin text?" (Chicago MSS; cf. *Letters,* p. 310). Reference to Wordsworth is clearly made at XII, 51 and should have warned critics that HOMAGE TO SEXTUS PROPERTIUS is something other than a literal translation (although it is only fair to point out that Hale never saw the sections containing the references to Yeats and Words-worth). As for the "parody of Yeats," Pound seems to have imitated the refrain from Yeats's poem "The Withering of the Boughs":

    No boughs have withered because of the wintry wind;
    The boughs have withered because I have told them my
    dreams.

    For other references to Yeats's poems, see the note to AMITIES. Parodies of Yeats are fairly common in *The Pisan Cantos* (79, 80, and 82).

24–43. The corrected typescript of this section is reproduced in facsimile by Stock in *Perspectives* (p. 137).

29. *many . . . equal:* Cf. line 10. Teubner *Aequalem multa,* Loeb *Et qualem nolo.*

[32a. *lacking* 49+; "She stews puffed frogs, snake's bones, the moulted *Faber and Faber*]

33. *rhombus:* The spinning of a rhombus wheel was reputed to bring back one's lover (cf. IX, 1).

[34. moulded 49–54; moulted 55+]

[43. twelve nights 49; twelve months 50+]

Section V.

[III, i] Sed tempus lustrare aliis Helicona choreis,
Et campum Emathio iam dare tempus equo.

Et Romana mei dicere castra ducis.
5 Quod si deficiant vires, audacia certe
Laus erit: in magnis et voluisse sat est.

Aetas prima canat Veneres, extrema tumultus.
Bella canam, quando scripta puella meast.
Nunc volo subducto gravior procedere voltu,
10 Nunc aliam citharam me mea Musa docet.
Surge, anima, ex humili iam carmine, sumite vires,
Pierides: magni nunc erit oris opus.
Iam negat Euphrates equitem post terga tueri
Parthorum et Crassos se tenuisse dolet:
15 India quin, Auguste, tuo dat colla triumpho,
Et domus intactae te tremit Arabiae:
Et siqua extremis tellus se subtrahit oris,
Sentiet illa tuas postmodo capta manus.
Haec ego castra sequar: vates tua castra canendo
20 Magnus ero: servent hunc mihi fata diem!

2.

[II, i] Quaeritis, unde mihi totiens scribantur amores,
Vnde meus veniat mollis in ora liber.
Non haec Calliope, non haec mihi cantat Apollo,
Ingenium nobis ipsa puella facit.
5 Sive lyrae carmen digitis percussit eburnis,
Miramur, faciles ut premat arte manus:
Seu vidi ad frontem sparsos errare capillos,

Sive illam Cois fulgentem incedere coccis,
10 Hoc totum e Coa veste volumen erit:
Seu cum poscentes somnum declinat ocellos,
Invenio causas mille poeta novas:
Seu nuda erepto mecum luctatur amictu,
Tum vero longas condimus Iliadas:
15 Seu quicquid fecit sivest quodcumque locuta,
Maxima de nihilo nascitur historia.
Quod mihi si tantum, Maecenas, fata dedissent,
Vt possem heroas ducere in arma manus,
Non ego Titanas canerem, non Ossan Olympo
20 Inpositam, ut caeli Pelion esset iter,
Non veteres Thebas, nec Pergama nomen Homeri,
Xerxis et imperio bina coisse vada,
Regnave prima Remi aut animos Carthaginis altae,
Cimbrorumque minas et benefacta Mari:
25 Bellaque resque tui memorarem Caesaris. . . .

Theseus infernis, superis testatur Achilles,
Hic Ixioniden, ille Menoetiaden.
Sed neque Phlegraeos Iovis Enceladique tumultus
40 Intonet angusto pectore Callimachus,
Nec mea conveniunt duro praecordia versu
Caesaris in Phrygios condere nomen avos.
Navita de ventis, de tauris narrat arator,
Enumerat miles volnera, pastor oves,
45 Nos contra angusto versantis proelia lecto:
Qua pote quisque, in ea conterat arte diem

3.

Laus in amore mori, laus altera, si datur uno
Posse frui: fruar o solus amore meo!
Si memini, solet illa leves culpare puellas,
50   Et totam ex Helena non probat Iliada.

([II, x] "But now 'tis time with other measures to range the
slopes of Helicon; 'tis time to launch the Haemonian steed
o'er the open plain . . . and tell of my chieftain's Roman camp.
But should strength fail me, yet my daring shall win me fame:
in mighty enterprises enough even to have willed success. Let
early youth sing the charms of love, life's later prime the storm
of war: war will I sing, now that I have set forth all my mistress' charms. Now would I go my way with grave frown
stamped on serious brow; my Muse now bids me strike another
lyre. Awake, my soul! Ye Pierid maids, leave these humble
strains and take a stronger tone; the work that waits you needs
a mighty voice. Now does Euphrates deny that the Parthian
aims his backward shaft, and grieves that ever he cut short the
return of the Crassi. Nay, even India, Augustus, bows her neck
to grace thy triumph, and the house of virgin Arabia trembles
before thee; and if there be any land withdrawn upon earth's
furthest rim, captured hereafter let it feel thy mighty hand.
This be the camp I follow. Great will I be among singers by
singing of thy wars. Let destiny keep that glorious day in store
for me.
[II, i] "You ask me, from what source so oft I draw my songs
of love and whence comes my book that sounds so soft upon
the tongue. 'Tis not Calliope nor Apollo that singeth these
things; 'tis my mistress' self that makes my wit. . . . or struck
she forth music from the lyre with ivory fingers, I marvel with
what easy skill she sweeps her hands along the strings. . . . or
have I seen her tresses stray disheveled o'er her brow. . . . If
thou wilt have her walk radiant in silks of Cos, of Coan raiment
all this my book shall tell; . . . or when she droops those eyes
that call for sleep I find a thousand new themes for song; or
if, flinging away her robe, she enter naked with me in the lists,
then, then I write whole Iliads long. Whate'er she does,
whate'er she says, from a mere nothing springs a mighty tale.
But if, Maecenas, the Fates had granted me power to lead the
hosts of heroes into war, I would not sing the Titans, nor Ossa
on Olympus piled, that Pelion might be a path to heaven. I'd
sing not ancient Thebes nor Troy's citadel, that is Homer's
glory, nor yet how at Xerxes' bidding sea met sundered sea,
nor, again, would I chant the primeval realm of Remus or the
fierce spirit of lofty Carthage, the Cimbrian's threats or the
service wrought by Marius for the State. But I would tell of
the wars and the deeds of thy master Caesar. . . . Theseus to

the shades below, Achilles to the gods above, proclaim a comrade's love, the one of Ixion's child, the other of the son of Menoetius. But neither would Callimachus' scant breath avail to thunder forth the strife 'twixt Jove and Enceladus on Phlegra's plains, nor has my heart power in verse severe to trace the line of Caesar to his Phrygian grandsires. The sailor talks of winds, the ploughman of oxen, the soldier counts o'er his wounds, the shepherd his sheep, while we for our part tell of lovers' wars upon a narrow couch! Let each man pass his days in that wherein his skill is greatest. To die for love is glory; and glory yet again to have power to joy in one love only; ah, may I, and I alone, joy in the love that's mine. If memory fails me not, she is wont to blame fickle-hearted maids, and on account of Helen frowns on the whole Iliad" —Loeb.)

V. Attempting the Virgilian and producing a grotesque parody of it, Propertius explains to his patron Maecenas why it is that he can write nothing but love poems.

2. *Emathian:* Macedonian (Teubner *Emathio,* Loeb *Haemonio*).

[5. In things   49+;   In the things   *Faber and Faber*]

10. *beak:* Ship's prow.

11. *gamut:* Musical scale. Pound's meaning is obscure: the sense (in Propertius) is that the poet will be instructed by his Muse to play a different kind of tune, i.e., to write martial instead of erotic poetry.

The Italian word *gambetto* means "gambit."

12. *cantilation:* Cf. COME MY CANTILATIONS.

14. *Pierides:* The muses.

16–17. *Euphrates . . . Parthian . . . Crassus:* Invading Roman armies had to cross the Euphrates to get into Mesopotamia. The Parthians lived in a country to the east of the Caspian Sea, and it was in battle against this people that Crassus (a member of the First Triumvirate) was killed in 53 B.C.

19. *Augustus:* The Emperor.

Virgin Arabia: Latin *intactae . . . Arabiae* (cf. I, 40n).

25. *you:* Maecenas.

28. *genius is . . . a girl:* Despite an early antipathy toward eroticism in poetry (THE CONDOLENCE, l. 3n), Pound became interested in the relationship between sexual activity, artistic creation, and intellectual advancement.

Propertius' "Ingenium nobis ipsa puella facit" marked for him the beginnings of a perception that passed through twelfth-century love poetry to the erotica of Remy de Gourmont. Midway in the tradition came the King of Navarre's "De Fine amour vient science e beautez," "Knowledge and beauty from true love are wrought" (*Quarterly Review* [Oct. 1913], 436). In the twentieth century the idea was elaborated characteristically by Remy de Gourmont: "Il y aurait peut-être une certaine corrélation entre la copulation complète et profonde et le développement cérébral" (*Natural Philosophy of Love* [1922], p. vii; the whole of Pound's introduction is relevant here). Similar speculations recur in Pound's letters to W. C. Williams, and with a frankness reminiscent of Charles Sackville's verse epistles to Etherege ("For what but prick and cunt doth raise/ Our thoughts to songs and roundelays . . . ?"). Aware of these things, one can understand why Pound should have asked Gaudier-Brzeska to carve an effigy of him in the form of a phallus (see also the note to SESTINA: ALTAFORTE and MŒURS CONTEMPORAINES, VII, 13).

32. *Cos:* Cf. I, 1*n*. In Roman times Cos was famous for the manufacture of light, transparent clothing.

39. *Maecenas:* The counselor of Augustus and patron of the literary circle that included Virgil, Horace, and Propertius.

41–43. *Ossa . . . Olympus . . . Pelion:* Otus and Ephialtes attempted to storm heaven by piling Mt. Ossa on Mt. Olympus, and Mt. Pelion on top of them both.

45. *Pergamus:* Troy.

46. *Xerxes:* King of Persia. He was responsible for cutting a canal across the promontory of Mt. Athus, thus making his kingdom "two-barreled."

Remus: Cofounder, with Romulus, of Rome.

48. *Welsh mines:* Propertius alludes to the victories of Gaius Marius (d. 86 B.C.) over a Germanic tribe called the Cimbri. Posidonius thought the Cimbri were Celts, and Pound similarly confuses *Cimbri* with *Cumbria* (Wales). He creates a bilingual pun on *minas* ("threats") by translating the word as "mines" (cf. I, 4*n*), and construes the last two words loosely as "a benefit to Marus."

51. *Callimachus:* Cf. line 1*n*.

52. *Theseus:* A mythical king of the Athenians.

[54. Moenetus   49;   Menoetius   50+]

54. *Ixion:* The king who, in Hades, was bound to a perpetually turning wheel of fire.

sons of Menoetius . . . Argo: Patroclus was one of the sons of Menoetius who sailed with Jason in the *Argo* in search of the Golden Fleece.

55. Latin *ore rotundo,* "with round mouth, full utterance" (cf. Horace, *Ars Poetica,* 323*f*; and II, 9*n*).

56. *Phrygian:* Propertius alludes to the Phrygian ancestry of Caesar.

Section VI.

[III, v]   1 Quandocumque igitur nostros mors claudet ocellos,

[IV, iv] 13 Haut ullas portabis opes Acherontis ad undas:
             Nudus ad infernas, stulte, vehere rates.
             Victor cum victis pariter miscebitur umbris:
             Consule cum Mario, capte Iugurtha, sedes.

[IV, iii]   1 Arma deus Caesar dites meditatur ad Indos,

            4 Tigris et Euphrates sub sua iura fluent:

            6 Adsuescent Latio Partha tropaea Iovi.

[IV, iv] 13 Haut ullas portabis opes Acherontis ad undas:
             Nudus ad infernas, stulte, vehere rates.
             Victor cum victis pariter miscebitur umbris:
             Consule cum Mario, capte Iugurtha, sedes.

[III, v]   Nec mea tunc longa spatietur imagine pompa,
             Nec tuba sit fati vana querela mei,
            5 Nec mihi tunc fulcro sternatur lectus eburno,
             Nec sit in Attalico mors mea nixa toro.
             Desit odoriferis ordo mihi lancibus, adsint
             Plebei parvae funeris exequiae.
             Sat mea sat magnast, si tres sint pompa libelli,
           10 Quos ego Persephonae maxima dona feram.
             Tu vero nudum pectus lacerata sequeris,
             Nec fueris nomen lassa vocare meum,
             Osculaque in gelidis pones suprema labellis,
             Cum dabitur Syrio munere plenus onyx.
                              'qui nunc iacet horrida pulvis,
           20 Vnius hic quondam servus amoris erat.'
                              'o mors, cur mihi sera venis?'
           35 Tu tamen amisso non numquam flebis amico:
             Fas est praeteritos semper amare viros.
             Testis, cui niveum quondam percussit Adonem
             Venantem Idalio vertice durus aper:
           40 Diceris effusa tu, Venus, isse coma.
             Sed frustra mutos revocabis, Cynthia, Manes:
             Nam mea quid poterunt ossa minuta loqui?

([II, xiiiA] "Wherefore, Cynthia, when at last death shall seal my eyes. . . . [III, v] Yet no wealth shalt thou carry to the waves of Acheron: naked, thou fool, thou shalt be borne to the ship of Hell. There victor and vanquished shades are mingled in equality of death: captive Jugurtha, thou sittest beside the consul Marius. . . . [III, iv] Caesar our god plans war against rich Ind. . . . Tiber, and Euphrates shall flow beneath thy sway. . . . Parthia's trophies shall become familiar with Latin Jupiter. [II, xiiiA] For me let no procession walk with long array of masks, let no trumpet make vain wailing for my end. Let no last bed on posts of ivory be strewn for me, let not my dead body lie on a couch of cloth-of-gold; no line of attendants with sweet-scented platters for me, only the humble obsequies that mark a poor man's death. Costly enough shall be my funeral train if three little books go with me to the grave, that I may bear them to Persephone as my most precious offering. And thou shalt follow, thy breast all bare and torn, nor shalt thou weary of calling upon my name, but shalt imprint the last kiss upon my clay-cold lips, when the casket of onyx with its gift of Syrian nard is bestowed upon me. . . . 'He that now lies naught but unlovely dust, once served one love and one love only.' . . . 'O death! why tarriest thou so late e'er thou come to me?' Yet thou, when thou hast lost thy friend, wilt sometimes weep for him; undying love is the due of the loved and lost. Witness the cruel boar that struck snow-white Adonis as he hunted on the Idalian peak. . . . 'tis said, thou wentest, Venus, thy tresses unbound. But in vain, Cynthia, shalt thou recall my voiceless shade to life; for what answer shall my crumbled bones have strength to make?"—Loeb.)

VI. Propertius meditates on his own death and considers the value of the poems he will bequeath to posterity.

2. *Acheron:* One of the rivers in Hades.

3. *one raft:* Cf. IX, 5.

4. *Marius . . . Jugurtha:* Gaius Marius (cf. V, 48n) captured and killed Jugurtha, the King of Numidia. The implication is that since death overtakes both victors and vanquished eventually, it is a waste of time for a poet to celebrate martial achievements.

6. *Caesar . . . India:* A reference to Augustus' projected expedition against the Parthians.

7. *Tigris:* Teubner *Tigris,* Loeb *Thybris* ("Tiber").

8. *Tibet . . . Roman policemen:* Pound's addition, needless to say. Juxtaposing ancient and modern ideas, Pound exploits

the incongruity for comic effect, as he does in Canto 48 ("At beatification / 80 loud speakers were used").

[16. Attalic   48, 49;   Atalic   50+]

16. Attalus was credited with the discovery of weaving cloth of gold. Sullivan restores the correct spelling "Attalic."

21. *Which . . . Persephone:* Pound used the original Latin as an epigraph to *Canzoni* (1911) and *Riposte* (1912): see page 261 below.

25. *Syrian onyx:* Syrian unguents preserved in an onyx container and used for embalming a dead body.

[30. sometime   48, 49;   sometimes   50+]

[33. Cytherean   48, 49;   Cytharean   50+]

33. *Adonis . . . Idalia:* Adonis was gored to death by a wild boar while hunting near Idalium, a hill town in Cyprus.

Cytharean: Sullivan restores the correct spelling "Cytherean," Venus.

36. *Cynthia:* Propertius' mistress.

Section VII.

[III, vii]   O me felicem! o nox mihi candida, et o tu
              Lectule deliciis facte beate meis!
              Quam multa adposita narramus verba lucerna,
              Quantaque sublato lumine rixa fuit!
         5   Nam modo nudatis mecumst luctata papillis,
              Interdum tunica duxit operta moram.
              Illa meos somno lapsos patefecit ocellos
              Ore suo et dixit 'sicine, lente, iaces?'
              Quam vario amplexu mutamus brachia! quantum
        10   Oscula sunt labris nostra morata tuis!
              Non iuvat in caeco Venerem corrumpere motu:
              Si nescis, oculi sunt in amore duces.
              Ipse Paris nuda fertur periisse Lacaena,
              Cum Menelaeo surgeret e thalamo,
        15   Nudus et Endymion Phoebi cepisse sororem
              Dicitur et nudae concubuisse deae.

              Dum nos fata sinunt, oculos satiemus amore:
              Nox tibi longa venit nec reditura dies.
        25   Atque utinam haerentes sic nos vincire catena
              Velles, ut numquam solveret ulla dies!

        29   Errat, qui finem vesani quaerit amoris:

        32   Et citius nigros Sol agitabit equos,

        31   Terra prius falso partu deludet arantes,

33 Fluminaque ad caput incipient revocare liquores,
Aridus et sicco gurgite piscis erit,

49 Tu modo, dum licet, o fructum ne desere vitae.

51 Ac veluti folia arentes liquere corollas,
Quae passim calathis strata natare vides,
Sic nobis, qui nunc magnum spiramus amantes,
Forsitan includet crastina fata dies.

50 Omnia si dederis oscula, pauca dabis.

35 Quam possim nostros alio transferre dolores:
Huius ero vivus, mortuus huius ero.
Quod mihi si secum tales concedere noctes
Illa velit, vitae longus et annus erit:
Si dabit haec multas, fiam inmortalis in illis:
40 Nocte una quivis vel deus esse potest.

([II, xv] "How happy is my lot! O night that was not dark for me! and thou beloved couch blessed by my delight! How many sweet words we interchanged while the lamp was by, and how we strove together when the light was gone! For now she struggled with me with breasts uncovered, now veiling herself in her tunic checked my advance. With a kiss she unsealed mine eyes weighed down with slumber and said: 'Dost thou lie thus, thou sluggard?' How oft we shifted our arms and varied our embrace; how long my kisses lingered on thy lips! There is no joy in spoiling love's delights by sightless motion: know, if thou knowest it not, that in love the eyes are guides. Paris himself is said to have been undone by love when he saw the Spartan naked, as she rose from the couch of Menelaus. Naked was Endymion when he impassioned Phoebus' sister, and naked they say he lay with the naked goddess. . . . While the Fates grant it, let us glut our eyes with love: the long night hasteneth on for thee that knows no dawning. And oh! that thou wouldst bind us in this embrace with such a chain that never the day might come to loose us! . . . He errs that seeks to set a term to the frenzy of love; true love hath no bound. Sooner will earth mock the ploughman by bearing fruit out of season, and the Sun-god drive the steeds of night, rivers begin to recall their waters to their fount, the deep dry up and leave its fish athirst. . . . Cynthia, do thou only while the light is yet with thee forsake not the joy of life! . . . and as leaves drop from withered wreaths and thou mayest see them bestrew the cups and float therein, so we that love and whose hopes are high perchance shall find to-morrow close our doom. . . . Give me all thy kisses, yet shall they be all too few. . . . than I shall be able to transfer my love to another; hers will I be in life and hers in death. But if she be willing again to grant me such nights as last, one year will be long life for me. If she give me many, they will make me immortal; one such night might make any man a god!"—Loeb.)

VII. Propertius spends a night with Cynthia.

13. *Paris . . . Helen . . . Menelaus:* Paris carried off Helen, the wife of Menelaus, thus bringing about the Trojan war.

14. *Endymion . . . Diana:* Selene (the Moon, Diana) fell in love with the handsome shepherd Endymion after seeing him sleeping on Mt. Latmos.

16. *Sate we:* See the introductory note to SATIEMUS.

30. *breath:* Teubner *spiramus* ("we breathe"), Loeb *speramus* ("we hope").

[33. but a few   50, 54;   but few   55+]

[36. confers   50, 54;   confer   55+]

Section VIII.

[III, xxiv] Iuppiter, adfectae tandem miserere puellae:
             Tam formosa tuum mortua crimen erit.
             Venit enim tempus, quo torridus aestuat aer,
             Incipit et sicco fervere terra Cane.
         5   Sed non tam ardoris culpast neque crimina caeli,
             Quam totiens sanctos non habuisse deos.
             Hoc perdit miseras, hoc perdidit ante puellas:
             Quidquid iurarunt, ventus et unda rapit.
             Num sibi collatam doluit Venus ipsa paremque?
        10   Per se formosis invidiosa deast.
             An contempta tibi Iunonis templa Pelasgae?
             Palladis aut oculos ausa negare bonos?

             Hoc tibi lingua nocens, hoc tibi forma dedit.
        15   Sed tibi vexatae per multa pericula vitae
             Extremo veniet mollior hora die.
             Io versa caput primos mugiverat annos:
             Nunc dea, quae Nili flumina vacca bibit.
             Ino etiam prima Thebis aetate fugatast:

        21   Andromede monstris fuerat devota marinis:
             Haec eadem Persei nobilis uxor erat.
             Callisto Arcadios erraverat ursa per agros:
             Haec nocturna suo sidere vela regit.
        25   Quod si forte tibi properarint fata quietem,
             Illa sepulturae fata beata tuae.
             Narrabis Semelae, quo sit formosa periclo,
             Credet et illa, suo docta puella malo;
             Et tibi Maeonias inter heroidas omnes
        30   Primus erit nulla non tribuente locus.
             Nunc, utcumque potes, fato gere saucia morem:
             Et deus et durus vertitur ipse dies.
             Hoc tibi vel poterit, coniunx, ignoscere Iuno:
             Frangitur et Iuno, siqua puella perit.

([II, xxviii] "Jupiter, at length have pity on my mistress, stricken sore; the death of one so fair will be accounted to thee for a crime. For the season has come when the scorching air seethes with heat and earth begins to glow beneath the parching Dog-star. But 'tis not so much the fault of the heat, nor hath heaven so much the blame for her illness, as that so oft she hath spurned the sanctity of the gods. This is it that undoes hapless girls, aye, and hath undone many; wind and water sweep away their every oath. Was Venus vexed that thou wast compared with her? She is a jealous goddess to all alike, that vie with her in loveliness. Or didst thou spurn the temple of Pelasgian Juno, or deny that Pallas' eyes were fair? . . . Cynthia, thou owest this thy sickness to thine offending tongue and to thy beauty. But anguished as thou hast been through many a deadly peril, at last hath come an hour of greater ease. So Io wore a strange guise and lowed all her earlier years; but now she is a goddess, that once drank Nilus' waters in likeness of a cow. Ino also wandered o'er the earth in her prime. . . . Andromeda was doomed to the monsters of the deep, yet even she became the far-famed wife of Perseus. Callisto wandered as a bear over the fields of Arcadia; now with her own star's light she guides the sails of mariners through the dark. Yet if it chance that the Fates hasten down on thee the eternal rest, the Fates of funeral made blest for thee, thou shalt tell Semele what dangers beauty brings; and she, taught by her own misfortune, will believe thee: and among all the Maeonian heroines thou by consent of all shalt have the foremost place. Now as best thou may, bear thyself reverently towards destiny on thy couch of pain; heaven and the cruel hour of death alike may change. Even Juno, the jealous wife, will forgive thee for thy beauty; even Juno is touched with pity for a maiden's death"—Loeb.)

VIII. Propertius reflects whimsically on what will happen to Cynthia when she dies.

8. *cupboard:* There is possibly a pun here on "cupboard love," but the Latin offers no clue to Pound's meaning.

12. *contempted:* Possibly a solecism for "contemned," but probably *logopœia:* to "contemn" Juno is to "tempt" providence.

Pelasgian: Argive. Argos, in the northeast of the Greek Peloponnese, was the chief center for the worship of Hera (Juno).

13. Pallas Athene was goddess of wisdom.

19–26. Propoundius is a man easily bored with the sort of routine mythological anecdotes expected in classical poems: hence the facetious tone of these lines. There is no such irony in the Latin.

19–20. *Io . . . Nile . . . god:* Because Zeus fell in love with Io, Hero had her turned into a cow. After many wanderings Io came to the Nile and was later worshiped in Egypt as Isis (cf. XI, 34).

21. *Ino . . . fled . . . Thebes:* Teubner *Thebis . . . fugast* ("fled from Thebes"), Loeb *terris . . . vagata est* ("wandered o'er the earth"). Ino fled from Thebes to escape her mad husband, and on plunging into the sea was metamorphosed into the goddess Leucothea.

22–23. *Andromeda . . . Perseus:* Andromeda was proclaimed more beautiful than the Nereids and accordingly aroused the anger of Poseidon, who sent a sea monster to ravage her homeland. Andromeda was exposed to the sea monster by way of appeasement, but was rescued by Perseus with the aid of the Gorgon's head.

24–26. *Callisto:* After bearing a son to Zeus, Callisto was changed by Hera into a she-bear.

Arcadia: The central region of the Greek Peloponnese.

26. *veil:* A bilingual pun on the Latin *vela* ("sails"). For other examples, see I, 4*n.*

31. *Semele:* Semele prayed that her lover might come to her in all his splendor. He did, and she was consumed with fire (cf. XI, 34).

34. *Maeonia:* Lydia, the region in the west of what is now Turkey.

42. This final line is Pound's addition.

Section IX.

[III, xxv] Deficiunt magico torti sub carmine rhombi,
    Et iacet extincto laurus adusta foco,
    Et iam Luna negat totiens descendere caelo,
    Nigraque funestum concinit omen avis.
5 Vna ratis fati nostros portabit amores
    Caerula ad infernos velificata lacus.
    Si non unius, quaeso, miserere duorum.
    Vivam, si vivet: si cadet illa, cadam,

10   'per magnum salva puella Iovem';
    Ante tuosque pedes illa ipsa adoperta sedebit,
    Narrabitque sedens longa pericla sua.

2.

[III, xxvi] Haec tua, Persephone, maneat clementia, nec tu,
Persephonae coniunx, saevior esse velis.
Sunt apud infernos tot milia formosarum:

5 Vobiscumst Iope, vobiscum candida Tyro,
Vobiscum Europe nec proba Pasiphae,
Et quot Troia tulit vetus et quot Achaia formas,

Et quaecumque erat in numero Romana puella,
10 Occidit: has omnes ignis avarus habet.
Nec forma aeternum aut cuiquamst fortuna
perennis:
Longius aut propius mors sua quemque manet.

3.

[III, xxvi] Tu quoniam es, mea lux, magno dimissa periclo,
Munera Dianae debita redde choros,
15 Redde etiam excubias divae nunc, ante iuvencae,
Votivas noctes et mihi solve decem.

([II, xxviii] "Now cease the wheels whirled to the magic chant,
the altar fire is dead and the laurel lies in ashes. Now the moon
refuses to descend so oft from heaven, and the bird of night
sings ominous of death. One murky boat of destiny shall bear
our loves together, setting sail to the pools of Hell. But pity
not one only, I pray thee, Jupiter; pity the twain of us. If she
lives, I will live; if she dies, I too will die. . . . 'The might of
Jove hath saved my mistress'; and she herself after she hath
sacrificed to thee will sit before thy feet, and seated there will
tell of the long perils she has passed.
[II, xxviiiA] "Persephone, may thy mercy endure, nor mayest
thou, that hast Persephone for spouse, be over-cruel. There
are so many thousand beauties among the dead. . . . With
you is Iope, with you snowy Tyro, with you Europe and impious
Pasiphae, and all the beauties that Troy and Achaea bore of
old, Troy the fallen realm of Phoebus and the old man Priam.
And all the fair, that Rome may rank with these, have perished: all these the greedy pyre hath taken for its own. Neither
beauty nor fortune abideth everlastingly for any; sooner or
later death awaiteth all.
"Since then, light of mine eyes, thou hast escaped from
mighty peril, render Diana the dance thou owest for offering;
and as is due, keep vigil in honour of her who, once a heifer,
is now a goddess, and on my behalf pay her ten nights of worship"—Loeb.)

IX. Continuing these speculations, Propertius asks that Cynthia might be spared death so that he can spend more
nights with her.

1. *rhombs:* Cf. IV, 33*n*.

[3. And the moon ——— declined wholly to   50;   The moon
   ——— declined to   54+]

4. *black . . . hoot:* Synaesthesia (cf. THE SPRING, l. 9*n*).

5. *one raft:* Cf. VI, 3.

[6. toward   50+;   towards   *Faber and Faber*]

6. *veiled:* Latin *velificata* ("sailed"). Other bilingual puns are listed at I, 4*n*.

   Avernus: A lake near Naples, regarded as the entrance to the infernal regions.

7. *Cerulean:* Sullivan emends to "cerulean."

   tears for two: Possibly *logopœia*, although the phrase "tea for two" may not have been common before the production of *No No Nanette* (1925). There is a similar phrase in PORTRAIT D'UNE FEMME (l. 17*n*).

14–22. Pound's earlier rendering is printed as PRAYER FOR HIS LADY'S LIFE.

14. *Persephone:* Carried off by Pluto while gathering flowers in the Vale of Enna.

   Dis: Pluto, god of the underworld.

17. *Iope:* Either Theseus' wife or Aeolus' daughter.

   Tyro: Loved by Poseidon in the form of a river.

   Pasiphae: Wife of Minos and mother of the Minotaur.

   formal: A Latinism in the Miltonic manner (*forma*, "beauty").

   Achaia: Achaea was the northern region of the Greek Peloponnese.

18. *Troad:* Troy.

   Campania: The area around Naples (Pound's substitution for Propertius' *Romana*).

[19. has its   50, 54;   has his   55+]

19. *tooth in the lot:* The same image appears in HOMAGE TO QUINTUS SEPTIMIUS FLORENTIS CHRISTIANUS (IV, 6).

Section X.

[III, xxvii] Extrema, mea lux, cum potus nocte vagarer,
        Nec me servorum duceret ulla manus,
        Obvia, nescioquot pueri, mihi turba minuta
        Venerat (hos vetuit me numerare timor),

5 Quorum alii faculas, alii retinere sagittas,
Pars etiam visast vincla parare mihi.
Sed nudi fuerunt. quorum lascivior unus,

'Hic erat, hunc mulier nobis irata locavit.'
10 Dixit, et in collo iam mihi nodus erat.
Hic alter iubet in medium propellere, et alter,
'Intereat, qui nos non putat esse deos!
Haec te non meritum totas expectat in horas:
At tu nescioquas quaeris, inepte, foris.
15 Quae cum Sidoniae nocturna ligamina mitrae
Solverit atque oculos moverit illa graves,
Adflabunt tibi non Arabum de gramine odores,

20 Et iam ad mandatam venimus ecce domum.'
Atque ita mi iniecto dixerunt rursus amictu
'I nunc et noctes disce manere domi.'
Mane erat, et volui, si sola quiesceret illa,
Visere: et in lecto Cynthia sola fuit.
25 Obstupui: non illa mihi formosior umquam
Visa, neque ostrina cum fuit in tunica,

Talis visa mihi somno dimissa recenti.
30 En quantum per se candida forma valet!
'Quo tu matutinus' ait 'speculator amicae?
Me similem vestris moribus esse putas?

35 Apparent non ulla toro vestigia presso,
Signa voluptatis, nec iacuisse duos.
Aspice, ut in toto nullus mihi corpore surgat
Spiritus admisso notus adulterio.'

27 Ibat et hinc castae narratum somnia Vestae,

42 Ex illo felix nox mihi nulla fuit.

([II, xxix] "Yesternight, light of mine eyes, when I wandered heavy with wine and with never a servant's hand to lead me home, a crowd of tiny boys met me; how many I know not, for fear forbade me to count them. Some carried little torches and others arrows, while some seemed even to make ready fetters for me. Yet naked were they all. Then one that was more wanton than the rest cried . . . 'This is he that the angry woman delivered to us.' He spake, and straightway a noose was about my head. Another then bade them thrust me into their midst, while a third cried: 'Perish the man that deems us not divine! Whole hours hath she waited thee, though little thou deservest it, while thou, fool, didst seek another's door. When she has loosened the strings of her nightcap of Sidonian purple and turns on thee her slumber-laden eyes, then will sweet odours breathe upon thee such as the herbs of Araby ne'er gave. . . . and lo! we have come to the house whither we were bidden.' Thus did they lead me back to my mistress' house. 'Go now,' they cried. . . . [II, xxixA] " 'Twas morn and I wished to see

if alone she took her rest, and behold Cynthia was in her bed
alone. I stood amazed; for never seemed she to mine eyes more
fair, not even when, clad in purple tunic . . . So seemed she
to me, as she woke from her fresh slumber. Ah, how great is
the power of beauty unadorned! 'What!' quoth she, 'thou that
spiest thus early on thy mistress, deemst thou that my ways are
like to thine? . . . There are no signs of impress on the couch,
the marks of lovers taking their delight, no signs that two have
lain therein. See! from my bosom springs no deep-drawn
breath, that, as thou knowest, might tell thee that I had been
untrue.' . . . she went hence to lay her dreams before chaste
Vesta. . . . since then no happy night has e'er been mine"—
Loeb.)

X. Propertius describes how he was kidnaped one night and
taken to Cynthia's room. L. J. Richardson has analyzed this
section (*Yale Poetry Review* [1947], 24–29).

1. *exceeding late hour:* Teubner *Extrema . . . nocte* ("late at
night"), Loeb *Hesterna . . . nocte* ("Yesternight").

11. *given to lust:* Propertius has *lascivior* ("more playful,
cheeky"). Pound emphasizes the secondary sense of the
word and connects it with "lasciviousness" (cf. I, 40n).

19. *Sidonian night cap:* Made of Phoenician crimson. Sidon is
now Beirut.

23. *enter . . . bail:* They take his purse (Pound's addition).

26. *yank to my cloak:* Teubner *atque ita mi iniecto dixerunt
rursus amictu* ("and so they said to me after I had thrown
on my cloak"), Loeb *atque ita me in tectum duxerunt rursus amicae* ("Thus did they lead me back to my mistress'
house").

33. *pure form has its value:* Pound brings Propertius up-to-
date by attributing to him a fundamental tenet of modern
abstract art. Selections from Kandinsky's *Über das Geis-
tige in der Kunst* (1912) appeared in *Blast* (1914) and
contained statements like the following: "Form alone,
even if it is quite abstract and geometrical, has its inner
timbre, and is a spiritual entity . . ." (p. 121). Pound
later advised his readers to "transpose [Kandinsky's] chapter on the language of form and colour and apply it to the
writing of verse" (*Fortnightly Review* [Sept. 1, 1914],
465). See IV, 23n for a similar modernization of the Latin.

37, 39. *incumbent . . . incubus:* The pun is Pound's addition.
The word "incumbent" (a person holding office) derives from *incumbere* ("to lie upon"); the perfect tense
of *incumbere* is *incubui,* which in turn suggests *in-*

cubus, a late Latin word for a demon ("nightmare")
having the power to produce supernatural births.

51. *Vesta:* Goddess of the hearth. There is a suggestion that
Cynthia sees herself as a Vestal Virgin.

Section XI.

[III, xxvii] Quo fugis a demens? nullast fuga: tu licet usque
    Ad Tanain fugias, usque sequetur Amor.
    Non si Pegaseo vecteris in aere dorso,
    Nec tibi si Persei moverit ala pedes,
   5 Vel si te sectae rapiant talaribus aurae,
    Nil tibi Mercurii proderit alta via.
    Instat semper Amor supra caput, instat amanti,
    Et gravis ipse super libera colla sedet.

[III, xxx] 18 Non urbem, demens, lumina nostra fugis:
    Nil agis, insidias in me conponis inanes,
    Tendis iners docto retia nota mihi.
   23 Nuper enim de te nostras me laedit ad aures
    Rumor, et in tota non bonus urbe fuit.
    Sed tu non debes inimicae credere linguae:
    Semper formosis fabula poena fuit.
    Non tua deprenso damnatast fama veneno:
    Testis eris puras, Phoebe, videre manus.

   31 Tyndaris externo patriam mutavit amore
    Et sine decreto viva reducta domumst.
    Ipsa Venus, quamvis corrupta libidine Martis,
    Nec minus in caelo semper honesta fuit.

[III, xxvii] 26 Roscida muscosis antra tenere iugis.
    Illic aspicies scopulis haerere sorores
    Et canere antiqui dulcia furta Iovis,
    Vt Semelast combustus, ut est deperditus Io,
    Denique ut ad Troiae tecta volarit avis.

[III, xxx] 35 Quamvis Ida palam pastorem dicat amasse
    Atque inter pecudes accubuisse deam.

[III, xxviii] 20 Et petere Hyrcani littora Eoa maris,

[III, xxx] 29 Sin autem longo nox una aut altera lusu
    Consumptast, non me crimina parva movent.

[III, xvii] 11 Et modo pavonis caudae flabella superbae

   14 Quaeque nitent Sacra vilia dona Via.

([II, xxx] "Whither fliest thou, mad heart? There is no escape.
Fly as far as Tanais; Love will hunt thee down. Thou shalt not
escape, though thou be borne aloft on the back of Pegasus, nor
though the pinions of Perseus wing thy feet. Or should the
cloven breezes sweep thee along on feathered sandals, yet will

the lofty path of Mercury avail thee naught. Love swoops ever above thy head; Love swoops down upon the lover, and sits a heavy burden on the neck that once was free.
[II, xxxii] " 'tis not the city, 'tis my eyes thou flyest. Thou strivest in vain; empty are the wiles thou spinnest against me; with little skill thou spreadst familiar snares for me, whom experience has taught. . . . For of late rumour spake ill of thee in mine ears, and a tale of evil ran through all the city. And yet thou shouldst not trust these bitter words; scandal has ever been the doom of beauty. Thine honour has ne'er been blasted by the crime of poisoning; thou, Phoebus, wilt bear witness that her hands are unsullied. . . . The daughter of Tyndareus left her fatherland for the love of a stranger, and yet was brought home alive without condemnation. Venus herself is said to have been seduced by the lust of Mars, yet none the less she had honour alway in heaven. . . . [II, xxx] And, Cynthia, be it thy joy to dwell with me in dewy grottoes on the mossy hills. There shalt thou see the Sisters clinging to the crags, while they chant the sweet loves of Jove in olden time, how he was consumed with fire for Semele, how madly he loved Io, and then how in likeness of a bird he flew to the abodes of Troy. . . . [II, xxxii] Though Ida's mount tell how a goddess loved the shepherd Paris, and lay with him among his flocks. . . . [II, xxx] and on shipboard seek the shores of the Hyrcanian sea? . . . [II, xxxii] And if thou hast spent one night or two in long-drawn wantoning, such petty crimes vex me not a whit. . . . [II, xxiv] [Cynthia] now demands a fan made from some proud peacock's tail. . . . and such worthless gifts as glitter in the Sacred Way"—Loeb.)

XI. Dismissed by Cynthia, Propertius regrets that he is unable to evade the torments of love.

1–3. Evidently Pound's addition.

5. *Ranaus:* All printings have this form, although the Latin word is *Tanais* ("River Don") in both Teubner and Loeb. Pound has sanctioned Sullivan's emendation to "Tanais."

7. *Pegasean:* Cf. II, 2n.

8. *Perseus:* Cf. VIII, 23.

25. *foreign lover:* Paris.

27. *Cytharean:* Cf. VI, 33n. Venus' affair with Mars was discovered by her husband Vulcan.

34. *Semele . . . Io:* Cf. VIII, 19, 31.

[35. Of how   50, 54, 56;   Oh how   55]

35. *bird:* Jove (eagle).

36. *Ida:* Personified by Pound. Ida is the name of a mountain in what is now central Turkey.

38. *Hyrcanian:* Hyrcania was the land to the south of the Caspian Sea.

   Eos: Goddess of the dawn.

40. *Via Sacra:* The approach to the temple of Saturn in Rome was frequented by prostitutes.

Section XII.

[III, xxxii] 1 Cur quisquam faciem dominae iam credit amico?

3 Expertus dico, nemost in amore fidelis:

5 Polluit ille deus cognatos, solvit amicos,
   Et bene concordes tristia ad arma vocat.
   Tros et in hospitium Menelao venit adulter:
   Colchis et ignotum nonne secuta virumst?
   Lynceu, tune meam potuisti, perfide, curam
10 Tangere?
12 Posses in tanto vivere flagitio?
11 Quid si non constans illa et tam certa fuisset?
13 Tu mihi vel ferro pectus vel perde veneno:

15 Te socium vitae, te corporis esse licebit,
   Te dominum admitto rebus, amice, meis:
   Lecto te solum, lecto te deprecor uno:
   Rivalem possum non ego ferre Iovem.

33 Nam cursus licet Aetoli referas Acheloi,
   [Fluxerit   . . .   liquor,]

37 Qualis et Adrasti fuerit vocalis Arion,
   Tristis ad Archemori funera victor equos:

41 Desine et Aeschyleo conponere verba cothurno,
45 Tu non Antimacho, non tutior ibis Homero:
   Despicit et magnos recta puella deos,
   Harum nulla solet rationem quaerere mundi,
   Nec cur fraternis Luna laboret equis,
   Nec si post Stygias aliquid restabimus undas,
   Nec si consulto fulmina missa tonent.

61 Actia Vergilium custodis littora Phoebi,
   Caesaris et fortes dicere posse rates,
   Qui nunc Aeneae Troiani suscitat arma
   Iactaque Lavinis moenia littoribus.
65 Cedite Romani scriptores, cedite Grai:
   Nescioquid maius nascitur Iliade.
   Tu canis umbrosi subter pineta Galaesi
   Thyrsin et attritis Daphnin harundinibus,
   Vtque decem possint corrumpere mala puellas,

70 Missus et inpressis haedus ab uberibus.
 Felix, qui viles pomis mercaris amores!
 Huic licet ingratae Tityrus ipse canat:
 Felix intactum Corydon qui temptat Alexin
 Agricolae domini carpere delicias!
75 Quamvis ille sua lassus requiescat avena,
 Laudatur faciles inter Hamadryadas.
 Tu canis Ascraei veteris praecepta poetae,
 Quo seges in campo, quo viret uva iugo.
55 Aspice me, cui parva domi fortuna relictast,
 Nullus et antiquo Marte triumphus avi,
 Vt regnem mixtas inter conviva puellas
 Hoc ego, quo tibi nunc elevor, ingenio.
 Me iuvet hesternis positum languere corollis,
60 Quem tetigit iactu certus ad ossa deus,

 Tale facis carmen, docta testudine quale
80 [Cynthius inpositis temperat articulis.]

 Nec minor his animis aut, si minor, ore canorus
 Anseris indocto carmine cessit olor.
85 Haec quoque perfecto ludebat Iasone Varro,
 Varro Leucadiae maxima flamma suae.
 Haec quoque lascivi cantarunt scripta Catulli,
 Lesbia quis ipsa notior est Helena.
 Haec etiam docti confessast pagina Calvi,
90 Cum caneret miserae funera Quintiliae.
 Et modo formosa quam multa Lycoride Gallus
 Mortuus inferna vulnera lavit aqua!
 Cynthia quin etiam versu laudata Properti,
 Hos inter si me ponere Fama volet.

([II, xxxiv] "Why should any one henceforth entrust his mistress' beauty to the care of Love? . . . I speak from experience; no man is ever faithful in love. . . . Love pollutes kinship, parts friends, and summons them, that are well agreed, to bitter strife. The adulterer, that was made welcome by Menelaus, was a stranger; and did not the woman of Colchis follow a lover whom she knew not? Lynceus, hadst thou the heart to touch my beloved? Did not thy hands, faithless friend, fall powerless then? . . . Couldst thou have lived in such guilt? . . . What if she had not been so constant and so true? . . . Take my life with poison or the sword. . . . Thou mayest be the comrade of my life and part never from my side; my friend, I make thee lord of all my fortune; 'tis only as partner in my love that I would have thee never: I cannot endure a rival, though he were Jove himself. . . . Now, though thou shouldst tell once more how the stream of Aetolian Achelous flowed shattered by the might of love. . . . how, mourning at the funeral of Archemorus, Adrastus' victorious steed Arion spake aloud. . . . Cease to frame verse shod with the buskin of Aeschylus. . . . Thou shalt not be safer in thy goings than

Antimachus or Homer: for a comely girl despises even the power of the gods. . . . Never will girl enquire concerning the system of the universe, nor ask why the labours of the moon depend on her brother's steeds, nor if in truth there is a judge beyond the waves of Styx, nor if the crashing thunderbolts be hurled by an aiming hand. . . . Be it for Vergil to sing the shores of Actium o'er which Phoebus watches, and Caesar's gallant ships of war; Vergil that now wakes to life the arms of Trojan Aeneas and the walls he founded on the Lavinian shore. Yield ye, bards of Rome, yield ye, singers of Greece! Something greater than the Iliad now springs to birth! Vergil, thou singest beneath the pine-woods of shady Galaesus of Thyrsis, and Daphnis with the well-worn pipe of reed, and how ten apples or a kid fresh from the udder of its dam may win the love of a girl. Happy thou that thus cheaply buyest thy love with apples; to such a love may even Tityrus sing, unkind though she be. Happy too, Corydon, who seeks to win Alexis, the darling of the farmer, his master, Alexis yet unwon; even though he weary and rest from his piping, yet is he praised by the wanton Hamadryads. Thou singest also the precepts of Ascra's poet old, telling in what plains the corn grows green, and on what hills the vine. . . . Look on me, to whom but a scanty fortune hath been left at home, whose ancestors ne'er triumphed for battles long ago, see how I reign at the banquet in the midst of a crowd of girls, thanks to the wit for which thou now makest light of me! Be it mine to lie languidly among the wreaths of yesterday, for the god hath stricken me with aim unerring even to the bone. . . . Such music makest thou as the Cynthian god modulates with fingers pressed upon his well-skilled lyre. . . . and the melodious 'swan,' less lofty of accent, yet no less inspired when he sings the songs of love, sinks not to tuneless cackle like the 'goose.' Such sportive themes also did Varro sing when his tale of Jason was all told; Varro, Leucadia's mightiest flame. Such are the songs that wanton Catullus wrote, whose Lesbia is better known than Helen. Such passion also the pages of learned Calvus did confess, when he sang of the death of hapless Quintilia; and dead Gallus too, that of late laved in the streams of Hell the many wounds dealt him by fair Lycoris. Nay, Cynthia also has been glorified by Propertius—if Fame shall grant me a place mid such as they"—Loeb.)

XII. Propertius discovers that his friend Lynceus, an ambitious minor poet, is Cynthia's latest lover. Surveying the prospect of a rival *Iliad* by Virgil, he once more affirms the power of his love for Cynthia and the value of love poetry.

1. *entrust . . . friend:* Teubner *credit amico* ("trusts a friend"), Loeb *credat Amico* ("entrust . . . to the care of Love").

4. *pomegranate:* Pound's addition. A poem by Dowson, based on Propertius and cited in the notes to SATIEMUS, mentions the "red pomegranate" of a "perfect mouth." This may be the source of Pound's more erotic use of the same image.

6. *Trojan and adulterous:* Paris (cf. VII, 13*n*). Teubner *Tros et . . . adulter* ("a Trojan and an adulterer"), Loeb *hospes . . . adulter* ("a stranger and an adulterer").

7. *woman in Colchis:* Medea, who helped her husband obtain the Golden Fleece. Colchis lay to the east of the Black Sea.

8. *Lynceus:* A minor poet, and Propertius' rival for Cynthia's affections.

18. *Achelous . . . Hercules:* Pound supplies his own gloss (cf. I, 38*n*). The river Achelous wrestled in the form of a bull with Hercules for the possession of Deianira.

19. *Adrastus:* King of Argos, whose horse was gifted with the power of human speech.

   Achenor: Propertius has *Archemorus*, at whose funeral Adrastus' horse first spoke. Pound seems content with a vaguely "classical" reference (cf. I, 33*n*), possibly making a deliberate misquotation to communicate his boredom with Lynceus' excursions into poesy.

21. *Antimachus:* Antimachus of Colophon, who wrote in the fifth century B.C. on the Theban legend.

26. *lunar eclipses:* Misspelled "lunar ellipses" in Pound's *Letters* (p. 225).

27. *any patch left of us:* Teubner *aliquid restabimus* ("anything remains of us"), Loeb *aliquid rest arbiter* ("there is a judge").

33. *Ilian:* Trojan.

35. *Lavinian beaches:* Latium was the coastal region to the south of Rome, where Aeneas settled after the fall of Troy.

[38. is in   50+;   is on   *Faber and Faber*]

38. *larger Iliad:* Virgil's *Aeneid.*

[41. "neath ――― shade   50+;   " 'neath ――― shade" (Sullivan)]

41. *Phrygian:* Cf. V, 56*n*.

42. *Thyrsis . . . Daphnis:* Pastoral figures from Virgil's *Eclogues.*

43. *sins:* The proximity of *corrumpere* ("to corrupt") to *mala* ("apples") led Pound to suppose that Propertius was punning on *mālum* ("apple") and *malum* ("evil"). Like the quibble on *canes* (I, 4n), puns on *malum* are of ancient origin (cf. Quintilian, *Institutio Oratoria*, I, vii, 2).

46–47. *Tityrus . . . Corydon . . . Alexis:* Pastoral figures. The first two are thought to be Virgil's personal pseudonyms in the *Eclogues.*

[49. Hamadryads" 50+; Hamadryads (Sullivan)]

49. *Hamadryads:* Tree nymphs.

50. *Ascraeus:* Hesiod, author of *Works and Days.*

51. *Wordsworthian:* Cf. IV, 23n. Conscious anachronizing is common among writers of imitations.

52. Another imagist passage (like III, 4–5).

55. *ladies of indeterminate character:* Pound read *conviva* ("guest") as "convivial" and associated the word with *puellas* ("girls")—thereby making possible the sort of *double entendre* achieved in I, 40.

59. *tortoise:* Cf. I, 4n. Pound puns on *testudo,* which could mean "tortoise" or "lyre." Sullivan (p. 102) reconstructs the process by which Pound achieved this "*collage* of sense" (cf. I, 17n).

60. *your fashion:* I.e., Virgil's.

60–65. Pound's interpolation. Only the "goose" comes from Propertius. Dante compares poetasters to geese in *De Vulgari Eloquio* (II, iv). Orphic swans are less noisy.

66–67. *Varro . . . Jason . . . Leucadia:* Varro (b. 82 B.C.) translated Apollonius of Rhodes's *Argonautica,* which tells the story of Jason's quest for the Golden Fleece. His love poems to Leucadia have not survived.

68–69. *Catullus . . . Lesbia:* See the note on TO FORMIANUS' YOUNG LADY FRIEND.

70–71. *Calvus . . . Quintilia:* Calvus (82–47 B.C.) wrote poems on his wife Quintilia, none of which has survived. The pages are "dyed" with the lover's blood.

72. *Gallus . . . Lycoris:* Gallus (b. 70 B.C.) wrote four (lost) books of *Amores* to his mistress Lycoris.

HORÆ BEATÆ INSCRIPTO
[NO. 35. PRINTINGS: 9, 42, 43, 55]

The Latin title means "an inscription for an hour of happiness." The savoring of selected experiences for their future value as pleasant memories is implicit in ERAT HORA.

See the introductory note to THE HOUSE OF SPLENDOUR.

HOUSE OF SPLENDOUR, THE
[NO. 36. PRINTINGS: 9, 42, 43, 55]

Originally this was the seventh piece in a poem of twelve sections called "Und Drang" after the *Sturm und Drang* ("storm and stress") of German Romanticism. The first six poems in the sequence describe the poet's weariness with trying to find a meaning in life, and have not been reprinted in *Personæ* (1926); but the rest (VII–XII) have been preserved in their original order: THE HOUSE OF SPLENDOUR, THE FLAME, HORÆ BEATÆ INSCRIPTO, THE ALTAR, AU SALON, AU JARDIN. Many of the poems in "Und Drang" are pastiches of Rossetti, whose sonnet sequence (*The House of Life*) may have suggested the title of THE HOUSE OF SPLENDOUR.

1. *Evanoe:* A fictitious name.

2. *house not made with hands:* "For we know that if our earthly house of this tabernacle were dissolved, we have a building of God, an house not made with hands, eternal in the heavens" (II Corinthians 5:1).

HUGH SELWYN MAUBERLEY
[NO. 177. PRINTINGS: 52, 54, 55, 56]

In *New Bearings in English Poetry* (1932) F. R. Leavis remarked that HUGH SELWYN MAUBERLEY had "almost wholly escaped recognition" (p. 139), and went on to offer in a few trenchant pages an evaluative interpretation of the whole sequence; since then, numerous commentaries have followed, the most influential being those of Kenner (1951), Friar and Brinnin (1951), and Espey (1955). In compiling the following notes I have drawn heavily on Espey's researches and incorporated the textual emendations he proposes, four of which were sanctioned by Pound.

HUGH SELWYN MAUBERLEY is in two main parts. The first section covers lines 1–245 and runs from the opening "Ode" through "Envoi (1919)" (Sections I–[XIII] in Pound's numbering). It deals with Pound's personal experience of the

London literary scene, attempts to account historically for discrepancies between private vision and public taste, and implies that the literary efforts of pre-Raphaelite and nineties poets were abortive. The second section, running from "Mauberley 1920" through the final "Medallion," deals with the *impasse* of aestheticism and concerns a fictitious minor poet called Hugh Selwyn Mauberley. In these two sections Pound describes the historical conditions and personal weaknesses that combine to frustrate his poetic ambitions. Historically, Pound saw himself as working in a tradition that had been notable recently for its failures ("The English Rubaiyat was still-born"; "The 'Nineties' tried your game / And died"); and he also detected within himself certain predilections and weaknesses that threatened to prevent him from producing major work, weaknesses that are cast in the terms of eroticism so as to emphasize their dangers for the young poet. Pound could scarcely alter the historical situation, but his personal life underwent a revolution: economics replaced aestheticism, and Pound abandoned a life of "selected perceptions" in order to put his "ideas into action." HUGH SELWYN MAUBERLEY, read in this way, dramatizes a conflict between the antithetical demands of aestheticism and politics, a conflict that Pound resolved successfully by rejecting his *Lustra* manner and going ahead with the *Cantos*.

Self-analysis produced the two personæ in the poem, Mauberley and E. P., each of whom is an oversimplification of radically different elements in Pound himself. E. P. is the sort of pragmatic person Pound would like to be, a man fully aware of his own historicity and working in difficult conditions at the task of restoring literature to a more central place than it holds at present in our civilization. Even in 1922, however, Pound feared (and perhaps rightly) that he was basically a *tour d'ivoire* aesthete like Mauberley, a man inordinately and helplessly attached to "nacre and objets d'art" (*Letters*, p. 234), and therefore incapable of anything more urgent or strenuous than subjective reveries. Ideally, Pound hoped to exorcise Mauberley and cultivate E. P. But in HUGH SELWYN MAUBERLEY it is Mauberley who triumphs: as Pound assured us in 1956, "Mauberley buries E. P. in the opening poem; gets rid of all his troublesome energies" (quoted by Davie in *The Modern Age* [1961], p. 320).

Readers who complain of crudities in the poem (naivety, factual inaccuracies, oversimplification) are commonly met with the objection that Pound intended these things to be taken ironically because he is not writing *in propria persona*: the weaknesses are Mauberley's, not Pound's. But as A. L. French points out, much of the crudity occurs in parts of the poem where E. P. is the author, and E. P.'s opinions are often identical with those expressed by Pound elsewhere. Nobody, as far as I know, has put forward the extreme (and absurd) argument that because E. P. is merely a persona, E. P.'s mistakes are not really Pound's responsibility, and that Pound is completely detached from the whole poem (refined, indifferent, paring his nails). Nevertheless, we have the curious state of affairs in which Pound is either ridiculed for being naive or praised for being ironically naive—both attack and defense resting on an unspoken assumption that good poems do not contain silly ideas (a proposition difficult to defend in the case of Yeats, to name only one example). Perhaps one ought to remember that there is a difference between *holding* ideas and *using* ideas, between ideas as such and ideas in literature. Pound's aim in writing HUGH SELWYN MAUBERLEY was not to versify literary history but to use this material in order to present the differences between the sort of writer who is Mauberley and the sort of writer who is E. P.; and then, having done so, to explore the poignancy of the situation that occurs when a man feels himself to be closer temperamentally to the Mauberley he despises than to the E. P. he admires. Literary history, as presented in the poem, is merely a *donnée*, a background against which to measure the difference between Mauberley and E. P. To say that it is inaccurate is quite true, but to notice that it is accurate enough is more helpful. Given this literary-historical situation, Mauberley reacts one way, E. P. another—and Pound is more interested in the nature of their reaction than in the situation that provokes it. To have got the facts right in the first place would have curtailed a lot of needless speculation, but the poem does not stand or fall by its accuracy as literary history. It depends, rather, on its subtle investigation of the intricate relationship between Pound, E. P., and Mauberley. There is no need to invent specious elaborations of the persona theory so as to protect the illusion of Pound's omniscience.

[*Subtitle:* (Life and Contacts)   52–55;   Contacts and Life 56]

On returning the corrected proofs of *Diptych Rome-London* (1957) to the publisher Pound wrote: "Note inversion in subtitle of Mauberley, NOT Life and Contacts but the actual order of the subject matter" (MacGregor). The original subtitle parodies the phrase "life and letters" and is an ironic comment on the modern formula for literary success.

[Footnote to the title page: [*lacking*]   52, 54, 56, *Faber and Faber;*   The sequence is so distinctly a farewell to London that the reader who chooses to regard this as an exclusively American edition may as well omit it and turn at once to page 205 [*where "Homage to Sextus Propertius" begins*]   55]

The Latin epigraph from the *Eclogues* (IV, 38) of Nemesianus, a Carthaginian poet of the third century B.C., means
"the heat calls us into the shade." A collection of Pound's early
poems appeared the same year as HUGH SELWYN MAUBERLEY
with the title *Umbra*.

[*Part One*]

I. An autobiographical section in which Pound regrets his
failure to reinstate poetry as one of the great arts. The subtitle is adapted from Ronsard's "De L'Élection de son Sépul-
chre" (*Odes*, IV, 5).

[*Subtitle:* E. P. Ode   52, 55+;   Ode   54]

1. *three years:* The phrase is echoed in line 262. The earliest
poems in *Lustra* (1916) date from 1913.

   out of key: Cf. line 136 and the musical analogy at line 262.

2–3. *resuscitate . . . poetry:* In *Provença* (1910) the section
headed "Canzoniere: Studies in Form" bears the epigraph: "Ma qui la morta poesi risurga" (p. 60; cf. Dante,
Purgatorio, I, 7). The metaphors are those of the Renaissance (Boccaccio describes Dante as having "suscitata
. . . la morta poesi"), and reveal the degree to which
Pound saw himself as participating in a new renascence
(see p. 17 above).

6. *half savage country:* Pound was born in Hailey, Idaho,
U.S.A.

   out of date: If it is E. P. who is out of date, the tone is one
of Romantic *mal du siècle* (the visionary Leonard in Tennyson's "The Golden Year," for example, feels himself out of
place in the scientific age, "born too late"). But if it is the
country that is out of date, Pound is simply reiterating the
complaint made in SALUTATION THE SECOND (l. 3*n*).

7. That is, attempting the impossible: trying to make pretty
poems ("lilies") from a nucleus of experience ("acorn")
that was not only unsuitable but potentially capable of yield-
ing something far greater. By 1920 the oak of the *Cantos*
had already supplanted the lilies of *Lustra*.

   The imagery is perhaps recalled in Canto 79: "Will the
scrub-oak burst into flower? . . . / Will you trade roses
for acorns . . . ?" On the erotic symbolism of acorn as
glans, see Espey (p. 80); also Martial (XII, lxxv) and
Shakespeare's *Cymbeline* (II, v, 16–17).

8. *Capaneus:* One of the Seven against Thebes, struck down
by Zeus on the city wall for his impiety. Pound approved of
Dante's idea (*Inferno*, XIV, 49–72) that Capaneus should,

even after death, be "unrelenting in his defiance of the su-
preme power" (*The Spirit of Romance* [1910], p. 123). In
Canto 79 Pound again refers to himself as Capaneus.

9. The Greek is quoted from the Syrens' song in the *Odyssey*
(XII 189): ἴδμεν γάρ τοι πάνθ' ὅσ ἐνὶ Τροίῃ εὑρείῃ ("For we know
all the toils that [are] in wide Troy"—Loeb). Part of the
Greek is quoted in Canto 79. Pound is the Odysseus figure
of his own *Cantos:* the earliest example of this identifica-
tion is probably in T. P.'s *Weekly* (June 6, 1913) where
Pound says he has " 'known many men's manners and seen
many cities' " (p. 707).

9,11. The rhyme "Τροίῃ / lee-way" is the first of several bilingual rhymes in the poem: "Flaubert / hair," "*trentiesme*
/ diadem," "θεόν / upon," "Milésien / Englishmen." The
device is Byronic. In *Don Juan* Byron rhymes Latin *ibis*
with "tribe is" (VI, xvii), Greek Ποιητικης with "critic
is" (III, cxi), French *ivresse* with "dress" (XI, xxxix),
German *Verfluchter* with "conductor" (X, lxxi) and
Italian *villeggiatura* with "might allure a" (XIII, lxxviii).
Bilingual rhymes do not occur in the Byronic satire
L'HOMME MOYEN SENSUEL, and Pound has here managed to purge them of their comic associations. Espey
traces the device to Gautier, but Pound was using it as
early as CINO (ll. 47, 49).

10. *Caught . . . ear:* The rhythm is taken from "Caught in the
rose-hued mesh," the second line of an uncollected poem
called "Donzella Beata" (*A Lume Spento* [1908], p. 29).

13. The whole line is repeated as lines 250–251.

Penelope: The wife to whom Odysseus returned after his
twenty years' wanderings, and an emblem of fidelity.

Flaubert: The French novelist Gustave Flaubert (1821–
1880), whose doctrine of the *mot juste* led to the formation
of one of the fundamental tenets of imagist theory: "Use
no superfluous word" (*Poetry* [March 1913], 201).

15–16. Instead of rehearsing platitudes, E. P. cultivated a
dangerous beauty (Circe was the sorceress with whom
Odysseus lived for a year).

[18. trentiesme   52–55;   trentuniesme   56, *Faber and Faber, 1968*]

18. The French is adapted from the opening of François Villon's *Le Testament:* "En l'an de mon trentiesme aage." On
the significance of thirty see SALUTATION THE THIRD (l.
16*n*) and MIDDLE-AGED. The revision (made in the interests of biographical accuracy: Pound was thirty-one when

he published *Lustra*) has brought the French phrase very close to a passage near the end of Canto 56, where the subject is Hong Vou, founder of the Ming dynasty: "En l'an trentunieme de son Empire / l'an soixante de son eage. . . ." The similarity is probably accidental.

II. The dedicated artist is unable to accommodate his art to the public taste.

21. See line 215*n.*

23. *modern stage:* In March 1920 Pound began reviewing plays for the *Athenæum.*

24. *Attic:* The word denotes a pervasive elegance of taste associated with Athens.

28. *classics in paraphrase:* Notably HOMAGE TO SEXTUS PROPERTIUS.

29–32. Pound's preference for the sculpted as against the modeled derives probably from Michelangelo and the artistic exploration of the scholastic concept of *eduction.* In the *Cantos* the two arts symbolize antithetical states of mind: the cut stone is associated with clarity of ideas, the modeled with muddle.

[31. alabaster   52+;   albaster   *Faber and Faber*]

31. *kinema:* "The cinema is not Art" (*New Age* [Sept. 26, 1918], 352) because it is a mechanized form of passive impressionism, and not of active instigation. This dictum was modified, apparently, after Pound had read Jean Cocteau's *Poésies 1917–1920:* "In a city," he remarked when reviewing this volume, "the visual impressions succeed each other, overlap, overcross, they are 'cinematographic'" (*Dial* [Jan. 1921], 110). In any case, Pound was using juxtaposition as a structural device before he saw Eisenstein's analogous experiments with the cinematic "cut."

III. Contrasts between an idealized past and a vulgarized present show what modernity is deficient in.

34. *mousseline . . . Cos:* Cf. HOMAGE TO SEXTUS PROPERTIUS (V, 32*n*).

36. *Sappho:* Pound's study of the European lyric began with Sappho (7th century B.C.), who mentions the barbitos or lyre in one of her poems (CLXXVIII).

37. *Dionysus:* This juxtaposition of pagan fertility cult with Christian asceticism was inspired probably by Théophile Gautier's poem "Bûchers et Tombeaux":

> Des dieux que l'art toujours révère
> Trônaient au ciel marmoréen;
> Mais l'Olympe cède au Calvaire,
> Jupiter au Nazaréen. . . .

See the introductory note to SURGIT FAMA.

38. *ambrosial:* Cf. lines 263, 332.

40. *Caliban . . . Ariel:* The gross supplants the ethereal in this brave new world (Shakespeare, *The Tempest*). "Caliban" was also a pseudonym under which Robert Buchanan wrote (cf. l. 100*n*).

42. Heracleitus of Ephesus was a Greek philosopher of the sixth century B.C. Line 41 translates a famous pronouncement attributed to him, the Greek version of which appears frequently in the *Cantos* (74, 80, 83, 96).

[44. Shall reign throughout our 52; Shall outlast our 54+]

46. *after Samothrace:* That is, "after the example of Samothrace": Christianity is becoming as extinct as the religious cults of Samothrace, its art as fragmentary as the Winged Victory now in the Louvre.

47. Greek τὸ καλόν means "the beautiful." This Greek ideal has in the twentieth century become merely the trade name for a brand of cosmetics, Cf. ΤΟ ΚΑΛΌΝ.

49. *faun's flesh:* Cf. "faun's head" (101) and "faun-like" (113). Without this pagan awareness of the flesh, art atrophies into mere aesthetic discriminations.

[54. Peisistratus 52, 54; Pisistratus 55+]

54. Peisistratus was a patron of the arts and tyrant of Athens in the sixth century B.C.

55. *knave:* Pound had a low opinion of Woodrow Wilson (president of the U.S.A., 1913–1921) and David Lloyd George (prime minister of England, 1916–1922). On Wilson see L'HOMME MOYEN SENSUEL (l. 16*n*). Surprisingly, Lloyd George was blessed in *Blast* (1914, p. 20)

eunuch: Canto 55 contains an attack on eunuchs in politics.

57. *Apollo:* On the significance of this appeal to the god of music and poetry, see page 4 above.

58. Adapted from Pindar (*Olympian Odes*, II, 2): τίνα θεόν, τίν' ἥρωα, τίνα δ' ἄνδρα κελαδήσομεν ("what god, what hero, aye, and what man shall we loudly praise?"—Loeb). In 1916 Pound used this line as an example of "Pindar's big rhetorical drum" (*Letters*, p. 143).

60. *tin:* A pun on the Greek τίν'. There is a similar trick of language in Canto 96:

> rather nice use of *aveu*, Professor,
> though you were looking at ἄνευ.

Bilingual puns are used in the *Cantos* occasionally as a means of progressing from one theme to another: " 'tis / Itys" (Canto 4), "Eleanor / ἑλέναυς / Helen" (Canto 5), "Otis / Οὖτις" (Canto 78). Yet Pound was scornful of the same device in Daniel and Petrarch: "long before Francesco Petrarca, he, Arnaut, had thought of the catch about *Laura,* laura, l'aura, and the rest of it, which is no great thing to his credit" (*Instigations* [1920], p. 289).

IV. The meaninglessness of the First World War, which is also the subject of the latter part of Canto 16.

63. The Latin *pro domo* ("for the home") is adapted from Cicero's *De Domo Sua.*

64 ff. Following up a hint in Pound's *Letters* (p. 249) and *ABC of Reading* (1934, p. 38), Espey shows (p. 44) how Pound's style has been influenced here by the rhythms of the "Lament for Adonis" by the Greek pastoral poet Bion:

> χὦ μὲν ὀϊστώς,
> ὃς δ' ἐπὶ τόξον ἔβαλλεν, ὃ δὲ πτερόν, ὃς δὲ φαρέπραν.
> χὦ μὲν ἔλυσε πέδιλον Ἀδώνιδος, οἳ δὲ λέβητι
> χρυσείῳ φορέουσιν ὕδωρ, ὃ δὲ μηρία λούει,
> ὃς δ' ὄπιθεν πτερύγεσσιν ἀναψύχει τὸν Ἄδωνιν.

("This flung upon him arrows, that a bow, this a feather, that a quiver. One hath done off Adonis' shoe, others fetch water in a golden basin, another washes the thighs of him, and again another stands behind and fans him with his wings"—Loeb.) There are, however, close parallels in Shakespeare to this passage, notably in *Richard II* (III, ii, 155–160); and in the *Cantos* anaphora is one of the most common rhetorical devices (e.g., the opening of Canto 9).

71–72. *pro patria:* Adapted from Horace's *Odes* (III, ii, 13): "dulce et decorum est pro patria mori" (" 'Tis sweet and glorious to die for fatherland"—Loeb). The phrase was used with savage irony by those with experience of trench warfare, like Wilfred Owen, who wrote a poem about a soldier whose death by poison gas was a terrible indictment against "The old Lie: Dulce et decorum est / Pro patria mori."

77. *lies . . . infamy:* Possibly a reference to Lloyd George's notorious promise that demobilized soldiers would have homes fit for heroes to live in. Pound was later to echo this line when writing about "the sins of Georgia" in Canto 34; "These are the lies / These are the infamies."

78. *usury:* An early mention of a theme that was to become axiomatic in the *Cantos,* where usury is the original sin which results in the spiritual destruction of civilization (Cantos 45 and 51). Pound's attitude to usury is primitivistic, deriving from Aristotle (*Politics,* 1258*b*) and Dante (*Inferno,* XI, 94–111).

82. *fair cheeks:* A. L. French censures the "Rupert Brookery" of these lines.

86. *hysterias:* Espey argues (p. 79) that Pound is here punning on the original Greek meaning of the word ὑστέρα, "womb."

87. *laughter . . . dead:* Pound is here writing very much under the influence of Wyndham Lewis. The way in which laughter and violent death are associated in Lewis' early short stories has provoked Geoffrey Wagner into Joycean speculations on the relationship between "manslaughter" and "man's laughter." See also POST MORTEM CONSPECTU (l. 5) and Lewis' "Inferior Religions" (*Little Review* [Sept. 1917], 3–8).

V. An epitaph for those killed in the war.

90. *bitch:* Britannia. The consonance in the pairing of "bitch" with "botched" is paralleled in THE NEEDLE ("bore / bear") and THE SPRING ("last / lost"). The device is common in the *Cantos* (e.g., Canto 4: "curved/carved").

93. *earth's lid:* This is a kenning of Pound's invention, a borrowing from the style of THE SEAFARER. The Old English word for "grave" is *eorþscræf* ("earth-cavern"), not *eorþhlid.*

94–95: *statues . . . books:* The bric-à-brac of an ancient and once vital tradition: but the civilization these men have died for is little more than a museum of shabby *objets d'art.*

VI. An attempt to account historically for the schism between public taste and aesthetic values: first, the case of the pre-Raphaelites.

Glauques: "The period was 'gla[u]que' and 'nacre'" (*Little Review* [Oct. 1918], 54). Beerbohm's Enoch Soames calls absinthe "la sorcière glauque"; on the art nouveau significance of marine imagery, see SUB MARE (1. 6*n*).

96. *Gladstone:* Pound's objection to W. E. Gladstone (1809–1898) is never made clear, although he was later to write that this liberal statesman's "general attitude to life" was "ridiculous" (*Guide to Kulchur* [1938], pp. 262–263). See the note on Swinburne below.

97. *Ruskin:* Ruskin's *Sesame and Lilies* (1865) opens with a chapter called "Of Kings' Treasuries."

[98. Kings   52;   Kings'   54, Espey, *Faber and Faber, 1968;*
    King's   55+]

98. *Swinburne:* Gosse says that Swinburne was prevented by Gladstone from being eligible for the poet laureateship after Tennyson's death in 1892.

99. *Rossetti:* D. G. Rossetti, whom Pound called a "smaragdite poet" (*New Age* [Dec. 1911], 201), was abused by Buchanan.

100. *Buchanan:* R. W. Buchanan (1841–1901) published a pseudonymous attack on the "Fleshly School of Poetry" (the pre-Raphaelite group) in the *Contemporary Review* in 1871. See line 40*n*.

101. *faun's head:* Cf. line 49n. The phrase alludes to a poem by Rimbaud: "In 'Tête de Faune' [Rimbaud] has produced an almost perfect example of almost exactly the sort of beauty that we are, in this particular month and year, in search of. I am not sure that we would notice the poem if we had not come, by our own route, to this precise desire" (*New Age* [Oct. 16, 1913], 726).

hers: Probably the pre-Raphaelite model Elizabeth Eleanor Siddal's.

104. *Burne-Jones:* Sir Edward Burne-Jones's painting *Cophetua and the Beggar Maid* was completed in 1884 and now is in the Tate Gallery in London.

cartons: Cartoons. The French spelling appears in all texts and represents studio pronunciation of the period.

110. *Rubaiyat:* Edward Fitzgerald's version of *The Rubáiyát of Omar Khayyám* was ignored by the reading public until it was discovered by some unknown person (possibly Whitley Stokes) and introduced to the pre-Raphaelites. See also FAMAM LIBROSQUE CANO (1. 38*n*).

still-born: Cf. "pickled fœtuses" (1. 120). On the art

nouveau origin of such images, see SUB MARE (l. 6n).
Pound uses them to suggest that pre-Raphaelite and
nineties poetry was an abortive production.

115. *Jenny:* Pound alludes to Rossetti's poem about a tired
prostitute, "Jenny," which Buchanan attacked in his article. Another famous pre-Raphaelite beauty, Jane Burden (Mrs. William Morris), was known to the group as
"Janey."

118. *maquero:* A sexual marauder, with something of the allure of a fictional bandit. What scandalized the Glad-
stonian epoch is of no concern to a later generation.

VII. Section VI continued: second, the case of the nineties.

The words of the subtitle are spoken by La Pia in Dante's
Purgatorio (V, 134): "Sienna gave me birth, Maremma death"
(Sinclair). The story of La Pia (who was condemned by her
husband to live in the disease-ridden Maremma marshes) is
the subject of a painting by Rossetti for which Jane Burden
was the model. The Italian line was later to be parodied in the
"Daughters of the Thames" section of *The Waste Land.*

123. *Verog:* Victor Plarr (1863–1929), a lyric poet who sur-
vives by becoming a cataloging machine. Plarr was born
in Strasbourg but lived in Britain after his parents' house
had been destroyed in the Franco-Prussian War of 1870
(his poem "Strasbourg" was published in the London
Times in December 1918). As a survivor from the nineties he is invoked again in Canto 16, Pound having described him earlier as "a survivor of the senatorial fami-
lies of Strasburg" (*Poetry* [April 1915], 44). In Pound's
mythopœic account of the nineties Plarr acquires some
of the conventional attributes of the decadent hero.
Huysmans' Des Esseintes similarly spends his life in
morbid surroundings, is the last scion of an ancient
family, and is out of step with his decade.

From 1897 until his death Plarr was Librarian of the
Royal College of Surgeons, where he prepared a *Cata-
logue of Manuscripts in the Library of the Royal College
of Surgeons of England* which he completed eventually
in 1928. Pound first met Plarr in 1909 and found him
"most congenial" (Edwards, p. 64). Verses written by
Henry Simpson for the Poets' Club suggest that Plarr was
liberal with his anecdotes:

> A comet from the Rhymers' Club afar,
> Still on our nights shines genial poet Plarr
> With quiet winks of humour, and a tale
> Of submerged poets fit to make us quail.

Poetry and Drama (June 1913), 169. "People whose minds have been enriched by contact with men of genius retain the effects of it," wrote Pound in *T. P's Weekly* (June 6, 1913), explaining his belief in a literary "sort of Apostolic Succession."

[124. Gallifet 52+; Galliffet Espey, *Faber and Faber, 1968*]

124. Gaston Alexandre Auguste de Gallifet (1830–1909) was a French general in the Franco-Prussian War, and this fragment from Plarr's conversation reappears in Canto 16:

> wall . . . Strasbourg
> Gallifet led that triple charge . . . Prussians
> and he said
> it was for the honour of the army.
> And they called him a swashbuckler.

In *The Spirit of Romance* (1910) Pound spells the name "Galiffet" (p. 74). The form "Gallifet" appears in the 14th and 15th editions of *Men and Women of Our Time* (1895 and 1899), both of which Plarr edited.

125. *Dowson:* There is no entry for Ernest Dowson (1867–1900) in the 1899 edition of *Men and Women of Our Time*, although Plarr included such people as Image, Johnson, and Headlam. Plarr later published a volume of reminiscences called *Ernest Dowson 1888–1897* (1914) in which he mentions how, for the "young Mr. Ezra Pound . . . Dowson is a kind of classical myth" (p. 28). This statement is supplemented by a letter Pound wrote to Floyd Dell early in 1911, explaining how Dowson was "a very fine craftsman" who "epitomized a decade" and holds "a very interesting position, strategically, in the development of the art" of poetry (Tansell, p. 118).

Rhymers' Club: Founded in 1890 or 1891 by W. B. Yeats, Ernest Rhys, and T. W. Rolleston. Among its members were John Davidson, Ernest Dowson, Selwyn Image, Lionel Johnson, Richard Le Gallienne, Victor Plarr, and Arthur Symons. In a letter to Dell in 1911 Pound said that "the whole set of 'The Rhymers' did valuable work in knocking bombast, & rhetoric & victorian syrup out of our verse" (Tanselle, p. 118).

126. *Johnson:* Lionel Johnson (1867–1902). Pound edited the *Poetical Works of Lionel Johnson* (1915) within a year of marrying Dorothy Shakespear, a relative of the Johnson family. Katherine Tynan seems to have been responsible for the erroneous story that Johnson died after falling from a stool. Yeats also in his poem "In Memory of

Major Robert Gregory" describes Johnson as "much falling" (the poem was first published in August 1918). Both
Pound and Yeats may allude to the poem by Johnson
cited in the notes to A VIRGINAL.

128. *no . . . alcohol:* Remarkable, as Johnson was an alcoholic.

129. *autopsy:* In his *Autobiographies* Yeats says that "Johnson
. . . at the autopsy after his death, was discovered never
to have grown, except in the brain, after his fifteenth
year" (pp. 310–311).

131. *Newman:* John Henry Newman (1801–1890). Dowson
was a heavy drinker, Johnson an alcoholic; both were
Roman Catholics (hence the submerged pun on "spirit").

132. *Dowson . . . harlots:* A detail which Pound probably obtained from Yeats (cf. *Autobiographies*, pp. 311, 312,
399). One cannot imagine Plarr transmitting such scan-
dalous information.

133. *Headlam . . . Image:* The line should read: "Headlam
impartially imbued" (an accuracy which would ruin that
fine sequence: "*Im*age *im*partially *im*bued"). It was however the Reverend Stewart Duckworth Headlam (1847–
1924) who took an unclerical interest in the art of the
dance, and who was compelled by the Bishop of London
to resign his curacy in 1878 because he had lectured on
theatres and dancing in a working-men's club. Headlam
survived to found the Church and Stage Guild with Selwyn Image (1849–1930), who was coeditor of the *Hobby
Horse* in the 1890's. Pound met Image in February 1909
and found him "one of the most worth while" of the
people he met in London (Edwards, p. 64). They both
contributed to *The Book of the Poets' Club* in December
of that year.

134. *Bacchus:* Image cultivates Christ *and* Dionysus (cf. l.
37).
Terpsichore: The Muse of Dancing.

135. *The Dorian Mood:* Plarr's single book of verse is called
In the Dorian Mood (1896).

136. *out of step:* Like E. P., Verog was "out of key with his
time."

VIII. Brennbaum is a contemporary of Pound's and a Jew who
adjusts to the society he lives in by choosing to ignore
the spiritual inheritance of his race.

140–141. The physical description fits Max Beerbohm (1872–1956).

144. *Horeb:* Where Moses saw the burning bush (Exodus 3:2).

Sinai: The mountain on which Moses received the Ten Commandments (Exodus 19:20 ff.).

forty years: The Children of Israel wandered in the wilderness for forty years (Joshua 5:6).

147. *Impeccable:* Beerbohm was a renowned dandy, and Pound had referred to him earlier as "the impeccable Beerbohm" (*Little Review* [Aug. 1918], 5). Kenner's suggestion that "Brennbaum" might be Beerbohm is qualified by Espey's reminder that Beerbohm was not a Jew; but Pound would not be alone in thinking Beerbohm Jewish.

Beerbohm, incidentally, had considered himself out of key with his time since 1895, and he too excluded himself from the world of letters by going to live in Italy in 1910.

IX. Nixon is another contemporary of Pound's who treats the writer's art as a commercial proposition. The model here is possibly Arnold Bennett (Kenner), although Bennett himself ridiculed the Nixon attitude to literature (see Stead's *The New Poetic* [1964], pp. 47–48).

151–152. *reviewer . . . you are:* An equally slovenly rhyme is associated with Bennett in L'HOMME MOYEN SENSUEL (ll. 65–66).

160. *Dundas:* Fraser suggests Robertson Nicoll, editor of the *British Weekly;* Espey thinks "Dundas" represents the "Waugh-Strachey-Gosse type of literary pontiff and editor" (p. 97).

[168. Bloughram 52+; Blougram *Faber and Faber, 1968*]

168. *friend of Bloughram's:* Gigadibs, the third-rate journalist in Browning's poem "Bishop Blougram's Apology." Friar and Brinnin print a note from Pound which reads: "reference to Browning's bishop, allegoric" (p. 529). Pound rejected Espey's proposal to emend *Bloughram* to *Blougram.*

169. *pricks:* Christ told Saul: "It is hard for thee to kick against the pricks" (Acts 9:5).

170. *Nineties:* Cf. lines 120–139.

X. In contrast to Nixon is the devoted stylist, probably modeled after Ford Madox Ford (Kenner). In *The Last Pre-Raphaelite* (1948) Douglas Goldring says that the cottage, in a wild and lovely part of West Sussex, in which Ford and Stella [Bowen] first set up housekeeping in May 1919, was picturesque, built of old red brick and old red tiles, charmingly situated, and, as it had a big hole in the roof, extremely damp. . . . [Ford] "was extraordinarily skilful with his hands when it was a question of making things grow, or concocting some of his famous dishes" (p. 209).

Some of the details were already precast in the neat quatrains of Théophile Gautier's "Fumée":

> Là-bas, sous les arbres s'abrite
> Une chaumière au dos bossu;
> Le toit penche, le mur s'effrite,
> Le seuil de la porte est moussu.

182. *succulent:* Perhaps Pound is hinting here at Ford's own distinction between novelists who speak of "dishes succulent" and those who can bring themselves to mention "saucepans" and "casseroles" (*Thus to Revisit* [1921], pp. 144, 151). Is Pound therefore suggesting that the stylist, for all his dedication, belongs essentially to the "dishes succulent" school of writers?

XI. The woman whose erotic instincts are stillborn or suppressed by her environment.

184. *Milésien:* The Greek *Milesian Tales,* famous for their licentiousness, have not survived. Pound has here adapted a phrase from "Stratagèmes," a short story in Remy de Gourmont's *Histoires Magiques* (1894): "Des femmes, au bon endroit, savent mordre. Elles ne doivent pas être méprisées, ces conservatrices des traditions milésiennes—mais c'est bien monotone et les artistes sont rares." Pound quotes the words "Femmes, conservatrices des traditions milésiennes" in the *Little Review* ([Feb.–March 1919], 7; cf. *Letters,* p. 201). In 1922 he paraphrased the French as "Woman, the conservator, the inheritor of past gestures" (*Natural Philosophy of Love,* p. xvi). Cf. line 345.

186. *Ealing:* A London suburb.

XII. The fashionable literary salon.

[188. Milésien 52; Milésian 54+; Milesian Espey]

192–193. Translated from Gautier's poem, "Le Château du Souvenir":

> Daphné, les hanches dans l'écorce,
> Étend toujours ses doigts touffus. . . .

Lady Valentine evidently possessed a copy of Bernini's statue *Apollo and Daphne* which depicts the scene from Ovid's *Metamorphoses* (I, 548–552) that Pound had recalled earlier in THE TREE. The associations it evokes (foiled rape and beautiful metamorphosis) are a mockery of this twentieth-century Apollo's contact with an unlikely Daphne.

195. *Lady Valentine:* Drawn from Lady Ottoline Morrel and Lady Geraldine Otter (Espey). Ronald Firbank's *Vainglory* (1915) established the taste for satirical sketches of fashionable salons.

196–199. E. P. has Prufrock's self-consciousness about his clothing.

212–213. Translated from the opening line of Laforgue's "Complainte des Pianos": "Menez l'âme que les Lettres ont bien nourrie." Pound quotes the whole poem in his survey of modern French poetry (*Little Review* [Feb. 1918], 11–13).

215. *Johnson:* Life was not so easy for Samuel Johnson (1709–1784) as Pound's lines suggest, but intelligent journalism was not nearly so difficult for him as it was for his nineteenth-century namesake. The tone of these lines suggests that Pound is again following Plarr:

> When first [Lionel Johnson] came from the University in 1890, with the reputation of being one of the best scholars of his year, he found a friend ready to receive him, who for some time had been enduring one of those bitter experiences that the lapse of years intensify in retrospect. The friend had been endeavouring to scale Parnassus in a Fleet Street where literature was anathema maranatha. . . . Despite Mr. Johnson's acknowledged talents and College reputation, it seemed to the friend that he brought nothing to Fleet Street or Paternoster that the age required.

Poetry Review (June 1912), 262.

219. *Pierian roses:* An allusion to Sappho, LXXI: οὐ γὰρ πεδέχεις βρόδων / τῶν ἐκ Πιερίας ("for you have no part in the roses that come from Pieria"—Loeb). Pieria was the place near Mt. Olympus where the muses were worshiped.

XIII. The lyric tradition Pound wanted to resurrect (*Letters*, p. 187) is accessible only in pastiche because English poetry since the time of the pre-Raphaelites has been stillborn.

220. *dumb-born:* A variation on "still-born" (l. 110*n*). This whole section is a pastiche of the song by Edmund Waller (1606–1687) which begins:

Goe lovely Rose,
  Tell her that wastes her time and me,
  That now she knowes
When I resemble her to thee,
  How sweet and fair she seems to be.

221. *her:* Norman writes: "I asked Pound in 1959, 'Who sang you once that song of Lawes?' He wrote from Rapallo: 'Your question is the kind of damn fool enquiry into what is nobody's damn business'" (p. 224).

Lawes: Henry Lawes (1596–1662) set Waller's poems to music (cf. Canto 81). A couple of years earlier Pound had said (pseudonymously) that he "would point out Lawes as an example of how the words of a poem may be set and enhanced by music" (*New Age* [March 7, 1918], 378). In *ABC of Reading* (1934) he says that "the great lyric age lasted while Campion made his own music, while Lawes set Waller's verses, while verses, if not actually sung or set to music, were at least made with the intention of going to music. . . . Poetry atrophies when it gets too far from music" (p. 45).

225–226. *lie . . . longevity:* On the origin of such rhymes, see PAN IS DEAD (ll. 2–3*n*).

231–245. Pound here imitates the Elizabethan "eternizing" conceit.

231. *I would bid them live:* The seventh section of Tennyson's *The Princess* (1847) is introduced by a pastiche of a famous poem by Carew, and contains this request: "Ask me no more, lest I should bid thee live."

232. *amber:* Cf. line 396.

[*Part Two*]

[*Subtitle:* 1920 Mauberley 52, 54; Mauberley 1920 55+]

I. Mauberley's limitations as an artist. The prototype of Mauberley was Walter Villerant, a persona Pound used when contributing "Imaginary Letters" to the *Little Review* in 1918.

[*Epigraph:* [*lacking*] 52, 54; Vacuos exercet aera morsus 55+]

The epigraph is adapted from Ovid's description of how Cephalus' dog Laelaps tried to bite the elusive monster which was ravaging Thebes (*Metamorphoses*, VII, 786: "vanos exercet in aera morsus" ["snaps at the empty air"—Loeb]). Pound rejected Espey's proposed emendation of the Latin, which is paraphrased in lines 295–298.

[247. Jaquemart 52+; Jacquemart Espey, *Faber and Faber, 1968*]

247. Jules Jacquemart (1837–1880) engraved the frontispiece for the 1881 edition of *Émaux et Camées.*

249. *Messalina:* It is ironic that the sexless Mauberley should be studying one of the most profligate Roman empresses. Pound told Friar and Brinnin "that he had in mind a particular portrait, but that he cannot now remember which" (p. 530).

250–251. Quoted from line 13.

254–257. Mauberley prefers the profile of aestheticism (with all its narrow perfections) to the full face of the complete life. Espey relates the chiseled quatrains of this section to Gautier's poetic manifesto, "L'Art."

259. *Pier Francesca:* The Umbrian painter, Piero della Francesca (1416?–1492). Yet Mauberley's imagination, as displayed in the final "Medallion," is far from "colourless." Reinach calls Piero "cold and impersonal" (*Apollo* [1904], p. 158).

260. *Pisanello:* Vittore Pisano (1397–1455), the Veronese painter and medalist who based his designs on Greek coinage but produced only high-class *objets d'art:* the medals he "forged" were "forgeries."

261. *Achaia:* Greece. This passage is recollected in Canto 74:

> Beloved the hours βροδοδάκτυλος
> as against the half-light of the window
> with the sea beyond making horizon
> le contre-jour the line of the cameo
> profile "to carve Achaia."

II. Mauberley realizes when it is too late that the woman he has regarded as merely a focus of aesthetic stimuli might in fact have been able to offer him the delights of physical love.

The epigraph is presumably in Pound's French. On the sexual symbolism of *tonnerre* see Espey (p. 75). Pound told Friar and Brinnin that Caid Ali is a pseudonym of his own (p. 530). Other pseudonyms include: M. D. Atkins, Alf Arpur, William Atheling, Claude Aveling, Sally Biggs, Cino, B. H. Dias, Thayer Exton, Ferrex, John Hall, Henery Hawkins, Hiram Janus, Weston Llewmys (and Weston St. Llewmys), Hermann Karl Georg Jesus Maria, Nemo, Old Glory, Raoul Root, Abel Sanders, Ben Tor, Alfred Venison, Walter Villerant, Baptiste von Helmholtz, and Bastien von Helmholtz.

262. *three years:* Cf. line 1.

diabolus in the scale: Espey explains (p. 76) that " 'the devil in music' is the augmented fourth, which gave the medieval musicians great difficulty and gave rise to the tag: *Mi contra Fa / Diabolus in Musica.*"

263. *ambrosia:* Mauberley's life is not *phallic* and ambrosial (l. 38).

265. *ANANGKE:* Greek ἀνάγκη ("necessity"). Pound has elsewhere described "the ἀνάγκη of modernity" as "cash necessity" (*Little Review* [Aug. 1918], 11). Traditionally, however, it was during the reign of Necessity that Eros (l. 294) was born.

Arcadia: There is no Arcadian Pan in Mauberley's idyllic dreamworld.

266. *moved . . . phantasmagoria:* In the *Little Review* (March 1918) Pound writes that "certain men move in phantasmagoria; the images of their gods, whole countrysides, stretches of hill land and forest, travel with them" (p. 57). Kenner cites a remark by Strether in Henry James's *The Ambassadors* (1903): "Of course I moved among miracles. It was all phantasmagoric." This is one of the allusions which enable Espey to identify Mauberley with the Jamesian aesthete, as represented by Gilbert Osmond in *The Portrait of a Lady* (1881).

[268. NUKTIS   52–55   NUKTOS   56, Espey]

268. The Greek phrase νυκτὸς ἄγαλμα ("night's jewel") is quoted from the Greek pastoral poet Bion (IX):

Ἕσπερε, τᾶς ἐρατᾶς χρύσεον φάος Ἀφρογενείας,
Ἕσπερε κυανέας ἱερὸν φίλε νυκτὸς ἄγαλμα, …

("Evening Star, which art the golden light of the lovely Child o' the Foam [Aphrodite], dear Evening Star, which art the holy jewel of the blue blue Night"—Loeb.)

272. *orchid:* See line 293n.

276. *final estrangement:* Cf. "last estrangement" (NEAR PERIGORD, l. 185).

277. *TO AGATHON:* Greek τὸ ἀγαθόν ("the good").

280. *sieve:* The metaphor recurs in Pound's introduction to *The Natural Philosophy of Love* (1922, pp. xvi, xvii).

seismograph: See THE NEEDLE (l. 3n).

[281. Given, that is, his urge   52;   Given that is his "fundamental passion"   54+]

[282. To convey   52;   This urge to convey   54+]

281–284. This passage is recollected in Canto 74:

> cheek bone, by verbal manifestation,
> her eyes as in "La Nascita" [Botticelli's *Birth of Venus*].

[284. manifestation   52, 56, *Faber and Faber, 1968;*   manifestations   54, 55]

284. *verbal manifestations:* This phrase is almost a cliché in Pound's writings: it occurs four times in *ABC of Reading* (1934).

[288. irises   52, 54;   irides   55+
wide-banded   52+;   wide-branded   *Faber and Faber*]

289–290. *botticellian sprays:* The allusion is to the painting of the *Birth of Venus* by Sandro Botticelli (1447–1510). Espey has an ingenious note (pp. 71–72) on how Pound used the literary source of Botticelli's painting (Poliziano's *La Giostra*).

292. *affect:* This word seems to be used in the sense of the medieval psychological term *affectus* ("emotions").

293. *Orchid:* Pound puns on the Greek meaning of the word ὄρχις ("testicle"). Cf. coitus (l. 1*n*). Epsey writes of this kind of symbolism (p. 51): "the poem moves throughout on two levels: one the level of orchid as aerial flower and iris as earthly flower, the other the level of orchid as ὄρχις (testicle) and the diastasis of the eyes as invitation to active love. . . ."

294. *Eros:* Cf. line 265*n*.

295–298. These lines translate and expand the Latin epigraph which precedes line 246: Mauberley "bites" ineffectually, without experiencing the erotic satisfactions of Catullus' *oscula mordenti*. It is also possible that the lines refer literally to the London scene, for Iris Barry later recalled "someone's account (Pound's, I think) of a row of houses discovered intact in Earl's Court outside the front door of each of which was a pair of stone dogs, large as life and no pair alike or even of the same species" (*Bookman* [Oct. 1931], 168). The Hudibrastic rhyme ("dogs / epilogues") recalls a passage from *Hudibras* (I, iii) quoted in *ABC of Reading* (1934, p. 164):

> Both are but several Synagogues
> Of *carnal* men, and *Bears* and Dogs. . . .

III. Unlike Pound, Mauberley is not driven to protest against "current exacerbations." Faced with the schism between public taste and artistic ambition, he lapses into subjective reveries.

301. *red-beaked steeds:* The chariot of Love is drawn by the doves of the Cytherean, Aphrodite.

311–347. The irony is sustained largely by the use of poly-syllables (see PIERROTS, ll. 7–9*n*).

313–314. See l. 322*n* and the note to QUIES. Mauberley is attacked for behaving as Pound used to behave.

315–318. An anticipation of the "scattered Moluccas" in the next section.

319. *neo-Nietzschean:* Possibly a reference to Pound's association with the *New Age,* a periodical which devoted a good deal of space to the ideas of Friedrich Wilhelm Nietzsche (1884–1900), whose *Collected Works* were translated into English 1909–1913. The Nietzsche cult was satirized by A. E. Randall in verses that begin: "Lo, I am the singer / Of Neo-Nietzscheans" (*New Age* [Feb. 1910], 317).

322. *exacerbations:* Another recollection of Pound's own aestheticism during his *Lustra* years (cf. ll. 313–314*n*). In the course of complaining about an inferior volume of poems by Sturge Moore, Pound remarked that "good poets are too few and the exacerbations of life are too many" (*Poetry* [June 1915], 139).

331. *Minoan:* Minos was the legendary king of Crete (cf. l. 395). Reinach says that the Minoan period (2000–1500 B.C.) was "characterised by a rapid advance in the arts of design and of work in metal, first towards realism and afterwards towards elegance" (*Apollo* [1904], p. 33).

undulation: Reinach notes "the marked undulation of the lips" of sculpted heads by Scopas. "We seem to divine in them the intensity of a struggle against desire, the anguish of unsatisfied aspirations" (*ibid.,* p. 59).

332. *ambrosial:* Cf. lines 38, 263.

337. *apathein:* Greek ἀπάθεια ("insensibility, apathy"), the divine indifference of Olympian gods to what is merely human.

342–343. *imaginary / Audition:* The genesis of this phrase is hinted at in a comment Pound made on Remy de Gourmont's *Litanies de la Rose:* "[This] is not a poem to lie on the page, it must come to life in audition, or in the finer audition which one may have in imagining sound" (*Little Review* [Feb. 1918], 27). See also MŒURS CONTEMPORAINES (VI, 4*n*). Mauberley's preference for the imagined as against the real indicates his withdrawal into revery.

343. *sea-surge:* Pound uses this word in THE SEAFARER (l. 6) and again in Canto 7:

> poor old Homer blind,
> blind as a bat
> Ear, ear for the sea-surge. . . .

345. *conservation . . . tradition:* Cf. line 184.

345–346. The lines express in brief Pound's aims as a writer. He had already spoken of the "better tradition" in the *Little Review* ([Oct. 1918], 23).

IV. Mauberley's reveries: escape from the pressures of the London scene, and oblivion in the South Sea islands of aesthetic fantasy.

360. *Moluccas:* The Molukka Islands are a group of spice-producing islands in the Malay Archipelago.

364, 371. *Simoon . . . Flamingoes:* Espey points out that there are no flamingoes in the Moluccas and that the sand-laden wind of Africa and Persia carries no farther than India: "what we have here is Carthage and Flaubert's African travels . . ." (p. 39). He concludes that the primary source of Mauberley's tropical vision is Flaubert's *Salammbô* (1862).

V. The single masterpiece produced by Mauberley, which transforms a living person into the metallic deadness of an *objet d'art,* and which synthesizes the limited perfections of Pound's *Lustra* manner.

385. *Luini:* Pound may allude to the portrait of *La Columbina* by Bernadino Luini (1475?–1532?). According to Salomon Reinach, Luini's "elegance is superficial, his drawing uncertain, and his power of invention limited" (*Apollo* [1904], p. 191).

391. *Anadyomene:* Pound seems to have in mind the "Head of Aphrodite" in the Leconfield collection, reproduced in Reinach's *Apollo* (fig. 83). Reinach's commentary on this work suggested many words and phrases to Pound, some of which are noted below. This particular quatrain may have been shaped also by the opening lines of Rimbaud's sonnet "Vénus Anadyomène," the octave of which Pound quotes in the *Little Review* ([Feb. 1918], 23).

393. *Honey-red:* "[Luini's] most characteristic trait is a certain honeyed softness" (Reinach, *ibid.*, p. 191).

face-oval: Reinach says of the "Head of Aphrodite" that "the form of the face, hitherto round, has become oval" (*ibid.*, p. 58).

395. *Minos:* A reference which confirms the earlier suggestion that Mauberley is preoccupied with "Minoan undulations" (l. 331).

396. *amber:* Cf. line 232.

398. *suave:* The word is a cliché of approbation in Reinach's book. The "Head of Aphrodite" is described as being "exquisitely suave in expression" (*ibid.*, p. 58; similarly p. 59).

IMAGE FROM D'ORLEANS
[NO. 131. PRINTINGS: 26, 39, 40, 42, 43, 55]

A translation of the first eight lines of a song by Charles d'Orléans (LXXIII):

> Jennes amoureux nouveaulx,
> En la nouvelle saison,
> Par les rues, sans raison,
> Chevauchent, faisans les saulx.

> Et font saillir des carreaulx
> Le feu, comme de cherbon,
> Jennes [amoureux nouveaulx,]
> [En la nouvelle saison.]

> Je ne sçay se leurs travaulx
> Ilz emploient bien ou non;
> Mais piqués de l'esperon
> Sont autant que leurs chevaulx,
> Jennes [amoureux nouveaulx!]

Pound's translation offers documentary support for his claim that "Imagisme exists in . . . 'Charles d'Orléans'" (*T. P.'s Weekly* [Feb. 20, 1915], 185). DIEU! QU'IL LA FAIT derives from a poem by the same writer.

'ΙΜΈΡΡΩ
[NO. 162. PRINTINGS: 38, 40, 42, 43, 55]

[TITLE: O Atthis   35;   ιμερρω   40+]

The Greek word ἱμείρω or ἱμέρρω means "to long for." Pound alludes to a poem by Sappho (LXXXVI):

πόλλα δὲ ζαφοίταισ' ἀγάνας ἐπι-
μνάσθεισ' Ἀτθίδος ἰμμέρω,
λέπταν ποι φρένα κῆρ' ἄσᾳ βόρηται.

("And oftentime while our beloved wanders abroad, when she calls to mind the love of gentle Atthis, her tender breast, for sure, is weighed down deep with longing"—Loeb.) A version of the Greek had been published recently by Edward Storer (*Egoist* [Oct. 1915], 153–154).

5–6. *long . . . long:* Cf. Sappho, XXIII: καὶ ποθήω καὶ μάομαι ("and I long and I yearn"—Loeb).

IMPRESSIONS OF FRANÇOIS-MARIE AROUET (DE VOLTAIRE)
[NO. 163. PRINTINGS: *38, 41, 42, 43, 55*]

In each of his adaptations from Voltaire (1694–1778) Pound omitted well over half of the original poem, translating only the lines italicized in the texts printed below. Pound admired Voltaire for the clarity with which he expressed his ideas, and also for his "method of annihilating imbecility" (*New York Herald Tribune Books* [Jan. 27, 1929], 1). Shortly after publishing these poems Pound was to turn his attention to the *Dictionnaire Philosophique*, from which he translated Voltaire's scornfully lucid examination of *Genesis* (*Little Review* [Nov. 1918], 50–64; cf. MŒURS CONTEMPORAINES, VII, 16*n*).

I. A translation of Voltaire's "Épitre Connue Sous le Nom des *Vous* et des *Tu*":

> *Philis, qu'est devenu ce temps*
> *Où, dans un fiacre promenée*
> *Sans laquais, sans ajustemens,*
> De tes grâces seules ornée,
> *Contente d'un mauvais soupé*
> Que tu changeais en ambroisie,
> Tu le livrais, dans ta folie,
> A l'amant heureux et trompé
> Qui t'avait consacré sa vie?
> Le Ciel ne te donnait alors,
> Pour tout rang et pour tous trésors,
> Que les agrémens de ton âge,
> Un cœur tendre, un esprit volage,
> Un sein d'albâtre et de beaux yeux.
> Avec tant d'attraits précieux,
> Hélas! qui n'eût été friponne?
> Tu le fus, objet gracieux,
> Et (que l'Amour me le pardonne)
> Tu sais que je t'en aimais mieux.

Ah! Madame! que votre vie,
D'honneur aujourd'hui si remplie,
Diffère de ces doux instants?
Ce large suisse à cheveux blancs
Qui ment sans cesse à votre porte,
Philis, est l'image du Temps:
Il semble qu'il chasse l'escorte
Des tendres Amours et des Ris;
Sous vos magnifiques lambris
Ces enfans tremblent de paraître.
Hélas! je les ai vus jadis
Entrer chez toi par la fenêtre,
Et se jouer dans ton taudis.

Non, Madame, tous ces tapis
Qu'a tissus la Savonnerie,
Ceux que les Persans ont ourdis,
Et toute votre orfèvrerie,
Et ces plats si chers que Germain
A gravés de sa main divine,
Et ces cabinets où Martin
A surpassé l'art de la Chine;
Vos vases japonais et blancs,
Toutes ces fragiles merveilles;
Ces deux lustres de diamans
Qui pendent à vos deux oreilles;
Ces riches carcans, ces colliers,
Et cette pompe enchanteresse,
Ne valent pas un des baisers
Que tu donnais dans ta jeunesse!

Subtitle: Pound's substitution of the classical "Phyllidula" for
Voltaire's *Philis* is in keeping with the epigrammatic nature of
his adaptations (cf. PHYLLIDULA). *Philis* is a soubriquet for a
former mistress of Voltaire's called Susanne de Livry, who
married the marquis de Gouvernet and then refused Voltaire
admission to her house. Pound may have altered the name to
avoid giving offense to Phyllis Reid and Phyllis Bottome, since
both women frequented the Pound circle at the time this poem
was written.

In alluding to Henry James's *The Spoils of Poynton* (1897)
Pound invites comparison between James's Mrs. Gereth and his
own Phyllidula, each of whom displays an excessive veneration
for material objects. "We may *conspuer* with all our vigour,"
Pound writes, "Henry James's concern with furniture, the
Spoils of Poynton . . ." (*Little Review* [Aug. 1918], 22; and
ibid., p. 31). The phrase "the spoils of Finlandia" occurs in
Canto 80.

[4. a cheap   38;   a soggy, cheap   41+]

4. The typescript from which 38 was printed reads "a bloody
   cheap," the word "bloody" being deleted (Chicago MSS)—

the canceled word having achieved notoriety recently in the
London production of Shaw's *Pygmalion* (1914). Other examples of Harriet Monroe's censorship of Pound's poems are
listed in TO A FRIEND WRITING ON CABARET DANCERS (l. 36n).

8 ff. The catalog is used as an ironic device with similar material in Canto 40:

> With our eyes on the new gothic residence, with our
> eyes on Palladio, with a desire for seigneurial splendours
> (AGALMA, haberdashery, clocks, ormoulo, brocatelli,
> tapestries, unreadable volumes bound in tree-calf,
> half-morocco, morocco, tooled edges, green ribbons,
> flaps, farthingales, fichus, cuties, shorties, pinkies
> et cetera
> Out of which things seeking an exit. . . .

II. Translated from Voltaire's *Stances:*

> *Si vous voulez que j'aime encore,*
> *Rendez-moi l'âge des amours;*
> *Au crépuscule de mes jours*
> *Rejoignez, s'il se peut, l'aurore.*
>
> Des beaux lieux où le dieu du vin
> Avec l'Amour tient son empire,
> *Le Temps, qui me prend par la main,*
> *M'avertit que je me retire.*
>
> De son inflexible rigueur
> Tirons au moins quelque avantage.
> Qui n'a pas l'esprit de son âge
> De son âge a tout le malheur.
>
> Laissons à la belle jeunesse
> Ses folâtres emportemens:
> *Nous ne vivons que deux momens;*
> *Qu'il en soit un pour la sagesse.*
>
> Quoi! pour toujours vous me fuyez,
> Tendresse, illusion, folie,
> Dons du Ciel, qui me consoliez
> Des amertumes de la vie!
>
> *On meurt deux fois, je le vois bien:*
> *Cesser d'aimer et d'être aimable,*
> *C'est une mort insupportable;*
> *Cesser de vivre, ce n'est rien.*
>
> *Ainsi je déplorais la perte*
> *Des erreurs de mes premiers ans;*
> *Et mon âme, aux désirs ouverte,*
> *Regrettait ses égaremens.*

Du ciel alors daignant descendre,
L'Amitié vint à mon secours;
Elle était peut-être aussi tendre,
Mais moins vive que les Amours.

Touché de sa beauté nouvelle,
Et de sa lumière éclairé,
Je la suivis; mais je pleurai
De ne pouvoir plus suivre qu'elle.

Subtitle: Mme. du Chatelet was Voltaire's mistress from about 1734 until 1749. During the later years of this liaison she was in the habit of consoling herself with other and younger lovers.

D. R. Guttery had recently published a translation of this poem in the *New Age* ([Oct. 1915], 603).

[4. out of   38–43;   out from   55]

5–10. Apparently Pound's addition.

9–10. *time . . . evil:* In Canto 30 "Time is the evil," and the phrase is repeated in Canto 74.

[20. Weeping that   38, 42+;   Lamenting that   41]

III. Adapted from one of Voltaire's *Stances* addressed "A Madame Lullin de Genève":

> *Hé quoi! vous êtes étonnée*
> *Qu'au bout de quatre-vingts hivers*
> *Ma muse faible et surannée*
> *Puisse encor fredonner des vers?*
>
> *Quelquefois un peu de verdure*
> *Rit sous les glaçons de nos champs;*
> Elle console la nature,
> Mais elle sèche en peu de temps.
>
> *Un oiseau peut se faire entendre*
> *Après la saison des beaux jours;*
> Mais sa voix n'a plus rien de tendre,
> Il ne chante plus ses amours.
>
> Ainsi je touche encor ma lyre,
> Qui n'obéit plus à mes doigts;
> Ainsi j'essaye encor ma voix
> Au moment même qu'elle expire.
>
> «*Je veux, dans mes derniers adieux,*
> *Disait Tibulle à son amante,*
> *Attacher mes yeux sur tes yeux,*
> Te presser de ma main mourante.

Mais quand on sent qu'on va passer,
Quand l'âme fuit avec la vie,
A-t-on des yeux pour voir Délie,
Et des mains pour la caresser?

Dans ces momens chacun oublie
Tout ce qu'il a fait en santé.
Quel mortel s'est jamais flatté
D'un rendez-vous à l'agonie?

Délie elle-même à son tour
S'en va dans la nuit éternelle,
En oubliant qu'elle fut belle,
Et qu'elle a vécu pour l'amour.

Nous naissons, nous vivons, bergère,
Nous mourons sans savoir comment;
Chacun est parti du néant:
Où va-t-il? . . . Dieu le sait, ma chère.

Wilfred Thorley had recently published a translation of this poem in the *New Age* ([April 29, 1915], 702).

3–4. Voltaire becomes an imagist as Pound cuts the original text and juxtaposes the salvaged parts.

4. *late . . . year:* This phrase recurs in EXILE'S LETTER (l. 42).

5–6. Voltaire alludes to Tibullus' *Elegies* (I, i, 59–60):

te spectem, suprema mihi cum venerit hora,
et teneam moriens deficiente manu.

("May I look on thee when my last hour comes; may I hold thy hand, as I sink, in my dying clasp"—Loeb.)

IN A STATION OF THE METRO
[NO. 71. PRINTINGS: *16, 17, 32, 39, 40, 42, 43, 55*]

[*In* 16 *and* 17 *only, the lines are spaced as follows:*

The apparition   of these faces   in the crowd   :
Petals   on a wet, black   bough   .]

It was in writing this poem that Pound first formulated the theory of juxtaposition as a structural device in poetry.

Three years ago in Paris I got out of a "metro" train at La Concorde, and saw suddenly a beautiful face, and then another and another, and then a beautiful child's face, and then another beautiful woman, and I tried all that day to find words for what this had meant to me, and I could not find any words that seemed to me worthy, or as lovely as that sudden emotion. And that evening, as I went home along the Rue Raynouard, I was still trying, and I found, suddenly, the expression. I do not mean that I found words, but there came an equation . . . not in speech, but in little splotches of colour.

That evening, in the Rue Raynouard, I realized quite vividly that if I were a painter, or if I had, often, *that kind* of emotion, or even if I had the energy to get paints and brushes and keep at it, I might found a new school of painting, of "non-representative" painting, a painting that would speak only by arrangements in colour. . . . The "one image poem" is a form of super-position, that is to say, it is one idea set on top of another. I found it useful in getting out of the impasse in which I had been left by my metro emotion. I wrote a thirty-line poem, and destroyed it because it was what we called work "of second intensity." Six months later I made a poem half that length; a year later I made the following hokku-like sentence [IN A STATION OF THE METRO]. I dare say it is meaningless unless one has drifted into a certain vein of thought. In a poem of this sort one is trying to record the precise instant when a thing outward and objective transforms itself, or darts into a thing inward and subjective.

This particular sort of consciousness has not been identified with impressionist art. I think it is worthy of attention.

Fortnightly Review (Sept. 1, 1914), 465, 467; there is a less elaborate version in *T. P's Weekly* (June 6, 1913), 707. Pound neglects to mention that he had already used the same image in an uncollected poem called "Laudantes Decem Pulchritudinis Johannae Temple":

> the perfect faces which I see at times
> When my eyes are closed—
> Faces fragile, pale, yet flushed a little, like petals of roses.

Exultations (1909), p. 30. Earl Miner thinks that the poetry of "superposition" derives from the Japanese *haiku* or *hokku* (*The Japanese Tradition in British and American Literature* [1958], pp. 112 ff.).

Richard Aldington's parody follows the original spacing:

> The apparition   of these poems   in a crowd:
> White faces   in a black   dead faint.

Egoist (Jan. 15, 1914), 36; cf. FURTHER INSTRUCTIONS (l. 1n). In trying "to indicate spaces between the rhythmic units" (*Letters*, p. 53) Pound succeeded in making the lines look as though they are composed of six detachable fragments; and as a means of getting the reader to regard the words on the page as "things," it is a typographical device similar to those used by Mallarmé, W. C. Williams, and e. e. cummings.

IN DURANCE
[NO. 17. PRINTINGS: 3, 42, 43, 53, 55]

The title alludes to a passage in Samuel Butler's *Hudibras* (II, i):

> And though I'm now in *durance* fast, . . .
> I'll make this low dejected *fate*
> Advance me to a greater height.

A few years later, in THE REST, Pound announced that he was no longer "in durance." IN DURANCE belongs to the period when Pound was "stranded in a most Godforsakenest area of the Middle West" and employed as an instructor in French and Spanish at Wabash College, Crawfordsville, Indiana.

[Epigraph: [lacking]   3–53;   (1907)   55]

4. *sell our pictures:* In Browning's "Pictor Ignotus" the speaker complains of the way in which art is debased by becoming a middle-class commodity:

> These buy and sell our pictures, take and give,
> Count them for garniture and household-stuff,
> And where they live needs must our pictures live
> And see their faces, listen to their prate,
> Partakers of their daily pettiness. . . .

6–7. *life . . . flame:* "To burn always with this hard, gem-like flame, to maintain this ecstasy, is success in life" (Pater, *The Renaissance* [1888], "Conclusion").

[7. reacheth   *3;*   reaches   42+]

[14. Yea, I   *3–43;*   And I   53+]

20. *S. T.:* Pound alludes here to Coleridge's essay "On the Principles of Genial Criticism": "the Greeks called a beautiful object καλόν quasi καλοῦν, i.e., *calling on* the soul, which receives instantly, and welcomes it as something connatural" (p. 243). In *The Spirit of Romance* (1910) Pound says this epigram (adapted from Plato's *Cratylus*, 416c) is "Coleridge's most magical definition of beauty" (p. 156). The allusion is made in a manner that prefigures the elliptical mode of the *Cantos*.

   Pound may have borrowed from the same essay by Coleridge the idea of dividing poetry into *melopœia*, *phanopœia*, and *logopœia* (see p. 11 above).

22. *mewards:* A poeticism of mid-nineteenth-century origin, according to the *O.E.D.* However, a poem in Herrick's *Hesperides* (1648) begins: "You say, to me-wards your

affection's strong." Pound uses the word again in HOMAGE TO SEXTUS PROPERTIUS (III, 14).

26. *All . . . sadness:* The line is quoted from an uncollected sonnet called "Masks," first printed in *A Lume Spento* (1908, p. 40). "They" are the singers, painters, poets, and wizards who "Ponder in silence o'er earth's queynt devyse."

[27. mock'ry   3–43;   mockery   53+]

[34. by echoes   3, 53+;   by the echoes   42, 43]

[37a, b. *These additional lines occur in 3 only:*

Of such a "Veltro" of the vasty deep
As bore my tortoise house scant years agone:]

[39. east us   3–53;   east of us   55]

IN EXITUM CUIUSDAM
[NO. 53. PRINTINGS: 15, 42, 43, 53, 55]

The title is translated in the epigraph.

1. *Time's bitter flood:* Quoted from the poem by Yeats which is printed in the note to AMITIES.

4. *your circle:* When in London Yeats held his literary gatherings at 18 Woburn Buildings, where he lived from 1896 to 1917. Pound met Yeats in 1909 and was in regular attendance at Yeats's "evenings" from about August 1911.

6. *my circle:* See the note on CAUSA and AU SALON (l. 18n).

"IONE, DEAD THE LONG YEAR"
[NO. 126. PRINTINGS: 25, 39, 40, 42, 43, 55]

[TITLE: Dead Iönè   25;   "Ione, Dead the Long Year"   39+]

Among Ben Jonson's *Epigrammes* (1616) is one "On Giles and Ione" (XLII), where "Ione" is disyllabic as in "Joan." Pound seems to have borrowed the name, however, from W. S. Landor, who had an affair in the 1790s with a girl called Nancy Jones, whose name he hellenized in various poems (none of which gave Pound his title) as "Iönè." Pound read Landor with Yeats in the winter of 1915–16 and later published an essay in which Landor is treated as potentially an English Gautier (*Future* [Nov. 1917], 10–12; cf. *Letters*, p. 140).
The title of this poem is quoted in Canto 7.

ITÉ
[NO. 82. PRINTINGS: *18, 39, 40, 42, 43, 55*]

[TITLE: [*untitled section VI of "Xenia"*]   *18;*   Ite   *39+*]

The Latin *ite* means "go." See the introductory note to A SONG OF THE DEGREES for the structure of "Xenia."

3. *hard Sophoclean light:* Pound's criticisms are frequently expressed in these terms. In 1915 he was hoping to see "a bit more Sophoclean severity" in contemporary writing (*Letters*, p. 92): "we have had so many . . . pseudo-glamours and glamourlets and mists and fogs since the nineties that one is about ready for hard light" (*Poetry* [May 1914], 67). The phrase may derive from the "dry light" (*lumen siccum*) of the medieval scholastics. Sophocles (5th century B.C.) evolved for his plays a plain style that was very different from the magniloquence of his senior contemporary Aeschylus.

JEWEL STAIRS' GRIEVANCE, THE
[NO. 136. PRINTINGS: *27, 39, 40, 42, 43, 55*]

See the introductory note to SONG OF THE BOWMEN OF SHU for the origin of Pound's translations from the Chinese. Alternative versions of this poem (*Li T'ai-po*, III, 5.13*b*–14*a* [Fang]) are available in H. A. Giles's *Chinese Poetry in English Verse* (1898, p. 72) and S. Obata's *Works of Li Po* (1923, p. 46).

2. *gauze stockings:* "silken shoes" (Obata).

Footnote: Chisolm prints a photocopy of a "Manuscript translation of a poem by Oshorei (in Fenollosa's hand)," to which the manuscript of THE JEWEL STAIRS' GRIEVANCE is probably similar: Chinese characters with a literal English gloss under each one, and a footnote explaining what is implicit in the poem. Believing that the subject of a poem should be presented with the maximum directness and economy, Pound could readily appreciate the virtues of THE JEWEL STAIRS' GRIEVANCE. In cases like this, Chinese poetry appeared to confirm the validity of imagist aesthetics; and it is not surprising, therefore, that Pound should have valued it largely for its imagist virtues: "It is because Chinese poetry has certain qualities of vivid presentation; and because certain Chinese poets have been content to set forth their matter without moralizing and without comment that one labours to make a translation . . ." (*To-Day* [April 1918], 54). In THE JEWEL STAIRS' GRIEVANCE "everything is there, not merely by 'suggestion' but by a sort of mathematical process of reduction" (*ibid.*, p. 55). In cases where imagist principles were not implicit Pound was ready to impose them, as he does in FAN-PIECE, FOR HER IMPERIAL LORD.

Rihaku: The Japanese form of Li Po.

LADIES
[NO. 121. PRINTINGS: 24, 39, 40, 42, 43, 55]

When Harriet Monroe objected to the polyglot nature of the original titles in this sequence Pound said she could "call 'Le Donne,' simply *'Ladies,'* tho' it don't mean the same thing. And call 'passante,' *'Passing.'* And call 'Agathas intacta,' simply 'Agathas'" (Chicago MSS, July 8, 1914). Having made this concession, he never restored the original titles when reprinting LADIES.

The simple contrast between *what was* and *what is* makes the first three of these epigrams identical in structure.

II. 1. The Latin *lar* means "household deity."

III. As its title indicates, this epigram is modeled on a poem by Catullus (LVIII):

> Caeli, Lesbia nostra, Lesbia illa,
> illa Lesbia, quam Catullus unam
> plus quam se atque suos amavit omnes,
> nunc in quadriviis et angiportis
> glubit magnanimi Remi nepotes.

("O, Caelius, my Lesbia, that Lesbia, Lesbia whom alone Catullus loved more than himself and all his own, now in the cross-roads and alleys serves the filthy lusts of the descendants of lordly-minded Remus"—Loeb.) An early draft of Canto 2 contained a version of the Latin:

> *Caelius, Lesbia illa—*
> That Lesbia, Caelius, our Lesbia, that Lesbia
> Whom Catullus once loved more
> Than his own soul and all his friends,
> Is now the drab of every lousy Roman.

Poetry (July 1917), 182. TO FORMIANUS' YOUNG LADY FRIEND is a version of another poem by Catullus.

LADIES was one of many poems Harriet Monroe thought improper, and it was an exasperated Pound who wrote to her: "Now WHO could blush at 'Lesbia Illa'?????????? WHO???" (*Letters*, p. 76). Other examples of her censorship of Pound's poems are mentioned in TO A FRIEND WRITING ON CABARET DANCERS (l. 36n).

The fate of Lesbia resembles that of the woman in HUGH

SELWYN MAUBERLEY who suppressed her Milesian habits upon
marrying the most bank-clerkly of Englishmen.

[6. Veneres *24–40, 55;* Venere *42, 43*]

6. The line is adapted from the opening of Catullus, III: "Lu-
gete, o Veneres Cupidinesque" ("Mourn, ye Graces and
Loves"—Loeb).

IV. Another canceled title of "Passing" was "Cytherea in
Furs." The poem concluded originally with the following lines,
canceled before publication (Chicago MSS):

> Neither upon you, unconscious,
> Nor upon that egoist who is longing to waste my time,
> Will I confer thought, or my hours.

4. *patchouli:* A nineties touch. Arthur Symons defended this
kind of subject matter ("Well, why not Patchouli?") in
his introduction to *Silhouettes* (1896, p. xiii).

LA FRAISNE
[NO. 6. PRINTINGS: *1, 3, 8, 53, 55*]

[*Epigraph:* Scene: the Ash Wood of Malvern. *1–53;* [*lacking*] *55*]

Originally this was to have been the title poem of what became *A Lume Spento* (1908), and a suppressed epigraph set
the monologue in the Ash Wood of Malvern, in Worcester-
shire. Pound also added an explanatory note to the poem in
which he drew attention to a metaphysical scheme that the
reader would scarcely have discerned for himself. This note
was retained until as late as 1920, and reads:

> When the soul is exhausted of fire, then doth the spirit
> return unto its primal nature and there is upon it a peace
> great and of the woodland
> > *"magna pax et silvestris."*
> Then becometh it kin to the faun and the dryad, a wood-
> land-dweller amid the rocks and streams
> > *"consociis faunis dryadisque inter saxa sylvarum."*
> > Janus of Basel.*
> Also has Mr. Yeats in his "Celtic Twilight" treated of
> such, and I because in such a mood, feeling myself divided
> between myself corporal and a self aetherial "a dweller by
> streams and in wood-land," eternal because simple in ele-
> ments
> > *"Aeternus quia simplex naturae."*
> Being freed of the weight of a soul "capable of salvation or
> damnation," a grievous striving thing that after much

straining was mercifully taken from me; as had one passed
saying as in the Book of the Dead,
>"I, lo I, am the assembler of souls,"

and had taken it with him, leaving me thus *simplex naturae,*
even so at peace and trans-sentient as a wood pool I made it.

The Legend thus: "Miraut de Garzelas, after the pains
he bore a-loving Riels of Calidorn and that to none avail,
ran mad in the forest.

Yea even as Peire Vidal ran as a wolf for her of Penautier
tho some say that twas folly or as Garulf Bisclavret so ran
truly, till the King brought him respite (see "Lais" Marie
de France), so was he ever by the Ash Tree.

Hear ye his speaking: (low, slowly he speaketh it, as one
drawn apart, reflecting) (*egare*)."

———

* Referendum for contrast. *Daemonalitas* of the Rev.
Father Sinistrari of Ameno (1600 *circ.*). "A treatise wherein
it is shown that there are in existence on earth rational
creatures besides man, endowed like him with a body and
soul, that are born and die like him, redeemed by our Lord
Jesus-Christ, and capable of receiving salvation or damna-
tion." Latin and English text. pub. Liseux, Paris, 1879.

A Lume Spento (1908), p. 2. The "Legend" Pound mentions
is of his own making, and "Miraut de Garzelas" is an invented
character. The story of Peire Vidal reappears in PIERE VIDAL
OLD. Marie de France, whose *Lai du Bisclaveret* is cited here,
also wrote a *Lai del Freisne* to which LA FRAISNE bears no
similarity. Seeing that Ludovico Maria Sinistrari was not born
until 1622, the date of his *De Daemonialitate* is wrong (perhaps "1600" is a misprint for "1700").

3, 23. *folly . . . wailing . . . bitterness:* The tone and vocabulary are those of Yeats's "In the Seven Woods":

> I have . . . put away
> The unavailing outcries and the old bitterness
> That empty the heart.

6. *sword-play:* Cf. FOR E. MCC.

13. *Mar-nan-otha:* Probably an imaginary name created by
crossing the biblical "Maranatha" (I Corinthians 16:22)
with Yeatsian Celtic forms such as "Pairc-na-lee" and
"Clooth-na-Bare."

15. *syne:* Time ago.

17–19. *hushed . . . flutters . . . leaves:* Pound seems to be
recollecting the refrain in Yeats's poem "The Madness
of King Goll": "They will not hush, the leaves a-flutter
round me, the beech leaves old."

25. *ellum:* A dialect form of the word "elm."

[35. That is   *1, 3, 53;*   Which is   8]

[52. mid   *1, 3;*   amid   8;   'mid   53+]

LAKE ISLE, THE
[NO. 164. PRINTINGS: *38, 42, 43, 55*]

The title alludes to that Yeatsian Shangri-La, "The Lake Isle of Innisfree."

9. *scales . . . greasy:* A "greasy till" is associated with the people Yeats mocks in "September 1913."

[10. the *volailles*   38;   the whores   42+]

10. *Volailles* is clearly a concession to Harriet Monroe (cf. TO A FRIEND WRITING ON CABARET DANCERS, l. 36*n*).

LAMENT OF THE FRONTIER GUARD
[NO. 137. PRINTINGS: *27, 39, 40, 42, 43, 55*]

See the introductory note to SONG OF THE BOWMEN OF SHU. LAMENT OF THE FRONTIER GUARD is translated from *Li T'ai-po*, II, 2.14*a* (Fang). Pound's version was set to music in 1923 by Granville Bantock.

3. *Trees fall:* "the trees [let] fall the leaves" (Lee and Murray).

[23. Rihoku   27+;   Rihaku   *Faber and Faber*]

23. *Rihoku:* Japanese *Riboku* from Chinese *Li Mu* (Fang). He defended China against the Tartars and died in 223 B.C. (Lee and Murray).

Footnote: Rihaku is Li Po (see the final note to THE RIVER SONG).

LANGUE D'OC
[NO. 172. PRINTINGS: *45, 46, 50, 54, 55*]

LANGUE D'OC and MŒURS CONTEMPORAINES form a diptych and were published as such in the *Little Review* after Harriet Monroe had declined to print them in *Poetry* on the grounds that they were too frank (*Letters*, p. 186). The reintroduction of an archaic style at this stage in Pound's career looks at first sight like a relapse into the Chattertonianism of his youth, when he "wallowed in archaisms" (*Letters*, p. 50). In LANGUE D'OC, however, the archaisms are functional: Pound wanted to create an idiom that would contrast sharply with the colloquial freedom of HOMAGE TO SEXTUS PROPERTIUS. "The point of the archaic language in the Prov. trans. is that the Latin is really 'modern.' We are just getting back to a Roman state of civilization, or in reach of it; whereas the Provençal feeling is archaic, we are ages away from it" (*Letters*, pp. 246–247). The original title of LANGUE D'OC ("Homage a la Langue d'Oc") enabled readers to see the affinity between this group of poems and HOMAGE TO SEXTUS PROPERTIUS; but the point was lost when Pound not only changed the title but bracketed LANGUE D'OC with the inferior MŒURS CONTEMPORAINES.

[*Title:* Homage a la Langue d'Or 45; — — — d'Oc 46;
  Langue d'Oc 50]

Alba. The Provençal text of this anonymous poem reads:

> Quan lo rossinhols escria
> Ab sa par la nueg e-l dia,
> Yeu suy ab ma bell' amia
>   Jos la flor,
> Tro la gaita de la tor
> Escria: drutz, al levar!
> Qu'ieu vey l'alba e-l jorn clar.

Florilège des Troubadours, ed. Berry (1930), p. 2. Pound's earlier prose version is printed in *The Spirit of Romance* (1910): "When the nightingale cries to his mate, night and day, I am with my fair mistress amidst the flowers, until the watchman from the tower cries 'Lover, arise, for I see the white light of the dawn, and the clear day!'" (p. 34).
  See the note to ALBA.

I. A translation from Guiraut de Borneil:

> Reis glorïos, verais lums e clartatz,
> Deus poderos, senher, si a vos platz,
> Al meu companh siatz fizels aiuda,
> Qu'eu non lo vi, pois la noitz fon venguda,
>   Et ades sera l'alba!
>
> Bel companho, si dormetz o veillatz?
> Non dormatz plus, suau vos ressidatz,
> Q'en orien vei l'estela creguda
> Qu'amena-l jorn, qu'eu l'ai ben coneguda;
>   Et ades sera l'alba!
>
> Bel companho, en chantan vos apel:
> Non dormatz plus, qu'en aug chantar l'auzel,
> Que vai queren lo iorn per lo boscatge,
> Et ai paor que-l gilos vos assatge;
>   Et ades sera l'alba!
>
> Bel companho, issetz al fenestrel
> Et regardatz las ensenhas del cel;

Conoisseretz si-us soi fizels messatge;
Si non o faitz, vostres n'er lo dampnatge;
Et ades sera l'alba!

Bel companho, pos me parti de vos,
Eu no-m dormi ni-m moc de genolhos,
Anz preguei Dieu, lo filh Santa María,
Que-us mi rendes per leial companhía;
Et ades sera l'alba!

Bel companho, la foras, als peiros,
Mi preiavatz qu'eu no fos dormilhos,
Enans veilles tota noit tro al día;
Ara no-us platz mos chans ni ma paría;
Et ades sera l'alba!

—Bel dos companh, tan soi en ric soiorn
Qu'eu no volgra mais fos alba ni jorn,
Car la gensor que anc nasques de maire,
Tenc e abras, per qu'eu non prezi gaire
Lo fol gelos ni l'alba!

Les Troubadours, ed. Nelli and Lavaud (1966), vol. 2, pp. 92, 94. Pound thought the poems of Guiraut de Borneil (1175–1220) "facile, diffuse, without distinction of style, without personality" (*The Spirit of Romance* [1910], p. 45). His earlier and more literal version of Guiraut's poem begins:

King Glorious, true light and clarity,
God powerful, Lord if it pleaseth Thee
To be my companion be thou faithful aid,
Him have I seen not since the night came on,
And straightway comes the dawn.

Fair companion, sleepest or art awakened?
Sleep no more, arise softly,
For in the East I see that star increasing,
That leadeth in the day; well have I known it.
And straightway comes the dawn.

The Spirit of Romance (1910), pp. 47–48.

The "gentleman" of the subtitle is the watchman on the tower, like the one in *Alba*.

1. *Plasmatour:* The word is used again in IV, 6. Old French *plasmateur* means "creator."

12. *plaineth:* Provençal *queren*. In defense of his earlier translation ("crying") Pound wrote:

The misinterpretation of this word seems to be one of the sacred traditions of Provençal scholarship. The form is not from the Latin *quaero*, but from *quaeror*, a deponent

with all four participles, habitually used of birds singing
or complaining (*vide* Horace, "C.S.," 43; Ovid, "Am.," i,
29).

The Spirit of Romance (1910), p. 47. Among the poems
omitted from *A Quinzaine for This Yule* (1909) is an untitled piece in which Pound distinguishes the visionary
poet (at home in darkness) from the "host of vagrants
crying the morn" (*A Lume Spento and Other Early Poems*
[1965], p. 98: "['queren lo jorn']," explains the footnote).

14. *swenkin:* Swinker, laborer. Pound makes the watchman
allude jokingly to the labors of love.

15. *welkin:* Sky.

[23. Bade   45, 46;   Badest   50+]

[25a. And day comes on."   45, 46;   [*lacking*]   50+]

[26. from within   45–54;   from inside   55]

28. *venust:* French *vénusté* ("charm, grace").

   make: Mate.

II. Translated from Guillaume de Poitiers (1071–1127), who
is considered to have been the first troubadour.

> Ab la dolchor del temps novel
> Foillo li bosc, e li aucel
> Chanton chascus en lor lati
> Segon lo vers del novel chan;
> Adonc esta ben c'om s'aisi
> D'acho don hom a plus talan.
>
> De lai don plus m'es bon e bel
> Non vei mesager ni sagel,
> Per que mos cors non dorm ni ri,
> Ni no m'aus traire adenan,
> Tro qe sacha ben de la fi
> S'el'es aissi com eu deman.
>
> La nostr'amor vai enaissi
> Com la branca de l'albespi
> Qu'esta sobre l'arbre en treman,
> La nuoit, a la ploja ez al gel,
> Tro l'endeman, que-l sols s'espan
> Pel las fueillas verz e-l ramel.
>
> Enquer me menbra d'un mati
> Que nos fezem de guerra fi,
> E que-m donet un don tan gran,
> Sa drudari'e son anel:
> Enquer me lais Dieus viure tan
> C'aja mas manz soz so mantel!

Qu'eu non ai soing d'estraing lati
Que-m parta de mon Bon Vezi:
Qu'eu sai de paraulas com van
Ab un breu sermon que s'espel;
Que tal se van d'amor gaban,
Nos n'avem la pessa e-l coutel.

Les Troubadours, ed. Nelli and Lavaud (1966), vol. 2, pp. 36, 38. There are useful French translations in Nelli and La-vaud's anthology and also in Jeanroy's edition of Guillaume's poems (1913, pp. 24–26).

[16. 'Till I have my hand 'neath her cloak   *45;*   'Till the sun come[,] and the green leaf on the bough   *46+*]

19. *gesning:* Hospitality, entertainment.

23–24. *clamour . . . charmer:* An example of syzygy "such as one finds in Arnaut's stanzas without internal rhyme: 'comba,' 'trembla,' 'po[m]a' followed in that strophe by rhyme in 'oigna'" (*Letters,* p. 247: the reference is to Arnaut Daniel's "Lancan Son Passat Li Giure").

III. Pound thought this translation from Cercamon the only satisfactory poem in the LANGUE D'OC sequence (*Letters,* p. 247). Cercamon was the pseudonym of a poet whose writings come chronologically after those of Guillaume de Poitiers, and who is said by early biographers to have taken the name because he had traveled widely ("cerquet tot lo mon"). The form of the name Pound uses (Cerclamon) does not occur in the manuscripts; in his earlier essay on troubadours he uses the correct form (*Quarterly Review* [Oct. 1913], 431).

The sequence of stanzas varies in different Provençal manuscripts, but none is recorded which might have served as a model for Pound's arrangement of the poem.

1 Quant l'aura doussa s'amarzis
E-l fuelha chai de sul verjan
E l'auzelh chanjan lor latis,
Et ieu de sai sospir e chan
D'Amor que-m te lassat e pres,
Qu'ieu anc no l'agui en poder.

2 Las! qu'ieu d'Amor non ai conquis
Mas cant lo trebalh e l'afan,
Ni res tant greu no-s covertis
Com fai so qu'ieu vau deziran;
Ni tal enveja no-m fai res
Cum fai so qu'ieu non posc aver.

4 Tota la genser qu'anc hom vis
Encontra lieys no pretz un guan;

Quan totz lo segles brunezis,
Delai on ylh es si resplan.
Dieu prejarai qu'ancar l'ades
O que la vej'anar jazer.

6 Ni muer ni viu ni no guaris,
Ni mal no-m sent e si l'ai gran,
Quar de s'amor no suy devis;
Non sai si ja l'aurai ni quan,
Qu'en lieys es tota la merces
Que-m pot sorzer o descazer.

5 Totz trassalh e bran et fremis
Per s'amor, durmen o velhan.
Tal paor ai qu'ieu mesfalhis
No m'aus pessar cum la deman,
Mas servir l'ai dos ans o tres,
E pueys ben leu sabra'n lo ver.

8 S'elha no-m vol, volgra moris
Lo dïa que-m pres a coman;
Ai, las! tan suavet m'aucis
Quan de s'amor me fetz semblan,
Que tornat m'a en tal deves
Que nuill'autra no vuelh vezer.

7 Bel m'es quant ilh m'enfolhetis
E-m fai badar e'n vau muzan;
De leis m'es bel si m'escarnis
O-m gaba dereir'o denan,
Qu'apres lo mal me venra bes
Be leu, s'a lieys ven a plazer.

9 Totz cossiros m'en esjauzis,
Car s'ieu la dopti o la blan,
Per lieys serai o fals o fils,
O drechuriers o ples d'enjan,
O totz vilas o totz cortes,
O trebalhos o de lezer.

11 Cercamons ditz: greu er cortes
Hom qui d'amor se desesper.

10 Mas, cui que plass'o cui que pes,
Elha-m pot, si-s vol, retener.

3 Per una joia m'esbaudis
Fina, qu'anc re non amiey tan;
Quan suy ab lieys si m'esbahis
Qu'ieu no-ill sai dire mon talan,
Et quan m'en vauc, vejaire m'es
Que tot perda-l sen e-l saber.

Les Troubadours, ed. Nelli and Lavaud (1966), vol. 2, pp. 38, 40, 42. For French translations see Nelli and Lavaud or Dejeanne's edition of the poem (1905, pp. 41–42).

[8. troubles   45–54;   trouble   55]

28. *shake . . . burn:* This conceit is used again in L'HOMME MOYEN SENSUEL (l. 123*n*).

29. *swevyn:* Dream.

[49. it is. Pleasure is 'neath her feet.   45–50;   it is.   54+]

50. *traist:* Trusty, faithful (cf. IV, 3, 18).

70 ff. A second version of the fourth stanza of the Provençal.

73. *rack:* A pun on two older meanings of the word: "destruction" and "cloud."

IV. The Provençal text of this anonymous poem reads as follows:

> En un vergier sotz fuella d'albespi
> Tenc la dompna son amic costa si,
> Tro la gayta crida que l'alba vi.
> Oy Dieus, oy Dieus, de l'alba! tan tost ve!
>
> Plagues a Dieu ja la nueitz non falhis
> Ni-l mieus amicx lonc de mi no-s partis
> Ni la gayta jorn ni alba no vis!
> Oy Dieus, oy Dieus, de l'alba! tan tost ve!
>
> Bels doux amicx, baizem nos yeu e vos
> Aval els pratz, on chanto-ls auzellos,
> Tot o fassam en despieg del gilos,
> Oy Dieus, oy Dieus, de l'alba! tan tost ve!
>
> Bels dous amicx, fassam un joc novel
> Yns el iardi, on chanton li auzel,
> Tro la gaita toque son caramelh.
> Oy Dieus, oy Dieus, de l'alba! tan tost ve!
>
> Per la doss' aura qu'es venguda de lay,
> Del mieu amic belh e cortes e gay,
> Del sieu alen ai begut un dous ray.
> Oy Dieus, oy Dieus, de l'alba! tan tost ve!
>
> La dompna es agradans e plazens,
> Per sa beutat la gardon mantas gens,
> Et a son cor en amar leyalmens.
> Oy Dieus, oy Dieus, de l'alba! tan tost ve!

Les Troubadours, ed. Nelli and Lavaud (1966), vol. 2, pp. 30, 32. Alternative English versions are to be found in F. Hueffer's *The Troubadours* (1878, pp. 91–92) and in B. Smythe's *Trobador Poets* (1911, pp. 183–184). In *The Spirit of Romance* (1910) Pound calls this poem the "finest alba" (p. 34) and first translated it in *Exultations* (1909, pp. 48–49). The tone of this earlier version may be gauged from the opening two stanzas:

> In a garden where the whitethorn spreads her leaves
> My lady hath her love lain close beside her,
> Till the warder cries the dawn—Ah dawn that grieves!
> Ah God! Ah God! That dawn should come so soon!
>
> "Please God that night, dear night should never cease,
> Nor that my love should parted be from me,
> Nor watch cry 'Dawn'—Ah dawn that slayeth peace!
> Ah God! Ah God! That dawn should come so soon!"

There is an amusing reminiscence of Pound reading this poem in F. M. Ford's *Return to Yesterday* (1931, p. 388).

3. *traist:* See III, 50n.

4. Swinburne's poem "In the Orchard (Provençal Burden)" has the refrain: "Ah God, ah God, that day should be so soon."

6. *Plasmatour:* See I, 1n.

21. *from her:* The earlier version has "from Far-Away."

[22. and pleasanter   45–50;   and thereby pleasanter   54+]

26. *Venust:* Cf. I, 28n.

L'ART, 1910
[NO. 112. PRINTINGS: 23, 39, 40, 42, 43, 55]

[TITLE: L'Art   23;   L'Art, 1910   39+]

The Post-Impressionist Exhibition opened in London at the Grafton Galleries in November 1910. Pound had little sympathy for the work of postimpressionist poets such as Horace Holly, whose *Creation: Post-Impressionist Poems* was published in the same year as L'ART, 1910.

Pound may have added the date to the title after remembering that he had already published a poem called "L'Art" in *Canzoni* (1911).

LES MILLWIN
[NO. 83. PRINTINGS: 18, 19, 39, 40, 42, 43, 55]

[TITLE: [*untitled section II of "Lustra"*]   18;   Les Millwin   19+]

The MS title, "(Les Millwin)," was deleted before the first publication of this poem (Chicago MSS).

1. *Russian Ballet:* Diaghilev's *Ballets Russes* performed in London during 1911 and 1912. His most famous dancer, Pavlova, is mentioned in THE GARRET (l. 7n).

6. *Slade:* The Slade School of Art in London.

9. *futuristic:* Slade students would have seen the Futurist Exhibition at the Sackville Gallery (March 1912) and heard lectures on futurism from the instigator of the movement, F. T. Marinetti (1876–1944), who was in London during 1912 and 1913. Futurism, conceived of in 1909 as an antidote to enervating *passéisme* in the arts, was the first European movement to evolve an aesthetic designed to cope with life in a mechanized twentieth century, and had some influence on Wyndham Lewis and the vorticist group with which Pound became involved in 1914 (cf. THE GAME OF CHESS). Futurist poetry (paratactic, anadjectival, and typographically mimetic) anticipated some of the most characteristically Poundian developments in poetic technique.

10. *Cléopâtre,* a ballet in one act, was first presented in Paris in June 1909, and was famous for its exotic sumptuousness. Pound was critical of Diaghilev's use of flamboyant spectacle: "The Russian dancers present their splendid, luxurious paganism, and everyone with a pre-Raphaelite or Swinburnian education is in raptures" (*New Age* [Sept. 12, 1912], 466).

14. Inconsequential endings are common in modernist poetry, which frequently deals with the casual and anticlimactic (THE STUDY IN AESTHETICS is written in the same vein).

LIU CH'E
[NO. 98. PRINTINGS: 21, 39, 40, 42, 43, 55]

LIU CH'E, like AFTER CH'U YUAN and FAN-PIECE, FOR HER IMPERIAL LORD, was written before Pound had access to the Fenollosa papers. Other versions of the original (*Ku-wen yüan,* II, 8.2b [Fang]) have been made by H. A. Giles in *Chinese Poetry in English Verse* (1898, p. 18) and Arthur Waley in *A Hundred and Seventy Chinese Poems* (1918, p. 49). When writing this poem Pound saw Liu Ch'e (156–87 B.C.) as a fellow imagist: "Ibycus and Liu Ch'e presented the 'Image'" (*Fortnightly Review* [Sept. 1, 1914], 462; on Ibycus, see THE SPRING).

5–6. On the function of the strophe division, see APRIL (ll. 4–5n). Pound invariably brought to his "Chinese" themes technical resources he had acquired elsewhere (see in this respect Pound's comment on the technical importance of PROVINCIA DESERTA).

6. *threshold:* In Canto 7 Pound recalls "My lintel, and Liu Ch'e's."

MARVOIL
[NO. 18. PRINTINGS: 3, 8, 53, 55]

"Marvoil" is the Provençal poet Arnaut de Mareuil (fl. 1170–1200). In this poem Pound tries to show that the gentle character of Arnaut as presented in his poetry is a mere persona, and that the real Arnaut was a Browningesque figure who possessed a Poundian capacity for abuse.

1–5. Adapted from the opening sentences of an early Provençal biography of Arnaut: "Arnautz de Meruoill si fo . . . clergues de paubra generacion. E car no podia viure per las soas letras, el s'en anet per lo mon" (Boutière and Schutz, *Biographies des Troubadours* [1950], p. 17).

1. *Arnaut the Less:* Petrarch refers to Arnaut as " 'l men famoso Arnaldo" in his *Trionfo d'Amore* (IV, 44). Pound speaks of the " 'Lesser Arnaut' . . . 'of Marvoil' " in *The Spirit of Romance* (1910), the Greater Arnaut being Arnaut Daniel (p. 53).

4. *Jaques Polin:* A fictitious name.

6. *Vicomte de Beziers:* Roger II Taillefer, vicomte de Beziers, married Azalais de Toulouse, with whom Arnaut is alleged to have been in love.

9. *Alfonso:* The Provençal biography tells how Alfonso became jealous of the affection Azalais showed for Arnaut, and stirred up so much gossip about her that she was compelled to dismiss Arnaut from her service (Boutière and Schutz, *op. cit.,* p. 20). Arnaut mentions Alfonso only once in his poems, where he politely calls him "cortes et pros" (ed. Johnson [1935], p. 123).

12. *Mont-Ausier:* The home of Tibors de Montausier (cf. "DOMPNA POIS DE ME NO'US CAL," l. 31*n*).

18. Pound explained that Tibors de Montausier "is contemporary with the other persons, but I have no strict warrant for dragging her name into this particular affair" (*Personæ* [1909], p. 59).

20. *Burlatz:* Azalais de Toulouse lived in the castle of Burlatz before her marriage.

22. *Quattro:* A misunderstanding on Pound's part. It was Alfonso II who was known to Arnaut, and not, as Pound writes in his gloss on the poem in the 1909 *Personæ,* "Alfonso IV of Aragon" (p. 59).

24. *this wall:* The real Arnaut will be known to posterity only by a parchment (the present poem) that Arnaut hides in the wall.

29. *kiss:* The kiss is mentioned in one of Arnaut's poems (p. 110).

48. *image in my heart:* This conventional image occurs in one of Arnaut's poems (p. 66).

49. The Latin phrase means "I do not have the parchment" (i.e., the parchment mentioned in l. 37: there is no documentary evidence for Pound's reconstruction of the "real" Arnaut). One of the subsections in *Guide to Kulchur* (1938) is called "Pergamena Deest."

MEDITATIO
[NO. 113. PRINTINGS: 23, 40, 42, 43, 55]

The habits of dogs have provoked philosophic musings since the time of Plato (*Republic*, II, 15–16). An inoffensive version occurs in Dostoevsky's *The Brothers Karamazov* (which had appeared recently in Constance Garnett's translation of 1912: Bk. X, chap. 3); but Mathews noted the obscene implications of MEDITATIO, and refused to print the poem in the trade edition of *Lustra* (1916).

There is another meditation on the curious habits of dogs in THE SEEING EYE.

[2. to admit   23;   to conclude   40+]

MESMERISM
[NO. 7. PRINTINGS: 1, 3, 8, 53, 55]

[*Epigraph: "And a cat's in the water-butt."* —Robt. Browning
     "Mesmerism"   1;   — — — Robert Browning.   3+]

MESMERISM takes the form of an homage to Robert Browning (1812–1889) from whom Pound learned a great deal about verse technique. As he admitted to René Taupin in 1928: "überhaupt ich stamm aus Browning. Pourquoi nier son père?" (*Letters*, p. 294; cf. CINO, l. 1*n*).

5. *water butt:* Pound admired Browning's ability to incorporate "unpoetical" words into his poetry.

7. *Master Bob:* The form of address is that of apprentice to master craftsman, and imitates the title of Browning's "Master Hugues of Saxe-Gotha."

9. *Calliope:* Normally the muse of epic poetry, but also the American name for an instrument consisting of a series of steam whistles toned to produce musical notes, played by a keyboard like that of an organ (*O. E. D.*).

15. The Latin *pluvius* means "rain-bringing."

MŒURS CONTEMPORAINES
[NO. 173. PRINTINGS: 45, 50, 54, 55]

This sequence of poems is meant to be read in connection with LANGUE D'OC, Pound's intention being to contrast the sexual *mœurs* of medieval Provence with those of twentieth-century London. In focusing on morals rather than manners, Pound aligns himself with the Goncourt brothers who, in a polemical preface to *Germinie Lacerteux* (1864), proclaimed "l'histoire morale contemporaine" as the proper concern of all serious writers. He takes his title, however, from a passage in Remy de Gourmont's *Le Problème du Style* (1902, p. 105) which he used as an epigraph to his review of Eliot's *Prufrock and Other Observations* (1917): "Il n'y a de livres que ceux où un écrivain s'est raconté lui-même en racontant les mœurs de ses contemporains—leurs rêves, leurs vanités, leurs amours et leurs folies" (*Poetry* [Aug. 1917], 264). Pound defined "mœurs contemporaines" as the "history . . . of national habit of our time and of the two or three generations preceding us" (*Little Review* [Aug. 1918], 36), and also used the similar English phrase "contemporary manners" (*New Age* [Aug. 5, 1920], 221). It is possible that he regarded the various portraits as Jamesian vignettes.

The technique of grouping short poems under a general title derives from earlier pieces such as AMITIES, LADIES, and THE SOCIAL ORDER. When MŒURS CONTEMPORAINES was first published in the *Little Review* it had nine sections, the last being a version of Horace (*Odes*, I, v).

I. 1. *Hecatomb Styrax:* Gum from the styrax tree is used in the manufacture of medicines and perfumes—hence, perhaps, "perfumed cigarettes" (l. 17). As the word "hecatomb" means "a sacrifice," it looks as though Pound has imitated Bunyanesque forms such as "Mr. Worldly Wiseman."

[14. aesthetics 45–54, *Faber and Faber, 1968;* asthetics 55, *Faber and Faber, 1952*]

18. *Machiavelli:* Observations on the cyclic repetition of events in history are common in the writings of Niccolo Machiavelli (1469–1527). Pound may be recalling the opening sentences of Book 5 of the *Florentine History*.

III. Pound had complained earlier about the difficulty of maintaining critical standards "in a capital where everybody's Aunt Lucy or Uncle George has written something or other, and where the victory of any standard save that of mediocrity would at once banish so many nice people from the temple of immortality" (*Poetry* [June 1914], 112).

V. The subtitle alludes to Théophile Gautier's poem, "Inès de las Sierras," which begins with the line "Nodier raconte qu'en Espagne" and goes on to describe a sinister beauty who is very unlike the two ladies of Pound's poem.

3. *sleeves:* A detail of dress that for Pound characterized a whole period. Whenever the muse visited Henry James, he once wrote, she "appeared doubtless in corsage, the narrow waist, the sleeves puffed at the shoulders, à la mode 1890–2" (*Little Review* [Feb.–March 1919], 4).

4. *lacertus:* Gourmont investigated the linguistic pedigree of this word in his *Esthétique de la Langue Française* (1899, pp. 190–192).

[19. And conservatory   45, 50;   Conservatory   54+]

20. *lilies . . . symbolical cups:* Similar floral symbolism occurs in COITUS.

[21. Their symbolical pollen is excerpted   45, 50;   Whence their symbolical pollen has been excerpted   54+]

24. *Hatha Yoga:* The systematic control of breathing for the purposes of meditation and ecstasy (*Hatha Yoga Pradipikā*), and which had a fashionable introduction into England in the late nineteenth century.

VI. 3. *Meleagar:* Meleagar's life-span was determined by the amount of time it took for a certain firebrand to be consumed by fire.

[4. sea-coast   45;   he lies by the poluphloisboious sea-coast   50+]

4. *poluphloisboious:* The word is anglicized from Homer (*Iliad*, I, 34): βῆ δ' ἀκέων παρὰ θῖνα πολυφλοίσβοιο θαλάσσης ("Forth he went in silence along the shore of the loud-resounding sea"—Loeb). The word recurs frequently in

Pound's writings, and what it meant to him is best explained in a letter he wrote to W. H. D. Rouse in 1935:

Para thina poluphloisboio thalasses: the turn of the wave and the scutter of receding pebbles.
Years' work to get that. Best I have been able to do is cross cut in *Mauberley*, led up to:
             . . . *imaginary*
     Audition of the phantasmal sea-surge
which is totally different, and a different movement of the water, and inferior.

Letters, p. 364; cf. HUGH SELWYN MAUBERLEY (ll. 342–343), and Pound's remark to Felix Schelling some thirteen years earlier: "And perhaps even now one has to over-stress the *au* in *au*dition before one gets the effect I was after" (*Letters*, p. 249).

[5. *The Greek line is lacking in 45 only*]

6. The Latin words *siste viator* ("stay, traveler") form the conventional opening for an epitaph. In *The Spirit of Romance* (1910) Pound translated from Andrea Navagero (1483–1529) the lines:

Stay here thy way, O voyager,
     for terrible is now the heat (p. 236).

The Latin reads: "Siste, viator, iter: nimio jam torridus aestu es."

VII. In the subtitle, the Italian *I Vecchi* means "old people."

6. *Blagueur:* The first of the two old men is Henry James, whom Pound elsewhere calls "the great blagueur" (*Little Review* [Aug. 1918], 30). Pound first met James in January 1912.

Con . . . tardi: Translated in *The Spirit of Romance* (1910) as "'with slow eyes and grave'" (p. 118), and adapted from Dante (*Purgatorio*, VI 63): "e nel mover delli occhi onesta e tarda" ("what dignity in the slow moving of thine eyes"—Sinclair). There are similar descriptions of James in the *Little Review* ([Aug. 1918], 6) and Canto 7:

And the great domed head, *con gli occhi onesti e tardi*
Moves before me, phantom with weighted motion,
Grave incessu, drinking the tone of things,
And the old voice lifts itself
     weaving an endless sentence.

8. Pierre Abélard (1079–1142) is referred to as "the knight-errant of learning" in *The Spirit of Romance* (1910, p. 90). In *Canzoni* (1911) the last of Pound's three "Victorian

Eclogues" (cf. SATIEMUS) is called "Abelard." For the view that Abelard is invoked as a symbol of sexual inadequacy, see Espey (p. 52).

10, 12. *Great Mary:* The novelist Mary Augusta Ward, usually called Mrs. Humphrey Ward (1851–1920). In some of his letters to her, James brought to a fine art that ambiguous and muffled criticism (the "mere twaddle of graciousness") which she thought implied a favorable view of her work.

13. *the other:* Probably "old Colonel Jackson," mentioned in Canto 80.

bust by Gaudier: Henri Gaudier-Brzeska sculpted in white marble a "Hieratic Head of Ezra Pound." The decision to make the effigy phallic in design was probably Pound's, for he was later to write sympathetically about "phallic religions" in which "man [is] really the phallus or spermatozoid charging, head-on, the female chaos; integration of the male in the male organ. Even oneself has felt it, driving any new idea into the great passive vulva of London, a sensation analogous to the male feeling in copulation" (*Natural Philosophy of Love* [1922], p. viii); hence the title of *Instigations* (1920)? See also HOMAGE TO SEXTUS PROPERTIUS (V, 28*n*) and the note to SESTINA: ALTAFORTE. The effigy was completed in 1915, but Pound preferred the unfinished work: "I do not mean to say that it was better, it was perhaps a *kinesis*, whereas it is now a *stasis*" (*Gaudier-Brzeska* [1916], p. 52). Plates i and iv in this book show the marble block at a very early stage; see also H. S. Ede's *Life of Gaudier-Brzeska* (1930, pl. xli).

[16. There once was 45; There was once 50+]

16. *Voltaire:* Pound translated the section on Genesis from Voltaire's *Dictionnaire Philosophique* because, as he wrote to Margaret Anderson in April 1918, "a reminder that 'There once was a man called Voltaire' can do no harm" (*Letters,* p. 194). See also the note to IMPRESSIONS OF FRANÇOIS-MARIE AROUET (DE VOLTAIRE).

17. *Verdi:* The Italian composer, Giuseppe Verdi (1813–1901).

There is a constant and irrefutable alliance between art and the oppressed. . . . The bitterest and most poignant songs have been often written in cipher—of necessity. It is not for nothing that Verdi's name was cheered hysterically after his operas; was cheered for its half-secret anagram V.E.R.D.I., Vittorio Emanuel *Re d'*Italia, cheered in cities where in Verdi's obscure, but not quite sufficiently obscure, chorus "Libertà" had been changed by the censors to "lealtà."

Egoist (Feb. 2, 1914), 54. The colonel may be alluding to the first performance in Rome of *La Battaglia di Legnano* (Jan. 27, 1849).

[20a, 22a, b. And that other, balancing on the edge of a gondola . . . 45; [*lacking*] 50+]

VIII. The Italian *ritratto* means "portrait."

2. *Lowell:* J. R. Lowell (1819–1891) was American minister in England from 1880 until 1885, the year Pound was born.

6–7. *stomped:* The word "stomp" was coined by Robert Browning, who uses it in his poem "The Englishman in Italy."

MONUMENTUM ÆRE, ETC.
[NO. 114. PRINTINGS: 23, 55]

The title is borrowed from Horace (*Odes,* III, xxx, 1–5):

> Exegi monumentum aere perennius
> regalique situ pyramidum altius,
> quod non imber edax, non Aquilo impotens
> possit diruere aut innumerabilis
> annorum series et fuga temporum.

("I have finished a monument more lasting than bronze and loftier than the Pyramids' royal pile, one that no wasting rain, no furious north wind can destroy, or the countless chain of years of the ages' flight"—Loeb.) Pound's translation of this ode was first printed in *Agenda* ([Sept. 1964], p. 3). The same poem, one of the most famous affirmations of the durability of art, also supplied the title of DUM CAPITOLIUM SCANDET.

The flippant curtailing of the Latin recalls Byron's burlesque of epic inductions: "Hail Muse! *et caetera*" (*Don Juan,* III, i, 1).

3. The Italian *buffo* means "clown."

[5. will not be present.   23;   will be absent.   55]

[6. will lie   23;   will rot   55]

MR. HOUSMAN'S MESSAGE
[NO. 37. PRINTINGS: 9, 42, 43, 55]

[TITLE: Song in the Manner of Housman   9;   Housman's Message to Mankind   42, 43;   Mr. Housman's Message   55]

Like Max Beerbohm, Pound regarded parody as a legitimate mode of criticism, and here he turned his attention to A. E. Housman's *A Shropshire Lad* (1896). "Good art thrives in an atmosphere of parody," he told Harriet Monroe in October 1912. "Parody is, I suppose, the best criticism—it sifts the durable from the apparent" (*Letters*, p. 47). For Pound's attitude toward parodies of his own work, see FURTHER INSTRUCTIONS (l. 1*n*). He seems to have thought it a mistake to change the original title of MR. HOUSMAN'S MESSAGE (Chicago MSS, April 1913).

8. *hung*: *A Shropshire Lad*, XVI and XLVII.

  shot: *A Shropshire Lad*, XLIV.

11, 12. *London . . . Shropshire*: *A Shropshire Lad*, XXXVII and XLI.

NA AUDIART
[NO. 8. PRINTINGS: *1, 3, 8, 53, 55*]

  Na is Provençal for "lady."

[*Epigraph*: Vicomptess of Chales   *1–53;*   Vicomtess of Chalais   *55*]

The Provençal epigraph is translated in line 33 as "though thou wish me ill" and adapted from a line by Bertran de Born ("N'Audiartz, sibem vol mal") which introduces the stanza that inspired the writing of NA AUDIART. Pound was afterwards to turn to Bertran's poem several times, translating it under the title of "DOMPNA POIS DE ME NO'US CAL" and making it one of the leading themes in NEAR PERIGORD.

The ladies mentioned in the somewhat pre-Raphaelite prose of the epigraph are identified in the notes to "DOMPNA POIS DE ME NO'US CAL."

love-lit glance: The same translation is given for Cavalcanti's phrase, "un amorosa sguardo" (*Sonnets . . . of . . . Cavalcanti* [1912], pp. 70, 71).

2. *Audiart*: See "DOMPNA POIS DE ME NO'US CAL" (l. 40*n*). Pound may have used the name as a pseudonym for the Beatrice of his *vita nuova* (THE ALCHEMIST, l. 12*n*).

7–8. *tender . . . render*: Farnell used this rhyme in her translation of Bertran's poem (*The Lives of the Troubadours* [1896], p. 117). Pound uses it again in *Sonnets . . . of . . . Cavalcanti* (1912, p. 107).

13. *Miels-de-Ben*: See "DOMPNA POIS DE ME NO'US CAL" (l. 47*n*).

20–22. The more anachronistic Pound becomes in his details, the more clearly does Audiart emerge as a pre-Raphaelite beauty.

[16. breathe *1+*; breath *Faber and Faber*]

[28. the phrase *1–53;* the praise *55*]

31. *Aultaforte:* Bertran's castle was called *Autafort* in Provençal. Pound is inconsistent in his spelling of the word, using the French *Hautefort* elsewhere (*Personæ* [1926], pp. 122, 154) as well as the Italian *Altaforte* (*ibid.,* p. 28) and the hybrid *Altafort* (*ibid.,* p. 151).

38. *bent and wrinkled:* The *carpe diem* theme does not appear in Bertran's poem.

NEAR PERIGORD
[NO. 153. PRINTINGS: *33, 39, 40, 42, 43, 55*]

A few months after contributing to *Des Imagistes* Pound began to consider the possibility of writing a long poem on imagist or vorticist principles (*Fortnightly Review* [Sept. 1, 1914], 471), and NEAR PERIGORD is one of the resulting experimental pieces which link the imagist poems with the *Cantos.* For his first attempt at a long poem Pound turned to Byron and produced L'HOMME MOYEN SENSUEL (written by April 1915). A couple of months later he completed NEAR PERIGORD, perhaps begun in June 1913 (*Letters,* p. 57), and the influence of Byron had clearly yielded to that of Browning, who was to remain a persistent influence on the *Cantos* (the earliest of which were begun in the autumn of 1915).

The technical challenge presented by NEAR PERIGORD was to write about an enigmatic subject in "plain, bald, pellucid statement" (Chicago MSS, June 28, 1915). Many years later Pound recalled this poem as being the ultimate in free verse (Norman, p. 444).

In NEAR PERIGORD, the last of the poems devoted to the writings and reputation of the Provençal poet Bertran de Born, Pound has attempted an imaginative reconstruction of the man and the legend in trying to discover how it was that the man who was allegedly responsible for so much of the political upheaval in his day could at the same time have written such a love poem as "DOMPNA POIS DE ME NO'US CAL."

By "Perigord" Pound means the town "Périgueux." "Périgord" is the name of the old French province of which Périgueux used to be the capital. The epigraph is quoted from a poem by Bertran (ed. Thomas [1888], p. 10):

> A Peiregors, pres del muralh,
> Tan quei posca om getar ab malh. . . .

Pound's translation in *The Spirit of Romance* (1910) reads:

> At Perigord near to the wall,
> Aye, within a mace throw of it . . . (p. 40).

2. *Cino:* Pound told T. E. Connolly that this is a fictional Cino (i.e., not Cino da Pistoia as in CINO). The name may be a pseudonym for Pound himself: a couple of the poems originally rejected from *A Quinzaine for This Yule* (1908) and first published in *A Lume Spento and Other Early Poems* (1965) are signed "Cino." Other pseudonyms are listed on page 142.

[3. Cire 33–40; Circ 42+]

3. Uc de Saint Circ is thought to have been the writer of the prose commentaries prefixed to some of Bertran's poems. In *The Spirit of Romance* (1910) Pound refers to him as "Hugh of St. Circ" (p. 35).

6–9. A paraphrase of "DOMPNA POIS DE ME NO'US CAL."

12. *one:* Tibors de Montausier.

another: Audiart de Malemort.

16–19. Pound has apparently misunderstood his Provençal source. The commentary says that Maent was "moiller d'En Talairan, qu'era fraire del comte de Peiregors" (Boutière and Schutz, *Biographies des Troubadours* [1950], p. 39). Seeing that Maent was married to Guillem Talairan (Pound's "Tairiran"), her husband would be the brother and not the brother-in-law of Hélias Talairan, comte de Périgord. According to Stroński, the comte de Périgord never had a brother called Talairan.

[19. hundreds 33–40; hundred 42+]

20. *Altafort:* Bertran's castle, Hautefort (see NA AUDIART, l. 31*n*).

21–27. Cf. lines 163–168 and *The Spirit of Romance* (1910), p. 39.

21. *stirrer-up of strife:* This is a common expression in *The Faerie Queene.*

23. *head . . . lamp:* From Dante (*Inferno*, XXVIII, 121–122):

> e 'l capo tronco tenea per le chiome,
> pèsol con mano a guisa di lanterna ...

("and it held the severed head by the hair swinging in its hand like a lantern"—Sinclair).

25. *set the strife:* Dante makes Bertran responsible for the animosity between the Young King Henry and his brother Richard Coeur de Lion (see the note to PLANH FOR THE YOUNG ENGLISH KING).

26. *had his way:* See lines 40–46n.

27. *counterpass:* Dante's *contrapasso* (*Inferno*, XXVIII, 142), "the laws of eternal justice" (*The Spirit of Romance* [1910], p. 116). Cf. "counterpart" (1. 168) and "counter-thrust" (1. 180). The importance of such link words was greatly increased when Pound changed the structural principles of his verse from narrative to juxtaposition.

28–37. Pound explains: "as to the possibility of a political intrigue behind the apparent love poem we have no evidence save that offered by my own observation of the geography of Perigord and Limoges" (*Poetry* [Dec. 1915], 145–146). The method of explaining history in terms of geography was popularized by H. T. Buckle's *History of Civilization in England* (1857).

[29. Rochechouart 33–43; Rochecouart 55]

29. *Poitiers:* Richard Coeur de Lion was comte de Poitiers.

Rochecouart: The home of Agnès, wife of the vicomte de Rochechouart.

35. *four brothers:* The four sons of Boson de Grignols, comte de Périgord *c.* 1140–1160, were allegedly Hélias Talairan (comte de Périgord *c.* 1160–1203), Guillem Talairan (husband of Maeut de Montagnac), Olivier de Mauriac, and Ramnulf (a monk). Stroński suggests (pp. 12–13) that Guillem and Olivier were names and personages invented by the early Provençal biographers, and that the two brothers of Hélias and Ramnulf were really called Audebert and Boson.

38–39. *Pawn . . . castles:* "De Born advises the barons to pawn their castles before making war, thus if they won they could redeem them, if they lost the loss fell on the holder of the mortgage" (*Pavannes and Divisions* [1918], p. 166). Pound alludes to Bertran's lines:

> Baro, metetz en gatge
> Chastels e vilas e ciutatz
> Enanz qu'usquecs nous guerrejatz.

("Barons! put in pawn castles, and towns and cities before anyone makes war on us"—*The Spirit of Ro-*

mance [1910], p. 43.) The first line of the Provençal reappears in Canton 85 (cf. THE ALCHEMIST, l. 3*n*).

40–46. *great scene:* In July 1183 Richard besieged Hautefort and captured Bertran. The Provençal commentary describes how Bertran made no attempt to excuse his treasonable activities when brought before Henry II, but moved the king to clemency by expressing his grief at the death of the Young King: "Seinger, dis en Bertrans, lo jorn qu-el valens joves reis, vostre fillz, mori, eu perdi lo sen e-l saber e la conoissensa" (Boutière and Schutz, p. 53). Pound comments: "The traditional scene of Bertrans before King Henry Plantagenet is well recounted in Smith's *Troubadours at Home* [1899]. It is vouched for by many old manuscripts and seems as well authenticated as most Provençal history, though naturally there are found the usual perpetrators of 'historic doubt' " (*Poetry* [Dec. 1915], 146; Smith [vol. 2, pp. 219–221] offers a melodramatic account).

51. *Talleyrands:* The modern name of the Talairan family.

[65. from thence   *33–43;*   from there   55]

66. *how could he do without her:* Bertran's needs are political, but they are expressed as though they were emotional.

69–70. Papiol was Bertran's jongleur (cf. ll. 104, 115–116, and the epigraph to SESTINA: ALTAFORTE). Pound alludes to the *envoi* of "Domna, pois de mi nous chal":

> Papiols, mon Aziman
> M'anaras dir en chantan
> Qu'amors es desconoguda
> Sai e d'aut bas chazeguda.

("Papiol, my lodestone, go, through all the courts sing this canzon, how love fareth ill of late; is fallen from his high estate"—*Poetry* [Dec. 1915], 145.)

70. *Anhes:* Agnès (cf. l. 29*n*).

Cembelins: Cf. "DOMPNA POIS DE ME NO'US CAL" (l. 21*n*).

83. *Born:* The pun is probably unintentional (cf. l. 153).

[86. much at   *33–40;*   much as   42+]

86. Polhonac is a place, not a person, and so the earlier reading must be the correct one.

86–87. *St. Leider:* Guillem de Saint Leidier, who was in love with the wife of the vicomte de Polignac (Boutière and Schutz, p. 178). Pound writes:

No student of the period can doubt that the involved forms, and especially the veiled meanings in the "trobar clus," grew out of living conditions, and that these songs played a very real part in love intrigue and in the intrigue preceding warfare. The time had no press and no theatre. If you wish to make love to women in public, and out loud, you must resort to subterfuge; and Guillaume St. Leider even went so far as to get the husband of his lady to do the seductive singing.

Quarterly Review (Oct. 1913), 426.

90–91. Pound quotes from "the sardonic Count of Foix" a song in which he finds "a livelier measure" than is usual in such pieces:

> Ben deu gardar lo sieu baston
> Car frances sabon grans colps dar
> Et albirar ab lor bordon. . . .

> Let no man lounge amid the flowers
> Without a stout club of some kind.
> Know ye the French are stiff in stours
> And sing not all they have in mind. . . .

Quarterly Review (Oct. 1913), 433.

92. *broken heaumes:* Bertran writes of "elm . . . faussat e romput" ("broken and shattered helmets"—*The Spirit of Romance* [1910], p. 41).

100. *al . . . ochaisos:* Rhyme words in the Provençal poem reproduced in the note to "DOMPNA POIS DE ME NO'US CAL."

101. *bilious:* Pound calls him a "dyspeptic curmudgeon" in an earlier essay (*New Age* [Dec. 1911], 201).

104. *magnet:* This translates the Provençal word *aziman* (cf. ll. 69–70n).

105. *Aubeterre:* Mentioned in PROVINCIA DESERTA (l. 19n).

110. *Aelis:* Hélis de Montfort.

115–116. Cf. lines 69–70n.

[116. Bertrand   33–43;   Bertrans   55]

[117. come   33;   came   39+]

117. *We:* Reconstructing what might have happened, Pound imagines himself accompanying Bertran's jongleur.

Ventadour: Maria de Turenne was the wife of the vicomte de Ventadorn, and allegedly Maent's sister.

119. *Arrimon Luc D'Esparro:* In one of Bertran's poems a man called Arramon Luc d'Esparro is mentioned, but nothing is known of him.

124. *smoked out:* Hautefort was surrendered to Richard after an eight days' siege.

127–128. The Provençal poet Arnaut Daniel lived in Richard's castle between 1194 and 1199. It was while Richard was besieging the castle of Chalûs in Limousin that he was mortally wounded by a crossbow bolt and died on the sixth of April 1199 (cf. ll. 157–159).

133. *leopards:* The heraldic term for a lion *passant.*

137–139. Pound's imaginary conversation takes place in April 1199, two years after Bertran had renounced secular ambitions by entering the abbey of Dâlon, near Hautefort. Bertran outlived Richard by some fifteen years.

140. *trobar clus:* Verse written in difficult and unusual rhymes. Daniel was an acknowledged master of the technique.

141. *best craftsman:* According to Dante (*Purgatorio*, XXVI, 117) Arnaut Daniel "fu miglior fabbro del parlar materno" ("was a better craftsman of the mother tongue"—Sinclair). Pound's essay on Daniel in *The Spirit of Romance* (1910) is entitled "Il Miglior Fabbro," words that Eliot was afterwards to apply to Pound in the dedication of *The Waste Land* (1922).

145. *her:* Maent.

146. *sister:* During the winter of 1182–1183 Bertran had for a short time sung the praises of a lady whom the Provençal commentator calls "Elena" but who was really Maeut —*not* Bertran's "Maent" but Richard's sister and wife of the Duke of Saxony.

149–152. The punctuation is faulty in all printings and in Pound's original typescript (Chicago MSS): line 152 must be spoken by Arnaut if the passage is to make sense. Perhaps the quotation marks should be deleted after "received" (149) or "man" (151).

153. *born:* Cf. line 83n and PROVINCIA DESERTA (l. 29n).

157–159. Cf. lines 127–128n.

161. *In sacred odour:* A hagiographic formula for describing the death of a holy man. Pound comments: "Nor is it known if Benvenuto da Imola speaks for certain when he says En Arnaut went in his age to a monastery" (*Make It New* [1934], p. 43).

163–168. Cf. lines 21–27. Pound translates from Dante (*Inferno,* XXVIII, 118–123, 139–142).

> Io vidi certo, ed ancor par ch'io 'l veggia,
> un busto sanza capo andar sì come
> andavan li altri della trista greggia;
> e 'l capo tronco tenea per le chiome,
> pèsol con mano a guisa di lanterna;
> e quel mirava noi, e dicea: 'Oh me!'

> Perch'io parti' così giunte persone,
> partito porto il mio cerebro, lasso!,
> dal suo principio ch'è in questo troncone.
> Così s'osserva in me lo contrapasso.'

> ("Verily I saw, and I seem to see it still, a trunk without a head going as were the others of the miserable herd; and it held the severed head by the hair swinging in its hand like a lantern, and that was looking at us and saying: 'Woe is me!' . . . Because I parted those so joined I carry my brain, alas, parted from its root in this trunk; thus is observed in me the retribution"—Sinclair.)

[169a, b. *In* 33 *only the following lines stand at the beginning of section III:*

> I loved a woman. The stars fell from heaven.
> And always our two natures were in strife.]

The canceled lines reveal that the third section is an imaginary monologue spoken by Bertran, who finds Maent as much an enigma as modern scholars do. They constituted a link between the poem's two images of Bertran as lover ("in strife" with Maent) and Bertran as troublemaker ("the stirrer-up of strife"). When Pound suppressed these lines in 1916 he must have been in the process of abandoning concatenation as a structural device in favor of the bolder juxtapositions of the ideogrammic method.

The epigraph to this concluding section means "And they were two in one and one in two" (Sinclair).

170. Auvézère is the name of a river near Hautefort.

171. *day's eyes:* Daisies, a Chaucerian etymology.

émail: French *émaillé* ("dotted with flowers").

180. *counter-thrust:* Cf. line 27n. The word also occurs in *Sonnets . . . of . . . Cavalcanti* (1912, p. 75).

181–184. The speaker is Maent. Perhaps she was incapable of loving Bertran (181f); or perhaps she loved everything about him except his scheming mind (183f).

185. *last estrangement:* Echoed in HUGH SELWYN MAUBERLEY (l. 276).

189. The "eternizing" conceit: Maent "lives" because of Bertran's poem about her.

NEEDLE, THE
[NO. 54. PRINTINGS: *15, 42, 43, 53, 55*]

To the traditional *carpe diem* theme Pound has here added the equally traditional image of the "tide of fortune," the most famous example of which occurs in a speech by Brutus in Shakespeare's *Julius Caesar* (IV, iii, 217 ff.).

3. *needle . . . soul:* Pound often writes as though intellectual and emotional states could be measured on instruments. The compass needle of the soul in this poem is followed in HUGH SELWYN MAUBERLEY by the seismograph on which Mauberley's delicate emotional disturbances are recorded. Similarly, in attempting to define the Jamesian sensibility, Pound rejected "the whole Wells-Bennett period" on the grounds that we can take no interest "in instruments which must of nature miss two-thirds of the vibrations in any conceivable situation" (*Egoist* [Jan. 1918], 2). In a different mood he protested against the "glucose christi-inanity" of certain periodicals, remarking that "Austin Harrison, and G. K. Chesterton, and the writers in the 'Bookman' . . . are not even daft seismographs" (*New Age* [Dec. 27, 1917], 168). "A nation's writers are the voltmeters and steam-gauges of that nation's intellectual life" (*English Journal* [Oct. 1934], 630). Such metaphors are anticipated in Gourmont's *Lettres à l'Amazone* (1914): "Les yeux sont le manomètre de la machine animale" (p. 202).

NEW CAKE OF SOAP, THE
[NO. 115. PRINTINGS: *23, 40, 42, 43, 55*]

This epigram was omitted from the English trade edition of *Lustra* (1916) and evidently caused the publishers of the American reprint similar anxieties, for we find Pound writing to Quinn in August 1917 in defense of his opinion "that one should name names in satire":

Chesterton is like a vile scum on the pond. The multitude of his mumblings cannot be killed by multitude but only by a sharp thrust (even that won't do it, but it purges one's soul).
All his slop—it is really modern catholicism to a great extent, the *never* taking a hedge straight, the mumbo-jumbo of superstition dodging behind clumsy fun and paradox.

If it were a question of cruelty to a weak man I shouldn't, of course, have printed it. But Chesterton *is* so much the mob, so much the multitude. It is not as if he weren't a symbol for all the mob's hatred of all art that aspires above mediocrity. . . . Chesterton has always taken the stand that the real thing isn't worth doing. . . . I should probably like G. K. C. personally if I ever met him. Still, I believe he creates a milieu in which art is impossible. He and his kind.

Letters, pp. 170–171. Pound seems to allude to Chesterton's epigram that if a thing is worth doing it is worth doing badly. He changed his mind about Chesterton (1874–1936) after meeting him at Rapallo in May 1935.

For other examples of Pound's troubles with censorship, see TO A FRIEND WRITING ON CABARET DANCERS (l. 36*n*).

NIGHT LITANY
[NO. 15. PRINTINGS: 2, 6, 8, 53, 55]

This celebration of Venice as a *civitas dei* (or at least, as a token of the divine presence) surprised even Pound: "for days the 'Night Litany' seemed a thing so little my own that I could not bring myself to sign it" (*T. P.'s Weekly* [June 6, 1913], 707). It was the product of "Impulse," not technique.

5. *Venice:* It was here that Pound published his first book of poems, *A Lume Spento* (1908). A few years later he was to see Venice as degraded by modernity (the opening of Canto 3).

22–23. *seen . . . glory:* The echo of the "Battle Hymn of the Republic" is surely unintentional?

[37a. And our lips to show forth thy praise,   2–53;   [lacking]   55]

[48a. (Fainter)   2;   [lacking]   6+]

N.Y.
[NO. 55. PRINTINGS: 15, 42, 43, 53, 55]

[TITLE: N.Y.   15, 53+;   New York   42, 43]

Pound lived in New York during the winter of 1910–1911, and considered the possibility of writing the poetry of cities:

And New York is the most beautiful city in the world?
It is not far from it. No urban night is like the nights there. I have looked down across the city from high windows. It is then that the great buildings lose reality and take on their magical powers. They are immaterial; that is to say one sees but the lighted windows.

Squares after squares of flame, set and cut into the aether.
Here is our poetry, for we have pulled down the stars to our
will.

New Age (Sept. 19, 1912), 492. N.Y. is roughly contemporary
with Eliot's "Preludes," a fact that illustrates the inadequacy
of Pound's approach to this subject. See also the note to DANS
UN OMNIBUS DE LONDRES.

[*Footnote:* [*lacking*]   *15–43, 55;*   Madison Ave., 1910   *53*]

OBJECT, AN
[NO. 56. PRINTINGS: *15, 42, 43, 53, 55*]

This sketch of a man who willfully withdraws from life has,
like QUIES, close affinities with the latter half of HUGH SELWYN
MAUBERLEY.

OF JACOPO DEL SELLAIO
[NO. 57. PRINTINGS: *15, 42, 43, 53, 55*]

1. *secret ways of love:* An allusion to the description of Venus
   in Swinburne's "A Ballad of Death":

   Upon her raiment of dyed sendaline
   Were painted all the secret ways of love. . . .

   Pound expressed his admiration of this poem when reviewing Gosse's biography of Swinburne in *Poetry* ([March
   1918], 326).

3–4. *Cyprian . . . Isles:* Venus was worshiped formerly on
   the island of Cyprus which, like Lesbos, was one of the
   more famous *îles d'amour.*

6. Cf. THE PICTURE (l. 1*n*).

OLD IDEA OF CHOAN BY ROSORIU
[NO. 156. PRINTINGS: *36, 39, 40, 42, 43, 55*]

[TITLE: Old Idea of Choan   *36;*   — — — Choan by Rosoriu
   39+
   Rosoriu   *36+;*   Rosorin   *Faber and Faber, 1968*]

See the introductory note to SONG OF THE BOWMEN OF SHU.
OLD IDEA OF CHOAN BY ROSORIU is a translation of the first
16 lines of a poem of 64 lines from *Yu-yu-tzu*, I, 2.3*a* (Fang).
"Choan" is Ch'ang-an (FOUR POEMS OF DEPARTURE, IV*n*).

"Rosoriu" is *Lu Chao-lin* (Japanese *Roshōrin*), a poet of the seventh century A.D. (Fang).

26. *Riu:* Roso-riu?

28. *Butei of Kan:* Wu-ti of Han (Fang).

ON HIS OWN FACE IN THE GLASS
[NO. 9. PRINTINGS: *1*, *6*, *53*, *55*]

A poem on the relationship between the poet and his personæ.

ORTUS
[NO. 72. PRINTINGS: *16*, *39*, *40*, *42*, *43*, *55*]

" 'Ortus' means 'birth' or 'springing out'—same root as in 'orient' " (*Letters*, p. 58). This is a poem about the nature of poetry, a small contribution to Romantic "metapoetry."

4. *name . . . centre:* Shakespeare describes the poet as someone who "gives to airy nothing / A local habitation and a name" (*A Midsummer Night's Dream*, V, i, 17–18).

7. *separation:* The successful poem must be self-contained, totally independent of its creator.

11. *stream . . . shadow:* Similar imagery is used in FISH AND THE SHADOW to evoke the elusiveness of personality.

OUR CONTEMPORARIES
[NO. 145. PRINTINGS: *28*, *39*, *40*, *42*, *43*, *55*]

The poet referred to in the footnote is Rupert Brooke (1887–1915), whom Pound thought the best of the Georgian poets (*Letters*, p. 103). Brooke spent the first three months of 1914 in Tahiti and then wrote a sequence of poems based on his experiences in the South Seas, first printed in its entirety in *1914 and Other Poems* (June 16, 1915). One of these ("Tiare Tahiti") is a love poem about a girl called Mamua who is probably the "princess" of Pound's anecdote.

The universality of the Brooke cult may be gauged from the fact that OUR CONTEMPORARIES is the only satirical poem about Brooke to be published in this period. When it first appeared in *Blast* in July 1915 it was considered a tasteless attack on the young Apollo of English literature who had died in the Dardanelles a couple of months previously. However, Pound's suggestion that lust and *wanderlust* are not incompatible (even in gods) was intended only to be mischievously iconoclastic:

> The verse contains nothing derogatory. It is a complaint against a literary method. Brooke got perhaps a certain amount of vivid poetry in life and then went off to associate with literary hen-coops like Lascelles Abercrombie in his writings. . . . If he went to Tahiti for his emotional excitements instead of contracting diseases in Soho, for God's sake let him have the credit of it.

> Of course the Brooke matter was an error. . . . However, admitting it is an error, I by no means consider it a felony, and I am not going into mourning. Other young men have gone, and will go, to Tahiti, and they will write Petrarchan verses, and they will be envied their enthusiastic princesses.

Letters, pp. 110, 112. Nor was it entirely Pound's fault that the poem came to be published after Brooke's death. Wyndham Lewis intended to bring out the second number of *Blast* in December 1914, in which case OUR CONTEMPORARIES would have been a timely comment on the South Seas poems that were printed in the Georgian satellite *New Numbers* in the August of that year. Unfortunately, seven more months elapsed before the second *Blast* appeared, by which time Brooke was dead.

3–5. *palm . . . sonnets:* Pound may be parodying a letter Brooke wrote to Edward Marsh from Fiji in November 1913:

> Perplexing country! At home everything is so simple, and choice is swift, for the sensible man. There is only the choice between writing a good sonnet and making a million pounds. Who could hesitate? But *here* the choice is between writing a sonnet, and climbing a straight hundred-foot cocoanut palm, or diving forty feet from a rock into pellucid blue-green water. Which is the better there? One's European literary soul begins to be haunted by strange doubts and shaken with fundamental, fantastic misgivings. I think I shall return home. . . .

The letter is printed in Marsh's edition of Brooke's *Collected Poems* (1918, pp. xc–xci), and Pound may very well have heard about it earlier.

[*Footnote: The French is more primitive in* 28:

> Foot-note. pour le lecteur francais: / Il s'agit — — — jusqu' a Taihayti meme, Etant — — — elle a montré son allegresse a la manière dont — — — parler, Malhereusement ses poèmes sont remplis seulement de ses — — — style Victorienne — — — Anthology,"]

Revising the footnote for 39 Pound added the parenthetic qualification that his "jeune poète" was still alive (in 1916) so that readers would not think he was writing specifically about Rupert Brooke.

PACT, A
[NO. 73. PRINTINGS: *16, 39, 40, 42, 43, 55*]

As a young American in Europe, Pound was greatly interested in the achievements of Whitman, Henry James, and Whistler, all of whom were Americans whose art was respected overseas (and two of whom, incidentally, were self-exiled like himself). The significance of James to an American writer is documented at length in the essays Pound wrote for the *Little Review* in 1918; that of Whistler in TO WHISTLER, AMERICAN. A PACT is a similar homage to Walt Whitman (1819–1892), who is the subject of an illuminating essay by Pound called "What I feel about Walt Whitman," written in February 1909 and first published by H. Bergman (*American Literature* [March 1955], 60):

> I honor [Whitman] for he prophesied me while I can only recognize him as a forebear of whom I ought to be proud. . . . Mentaly I am a Walt Whitman who has learned to wear a colar and a dress shirt (although at times inimical to both). . . . Like Dante he wrote in the "vulgar tongue," in a new metric. The first great man to write in the language of his people.
> Et ego Petrarca in lingua vetera scribo, and in a tongue my people understand not.

[1. make truce with *16;* make a pact with *39+*]

2. *detested:* In June 1913 Pound wrote that "Whitman is a hard nutt. The *Leaves of Grass* is the book. It is impossible to read it without swearing at the author almost continuously" (*Letters*, p. 57). The few references to Whitman in *The Spirit of Romance* (1910) are all unfavorable.

PAGANI'S, NOVEMBER 8
[NO. 165. PRINTINGS: *38, 42, 43, 55*]

[TITLE: Pagani's *38;* Pagani's, November 8 *42+*]

When in London, Pound and his friends used to dine at Pagani's Restaurant in Great Portland Place, and also at Bellotti's (see BLACK SLIPPERS: BELLOTTI).

[3. learned museum *38;* learned British Museum *42+*]

3. *assistant:* Possibly Lawrence Binyon (1869–1943), poet and Keeper of the Prints and Drawings in the British Museum (Norman, p. 158).

PAN IS DEAD
[NO. 58. PRINTINGS: *15, 42, 43, 53, 55*]

The story of the death of Pan is recorded by Plutarch (*Moralia*, V, 419) and has been a recurrent theme in European literature, as essays by Irwin and Merivale testify. For Pound, the death of Pan symbolized the end of the paganism he admired so much in the ancient world; and this is why in many of his poems he seeks to resurrect the pagan deities obliterated by Christianity. See in this respect the introductory note to SURGIT FAMA.

In Canto 23 the death of Pan is conflated with the death of Adonis.

2–3. *all . . . coronal:* The trick of rhyming native monosyllabic words with polysyllabic words of foreign origin is reminiscent of seventeenth-century practice (Herrick, for example, was fond of rhyming "set" with "coronet"). The presence of rhymes like "lie / longevity" and "alone / oblivion" in such a deliberate pastiche of seventeenth-century poetry as the "Envoi (1919)" of HUGH SELWYN MAUBERLEY suggests that Pound identified this mode of rhyming as one of the characteristic techniques of Renaissance English lyrics. He could, of course, have picked up the rhyme "all / coronal" from Wordsworth's *Immortality* ode or (more remotely) from Barnes' *Parthenophil and Parthenophe* (1593, Ode 6); but his source was probably Herrick.

13. *hollow season:* See VILLONAUD FOR THIS YULE (ll. 1–4*n*). The death of Pan allegedly coincided with the birth of Christ.

PAPYRUS
[NO. 168. PRINTINGS: *39, 40, 42, 43, 55*]

Hughes regards PAPYRUS as "a satire on H. D. and her Sapphics," and uses the poem as evidence for his opinion that the "comic aspect of the poetic fragment was fully realized by some of the imagists themselves" (*Imagism and the Imagists* [1931], p. 123). Fang noted in 1952 that PAPYRUS is based on a Sapphic fragment which was not published until 1902 and which Pound probably came upon in J. M. Edmonds' *The New Fragments of Alcaeus, Sappho and Corinna* (1909).

The texts of several Sapphic fragments have survived only on papyri. One of them (LXXXV) begins:

ἦρ’ ἀ[. . .
δῆρα το[. . .
Γογγύλα τ[. . .

In defense of Pound’s rendering, Collinge writes: “As for the broken words er-, derar, the suppletions eri (‘in spring’ [cf. the epigraph to THE SPRING]) and some by-form of deros (cf. deron, ‘all too long,’ often in Homer) are at least feasible” (Notes and Queries [June 1958], 265).

3. Gongula: One of Sappho’s “pupils or disciples,” according to Suidas (Sappho, XLV).

PARACELSUS IN EXCELSIS
[NO. 26. PRINTINGS: 7, 8, 9, 55]

Bombastes Paracelsus (1493–1541) was a Swiss alchemist who is acknowledged as one of the founders of modern chemistry. Pound’s poem is an epilogue to Robert Browning’s “Paracelsus,” and his title is adapted from the hymn “Gloria in Excelsis Deo” (“glory to God in the highest”).

Pound later translated a dialogue by Fontenelle in which Bombastes comes off much the worse in conversation with Molière (Egoist [June 1917], 70–71).

1. no longer human: Browning ends with the death of Paracelsus.

4. essence: Used, like “element” in the following line, as a technical term in alchemy.

PATTERNS, THE
[NO. 149. PRINTINGS: 31, 35, 40, 42, 43, 55]

Erinna’s namesake was a Greek poetess of the fourth century B.C. who died unmarried at the age of nineteen. Lalage is a courtesan in Horace’s Odes (I, xxii, II, xv). “Lalage’s shadow moves in the fresco” described in Canto 50.

PHANOPŒIA
[NO. 175. PRINTINGS: 47, 53, 55]

[TITLE: Φανοποεια 47; Phanopœia 53+]

PHANOPŒIA makes use of freely associated images which, remaining undefined, are nevertheless capable of evoking a mood. The technique of this poem, like that of HEATHER, is more symbolist than imagist. It is possible that PHANOPŒIA represents an attempt to get away from the sculpturesque effects of pure imagism by introducing what Pound was later to call "the moving image" (*ABC of Reading* [1934], p. 36).

There is an elaborate Neoplatonic interpretation of the poem by E. Hombitzer (*Neueren Sprachen* [July 1965], 568–578). The term *phanopœia* is discussed on page 11 above.

I. The colors of the subtitle evoke images that provide the material for this section. The method may derive from contemporary interest in "color music" like Scriabin's *Prometheus, the Poem of Fire* (New York, 1915): see Steadman's essay (*Image* [1964], 17–22).

5. *descend . . . æther:* There is a similar phrase in HOMAGE TO SEXTUS PROPERTIUS (I, 14).

II. Latin *saltus* means "a leap."

11. *Io:* This Greek exclamation is used again in TEMPORA.

III. Latin *concava vallis* means "a hollow valley."

21. *AOI:* An unglossed word in the *Chanson de Roland*.

22. *whirling . . . light:* An uncollected poem called "A Prologue" contains the phrase "whirling light" (*Canzoni* [1911], p. 34). Cf. "whirling laughter" (PROVINCIA DESERTA, l. 32n).

22–23. *light . . . solid:* Cf. Canto 93 (and THE ALCHEMIST, l. 3n):

> that the child
> walk in peace in her basilica,
> The light there almost solid.

"PHASELLUS ILLE"
[NO. 59. PRINTINGS: 15, 42, 43, 53, 55]

The title and opening lines are adapted from Catullus (IV):

> Phasellus ille quem videtis, hospites,
> ait fuisse navium celerrimus. . . .

("The pinnace you see, my friends, says that she was once the fleetest of ships"—Loeb.)

1. *papier-mâché:* Pound's term for the literary establishment that evolved during the late Victorian period. "Perched on the dry rim of the cauldron the naive transpontine observes

the 'British institutions,' Gosse, Thackeray, Garnett, and their penumbra, the 'powers in the world of letters.' . . . One knows that if one ascend up into height the manifestations of the *papier mâché* are before him . . ." (*New Age* [Jan. 30, 1913], 300); the same sentiment reappears in *Poetry* (Sept. 1916), 310, and *ibid.* (March 1918), 327.

3. *seventies:* Explained in l'homme moyen sensuel (ll. 53–55).

6. *hair-cloth:* Pound tends to characterize the Victorian period as "the horse-hair period" (*Poetry* [Sept. 1916], 311).

7. *Shaw:* Pound's attitude toward G. B. Shaw (1856–1950) changed from enthusiasm in his student days (*Letters,* p. 248) to antipathy in later life. Shaw's unforgivable offense was to refuse to subscribe to Joyce's *Ulysses* (1922).

9. *deathless . . . world:* Possibly a recollection of the "Dedication" to Shelley's *Laon and Cythna:* "Truth's deathless voice pauses among mankind!" See also *Letters* (p. 138) and silet.

12. *Cyclades:* A group of islands in the Grecian Archipelago, encircling the sacred island of Delos. The name occurs in Catullus' poem.

13. *St. Anthony:* A type of resistance to temptation.

PHYLLIDULA
[NO. 150. PRINTINGS: *31, 35, 40, 42, 43, 55*]

[TITLE, 1. Phylidula   *31, 35;*   Phyllidula   *40+*]

Pound thought this poem demonstrated his mastery of the epigrammatic style. Among the Chicago mss is a typescript of PHYLLIDULA on which he has written part of the Greek epigram by Parrhasius that he quotes in his preface to the *Poetical Works of Lionel Johnson* (1915, p. xvi): "The limits, I say, of this art, have now been discovered plain by my hand" (Loeb). A canceled subtitle acknowledges that PHYLLIDULA is a translation from "Antipater of Cos," but I have been unable to trace the Greek original (for other translations from the *Greek Anthology,* see HOMAGE TO QUINTUS SEPTIMIUS FLORENTIS CHRISTIANUS).

Phyllidula reappears in IMPRESSIONS OF FRANÇOIS-MARIE AROUET (DE VOLTAIRE).

3. *receives . . . give:* This parodies a line from Coleridge's "Dejection: an Ode": "O Lady! we receive but what we give."

PICTURE, THE
[NO. 160. PRINTINGS: 15, 42, 43, 53, 55]

There are two pictures by Jacopo del Sellaio called *Venus Reclining,* one in the National Gallery, the other in the Louvre.

1. The line is repeated in OF JACOPO DEL SELLAIO. A French version of this line appears as the opening of DANS UN OMNIBUS DE LONDRES.

PIERE VIDAL OLD
[NO. 24. PRINTINGS: 6, 42, 43, 53, 55]

"It would be most immoral of me," Pound wrote to a friend early in 1908, "to present Piere Vidal's ravings as a spiritual extacy. What the poem says is simply this: 'Animal passion is very near—in its extreme form, that is—to insanity, or dipsomania!" (Edwards, p. 41). In this Browningesque piece Pound's note on the Provençal poet Peire Vidal is taken from an early biography:

La Loba si era de Carcases, e Peire Vidal si se fazia apelar Lop per ela e portava armas de lop. Et en la montanha de Cabaretz si se fes cassar als pastors ab los mastis et ab los lebrers, si com hom fai lop. E vesti una pel de lop per donar az entendre als pastors et als cans qu'el fos lop. E li pastor ab lur cans lo casseron e-l barateron si en tal guiza qu'el en fo portatz per mort a l'alberc de la Loba de Pueinautier.

Quant ela saup que aquest era Peire Vidal, ela comenset a far gran alegreza de la folia que Peire Vidals avia faita et a rire molt, e-l marit de leis autressi. E reseubron lo ab gran alegreza; e-l maritz lo fes penre e fes lo metre en luec rescos, al meils qu'el saup ni poc. E fes mandar pel metge e fes lo metgar, entro tant qu'el fo gueritz.

Boutière and Schutz, *Biographies des Troubadours* (1950), pp. 247–248. The nature of Peire Vidal's love for the *Loba* is not known. Modern scholars think that the whole legend may have been prompted by a literal reading of these lines from one of Peire's poems (XXXIII):

E sitot lop m'appellatz,
No m'o tenh a dezonor,
Ni si-m cridan li pastor
Ni si sui per lor cassatz. . . .

See also the note to LA FRAISNE.

Henri Gaudier-Brzeska's drawing for PIERE VIDAL OLD is reproduced in Pound's memoir of the artist (1916, pl. xxvii).

Pennautier is in the south of France, in the department of

Carcassonne, to the north of which lie the mountains of Le Cabardes (Pound's "Cabaret").

23. *guerdon:* Reward.

35. *Silent as fate:* A preimagist example of facile abstraction. Pound was later to exhort poets to "go in fear of abstractions" (*Poetry* [March 1913], 201).

[51. run-way   6–43;   run-away   53+
through that   6, 53+;   through the   42, 43]

PLANH FOR THE YOUNG ENGLISH KING
[NO. 25. PRINTINGS: 6, 8, 53, 55]

Planh is Provençal for "lament." Prince Henry Plantagenet, the eldest son of Henry II, had been crowned in 1170 and was known throughout Provence as the Young King. His friendship with Bertran de Born achieved almost legendary fame even during his lifetime, and it used to be thought that Bertran was responsible for encouraging the Young King to declare war on his brother Richard (NEAR PERIGORD, l. 25). Before the fighting broke out, however, Henry caught fever and died at Martel in June 1183. The poem which Pound has translated is the second of two that Bertran wrote shortly after Henry's death.

> Si tuit li dol e-lh plor e-lh marrimen
> E las dolors e-lh dan e-lh chaitivier
> Qu'om anc auzis en est segle dolen
> Fossen ensems, sembleran tuit leugier
> Contra la mort del jove Rei engles,
> Don rema Pretz e Jovens doloros
> E-l mons oscurs e teintz e tenebros
> Sems de tot joi, ples de tristor e d'ira.
>
> Dolen e trist e ple de marrimen
> Son remazut li cortes soudadier
> E-lh trobador e-lh joglar avinen;
> Trop an agut en Mort mortal guerrier;
> Que tòut lor a lo jove rei engles,
> Ves cui eran li plus larc cobeitos;
> Ja non er mais ni no crezatz que fos,
> Ves aquest dan, e-l segle, plors ni ira.
>
> Estóuta Mortz! plena de marrimen
> Vanar ti potz que-l melhor chavalier
> As tòut al mon qu'anc fos de nula gen,
> Quar non es res qu'a Pretz aia mestier
> Que tot no fos el jove Rei engles;
> E fora mielhs, s'a Dieu plagues razos,

Que visques el que maint autr'enoios
Qu'anc no feiron als pros mas dol et ira.

D'aquest segle flac, ple de marrimen,
S'amors s'en vai son joi tenh menzongier,
Que re no-i a que no torn en cozen;
Totz jorns veuzis e val mens huoi que hier;
Chascus si mir el jove Rei engles,
Qu'era del mon lo plus valens dels pros;
Ar es anatz sos gens cors amoros,
Don es dolors e desconortz et ira.

Celui que plac, pel nostre marrimen,
Venir el mon nos traire d'encombrier
E receup mort a nostre salvamen,
Cum a senhor humil e drechurier
Clamem merce, qu'al jove Rei engles
Perdo, si-l platz, si com es vers perdos,
E-l fass'estar ab honratz companhos
Lai on anc dol non ac ni aura ira.

Les Troubadours, ed. Nelli and Lavaud (1966), vol. 2, pp. 542, 544. The poem is translated in Farnell's *The Lives of the Troubadours* (1896, pp. 110–112), in Smythe's *Trobador Poets* (1911, pp. 79–80), and in Hueffer's *The Troubadours* (1878, p. 201: stanzas 1, 3, and 4 only).

1. The Provençal is quoted in Canto 80.

5. This is Farnell's translation.

8. *void . . . joy:* This is Hueffer's translation.

10. *teen:* Grief. An archaism resurrected mainly for its sound value, as a word was needed which could be linked with "Grieving" and "liegeman" and thus echo the sequence "grief-evil-grieving-seem" of the first stanza.

11. *joglars supple:* The Provençal *joglar avinen* means "handsome jongleurs." Pound evidently associated *joglar* with "juggler."

18. *Well mayst thou boast:* The same phrase is used by both Farnell and Smythe.

[25. how full   6, 53+;   now full   8]

PLUNGE, THE
[NO. 61. PRINTINGS: *15, 42, 43, 53, 55*]

[TITLE: Plunge   *15–53;*   The Plunge   *55*]

Many of Pound's contemporaries have commented on his restlessness and inability to stay with any one group of writers for very long. Here Pound gives expression to that yearning for new experience which probably motivated his restlessness.

6. *this:* The London literary world.

9. *you:* Probably Dorothy Shakespear, whom Pound was to marry in April 1914.

11–13. The trials of the London winter are treated humorously in ANCIENT MUSIC.

[15. Oh, but far out   *15, 53+;*   Oh, to be out   *42, 43*]

16 ff. Pound resisted the temptation to seek out a more favorable climate than the English one until the summer of 1921, when he decided to settle in Paris.

POEM BY THE BRIDGE AT TEN-SHIN
[NO. 138. PRINTINGS: 27, 39, 40, 42, 43, 55]

See the introductory note to SONG OF THE BOWMEN OF SHU. POEM BY THE BRIDGE AT TEN-SHIN is translated from *Li T'ai-po*, II, 2.18*b*–19*b* (Fang). *Ten-Shin* is the Japanese form of *T'ien-chin* (Fang).

11. *Sei-go-yo:* Japanese *Sei-jō-yō* from Chinese *Hsi-Shang-yang* (Fang).

14. *far borders:* "capital" (Lee and Murray).

28. *yellow dogs:* An allusion to the nostalgic words spoken by a once powerful minister, Li Su, as he was about to be executed: "Now it is impossible for us to go rabbiting out of the East Gate with our yellow dogs!" (Lee and Murray).

29. *Riokushu:* Japanese *Ryokushu* from Chinese *Lu-chu* (Fang).

31. Japanese *Han-rei* from Chinese *Fan-Li* (Fang).

32. *with his mistress:* Pound's romantic interpolation.

33. *hair unbound:* Han-rei unbound his own hair in order to disguise himself (Lee and Murray).

Footnote: Rihaku is Li Po.

PORTRAIT D'UNE FEMME
[NO. 62. PRINTINGS: 15, 42, 43, 53, 55]

An attempt to describe a woman who has lost her individuality, and whose personality consists entirely of the ideas and attitudes she has acquired as a result of twenty years' acquaintance with the London intelligentsia.

PORTRAIT D'UNE FEMME is one of the two poems Edward

Marsh wanted to include in *Georgian Poetry 1911–1912* (see the note to BALLAD OF THE GOODLY FERE). Blank verse was soon to come under attack: according to Pound, "to break the pentameter . . . was the first heave" in the metrical revolution (Canto 81).

1. *are our Sargasso:* A rotacism which caused the editors of an unnamed periodical to reject this poem. Pound used the incident as an example of the degenerate criticism of the time: "I sent them a real poem, a modern poem, containing the word 'uxorious,' and they wrote back that I used the letter 'r' three times in the first line, and that it was very difficult to pronounce, and that I might not remember that Tennyson had once condemned the use of four s's in a certain line of a different metre" (*New Age* [Oct. 3, 1912], 540; Tennyson found the sibilants "horrible" in the opening line of Pope's *The Rape of the Lock:* "What dire Offence from am'rous Causes springs").

The Sargasso, in the North Atlantic, is choked with gulfweed.

[4. Ideas   *15–43, 55;*   Ideals   *53*]

[17. tale for   *15–53;*   tale or   *55*]

17. The earlier reading "tale for two" compares with "tears for two" in HOMAGE TO SEXTUS PROPERTIUS (IX, 7).

POST MORTEM CONSPECTU
[NO. 116. PRINTINGS: 23, 55]

[TITLE: His Vision of a Certain Lady Post Mortem   *23;*   Post Mortem Conspectu   *55*]

Rejected from *Poetry,* this poem was entitled originally " 'Madonna e desiato in sommo cielo' " ("my lady is desired in heaven": adapted from the fourth canzone in Dante's *Vita Nuova*) and began: "They call you dead, but I saw you: / A brown, fat babe . . . ," etc. (Chicago MSS). If the present title is meant to translate the earlier one, *conspectu* must be a mistake for *conspecta.*

5. *laughter . . . end:* The idea is Bergsonian but is common also in the writings of Wyndham Lewis, in whose *Blast* this poem was first published. See HUGH SELWYN MAUBERLEY (l. 87n).

PRAISE OF YSOLT
[NO. 10. PRINTINGS: *1* (ll. 1–20 only), 3, 53, 55]

Iseult was, of course, Tristram's lady (cf. THRENOS), but Pound's Ysolt is more in the nature of a personal muse of

poetry. PRAISE OF YSOLT describes how the desire to write over-
comes the sense of one's own inadequacy: the knowledge that
"there be many singers greater than thou" cannot suppress the
desire to make fresh songs; Ysolt embodies the poet's irrepress-
ible urge to create beauty.

Among the pieces originally rejected from *A Quinzaine for
This Yule* (1908) is one called "To Ysolt, For Pardon" in which
Pound laments the fact that his poems are inferior to what
inspired them: Ysolt sent him the inspiration "freighted with
fragrance," but he has turned it into so many dead leaves (*A
Lume Spento and Other Early Poems* [1965], p. 119). There
is also an uncollected "Sestina for Isolt" in *Exultations* (1909,
pp. 23–24).

5. *lutany:* Lute music. The *O. E. D.* traces the word to Francis
   Thompson's *New Poems* (1897).

12. *roads:* Probably a reference to Pound's incursions into
    ancient and Romance literatures.

[15–18. *Set up as follows in* 1, 3, *and* 53:

— — — words   crying — — —
— — — words   crying — — —
— — — words   crying — — —
— — — words   crying — — —]

[22. lip   3, 55;   lips   53]

38. *soul . . . woman:* The image is Rossetti's (DE ÆGYPTO, l.
    5n).

[50. the song-drawer   3;   the mother of songs   53+]

58. *heart art:* It was Robert Bridges, author of the S.P.E. tract
    On English Homophones (1919), who first cautioned
    Pound on the subject of awkward homophones in poetry
    (*Criterion* [Jan. 1923], 144). The lesson was well learnt,
    for Pound later commented on a detail in Binyon's trans-
    lation of Dante's *Purgatorio:* "I dunno about 'Gryphon'
    and 'griped' so near together, sound, etc." (*Letters*, p.
    412).

PRAYER FOR HIS LADY'S LIFE
[NO. 38. PRINTINGS: 9, 42, 43, 55]

Readers who found themselves agreeing with W. G. Hale
that Pound must have been incredibly ignorant of Latin in
order to write HOMAGE TO SEXTUS PROPERTIUS had their attention directed to PRAYER FOR HIS LADY'S LIFE for proof that
Pound was quite capable of producing "a perfectly literal, and,
by the same token, perfectly lying and 'spiritually' mendacious

translation" (*New Age* [Dec. 1919], 82). In the epigraph here Pound cites the Teubner text which is numbered differently from the Loeb Propertius; the original Latin is printed in the notes to HOMAGE TO SEXTUS PROPERTIUS (IX, 13–21).

2. *do thou:* Translators' jargon (as in SURGIT FAMA, l. 15).

3. *Avernus:* A lake in Campania, thought to be the entrance to the underworld of which Pluto was king.

4. Omitted from HOMAGE TO SEXTUS PROPERTIUS. Propertius: "Pulchra sit in superis, si licet, una locis" ("let one fair one, if so it may be, abide on earth"—Loeb).

6. Europa was loved by Zeus in the form of a bull.

8. Also omitted from HOMAGE TO SEXTUS PROPERTIUS. Propertius: "Et Thebe et Priami diruta regna senis" (the Loeb editor reads *Phoebi* for *Thebe* and translates: "Troy the fallen realm of Phoebus and the old man Priam"). Priam was king of Troy.

PROVINCIA DESERTA
[NO. 132. PRINTINGS: 26, 39, 40, 42, 43, 55]

The title of this topographical poem alludes to C. M. Doughty's *Travels in Arabia Deserta* (1888). One of the sections in *Guide to Kulchur* (1938) is subtitled "Arabia Deserta" (XI, 48) and opens with the qualified acknowledgment that "Doughty's volume is a bore, but one ought to read it. . . ."

In the spring of 1914 Pound married Dorothy Shakespear and took his bride off to Provence to see the land of the troubadours. Before this he had written an essay on troubadours which gives a useful account of the writers and legends that were to have a lasting influence on his poetry; and it is here also that one finds what is probably the germ of the idea which resulted in the writing of PROVINCIA DESERTA: "a man may walk the hill-roads and river-roads from Limoges and Charente to Dordogne and Narbonne and learn a little, or more than a little, of what the country meant to the wandering singers. He may learn, or think he learns, why so many canzos open with speech of the weather; or why such a man made war on such and such castles" (*Quarterly Review* [Oct. 1913], 427). In describing Provence Pound wanted to convey the feeling for "ancient associations" that he felt was lacking in Henry James's *A Little Tour in France* (James had gone "only by train" and had therefore overlooked qualities discernible to the *piéton* [*Little Review* (Aug. 1918), 38]). Before visiting Provence Pound had known it only through medieval poetry, and in PROVINCIA DESERTA he observes nostalgically that although the names have survived, the spirit of Provence as he had known it in literature has disappeared completely. *Provincia Felix* exists only in the imagination of someone for whom the names of towns and villages have the sort of literary resonances recorded in this poem.

The main structural device of PROVINCIA DESERTA derives from A SONG OF THE DEGREES (ll. 6–8). On the technical importance of PROVINCIA DESERTA Pound wrote to Kate Buss in January 1917: "I think you will find all the verbal constructions of *Cathay* already tried in 'Provincia Deserta'" (*Letters*, p. 154; cf. LIU CH'E, ll. 5–6*n*).

1. Lady Agnès lived at Rochechouart (cf. "DOMPNA POIS DE ME NO'US CAL," ll. 35–36).

9. *Chalais:* The home of Tibors de Montausier ("DOMPNA POIS DE ME NO'US CAL," l. 31).

16–17. Cf. NEAR PERIGORD (l. 56).

19. *Aubeterre:* A church just outside Poitiers (NEAR PERIGORD, l. 105).

22. *Mareuil:* Where Arnaut de Mareuil lived (MARVOIL).

23. *La Tour:* The home of Miquel de la Tour, who was one of the writers of the Provençal biographies.

29. *Perigord:* Bertran de Born, Arnaut de Mareuil, and Arnaut Daniel all came from the diocese of Périgord (NEAR PERIGORD, note on the title).

[32. And, under 26–40; Heard, under 42+]

32. *whirling laughter:* Another epithet of "emotional apparition" (THE SPRING, l. 9*n*). The phrase is borrowed from Joyce's poem "I Hear an Army": "I moan in sleep when I hear afar their whirling laughter" (*Des Imagistes* [1914], p. 40). PHANOPŒIA has "whirling light" (l. 22*n*).

36. *Ribeyrac:* Arnaut Daniel came from Ribérac.

37. "Elias Cairels was of Sarlat" (*Quarterly Review* [Oct. 1913], 430); so was Aimeric de Sarlat.

38. A similar pilgrimage is recorded in Canto 7:

We also made ghostly visits, and the stair
That knew us, found us again on the turn of it,
Knocking at empty rooms, seeking for buried beauty. . . .

39. *layout:* Hautefort, the castle of Bertran de Born.

40. *Narbonne:* The home of Guiraut de Riquier (cf. l. 63).

Chalus: Richard Coeur de Lion was killed at Chalûs (cf. l. 44 and NEAR PERIGORD, ll. 157–159).

48. *Hautefort:* See line 39n.

49. *Montaignac:* Lady Maent lived at Montagnac ("DOMPNA POIS DE ME NO'US CAL," l. 1n).

[57. by such and such valleys   26+;   by such valleys   *Faber and Faber*]

[58. halls are   26–43;   halls were   55]

[59. rocks   26;   rock   39+]

59. *Foix:* The home of Raimon-Roger de Foix (NEAR PERIGORD, l. 91n).

Toulouse: The home of the "sensitive and little known Joios of Tolosa" (*Quarterly Review* [Oct. 1913], 433). The Pounds used Toulouse as their base when touring the area.

61. *Dorata:* The church of La Daurade, Toulouse. "The Golden Roof, la Dorata" is recalled in Canto 52 (and mentioned in *Sonnets . . . of . . . Cavalcanti* [1912], pp. 108, 109).

63. *Riquier . . . Guido:* Guiraut de Riquier and the Italian poet Guido Cavalcanti. "There is no reason why Cavalcanti and Riquier should not have met while the former was on his journey to Campostella" (*Quarterly Review* [Oct. 1913], 435). Guiraut is acknowledged as " 'the last of the troubadours' " in *The Spirit of Romance* (1910, p. 60). A meeting between Guiraut and Cavalcanti would therefore symbolize the transmission of lyric poetry from Provence to Tuscany, since Pound believed that "the poetic art of Provence paved the way for the poetic art of Tuscany" (*Quarterly Review* [Oct. 1913], 434).

64. *second Troy:* Pound quoted part of Yeats's poem "No Second Troy" when reviewing *Responsibilities* in *Poetry* ([May 1914], 66). The phrase is an early example of what Pound was later to call a "subject-rhyme" or "repeat in history" (*Letters*, p. 285)—a poetic device originating in the ancient historiographical theory of cyclic repetition, and one that was to be structurally important in the early Cantos. The Virgilian motif of a "second Troy" (cf. the epigraph to ROME) reappears in Canto 5:

> And Piere won the singing, Piere de Maensac,
> Song or land on the throw, and was *dreitz hom*
> And had De Tierci's wife and with the war they made:
> Troy in Auvergnat
> While Menelaus piled up the church at port
> He kept Tyndarida. Dauphin stood with de Maensac.

There is a prose version of this episode, based on an early Provençal biography of Peire, in Pound's essay on troubadours (*Quarterly Review* [Oct. 1913], 429). Here again the Homeric parallel is stressed: Peire ran off with another man's wife, "and the husband," writes Pound, " 'in the manner of the golden Menelaus,' demanded her much"; but all the Provençal text says is that the "marritz la demandet molt" (Boutière and Schutz, *Biographies des Troubadours* [1950], p. 228).

On the superficial difficulties of this kind of poetry Amy Lowell's strictures in "A Critical Fable" (1922) are still relevant:

There is Pierre de Maensac, and Pierre won the singing—
Where or how I can't guess, but Pound sets his fame
  ringing
Because he was *dreitz hom* (whatever that is)
And had De Tierci's wife; what happened to his
We don't know, in fact we know nothing quite clearly,
For Pound always treats his ghosts cavalierly.

66. *two men:* Peire and Austors de Maensac.

tossing a coin: Pound's interpolation.

71–73. Adapted from the Provençal biography: "Lo castel ac Austors e-l trobar ac Peire. . . . Fort fo adregs [Pound's *dreitz*] hom e de bel solatz" (Boutière and Schutz, *op. cit.*, p. 228).

74. *lady:* The wife of Bernart de Tierci.

QUIES
[NO. 63. PRINTINGS: *15, 42, 43, 53, 55*]

The Latin *quies* means "rest." Pound was later to dissociate himself from such preciosity by criticizing similar traits in Hugh Selwyn Mauberley. The values represented by the words "the month was more temperate / Because this beauty had been . . ." are essentially those of QUIES, ERAT HORA and several other poems in *Ripostes* and *Lustra*. In HUGH SELWYN MAUBERLEY, however, they stand as an indictment of Mauberley's apathy and aestheticism.

REST, THE
[NO. 84. PRINTINGS: *18, 19, 39, 40, 42, 43, 55*]

[TITLE: [*untitled section I of "Lustra"*]   *18;*   The Rest   *19+*]

Addressed to all Americans who feel as frustrated as Pound had felt some six years previously when writing IN DURANCE, THE REST is in some ways a sequel to the earlier poem and a defense of self-imposed exile. It is Pound's *Look! We Have*

Come Through! Within a few weeks of publishing THE REST he praised J. G. Fletcher for having taken "the step which would seem to be imperative for any American who has serious intentions toward poetry. He left the virgin republic of the west as a duckling departs from a hen" (*Poetry* [Dec. 1913], 111). As precedents, Pound invariably cites the case of Whistler and Henry James (see the note to A PACT).

7–8. *systems . . . control:* The case against the American literary establishment and the debilitating effects of the American way of life is given in more detail in L'HOMME MOYEN SENSUEL.

RETURN, THE
[NO. 51. PRINTINGS: *14, 15, 42, 43, 53, 55*]

A couple of years after publishing THE RETURN Pound stated cryptically that the poem "is an objective reality and has a complicated sort of significance, like Mr. Epstein's 'Sun God,' or Mr. Brzeska's 'Boy with a Coney'" (*Fortnightly Review* [Sept. 1, 1914], 464). The poem seems to be about the pagan gods who, vigorous in antiquity, have managed to survive only as shadows of their former selves. See the introductory note to SURGIT FAMA.

Taupin says (pp. 142, 144) that THE RETURN was written in a quarter of an hour and composed to the rhythms of the introductory poem in Henri de Régnier's *Les Médailles d'Argille* (1900). Yeats described THE RETURN as "the most beautiful poem that has been written in the free form, one of the few in which I find real organic rhythm" (*Little Review* [April 1914], 48); and Goodwin has suggested that it provided Aldington and H. D. with the rudiments of their "Greek" style. In 1913 it was set to music by Walter Morse Rummel.

5–6. Pound parodied these lines years later when describing the experiments of the Abbé Rousselot, a French phonetician who

had made a machine for measuring the duration of verbal components. A quill or tube held in the nostril, a less shaved quill or other tube in the mouth, and your consonants signed as you spoke them.
They return, One and by one, With fear, As half awakened each letter with a double registration of quavering.

Polite Essays (1937), pp. 129–130. Stock (p. 90) thinks that Pound is here describing how a reading of THE RETURN was registered on Rousselot's machine.

[10. Winged *14;* Wing'd *15+*]

10. *Wing'd-with-Awe:* Evidently a Dantesque personification. Pound had observed that Dante's personifications "are real and not artificial. Dante's precision . . . comes from the attempt to reproduce exactly the thing which has been clearly seen. The 'Lord of terrible aspect' is no abstraction" (*The Spirit of Romance* [1910], p. 114; "Lord of Terrible Aspect" is Rossetti's translation of "signore di pauroso aspetto" in the *Vita Nuova*, IV). Even so, such effects were later to be prohibited by the imagist exhortation to "go in fear of abstractions" (*Poetry* [March 1913], 201).

12. *Gods . . . wingèd shoe:* The citation is Homeric (THE COMING OF WAR: ACTÆON, l. 15*n*).

17, 20. *These the keen-scented . . . pallid the leash-men:* Carne-Ross suggests (p. 222) that the metre of these lines is the classical five-syllabled *adonius*, as it is in THE SEAFARER: "coldly afflicted" (l. 8). But the rhythm is common in English, corresponding to the *cursus planus* in liturgical writings ("Lord is my shepherd") as well as to Type *A* in Sievers' system of Old English verse scansion ("Calde geþrungen").

RIVER-MERCHANT'S WIFE: A LETTER, THE
[NO. 139. PRINTINGS: 27, 39, 40, 42, 43, 55]

See the introductory note to SONG OF THE BOWMEN OF SHU. The title was invented by Pound or Fenollosa. In Chinese this is the first of "Two Letters from Chang-kan" (Obata), and is translated from *Li T'ai-po*, III, 4.26*b*–27*a* (Fang).

Pound thought his version "might have been slipped into Browning's work without causing any surprise save by its simplicity and its naive beauty" (*To-Day* [May 1918], 94).

3. *bamboo . . . horse:* "riding on your bamboo horse" (Obata).

4. *blue plums:* "green plums" (Obata). See THE BEAUTIFUL TOILET (l. 1*n*).

5. Japanese *Chōkan* from Chinese *Ch'ang-kan* (Fang), a suburb of Nanking.

8. *laughed:* "could never bare my face" (Obata).

13. Pound's addition, modeled on Shakespeare's line, "To-morrow and to-morrow, and to-morrow" (*Macbeth*, V, v, 19).

14. *Why should I climb:* "I never knew I was to climb the Hill of Wang-fu / And watch for you these many days" (Obata).

16. *Ku-to-yen:* Japanese *Ku-tō-en* from Chinese *Yen-yü-tui,* an island in the river *Ch'ü-t'ang* (Fang); "the Keu-Tang Gorge" (Obata). See line 26*n.*

17. *gone five months:* "the rapids are not passable in May" (Obata). Pound may have misread "the fifth month" as "five months."

23. *August:* "October" (Obata).

26. Japanese *Kiang* from Chinese *Ch'ü-t'ang* (Fang). See line 16*n.*

29. Japanese *Chō-fū-sa* from Chinese *Ch'ang-feng-sha* (Fang), "the long Wind Beach . . . in An-hwei, several hundred miles up the river from Nanking" (Obata).

Footnote: Rihaku is Japanese for Li Po.

RIVER SONG, THE
[NO. 140. PRINTINGS: 27, 40, 42, 43, 55]

See the introductory note to SONG OF THE BOWMEN OF SHU. Following another man's notes, Pound may not have known that in writing THE RIVER SONG he was translating not one but two poems by Li Po. Kenner tells me the conflation occurred because in the notebook that contains the transcript for THE RIVER SONG Fenollosa was in the habit of putting all his text on right-hand pages and keeping the left-hand pages for Mori's comments. Pound mistook a blank leaf opposite the long title of the second poem for mere absence of comment by Mori. Similar conflations occur in *"Noh," or Accomplishment* (1916): as Teele observes (*Comparative Literature* [Fall 1957], 355), the text of *Kakitsubata,* for example, contains extraneous material which Fenollosa probably intended to use in footnotes.

Fang says THE RIVER SONG is made up as follows: lines 1–18 from *Li T'ai-po,* IV, 7.3*b;* lines 19–22 translate the title of another poem that forms lines 23–40; and lines 23–40 are from *Li T'ai-po,* IV, 7.4*a–b.* Both poems are translated in Obata's *The Works of Li Po* (1923, pp. 25, 34–35).

1. *shato:* Japanese *satō* from Chinese *Sha-t'ang* (Fang); "spice-wood" (Obata).

6. Japanese *sennin* from Chinese *hsien-jen* (Fang); "fairy of the air" (Obata). Names such as this have no connotations for the western reader, but in defense of them Pound wrote: "Sennin are the Chinese spirits of nature or of the air. I don't see that they are any worse than Celtic Sidhe" (*Letters,* p. 247) Sennin recur in EXILE'S LETTER (l. 26) and SENNIN POEM BY KAKUHAKU.

9. Japanese *Kutsu* (from Chinese *Chu'ü*) is Ch'ü P'ing or Ch'ü Yüan (Fang: see the note to AFTER CH'U YUAN).

11. Japanese *So* from Chinese *Ch'u*, i.e., the Chu state. Fang thinks Pound misunderstood his crib. Obata has: "The songs of Chu-ping are vanished from the hills."

16. *joy of blue islands:* "my delight is vaster than the sea" (Obata).

18. *Han:* A large tributary of the Yangtse (Obata).

23. *Yei-shu:* Japanese *Ei-shū* from Chinese *Ying-chou* (Fang).

24. *crimson:* "crimson towers" (Obata).

25. *half-blue:* "half-green" (Obata). See THE BEAUTIFUL TOILET (l. 1*n*).

27. *railings:* "pillars" (Obata).

29. *Kwan, Kuan:* Japanese *Ken-k(w)an* from Chinese *Chien-kuan* (Fang), an onomatopoeic imitation of a birdcall.

31. *thousand doors:* "ten thousand doorways" (Obata). The numerical discrepancy occurs again in FOUR POEMS OF DEPARTURE (II, 4*n*).

32. Japanese *Kō* from Chinese *Hao* (Fang). Obata renders the word "Hao-king" and explains that it was a former name for Chang-an, the ancient capital of China.

36. *Hori:* Japanese *Hōrai* from Chinese *P'eng-lai* (Fang), "the Peng-lai garden" (Obata).

37. *Sei:* Japanese *Shi* from Chinese *ch'ih* (Fang), "the garden of Yi-shih" (Obata).

38. *Jo-run:* Japanese *Jō-rin* from Chinese *Shang-lin* (Fang). *new nightingales:* "first songs of nightingales" (Obata).

39–40. "Desiring to mingle their notes with the mouth-organs, / And join the imperial concert of the phoenix-flutes" (Obata).

Footnote: Rihaku is the Japanese form of Li Po (A.D. 701–762), who is the author of many of the poems selected from among the Fenollosa transcripts.

ROME
[NO. 39. PRINTINGS: 9, 42, 43, 55]

The epigraph is from Propertius (*Elegies*, IV, i, 87): "dicam: 'Troia cades, et Troica Roma resurges'" ("I will cry, 'Troy, thou shalt fall, and thou, Trojan Rome, shalt arise

anew!' "—Loeb). Pound uses the motif of a "second Troy" in
PROVINCIA DESERTA (l. 64n).

ROME is a translation from the *Antiquetez de Rome* (1558,
I, iii) of Joachim du Bellay (1522–1560):

> Nouveau venu, qui cherches Rome en Rome
> Et rien de Rome en Rome n'apperçois,
> Ces vieux palais, ces vieux arcz que tu vois,
> Et ces vieux murs, c'est ce que Rome on nomme.

> Voy quel orgueil, quelle ruine: & comme
> Celle qui mist le monde sous ses loix,
> Pour donter tout, se donta quelquefois,
> Et devint proye au temps, qui tout consomme.

> Rome de Rome est le seul monument,
> Et Rome Rome a vaincu seulement.
> Le Tybre seul, qui vers la mer s'enfuit,

> Reste de Rome. O mondaine inconstance!
> Ce qui est ferme, est par le temps destruit,
> Et ce qui fuit, au temps fait resistance.

Among the poems originally rejected from *A Quinzaine for
This Yule* (1908) is one called "Roundel After Joachim du
Bellay" (*A Lume Spento and Other Early Poems* [1965], p.
117). Pound saw Du Bellay as an important figure in the
transference of lyric poetry from Italy to England:

> The Italians . . . had renewed the art [of lyric poetry], they
> had written in Latin, and some little even in Greek, and had
> used the Hellenic meters. DuBellay translated Navgherius
> into French, and Spenser translated DuBellay's adaptations
> into English, and then as in Chaucer's time and times since
> then, the English cribbed their technique from over the
> channel.

Poetry (Jan. 1914), 138. ROME is a particularly useful illus-
tration in this case. Du Bellay's poem is itself a translation of
a Renaissance Latin poem by Giovanni Vitali (reprinted in
Chamard's Du Bellay [1910], vol. 2, pp. 5–6); and Du Bellay's
poem was in turn translated by Edmund Spenser in *The
Ruines of Rome* (*Complaints*, 1591).

[9. that art   9–55;   that are   42, 43;   thou art   *Faber and
      Faber*
      Rome's   9+;   Romes's   *Faber and Faber*]

9. *Rome . . . ornament:* The rhythm is borrowed from Shake-
    speare's first sonnet (l. 9): "Thou that art now the world's
    fresh ornament."

SALUTATION
[NO. 74. PRINTINGS: *16, 17, 39, 40, 42, 43, 55*]

Uncluttered by private property, the fishermen enjoy a peace of mind denied the bourgeoisie. SALUTATION draws on the conventional primitivism of pastoral literature. It was set to music in 1922 by J. C. Holbrooke.

[3. seen fishermen   *16, 39+*;   seen the fishermen   *17*]

SALUTATION THE SECOND
[NO. 75. PRINTINGS: *16, 17, 40, 42, 43, 55*]

3. *twenty years behind the times:* "The London nineties were maintained in New York up to 1915" (*English Journal* [Oct. 1934], 635). On the drawbacks of being "behind the times," Pound has said that "no good poetry is ever written in a manner twenty years old, for to write in such a manner shows conclusively that the writer thinks from books, convention and *cliché,* and not from life" (*Poetry Review* [Feb. 1912], 75).

[8a–c. *The following additional lines appear in* 16–43:

> Watch the reporters spit,
> Watch the anger of the professors,
> Watch how the pretty ladies revile them:]

[9. [*lacking*]   *16–43;*   Observe the irritation in general: *55*]

16. *naked . . . songs:* SALUTATION THE SECOND was published over a year before Yeats's famous poem on the stylistic advantages of "walking naked" ("A Coat"). In FURTHER INSTRUCTIONS the songs are "devoid of clothing."

25. Pound's contempt for the "stupendous vacuity" of the *Spectator* is expressed at length in the *New Age* ([Sept. 6, 1917], 406–407). Eliot's poem "Le Directeur" (first published in the *Little Review* [July 1917], 8) mocks "Le Directeur / Conservateur / Du Spectateur."

27. *make people blush:* Modernists aim to *épater le bourgeois.*

28. *dance of the phallus:* Probably the cordax. Pound contributed to the 1915 *Blast* some verses

> In praise of Monsieur Laurent Tailhade,
> Whose "Poemes Aristophanesques" are
> So-very-odd.
> Let us erect a column and stamp with our feet
> And dance a Zarabondilla and a Kordax . . . (p. 21).

The poem ("Our Respectful Homages to M. Laurent Tail-hade") is now reprinted in the Faber and Faber *Collected Shorter Poems by Ezra Pound* (1968).

29. *Cybele:* An Asiatic fertility goddess.

[31. (Tell it to Mr. Strachey)   *16+;   [lacking]   Faber and Faber]

31. John St. Loe Strachey (1860–1927) was editor of the *Spectator* from 1898 until 1925. "I use him as the type of male prude, somewhere between Tony Comstock and Hen. Van Dyke. Even in America we've nothing that conveys his exact shade of meaning. I've adopted the classic Latin manner in mentioning people by name" (*Letters*, p. 58). Strachey is blasted in *Blast* ([June 20, 1914], 21).

33. *knees:* See ANCORA (l. 13*n*).

[35. go! jangle their door-bells   *16+;   [lacking]   Faber and Faber]

36. *no work:* The songs in FURTHER INSTRUCTIONS are "very idle."

SALUTATION THE THIRD
[NO. 117. PRINTINGS: 23, 55]

In 1927 Wyndham Lewis was still gibing at Pound for having supplied "some nice quiet little poems" in response to a request for "something nasty for *Blast*" (*Time and Western Man*, p. 55; Rose, p. 81). SALUTATION THE THIRD (which Harriet Monroe refused to print) is a fair answer to Lewis' criticisms and quite in the style of *Blast* abuse. The original printing is heavily strewn with capital letters.

2. *gagged reviewers:* Only a few months later the London *Times* was to surprise Pound by printing a favorable review of his *Cathay* (*Letters*, p. 105).

[3. much the   *23;*   much for the   *55*]

[5. These were   *23;*   These are   *55*]

[14. with Jews and Jobbery   *23;*   with pandars and jobbery   *55*]

[15. who fawn on the JEWS for their money,   *23;*   who pat the big bellies for profit,   *55*]

14–15. The antisemitic element, excised in 1926, was to appear again in the *Cantos*.

[16. us out to the pastures.   *23;*   us go out in the air for a bit.   *55*]

16. *thirty:* Pound was twenty-eight when SALUTATION THE
THIRD was published and he regarded the age of thirty as
a turning point in both his life and art (in the original
version of HUGH SELWYN MAUBERLEY, E. P. "passed from
men's memory in *l'an trentiesme / De son eage*"; see also
MIDDLE-AGED). Before this, he had rejected "the saying
'that a lyric poet dies at thirty'" and showed himself more
sympathetic to the idea "that the emotions increase in
vigour as a vigorous man matures" (*New Freewoman*
[Nov. 1, 1913], 195).

[17. Perhaps 23; Or perhaps 55]

[21. with true poets 23; with good writers 55]

[28a–d. *In 23 are the following additional lines:*

And I will laugh at you and mock you,
And I will offer you consolations in irony,
O fools, detesters of Beauty.
I have seen many who go about with supplications,]

[29–31. [*lacking*] 23]

[32. say how 23; say that 55]

[33. [*lacking*] 23]

SALVATIONISTS
[NO. 122. PRINTINGS: 24, 39, 40, 42, 43, 55]

1–2. Reviewing Ford's *Collected Poems* a couple of months
before SALVATIONISTS was published, Pound complained
that "it is impossible to talk about perfection without getting yourself very much disliked" (*Poetry* [June 1914],
112).

4. Latin *rusticus* means "countrified, boorish."

12. *take arms:* "to take arms against a sea of troubles, / And
by opposing end them" (*Hamlet*, III, i, 59–60).

13, 15. *Mumpodorus . . . Nimmim:* Pound was soon to decide
that "one should name names in satire" (see the note
to THE NEW CAKE OF SOAP).

17. Bulmenia is Bloomsbury?

SATIEMUS
[NO. 40. PRINTINGS: 9, 55]

The title alludes to Propertius' *Elegies* (II, xv, 23): "Dum
nos fata sinunt, oculos satiemus amore" ("while the Fates

grant it, let us glut our eyes with love"—Loeb; cf. HOMAGE TO
SEXTUS PROPERTIUS, VII, 16). The Latin forms the title of a
poem by Ernest Dowson which Pound echoes in SATIEMUS. For
similar "answers," see the note to AMITIES.

SATIEMUS was published in *Canzoni* (1911) as the second
of three "Victorian Eclogues." The first is called "Excuses" and
is a complaint by a rejected lover, the third "Abelard" and is a
prayer for a spiritual relationship with a woman; neither poem
is reprinted in *Personæ* (1926).

6. *Sighing:* Dowson writes of "sighing boughs."

8. *crushed lips:* "we shall lie, / Red mouth to mouth" (Dowson).

10. *fair dead:* An image borrowed from THRENOS.

18. *laughter:* Dowson asks the girl to "Cease smiling. . . ."

SEAFARER, THE
[NO. 43. PRINTINGS: *10, 15, 27, 42, 43, 53, 55*]

[*Subtitle:* A Translation from the early Anglo-Saxon text *10;*
From the ———— *15–53;* From the Anglo-Saxon
55]

This Old English poem is included in Pound's various short
lists of essential literary masterpieces because it manifests
what he once called "the English national chemical," meaning
by this phrase "that quality which seems . . . to have trans-
formed the successive arts of poetry that have been brought to
England from the South" (*New Age* [Nov. 14, 1912], 33).
Pound's aim in writing THE SEAFARER was to invent a language
that would be akin in sound and rhythm to Old English and be
at the same time completely intelligible to the modern reader.
It must have become clear to him at an early stage that either
the sound or the sense of the original would have to be sacrificed if the poem were ever to be finished; and by choosing to
duplicate the sound of "The Seafarer" he inevitably antago-
nized readers who value literal accuracy in translations.

When thinking about this poem it helps if one distinguishes
between what are obviously misunderstandings on Pound's part
and what are only apparent misreadings of the text. Among
obvious misunderstandings one can include misconstrued
syntax (as at ll. 12, 40–44, 65–70, 73–77, 89–101) and literal
mistranslations: for example, when Pound translated *læne*
("transitory") as "loan" (67) he probably confused *læne* with
læn; and when he translated *þurh* ("through") as "tomb" (90)
he most certainly misread *þurh* as *þruh* ("coffin"). In a number
of cases, however, Pound seems deliberately to have disre-

garded the literal sense of some Old English words, treating them as units of sound for which modern English homophones might be substituted.

As a result he has given us "reckon" (1) for *wrecan* ("to make, compose"); "stern" (23) for *stearn* ("a tern"), "moan-eth" (37) for *monað* ("makes mindful of, urges"; in l. 51 *gemoniað* is translated literally as "admonisheth"); "berries" (49) for *byrig* (dative of *burh*, "a town"); "twain" (70) for *tweon* ("to doubt"); "mirth" for *mærþo* ("glory"); and "blade" (90) for *blæd* ("glory," translated literally as "blast" in l. 80). This technique can cope not only with single words but also with phrases: *on eorþan* becomes "on earth then" (33; "then" is superfluous); *sumeres weard* ("guardian of summer") becomes "summerward" (55); and *eorþan rices* ("kingdom of the earth") becomes "earthen riches" (83). As well as retaining the sounds of "The Seafarer" in details like these, Pound also gave his poem something of the strangeness of Old English by preserving some of the kennings in literal translation: hence *hreþerloca* ("breast") became "breastlock" (59); *hwæl-weg* ("ocean") became "whale-path" (64; the translation "whale-ways" occurs in another uncollected poem in *Personæ* [1909, p. 35]); *ecghete* ("violence") became "sword-hate" (71); and *flæschoma* ("body") became "flesh-cover" (96). To these he added coinages of his own, such as "hail-scur" (17) for *hægl scurum* ("hail in showers") and "earth-weal" (68) for *eorðwe-lan* ("earthly possessions"). Occasionally the technique results in unnecessary obscurity, as when *nearo nihtwaco* ("on a night-watch full of hardship") is rendered as "narrow night-watch" (7), or *merewerges mod* ("the heart of a man weary with the sea") as "Mere-weary mood" (12); but on the whole the successes outweigh the failures. Pound's methods are inconsistent with the demands of literal translation, but as a means of echoing the sound of the Old English poem they are certainly defensible.

The academic opposition to THE SEAFARER would scarcely have mattered had Pound been content to let his translation stand simply as a free version of the Old English and as a poem in its own right. But he wanted more than that. He wanted it to be an example of " 'The New Method' in Literary Scholarship"—and it was under this heading that the translation first appeared in the *New Age*. A few weeks later he was saying that THE SEAFARER is "as nearly literal, I think, as any translation can be" (*New Age* [Feb. 15, 1912], 369); and in printing such a statement he was clearly inviting hostile criticism.

Appended to the *New Age* text of THE SEAFARER is a "Philological Note" by Pound, which reads:

The text of this poem is rather confused. I have rejected half of line 76 [77], read "Angles" for angels in line 78 [79], and stopped translating before the passage about the soul and the longer lines beginning, "Mickle is the fear of the Almighty [*Micel biþ se Meotudes egsa*], and ending in a dignified but platitudinous address to the Deity: "World's elder, eminent creator, in all ages, amen" [*wuldres Ealdor, / ece Dryhten, in ealle tid. / Amen*]. There are many conjectures as to how the text came into its present form. It seems most likely that a fragment of the original poem, clear through about the first thirty lines, and thereafter increasingly illegible, fell into the hands of a monk with literary ambitions, who filled in the gaps with his own guesses and "improvements." The groundwork may have been a longer narrative poem, but the "lyric," as I have accepted it, divides fairly well into "The Trials of the Sea," its Lure and the Lament for Age.

In this short passage theories picked up from various scholars are synthesized and overlaid with Pound's own opinions. Thus the idea of a "monk with literary ambitions" appears to derive from Kluge; that of a threefold division of the poem from Ehrisman; and that of an *ur-*"Seafarer" from Boer. On the other hand, Pound's stress on the poem's lyric rather than dramatic qualities seems to have anticipated orthodox academic opinion by some ten years.

In a note to *Umbra* (1920) THE SEAFARER shares with EXILE'S LETTER and HOMAGE TO SEXTUS PROPERTIUS the distinction of being a "major persona" (p. 128). Seen in the context of Pound's later work THE SEAFARER is important in that it looks forward to the alliterative style of Canto 1, where the beginning of the *Cantos* is treated as a linguistic problem and represented symbolically in a style that suggests the beginnings of the English language.

The Old English text is reprinted from Sweet's *Anglo-Saxon Reader in Prose and Verse* (1946, pp. 152–155):

```
   Mæg ic be me sylfum    soðgied wrecan,
   siþas secgan,    hu ic geswincdagum
   earfoðhwile    oft þrowade,
   bitre breostceare    gebiden hæbbe,
 5 gecunnad in ceole    cearselda fela,
   atol yþa gewealc.    Þær mec oft bigeat
   nearo nihtwaco    æt nacan stefnan,
   þonne he be clifum cnossað.    Calde geþrungen
   wæron fet mine    forste gebunden,
10 caldum clommum;    þær þa ceare seofedun
   hat[e] ymb heortan;    hungor innan slat
   merewerges mod.    Þæt se mon ne wat,
   þe him on foldan    fægrost limpeð,
   hu ic earmcearig    iscealdne sæ
15 winter wunade    wræccan lastum
   winemægum bidroren    *    *    *
   bihongen hrimgicelum:    hægl scurum fleag.
```

Þær ic ne gehyrde   butan hlimman sæ,
iscaldne wæg,   hwilum ylfete song:
20 dyde ic me to gomene   ganetes hleoþor
and huilpan sweg   fore hleahtor wera,
mæw singende   fore medodrince.
Stormas þær stanclifu beotan,   þær him stear[n] oncwæð
isigfeþera;   ful oft þæt earn bigeal
25 urigfeþra.   Nænig hleomæga
feasceaftig ferð   frefran meahte.
For þon him gelyfeð lyt   se þe ah lifes wyn
gebiden in burgum,   bealosiþa hwon,
wlonc and wingal,   hu ic werig oft
30 in brimlade   bidan sceolde.
Nap nihtscua,   norþan sniwde,
hrim hrusan band;   hægl feol on eorþan,
corna caldast.   For þon cnyssað nu
heortan geþohtas,   þæt ic hean streamas,
35 sealtyþa gelac   sylf cunnige;
monað modes lust   mæla gehwylce
ferð to feran,   þæt ic feor heonan
elþeodigra   eard gesece.
For þon nis þæs modwlonc   mon ofer eorþan,
40 ne his gifena þæs god,   ne in geoguþe to þæs hwæt,
ne in his dædum to þæs deor,   ne him his Dryhten to þæs
    hold,
þæt he a his sæfore   sorge næbbe,
to hwon hine Dryhten   gedon wille.
Ne biþ him to hearpan hyge,   ne to hringþege,
45 ne to wife wyn,   ne to worulde hyht,
ne ymbe owiht elles   nefne ymb yða gewealc;
ac a hafað longunge   se þe on lagu fundað.
Bearwas blostmum nimað,   byrig fægriað,
wongas wlitig[i]að,   woruld onetteð:
50 ealle þa gemoniað   modes fusne
sefan to siðe,   þam þe swa þenceð
on flodwegas   feor gewitan.
Swylce geac monað   geomran reorde,
singeð sumeres weard,   sorge beodeð
55 bittre in breosthord.   Þæt se beorn ne wat,
secg esteadig,   hwæt þa sume dreogað,
þe þa wræclastas   widost lecgað!
For þon nu min hyge hweorfeð   ofer hreþerlocan,
min modsefa   mid mereflode
60 ofer hwæles eþel,   hweorfeð wide
eorþan sceatas,   cymeð eft to me
gifre and grædig;   gielleð anfloga,
hweteð on [h]wælweg   hreþer unwearnum
ofer holma gelagu.
                For þon me hatran sind
65 Dryhtnes dreamas   þonne þis deade lif,
læne on londe: ic gelyfe no
þæt him eorðwelan   ece stondað.
Simle þreora sum   þinga gehwylce

ær his tid aga   to tweon weorþeð:
70 adl oþþe yldo   oþþe ecghete
    fægum fromweardum   feorh oðþringeð.
    For þon þæt [is] eorla gehwam   æftercweþendra
    lof lifgendra,   lastworda betst,
    þæt he gewyrce,   ær he onweg scyle,
75 freme on foldan   wið feonda niþ
    deorum dædum   deofle togeanes,
    þæt hine ælda bearn   æfter hergen
    and his lof siððan   lifge mid englum
    awa to ealdre,   ecan lifes blæd
    dream mid dugeþum!
80   Dagas sind gewitene,
    ealle onmedlan   eorþan rices;
    nearon nu cyningas   ne caseras
    ne goldgiefan,   swylce iu wæron,
    þonne hi mæst mid him   mærþa gefremedon
85 and on dryhtlicestum   dome lifdon:
    gedroren is þeos duguð eal,   dreamas sind gewitene;
    wuniað þa wacran   and þas woruld healdaþ,
    brucað þurh bisgo.   Blæd is gehnæged;
    eorþan indryhto   ealdað and searað
90 swa nu monna gehwylc   geond middangeard:
    yldo him on fareð,   onsyn blacað,
    gomelfeax gnornað,   wat his iuwine,
    æþelinga bearn   eorþan forgiefene.
    Ne mæg him þonne se flæschoma,   þonne him þæt ferog
    losað,
95 ne swete forswelgan   ne sar gefelan
    ne hond onhreran   ne mid hyge þencan.
    Þeah þe græf wille   golde stregan,
    broþor his geborenum   byrgan be deadum
    maþmum mislicum,   þæt hine mid wille:

The Old English poem continues for a further 25 lines in the manuscript, and in an increasingly corrupt state. Modern editors usually terminate the poem at line 108.

6. *sea-surge:* The word reappears in HUGH SELWYN MAUBER-LEY (l. 343*n*).

8. *Coldly afflicted:* On the meter of such lines, see THE RETURN (ll. 17, 20*n*).

[13. lovlieth *10;* loveliest *15+*]

[37. alway *10–27, 53+*; away *42, 43*]

73–80. Sisam comments (*Times Literary Supplement* [June 25, 1954], 409: "So he eliminates the blend of Christian thought which is a main source of difficulty in the general interpretation of *Seafarer,* and makes malice the source of everlasting renown among the English. The Anglo-Saxon poet urges men to fight against the malice of devils, so that their good fame may last for ever with the angels."

17. *hail-scur:* Cf. "snow scur" (Canto 49).

59. *so that . . . burst:* The phrasing is echoed in the opening line of Canto 17: "So that the vines burst from my fingers. . . ."

79. *English:* Old English *engel* means "angel." Pound's rendering refutes (with characteristic Anglophobia) Pope Gregory's observation, "Not *Angli* but *Angeli.*"

82 ff. The elegiac tone of this concluding section is parodied in an uncollected poem called "Et Faim Sallir Le Loup Des Boys," where Pound describes the Villonesque rigors of the avant-garde life: "Cowardly editors threaten, / Friends fall off at the pinch, the loveliest die" (*Blast* [July 1915], 22).

84. *Caesar:* Old English *caseras* ("emperors"). The scholar in Pound here acknowledges the presence of a loanword.

[90. layed   10, 15, 42+;   laid   27]

92. *earth's gait:* Old English *middangeard* ("earth"). The word "Middan-gard" appears in one of Pound's uncollected poems and is glossed by him as "Anglo Saxon 'Earth'" (*Personæ* [1909], p. 35).

95. *Lordly men . . . o'ergiven:* The whole line is introduced into Canto 74 as Pound recollects the death of the "lordly men" he has known in the literary world—F. M. Ford, W. B. Yeats, James Joyce, Henry James, etc.

96. *flesh-cover:* Old English *flæschoma* ("body"). Pound had earlier used the word "body-house" in an uncollected poem called "An Idyll for Glaucus" (*Personæ* [1909], p. 37).

SEEING EYE, THE
[NO. 123. PRINTINGS: 24, 40, 42, 43, 55]

What Pound means by the title is explained in a passage describing his American forefathers and their friends: "When I say they hadn't the 'seein' eye' I mean that they never succeeded in conveying the visual appearance of any one of their characters as distinct from any other. There was an almost complete lack of detail" (*New Age* [July 15, 1920], 173). MEDITATIO has a similar theme to THE SEEING EYE.

8. *Tsin-Tsu:* Probably an invented name (Fang).

SENNIN POEM BY KAKUHAKU
[NO. 157. PRINTINGS: *36, 39, 40, 42, 43, 55*]

[TITLE: Sennin Poem *36;* Sennin Poem by Kakuhaku *39+*]

See the introductory note to SONG OF THE BOWMEN OF SHU. SENNIN POEM BY KAKUHAKU is translated from *Wen-hsüan,* XI, 21.28*a* (Fang). The "sennin" are introduced into the poem by Pound and defended in THE RIVER SONG (l. 6*n*). *Kakuhaku* is Japanese for Kuo P'u, a Chinese poet who died in A.D. 324 (Fang).

[11. looks on *36–43;* looks at *55*]

[*Footnote:* Name of a Sennin. Sennin—an air spirit. *36;* ———— a sennin. *39+*]

SESTINA: ALTAFORTE
[NO. 20. PRINTINGS: *4, 6, 8, 53, 55*]

On the genesis of this poem Pound has written:

I had had De Born in my mind. I had found him untranslatable. Then it occurred to me that I might present him in this manner. I wanted the curious involution and recurrence of the Sestina. I knew more or less of the arrangement. I wrote the first strophe and then went to the Museum to make sure of the right order of the permutations. . . . I did the rest of the poem at a sitting. Technically it is one of my best, though a poem on such a theme could never be very important.

T. P.'s Weekly (June 6, 1913), 707. The poem is very similar in tone (and occasionally in phrasing) to Lionel Johnson's "Enthusiasts."

The reputation of SESTINA: ALTAFORTE is already legendary. It was with this poem—known colloquially as "The Bloody Sestina"—that Pound made his debut with the T. E. Hulme group on the twenty-second of April 1909, and four years later F. S. Flint still remembered the Marinettilike rendering and "the excitement with which the diners on the other side of our screen heard [Pound] declaim the 'Sestina: Altaforte'. . . how the table shook and the decanters and cutlery vibrated in resonance with his voice" (*Poetry and Drama* [March 1913], 61). Pound has himself recalled how, when he wanted to impress the young sculptor Henri Gaudier-Brzeska, he "opened fire with 'Altaforte,' 'Piere Vidal,' and such poems as I had written when about his own age. And I think it was the 'Altaforte' that convinced him that I would do to be sculpted" (*Gaudier-Brzeska* [1916], p. 47; *Letters*, p. 65). A rather different view of the matter is given in the *Autobiography* (1935) of John Cournos, who introduced Pound to Gaudier:

> In his room in Church Walk, Kensington, Ezra picked up one of his poems and read it aloud to us. When Gaudier and I left, the sculptor was enthusiastic because Ezra had dared to use the word "piss" in a poem. When I told this to Ezra, he was delighted; actually, however, Ezra did not use the word in his poem, but some other quite innocent word which had a similar sound! (p. 260).

The outcome of this creative misunderstanding (Pound's pronunciation of the word "peace" reverberating in the Frenchman's ears) was the celebrated phallic effigy of Pound which is referred to in MŒURS CONTEMPORAINES (VIII, 13*n*).

In *The Spirit of Romance* (1910) Pound describes "the sestina form invented by Arnaut Daniel" as "a form like a thin sheet of flame folding and infolding upon itself" (p. 18). There is an uncollected "Sestina for Isolt" in *Exultations* (1909, pp. 23–24) and an uncollected translation in *Canzoni* (1911, pp. 25–27) of "The Golden Sestina" by Pico della Mirandola.

Epigraph: Latin *loquitur* means "he speaks"; *en* is Provençal for "lord," and *eccovi* Italian for "here you are." On Bertran de Born, see the note to "DOMPNA POIS DE ME NO'US CAL"; on Dante, NEAR PERIGORD (ll. 163–168); on Altaforte, NA AUDIART (l. 31*n*); on Papiols, NEAR PERIGORD (ll. 69–70*n*); on the Leopard, NEAR PERIGORD (l. 133*n*).

1. CINO has a similarly Browningesque opening.

4. Adapted from the opening lines of a poem by Bertran (ed. Thomas [1888], p. 49):

> Quan vei pels vergiers desplejar
> Los sendatz grocs, indis e blaus. . . .

Pound's translation in *The Spirit of Romance* (1910): "When I see spread through the gardens / The standards yellow and indigo and blue" (p. 41).

14. *destriers:* War-horses.

21–22. The lines ought to be reversed, as the rhyme pattern in the fourth stanza of a sestina is ECBFAD, not ECFBAD.

25–28. The sentiment derives from Bertran's lines (*op. cit.*, p. 134):

> Que nuls om non es re prezatz
> Tro qu'a maintz colps pres e donatz.

("For no man is worth a damn till he has taken and given many a blow"—*The Spirit of Romance* [1910], p. 43.)

35. *charges 'gainst "The Leopard's":* Bertran was reputedly the instigator of the Limousin League against Richard, and wrote several poems urging other barons to join him. See the introductory note to PLANH FOR THE YOUNG ENGLISH KING.

37–39. The *envoi* of a sestina is supposed to contain all the rhyme words. Pound omits "opposing" and "rejoicing."

[39. alway   4+;   always   *Faber and Faber*]

SHOP GIRL
[NO. 151. PRINTINGS: *31, 35, 39, 40, 42, 43, 55*]

2. *blown:* Pound uses the same word of the lady in THE GARDEN.

3. A. C. Swinburne (1837–1909) shocked his contemporaries with poems like "Dolores."

4. *shepherdess . . . Guido:* A *pastourelle* by Guido Cavalcanti (1250–1300) begins: "In un boschetto trovai pastorella" ("In wood-way found I once a shepherdess"—*Sonnets . . . of . . . Cavalcanti* [1912], pp. 114–117).

5. Pound may be alluding to the poem by Charles Baudelaire (1821–1867) called "Confession":

> Une fois, une seule, aimable et douce femme,
>   A mon bras votre bras poli
> S'appuya (sur le fond ténébreux de mon âme
>   Ce souvenir n'est point pâli).

SILET
[NO. 49. PRINTINGS: *13, 15, 42, 43, 53, 55*]

[TITLE: Silet   *13, 15, 53*+;   [*lacking*]   *42, 43*]

The Latin *silet* means "he is silent." In *The Spirit of Romance* (1910, p. 237) Pound quotes the last line of a poem by Andrea Navagero (1483–1529): "Sed veteri obstrictus religione, silet" ("held from [by?] the older cult, he doth not speak"—Pound's translation). In this line, he writes, "*silet* suggests the *silentes anni* of the Pythagorean disciples" (*ibid.*, p. 238).

[2. well-a-way *13*; well-away *15+*]

2. *deathless pen:* Cf. "deathless voice" ("PHASELLUS ILLE").

8. *harsh northwindish time:* In *The Spirit of Romance* (1910) Pound asks the reader to consider Arnaut Daniel's line, "Al brieu brisaral temps braus," and notice "how unmistakably the mere sound suggests that 'harsh north-windish time'" (p. 31).

[12. Time hath *13*; Time has *15+*]

[*Footnote:* [*lacking*] *13–43*; Verona 1911 *53+*]

SIMULACRA
[NO. 93. PRINTINGS: 20, 39, 40, 42, 43, 55]

Simulacra is Latin for "images." Self-contained and enigmatic, each of these is an example of the nucleus from which the imagist derives his poems, the "luminous detail" to be presented without comment (*New Age* [Dec. 7, 1911], 130).

2. *Swinburne:* Cf. SHOP GIRL (l. 3*n*).

2, 5. The location is London.

[5. handsome prostitute approach 20; handsome young woman approach *39+*]

5. The alteration was made probably at the request of the publisher Elkin Mathews, who was troubled by the impropriety of several of the poems in *Lustra* (see the note to COITUS). The original reading has never been restored.

SOCIAL ORDER, THE
[NO. 146. PRINTINGS: 28, 39, 40, 42, 43, 55]

Stylistically, this poem anticipates MŒURS CONTEMPORAINES.

12. *Avernus:* A lake in Campania, once regarded as the entrance to the infernal regions.

SOCIETY
[NO. 105. PRINTINGS: 22, 39, 40, 42, 43, 55]

There is a similar protest in Canto 14 against the implicit prostitution of the *mariage de convenance:* among the perverters of language and those who are driven by lust for money one finds "sadic mothers driving their daughters to bed with decrepitude." In COMMISSION Pound communicates to "the bought wife" his "contempt of oppressors."

The Latin personal names are to remind the reader that SOCIETY is written in the manner of the Roman epigram (cf. THE TEMPERAMENTS).

SONG OF THE BOWMEN OF SHU
[NO. 141. PRINTINGS: 27, 39, 40, 42, 43, 55]

In 1928 Eliot acclaimed Pound as "the inventor of Chinese poetry for our time" (*Selected Poems*, p. xvi), basing his judgment on the poems printed in *Cathay* (1915). Pound received no formal instruction in the Chinese language, and would never have produced *Cathay* but for acquiring the unpublished papers of the sinologist Ernest Fenollosa, who had been engaged in translating Chinese literature shortly before he died in September 1908. Pound never met Fenollosa. In 1912, however, he was introduced to Mary Fenollosa who was in London for the Heinemann publication in October of her husband's *Epochs of Chinese and Japanese Art*. Mrs. Fenollosa herself published *Blossoms from a Japanese Garden: a Book of Child Verses* (1913), but could make nothing of the extremely rough notes on Chinese poetry that Fenollosa had made purely for his own use in the course of sessions with Mori and other tutors. Pound "was so enthusiastic about Fenollosa's literary researches that Mrs. Fenollosa promised, on her return to America, to send him whatever translations and notes she had" (Chisolm, p. 222). In this way Pound became Fenollosa's literary executor and gained possession of the manuscripts toward the end of 1913 (*Letters*, p. 65).

For a time it seemed to him that the Fenollosa papers would have a seminal influence on English poetry. "Liu Ch'e, Chu Yuan, Chia I, and the great *vers libre* writers before the Petrarchan age of Li Po," he wrote, "are a treasury to which the next century may look for as great a stimulus as the renaissance had from the Greeks" (*Poetry* [Feb. 1915], 233). He worked on the Fenollosa papers throughout 1914 and the following year, producing the poems selected for *Cathay* (1915) after he had finished the plays in *"Noh," or Accomplishment* (1916) that Yeats found so interesting. By 1916, however, he had already begun work on the *Cantos*, and his creative interest in Chinese poetry dwindled; what had promised in 1913 to be a totally new departure—possibly a second renaissance (see p. 17 above)—became in retrospect simply his *Cathay* period.

In assembling his translations Fenollosa made use of cribs prepared by two Japanese scholars, Mori and Ariga, and this is why the proper nouns in *Cathay* are given not in Chinese but in Japanese transliterations.

SONG OF THE BOWMEN OF SHU is a version of *Mao-Shih*, II, 9.8*a* (Fang) which Legge had translated in 1871 in *The Chinese Classics* (vol. 4, part 2, pp. 258–261); Waley's version appears in *The Book of Songs* (1937, p. 122). Chisolm reprints "Fenollosa's Literal Version as Taken from His Notes" (p. 252). Pound was to return to this poem forty years later and produce a new version that takes as its starting point the nursery rhyme beginning "Pat-a-cake, pat-a-cake, baker's man" (*Classic Anthology* [1954], pp. 86–87):

> Pick a fern, pick a fern, ferns are high,
> "Home," I'll say: home, the year's gone by,
> no house, no roof, these huns on the hoof.
> Work, work, work, that's how it runs,
> We are here because of these huns. . . .

The *Cathay* version was set to music in 1923 by Granville Bantock. *Shu* (Legge's "Chow") is the modern state of Ssu-chuan.

3. *Ken-nin:* Japanese *Ken-in* from Chinese *Hsien-yün* (Fang). Legge transliterates the word as "Hëen-yun" and translates it as "wild tribes." He also equates it with the modern English sense of "Huns" (p. 259), a reading that Pound incorporated into his later version of the poem.

13. *flower:* In a line Pound omits here (but includes in his *Classic Anthology* version) "the cherry flower" is specified.

17. *horses . . . tired:* "Those four horses are tied" (Fenollosa), "the four steeds are strong" (Legge).

19. *fish-skin:* "seal-skin" (Legge).

[*Footnote:* By Kutsugen. / 4th Century B.C. 27; By Bunno. / Very early 39, 40; By Bunno / Reputedly 1100 B.C. 42+]

Bunnō is Japanese for Chinese *Wen-Wang*, "King Wen of the Chou dynasty" (Fang).

SONG OF THE DEGREES, A
[NO. 85. PRINTINGS: 18, 19, 39, 40, 42, 43, 55]

[TITLE: [*untitled sections III–V of "Xenia"*] 18; Convictions 19; A Song of the Degrees 39+]

Psalms 120–134 in the King James Bible are subtitled "A Song of Degrees," but the exact meaning of this phrase is uncertain. A SONG OF THE DEGREES was originally the middle of a poem in seven parts called "Xenia" after the *Xenien* ("epigrams") by Goethe and Schiller in their *Musenalmanach* (1796). The first two sections have never been reprinted by Pound, and read as follows:

I. *The Street in Soho*
Out of the overhanging gray mist
There came an ugly little man
Carrying beautiful flowers.

II.
The cool fingers of science delight me;
For they are cool with sympathy,
There is nothing of fever about them.

Poetry (Nov. 1913), 58–59. The original sixth section is now ITÉ and the seventh DUM CAPITOLIUM SCANDET. The "degrees" in "Xenia" are easily discernible as Pound progresses from the "gray mist" of the canceled first section to the sunlight of DUM CAPITOLIUM SCANDET, from an art of shadowy evocation ("the crepuscular spirit") to an art of clearly defined contours; but by 1916 Pound had cut and rearranged the text of "Xenia" in the form it takes in *Personæ* (1926), and the reference to degrees was obscured. What happened here is symptomatic of what was to happen later to the early Cantos, which are much more obscure in their present revised state than they were in 1917 when published in *Poetry*.

Richard Aldington parodied the opening five lines of A SONG OF THE DEGREES:

> Rest me with mushrooms,
> For I think the steak is evil.
>
> The wind moves over the wheat
> With a silver crashing,
> A thin war of delicate kettles.

Pound approved of Aldington's parodies (FURTHER INSTRUCTIONS, l. 1*n*) and also wrote his own (Chicago MSS, April 1913):

> Come, mix yourself a hot julep
> For I think the soup is colder.

Parody, he adds, should be based "not on a general impression but on minute analysis of some particular detail" (*ibid.*).

1. *Chinese colours:* See FURTHER INSTRUCTIONS (ll. 17–18*n*).

2. *glass is evil:* A looking glass mercilessly records changes in a world subject to time. Selected aesthetic experiences— Chinese colors, sunlight on stone—are in some ways compensatory for this.

3–4. *wheat . . . silver crashing:* The image derives from THE ALCHEMIST (l. 15).

6–8. *I have known . . . seen . . . known:* This was later to be the main structural device of PROVINCIA DESERTA.

8. *stone-bright:* See HUGH SELWYN MAUBERLEY (ll. 29–32*n*).

15. *two-faced:* A pun an "amber" and the Latin *ambo* ("two together").

SOUTH-FOLK IN COLD COUNTRY
[NO. 142. PRINTINGS: 27, 39, 40, 42, 43, 55]

See the introductory note to SONG OF THE BOWMEN OF SHU. SOUTH-FOLK IN COLD COUNTRY is translated from *Li T'ai-po,* II, 2.6*b* (Fang), and Pound admired it because it contains "no mellifluous circumlocution, no sentimentalizing of men who have never seen a battlefield and who wouldn't fight if they had to. You have war, campaigning as it has always been, tragedy, hardship, no illusions" (*To-Day* [April 1918], 57). In general, Pound seems to have shared Yeats's distaste for war poems (Chicago MSS).

There is a musical setting of Pound's version by Granville Bantock.

1. Japanese *Dai* and *Etsu* from Chinese *Tai* and *Yueh* (Fang). "The writer expects his hearers to know that Dai and Etsu are in the south," says Pound in his note on this poem (*To-Day* [April 1918], 56); but Lee and Murray point out that *Dai* means "north" and *Etsu* "south."

2. Japanese *En* from Chinese *Yen* (Fang).

9–10. Shortly before SOUTH-FOLK IN COLD COUNTRY was published for the first time in *Cathay,* Pound quoted lines 8–14 in a review article. Lines 9–10 in this earlier draft read:

> Our mind is on getting forward the feather-silk banners.
> Hard fighting gets no reward.

Egoist (Jan. 1, 1915), 11.

12. *Rishogu:* Japanese *Rishōgun* from Chinese *chiang-chun,* which "alludes to the nickname . . . 'The Winged General,' that Li Kuang of Han obtained from Hsiung-nu; 'General Rishogu[n]' may be improved by substituting 'General Rikō' " (Fang).

SPEECH FOR PSYCHE IN THE GOLDEN BOOK OF APULEIUS
[NO. 41. PRINTINGS: 9, 55]

Lucius Apuleius' *Golden Ass* (2nd century A.D.) contains a long digression which describes Psyche's affair with Cupid (IV,

28–VI, 24; cf. *The Spirit of Romance* [1910], pp. 7–10). Because Psyche was mortal, the divine Cupid had to remain invisible even when making love to her; this gave Pound the subject of his poem.

Pater, who translated the story of Cupid and Psyche as the fifth chapter of *Marius the Epicurean*, was the first to speak of Apuleius' romance as a "Golden Book," the term having been reserved previously for Marcus Aurelius' *Meditations* (Frean, p. 106). By the 1890s any admired book was likely to be styled a Golden Book: this was how George Moore described Gautier's *Mademoiselle de Maupin* and Wilde Pater's *Renaissance*. The title Pound chose for his poem suggests that he approached the "scurrilous, bejewelled prose" of Apuleius by way of Pater (*The Spirit of Romance* [1910], p. 10). It is also worth noting that SPEECH FOR PSYCHE IN THE GOLDEN BOOK OF APULEIUS usually accompanies "BLANDULA, TENULLA, VAGULA," the title of which echoes a chapter heading in *Marius the Epicurean*. The two poems may have been written as marginalia on Pater's book (another Paterian motif appears in COITUS).

1–2. *as the wind . . . he lay:* Pound has imagined Cupid in terms of the "gentle Zephyrus" who transports Psyche from the mountain to Cupid's palace in the valley (*Golden Ass*, IV, 35). A passage on sexual initiation in Canto 47 similarly emphasizes the lightness and deftness of the lover:

> By prong have I entered these hills:
> That the grass grow from my body,
> That I hear the roots speaking together,
> The air is new on my leaf,
> The forked boughs shake with the wind.
> Is Zephyrus more light on the bough, Apeliota
> more light on the almond branch?

SPRING, THE
[NO. 133. PRINTINGS: 26, 39, 40, 42, 43, 55]

[*Epigraph:* [*lacking*]   26–43]

Ibycus was a Greek lyric poet of the sixth century B.C. THE SPRING is a version of the first of his poems, the opening line of which Pound uses as an epigraph:

> Ἦρι μὲν αἵ τε Κυδώνιαι
> μαλίδες ἀρδόμεναι ῥοᾶν
> ἐκποτάμων ἵνα Παρθένων
> κᾶπος ἀκήρατος, αἵ τ' οἰνανθίδες
> αὐξόμεναι σκιέροισιν ὑφ' ἔρνεσιν
> οἰναρέοις θαλέθοισιν· ἐμοὶ δ' Ἔρος

οὐδεμίαν κατάκοιτος ὥραν,
<ἀλλ' ἅ >θ' ὑπὸ στεροπᾶς φλέγων
Θρηίκιος Βορέας ἀΐσσων
παρὰ Κύπριδος ἀζαλέαις μανίαισιν ἐρεμνὸς ἀθαμβὴς
ἐγκρατέως πέδοθεν σαλάσσει
ἀμετέρας φρένας.

(" 'Tis but in Spring the quince-trees of the Maids' holy garden grow green with the watering rills from the river, and the vine-blossoms wax 'neath the mantling sprays of the vines; but for me Love's awake the year round, and like the Northwind from Thrace aflame with the lightning, comes with a rush from the Cyprian, with shrivelling frenzies baleful and bold, and with masterful power shakes me to the bottom of my heart"—Loeb.) The opening line of the Greek reappears in Canto 39.

Ibycus' lyric was among those Arnoldian touchstones by means of which Pound assessed literary excellence: "If a man knew Villon and the *Sea-farer* and Dante, and that one scrap of Ibycus, he would, I think, never be able to be content with . . . pretentious and decorated verse" (*Poetry* [Feb. 1915], 230). He also seems to have thought of Ibycus as a fellow imagist (see the note to LIU CH'E).

1. Cydonia (Κυδωνία) was the name of a Cretan town after which the quince (κυδών) was named.

[2. Maelids   26–40, 55;   Meliads   42, 43]

2. The Greek word μελιαδής means "honey-sweet." The correct spelling "Meliads" is probably due to John Quinn's editorial vigilance; Pound seems to prefer "Maelids," the form that occurs again in Canto 3.

3. *Thrace:* The land to the northeast of Greece.

5. *bright tips:* The phrase recurs in HOMAGE TO SEXTUS PROPERTIUS (III, 5).

9. *black lightning:* Synaesthesia is a symbolist mannerism usually avoided by Pound, who two years before writing THE SPRING had advised young poets not to "mess up the perception of one sense by trying to define it in terms of another. This is usually only the result of being too lazy to find the exact word. To this clause there are possibly exceptions" (*Poetry* [March 1913], 206). Among the exceptions was Yeats's line, "Under a bitter black wind that blows from the left hand," which Pound had commended in *The Spirit of Romance* (1910), the word "black" here being considered an epithet of " 'emotional apparition,' transensuous, suggestive" (p. 167). Other examples of synaesthesia occur in HOMAGE TO SEXTUS PROPERTIUS (IX, 4) and PROVINCIA

DESERTA (l. 32). Despite his strictures on this subject, some of Pound's most characteristic ideas are modes of synaesthesia (*melopœia* and *phanopœia*, for example). An important section of the *Cantos* derives from Pound's almost Ruskinian ability to "tell the bank-rate and component of tolerance for usury . . . by the quality of *line* in painting" (*Letters*, p. 397).

10. *last . . . lost:* Other examples of consonance are listed in HUGH SELWYN MAUBERLEY (l. 90n).

STUDY IN AESTHETICS, THE
[NO. 124. PRINTINGS: 24, 32, 39, 40, 42, 43, 55]

5. The Italian phrase means "Look! Hey, look! She's beautiful!"

8. *Sirmione:* A town on the Lago di Garda in northern Italy, the "Sirmio" of "BLANDULA, TENULLA, VAGULA" (l. 5n).

12. The city of Brescia is to the west of the Lago di Garda.

14. *getting in both of their ways:* In the *Metamorphoses* Ovid describes how Icarus made a nuisance of himself while his father was constructing a pair of wings: "lusuque suo mirabile patris / impediebat opus" (VIII, 199–200). Pound mentions this passage in *The Spirit of Romance* (1910) and translates: "and with his play hinders the wonderful work of his father" (p. 6). In 1917 he returned to the same passage, this time rendering the lines as "Getting in both of their ways," and commenting: "My plagiarism was from life and not from Ovid" (*Egoist* [Nov. 1917], 155).

15. The Italian *sta fermo* means "keep quiet, be still."

22. LES MILLWIN ends in a similarly inconsequential manner.

SUB MARE
[NO. 47. PRINTINGS: 12, 15, 42, 43, 53, 55]

Sub mare is Latin for "under the sea." The poem attempts to evoke the indefinable turmoil of love.

6. *Algæ:* A favorite image, used again in COMMISSION and Canto 2. The eurhythmic movements of underwater plants is a dominant motif in art nouveau. The foetal imagery of HUGH SELWYN MAUBERLEY similarly derives from what Schmutzler calls the "biological Romanticism" of art nouveau, the expression of nostalgia for an interuterine stage of life.

7. The words are probably arranged so as to evoke a specific movement in the water (cf. MŒURS CONTEMPORAINES, VI, 4n).

SURGIT FAMA
[NO. 86. PRINTINGS: *18, 19, 39, 40, 42, 43, 55*]

[*Subtitle:* Fragment from an unwritable play   *18*;   [*lacking*] *19+*]

The Latin *surgit fama* means "there is a rumor." Pound's interest in classical literature was not limited to an appreciation of its technical resources. Finding Christianity excessively prohibitive and life-denying, he was attracted by what he considered to be the healthier and saner paganism of ancient Greece. The transition from one to the other appears in a canceled poem called "Printemps," where he invites his songs to

> subvert the established churches,
> And say to that bald-headed djinn Gehovah
> That we will take no more of his nonsense,
> For we have seen the fair meadows,
> We have seen the old gods at their furrow
> And the peach-trees in magical blossom,
> What else can possibly matter!

Chicago MSS. "Jehoveh is a swine," he added in an accompanying letter to Harriet Monroe, "a low grade anthropomorphic deity invented by the most loathsome of semites . . . America needs some definitely pagan publication" (Chicago MSS, July 8, 1914). This is why so many of his poems affirm the survival of the pagan deities and pagan concepts that Christianity is supposed to have supplanted: see ANCORA, BEFORE SLEEP, COITUS, PAN IS DEAD, THE RETURN, and his comments on Renaissance paganism in the closing chapter of *The Spirit of Romance* (1910). This whoring after strange gods may have been stimulated by the neopaganism of D'Albert in Gautier's *Mademoiselle de Maupin* (1835).

In SURGIT FAMA Pound writes as though the pagan gods are still discernible to those who take the trouble to look for them, which is one of the themes of Canto 3:

> Gods float in the azure air,
> Bright gods and Tuscan, back before dew was shed.
> Light: and the first light, before ever dew was fallen.
> Panisks, and from the oak, dryas,
> And from the apple, maelid,
>> Through all the wood, and the leaves are full of voices. . . .

[1. is a truce   *18, 39+*;   is truce   *19*]

2. *Kore:* Greek κόρε means "virgin." Pound gave a conventional explanation of the name when glossing an uncollected poem

called "Canzon: the Yearly Slain" (an answer to Frederick
Manning's "Koré"): "The name 'Korè' or 'the Maiden' is
especially used of Persephone with regard to her being
stolen by Lord of Dis and thereby causing the death of summer" (*English Review* [Jan. 1910], 194).

4. *russet mantle:* Borrowed from *Hamlet* (I, i, 166*f*):

> But, look, the morn in russet mantle clad,
> Walks o'er the dew of yon high eastern hill.

"When Shakespeare talks of the 'Dawn in russet mantle
clad' he presents something which the painter does not
present. There is in this line of his nothing that one can
call description; he presents" (*Poetry* [March 1913], 203).

5. *Leuconoë:* The girl appears in Horace (*Odes*, I, xi, 2).

8. *Hermes:* Mercury, the messenger and herald of the gods.

15. *do thou:* Translators' jargon, as used in PRAYER FOR HIS
LADY'S LIFE.

16. *Delos:* One of the Cyclades islands in the Aegean, the
birthplace of Apollo and Artemis.

altar a-quiver: A sign that the deity is approaching (Callimachus, *Hymns*, II, 1–2).

TAME CAT
[NO. 94. PRINTINGS: 20, 39, 40, 42, 43, 55]

TAME CAT was set to music in 1923 by J. C. Holbrooke.

1. An example of those "perfectly plain statements" with
which Pound was experimenting in the *Lustra* volume (TO
A FRIEND WRITING ON CABARET DANCERS, ll. 24–25*n*). In
this case the model was provided by the twelfth-century
Provençal poet Arnaut Daniel: "Daniel has moments of
simplicity. 'Pensar de lieis m'es repaus'—'It rests me to
think of her.' You cannot get statement simpler than that,
or clearer, or less rhetorical" (*New Age* [Feb. 15, 1912],
370; the Provençal reappears in Canto 91). Other experiments in simplicity are noted in HOMAGE TO QUINTUS
SEPTIMIUS FLORENTIS CHRISTIANUS (III, 4*n*).

6. *antennæ:* The image is borrowed from Gourmont's *Lettres
à l'Amazone* (1914, p. 101) and recurs in PIERROTS.

TEA SHOP, THE
[NO. 152. PRINTINGS: 31, 35, 39, 40, 42, 43, 55]

Sending the poem to Harriet Monroe, Pound explained that
he had tried to express in it that "peculiar combination of

sensuality and sentimentality to which we grossly apply the term 'post-Victorian'" (Chicago MSS, Dec. 3, 1912). This is why he suggested to A. C. Henderson that THE TEA SHOP should be subtitled, "A poem still touched with Victorian Sentimentality" (Chicago MSS, April 1913). The poem was set to music in 1923 by J. C. Holbrooke.

4–6. Pound originally had the following lines between lines four and six (five was lacking):

> And this teaches me
> Or at least draws my mind toward
> The thought here following,
> To wit:
>
> Not only do the lights of love
> Go dim with the years sliding by us,
> But even these incidental girls,
> To whom we have not spoken,
> Lose their gay grace.

Chicago MSS (canceled before publication).

5. *middle-aged:* See the note on MIDDLE-AGED.

[8. She will spread   *31, 35;*   Will be spread   *39+*]

8. Pound's revision is rhythmically an improvement, although it ignores Fenollosan doctrine on the inferiority of passive constructions and intransitive verbs.
After line eight, the poem originally went on:

> They will have just that slight stiffness
>   in moving
> Which tells that the sap of youth
>   is drying.
>
> They will turn middle-aged
>
> And in them we shall find a constant
>   reminder
>
> That she, whom we most desire,
> Turns also her face toward the winter.

Chicago MSS (canceled before publication).

TEMPERAMENTS, THE
[NO. 170. PRINTINGS: *43, 55*]

1–2. Enumeration for ironic effect is a technique Pound learned from Martial (*Epigrams,* VI, viii):

> Praetores duo, quattuor tribuni,
> septem causidici, decem poetae

cuiusdam modo nuptias petebant
a quodam sene.

("Two praetors, four tribunes, seven lawyers, ten poets,
lately sued a certain old man for the hand of a certain maid"—Loeb.) The same device is used in THE
BELLAIRES.

2, 5. *Florialis . . . Bastidides:* Unidentified. "Bastidides is
such a perfect portrait of a certain distinguished author
who wouldn't recognize it, that I should greatly regret
not giving it, sometime, to the light of day" (*Letters*, p.
100).

[4–5. he is held to be both ——— nothing but   43;   he
passes for both ——— nothing save   55]

TEMPORA
[NO. 106. PRINTINGS: *22, 39, 40, 42, 43, 55*]

The Latin *tempora* means "the times," and Pound may be
alluding (as in Canto 76) to Cicero's first Catiline oration (I,
i, 2): "O tempora, o mores!" ("What an age! What morals!"
—Loeb).

1. *Io:* Greek ἰώ (an exclamation).

Tamuz: Thamuz, the Syrian equivalent of Adonis.

2. *Dryad:* Pound's nickname for "H. D.," Hilda Doolittle
(1886–1961), a contemporary of his at the University of
Pennsylvania who married Richard Aldington and contributed to *Des Imagistes* (1914). Pound wrote several
poems for her, some of them love poems, which are collected in the unpublished *Hilda's Book* now in Harvard
University Library.

5. That is, she is not offering him what Venus offered Adonis.

8. By the time TEMPORA was published, Pound's opinion in
literary matters was respected by editors of various little
magazines: hence the girl's interest in him.

TENZONE
[NO. 76. PRINTINGS: *16, 17, 39, 40, 42, 43, 55*]

The Italian *tenzone* derives from Provençal *tenson,* the
technical term for a contention in verse between rival troubadours. It is a borrowing that points to the transference of poetic
technique from Provence to Italy (*Poetry* [Jan. 1914], 138).
Lustra was a new departure from Pound's early work. This

explains the programmatic quality of TENZONE, which in April 1913 introduced readers of *Poetry* to a selection of poems in the new style. It is typical of the *Lustra* manner in that it uses a façade of arrogant indifference toward the reader in order to protect a statement of personal values at once vulnerable and precious. Pound's abusiveness is frequently brought to the defense of lyric prettiness.

3. *centaur:* "Poetry is a centaur" insofar as it "must move and leap with the energizing, sentient, musical faculties" (*New Freewoman* [Nov. 1913], 195).

[6. the truth *16, 17;* the verisimilitudes *39+*]

THREE POETS, THE
[NO. 166. PRINTINGS: *38, 39, 40, 42, 43, 55*]

A parable illustrating the kind of poetry Pound most admired at the time of writing *Lustra*.

THRENOS
[NO. 11. PRINTINGS: *1, 9, 55*]

Shakespeare's *The Phoenix and Turtle* concludes with a *threnos* or "dirge" (Greek θρῆνος).

1. *us:* Probably Tristram and Iseult.

[6. whirred the *1;* whirred in the *9+*]

18. *Tintagoel:* Tintagel is a castle on the north coast of Cornwall associated with the Arthurian legend. The same unusual spelling (not recorded in Ackerman's *Index to Arthurian Names*) occurs also in an uncollected poem called "Li Bel Chasteus" (*A Lume Spento* [1908], p. 31).

3. *fair dead:* The phrase recurs in SATIEMUS.

12. *wine . . . lips:* A Swinburnian image.

TO A FRIEND WRITING ON CABARET DANCERS
[NO. 169. PRINTINGS: *39, 40, 42, 43, 55*]

The friend is Hermann Hagedorn (1882–1964), who later became known for his biographical studies of Theodore Roosevelt. The Latin *vir quidam* means "a certain man," and the line of verse Pound quotes is the opening of Hagedorn's sonnet, "The Cabaret Dancer" (*Poetry* [Dec. 1915], 125).

1. *Hedgethorn:* German *Hagedorn* is usually translated as "hawthorn."

9. *Pepita:* Pound possibly got the name from the famous Spanish dancer Pepita Oliva (d. 1871), whose liaison with Lionel Sackville-West is the subject of a book by Violet Sackville-West (1937).

24–25. *Carmen . . . gitana:* These are the opening lines of Théophile Gautier's poem "Carmen," which both Eliot and Pound found technically interesting:

> Carmen est maigre,—un trait de bistre
> Cerne son oeil de gitana.
> Ses cheveux sont d'un noir sinistre,
> Sa peau, le diable la tanna.

Eliot parodies the lines in the fifth stanza of "Whispers of Immortality"; to Pound, Gautier's lines showed how it was possible to get simple and clear statements into poetry: " 'Carmen est maigre—un trait de bistre . . .' wrote Gautier. I think this sort of clear presentation is of the noblest traditions of our craft" (*New Age* [Oct. 2, 1913], 662; and he told Iris Barry in July 1915 that "perfectly plain statements like 'Carmen est maigre' should teach one a number of things" (*Letters,* p. 139). Other "perfectly plain statements" occur in TAME CAT (l. 1*n*) and EPILOGUE.

26. *rend la flamme:* Quoted from the fifth stanza of "Carmen":

> Ainsi faite, la moricaude
> Bat les plus altières beautés,
> Et de ses yeux la lueur chaude
> Rend la flamme aux satiétés.

33. Spanish *bonita* means "pretty," and *chiquita* is coined from the French *chic* ("smart"). Both words are possible rhymes in what promises to be a banal poem.

34. *spade:* Pound originally wrote "bitch" before offering to change the word to "spay'd" (Chicago MSS, May 3, 1916). To "spay" is to remove the ovaries: "Sows and Bitches may be spay'd" (*Hudibras,* II, iii).

35. *intaglio:* "The intaglio is in real life a beauty in the Museo Civico in Venice" (Chicago MSS, May 29, 1916).

36. *Cupid . . . phallus:* An indecorous detail that made Harriet Monroe refuse to print the poem. Pound complained (June 5, 1916):

What you object to in the "Cabaret" is merely that it isn't bundled up into slop, sugar and sentimentality, the underlying statement is very humane and most moral. It simply says there is a certain form of life, rather sordid, not gilded with tragedy any more than another, just as dull as another, and possibly quite as innocent and innocuous, vide, my singers in Venice. The thing the bourgeois will always hate is the fact that I make the people *real*. I treat the dancers as human beings, not as "symbols of sin." That is the crime and the "obscenity."

Letters, p. 131. For further examples of Harriet Monroe's censorship of his poems, see the notes to ANCORA, COMMISSION, LADIES, IMPRESSIONS OF FRANÇOIS-MARIE AROUET (DE VOLTAIRE), THE LAKE ISLE, and LANGUE D'OC. FRATRES MINORES and THE NEW CAKE OF SOAP proved troublesome to other publishers—all of which explains Pound's comment on printers in COME MY CANTILATIONS (l. 5).

[55. Pauvre   39–43;   Paunvre   55, *Faber and Faber*]

65. *Weehawken:* A town on the Hudson river, northeast of Jersey City.

67. Spanish *fonda* means "restaurant."

Orbajosa: Unidentified.

69. *preacher:* Isaiah: "Wherefore do ye spend money for that which is not bread? and your labor for that which satisfieth not? hearken diligently unto me, and eat ye that which is good, and let your soul delight itself in fatness" (55:2). The jocular invocation of scriptural authority is a Byronic device.

70. Latin *mica salis* means "a grain of salt" (Catullus, LXXXVII).

72. Eleanor Gwyn (1650–1687), actress and mistress of Charles II, has long been a type of one sort of theatrical success.

73. *Edward:* Edward VII, King of England 1901–1910. In Canto 80 Pound refers to him as Edward the Caressor.

79. The Italian *Ristorante al Giardino* means "the Garden Restaurant."

83. The Italian phrase means "one and two make three."

85–85. Quoted from F. M. Piave's libretto to Verdi's *Rigoletto* (1851): "La donna è mobile / Qual piuma al vento" ("Woman is fickle as a feather in the wind").

TO DIVES

[NO. 95. PRINTINGS: 20, 39, 40, 42, 43, 55]

[TITLE: [*untitled section I of "Zenia"*] 20; To Dives 39+]

Cf. FAMAM LIBROSQUE CANO (l. 32n).

TO-EM-MEI'S "THE UNMOVING CLOUD"
[NO. 158. PRINTINGS: 36, 37, 39, 40, 42, 43, 55]

See the introductory note to SONG OF THE BOWMEN OF SHU. TO-EM-MEI'S "THE UNMOVING CLOUD" is a translation from *T'ao Yüan-ming*, I, 1.1*b* (Fang). An alternative version is given by W. Acker in *T'ao the Hermit* (1952, p. 135). *To-em-mei* is Japanese for *T'ao Ch'ien*, who died in A.D. 427 (Fang).

[6. towards   *36, 37;*   toward   *39+*]

22. *The birds flutter:* This is the opening line of the fourth stanza of the Chinese (Fang).

[26–27. Yet however ——— cannot   *36, 37;*   But however ——— can not   *39+*]

TO FORMIANUS' YOUNG LADY FRIEND
[NO. 107. PRINTINGS: 22, 39, 40, 42, 43, 55]

Pound thought Catullus (*c.* 84–*c.* 54 B.C.) the most important of the Roman poets (*Letters*, p. 138). In 1938 he began to write an opera called "Collis o Heliconii [Cultor]" (based on Catullus, LXI), but it has never been published and may never have been completed. TO FORMIANUS' YOUNG LADY FRIEND is a version of Catullus (XLIII):

> Salve, nec minimo puella naso
> nec bello pede nec nigris ocellis
> nec longis digitis nec ore sicco
> nec sane nimis elegante lingua,
> decoctoris amica Formiani.
> ten Provincia narrat esse bellam?
> tecum Lesbia nostra comparatur?
> o saeclum insapiens et infacetum!

("I greet you, lady, you who neither have a tiny nose, nor a pretty foot, nor black eyes, nor long fingers, nor dry mouth, nor indeed a very refined tongue, you mistress of the bankrupt of Formiae. Is it you who are pretty, as the Province tells us? is it with you that our Lesbia is compared? Oh, this age! how tasteless and ill-bred it is!"—Loeb.) Catullus also inspired the poems in LADIES. Pound thought him a difficult poet to translate (*Letters*, pp. 116–117).

7. *vendor of cosmetics:* A mistranslation of the sort one expects to find in HOMAGE TO SEXTUS PROPERTIUS. It is Pound's first published example of what C. A. Forbes was later to call "Rappalatinitas," and shows that the technique

of distorting Latin for ironic effect was evolved as early as 1914.

TO ΚΑΛΟΝ

[NO. 125. PRINTINGS: 24, 39, 40, 42, 43, 55]

Pound returned to the ambiguities of "the beautiful" (τὸ καλόν) in HUGH SELWYN MAUBERLEY (l. 47n).

[2. You have sent   24;   And sent   39+]

TOMB AT AKR ÇAAR, THE

[NO. 64. PRINTINGS: 15, 42, 43, 53, 55]

An address by the soul of a fictitious character called Nikoptis to his dead and mummified body. Unrelated to DE ÆGYPTO, the poem is roughly contemporary with T. E. Hulme's interest in the geometrical qualities of Egyptian art.

Pound did not share the modern interest in Egyptology until comparatively late in life. Egyptian hieroglyphs begin to appear in the Cantos in Section: Rock-Drill (1955), and in 1960 Pound began a series of translations that were published a couple of years later as Love Poems of Ancient Egypt.

[2. millennia   15–53, Faber and Faber;   millenia   55]

10. signs: The hieroglyphic inscriptions on the walls of the tomb.

15 ff. This section is obscure, but apparently describes a struggle between disembodied souls for the body of the newborn Nikoptis.

18. There are "three spirits" in APRIL (l. 1n).

24. thee and Thee: "Was I not part of you and in fact the essential part?"

25. sun . . . to rest me: Disembodied souls are reputed to return to their graves at dawn.

30. crafty work: Tombs were sealed and stamped with cartouches bearing the name of the occupant. It was impossible to break into a tomb without disturbing the seal.

TRANSLATIONS AND ADAPTATIONS FROM HEINE

[NOS. 42 [I–VII], 48 [VIII]. PRINTINGS: 9 [I–VII], 12 [VIII], 42 [I–VIII], 43 [I–VIII], 53 [VIII], 55 [I–VIII]]

[TITLE: Translations from Heine   9, 42, 43;   Translations and Adaptations from ——— 55]

[Subtitle: Von "Die ———   9–43;   From "Die ———   55]

Pound has often praised Heinrich Heine (1797–1856) for his lyric qualities and the clarity of his imagery. In this sequence of preimagist translations, however, Pound seems to be more interested in Heine's irony than in his *melopœia* or *phanopœia*. His best translation (VI) uses Latinate polysyllables for ironic effect, which suggests that the famous "cosmopolitan" style of HUGH SELWYN MAUBERLEY derives ultimately from Heine by way of Laforgue.

The German texts printed here are from editions of the *Buch der Lieder* by Elster (1887) and Lees (1920). An uncollected version of the poem beginning "Diese Damen, sie verstehen" (the first of the *Nolante und Marie* sequence in Heine's *Verschiedene*) appears in *EP to LU* (ed. Robbins), pp. 20–23.

I. From *Die Heimkehr*, LXXVI:

> Bist du wirklich mir so feindlich,
> Bist du wirklich ganz verwandelt?
> Aller Welt will ich es klagen,
> Dass du mich so schlecht behandelt.
>
> O ihr undankbaren Lippen,
> Sagt, wie könnt ihr Schlimmes sagen
> Von dem Manne, der so liebend
> Euch geküsst, in schönen Tagen?

[4. Of how   *9, 55;*   Oh how   *42, 43*]

II. From *Lyrisches Intermezzo*, XXI:

> So hast du ganz und gar vergessen,
> Dass ich so lang dein Herz besessen,
> Dein Herzchen so süss und so falsch und so klein,
> Es kann nirgend was süss'res und falscheres seyn.
>
> So hast du die Lieb' und das Leid vergessen,
> Die das Herz mir thäten zusammenpressen.
> Ich weiss nicht, war Liebe grösser als Leid?
> Ich weiss nur, sie waren gross allebeid'!

5, 7. *lay:* Pound misread *Leid* ("sorrow") as *Lied* ("song").

III. From *Die Heimkehr*, LXXXVIII:

> "Sag', wo ist dein schönes Liebchen,
> Das du einst so schön besungen,
> Als die zaubermächt'gen Flammen
> Wunderbar dein Herz durchdrungen?"
>
> Jene Flammen sind erloschen,
> Und mein Herz ist kalt und trübe,
> Und dies Büchlein ist die Urne
> Mit der Asche meiner Liebe.

IV. From *Die Heimkehr*, LXVI:

> Mir träumt': ich bin der liebe Gott,
> Und sitz' im Himmel droben,
> Und Englein sitzen um mich her,
> Die meine Verse loben.

There are twelve more stanzas in Heine's poem.

V. From *Die Heimkehr*, LXXIX:

> Doch die Kastraten klagten,
> Als ich meine Stimm' erhob;
> Sie klagten und sie sagten:
> Ich sänge viel zu grob.
>
> Und lieblich erhoben sie alle
> Die kleinen Stimmelein,
> Die Trillerchen, wie Kristalle,
> Sie klangen so fein und rein.
>
> Sie sangen von Liebessehnen,
> Von Liebe und Liebeserguss;
> Die Damen schwammen in Thränen,
> Bei solchem Kunstgenuss.

1. *mutilated:* Demetz points out that Heine's *Kastraten* are both "eunuchs" and "critics" (*castrati*).

VI. From *Die Heimkehr*, LXV:

> Diesen liebenswürd'gen Jüngling
> Kann man nicht genug verehren;
> Oft traktirt er mich mit Austern,
> Und mit Rheinwein und Liquören.
>
> Zierlich sitzt ihm Rock und Höschen,
> Doch noch zierlicher die Binde,
> Und so kommt er jeden Morgen,
> Fragt, ob ich mich wohl befinde;
>
> Spricht von meinem weiten Ruhme,
> Meiner Anmuth, meinen Witzen;
> Eifrig und geschäftig ist er
> Mir zu dienen, mir zu nützen.
>
> Und des Abends, in Gesellschaft,
> Mit begeistertem Gesichte,
> Deklamirt er vor den Damen
> Meine göttlichen Gedichte.
>
> O, wie ist es hoch erfreulich,
> Solchen Jüngling noch zu finden,
> Jetzt in unsrer Zeit, wo täglich
> Mehr und mehr die Bessern schwinden.

Pound alludes to the poem in AMITIES (II).

16. *god-like compositions:* Pound used the German line of his own *Ripostes* (Chicago MSS, Dec.? 1912).

[17. comfort is it   9, 55;   comfort it is   42, 43]

Translator to Translated.

4. *Philistia:* The modern sense of "Philistine" derives from Heine (via Matthew Arnold).

VII. From *Die Harzreise,* "Die Ilse":

Ich bin die Prinzessin Ilse,
Und wohne im Ilsenstein;
Komm mit nach meinem Schlosse,
Wir wollen selig seyn.

Dein Haupt will ich benetzen
Mit meiner klaren Well',
Du sollst deine Schmerzen vergessen,
Du sorgenkranker Gesell!

In meinen weissen Armen,
An meiner weissen Brust,
Da sollst du liegen und träumen
Von alter Mährchenlust.

Ich will dich küssen und herzen,
Wie ich geherzt und geküsst
Den lieben Kaiser Heinrich,
Der nun gestorben ist.

Es bleiben todt die Todten,
Und nur der Lebendige lebt;
Und ich bin schön und blühend,
Mein lachendes Herze bebt.

Und bebt mein Herz dort unten,
So klingt mein kristallenes Schloss,
Dort tanzen die Fräulein und Ritter,
Es jubelt der Knappentross.

Es rauschen die seidenen Schleppen,
Es klirren die Eisenspor'n,
Die Zwerge trompeten und pauken,
Und fiedeln und blasen das Horn.

Doch dich soll mein Arm umschlingen,
Wie er Kaiser Heinrich umschlang;—
Ich hielt ihm zu die Ohren,
Wenn die Trompet' erklang.

Demetz calls this poem the "showpiece of the American Heine tradition" (*Germanic Review* [Dec. 1956], 290).

17–18. Cf. Housman, *Last Poems* (1922), XIX: "The living are the living / And dead the dead will stay."

VIII.

[*Title:* After Heine   12, 53;   [*untitled: referred to in the Contents Table as "Extra Poem from Heine"*]   42, 43; Night Song   55]

From a group of supplementary poems appended to the *Buch der Lieder:*

> Hast du die Lippen mir wund geküsst,
> So küsse sie wieder heil,
> Und wenn du bis Abend nicht fertig bist,
> So hat es auch keine Eil.
>
> Du hast mich ja noch die ganze Nacht,
> Du Herzallerliebste mein!
> Mann kann in solch einer ganzen Nacht
> Viel küssen und selig seyn.

[2. particular haste   12, 53, 55;   particular waste   42, 43]

TREE, THE
[NO. 12. PRINTINGS: *1, 8, 9, 53, 55*]

[*Epigraph:* [lacking]   1, 9+;   From "A Lume Spento"   8]

Commenting on THE TREE in a footnote to an uncollected poem called "Aube of the West Dawn. Venetian June," Pound said he thought "from such perceptions as this arose . . . the myths of metamorphosis" (*A Quinzaine for This Yule* [1908], p. 12). The theory was elaborated subsequently in the *New Age* ([Jan. 7, 1915], 246):

> The first myths arose when a man walked sheer into "nonsense," that is to say, when some very vivid and undeniable adventure befell him, and he told someone else who called him a liar. Thereupon, after bitter experience, perceiving that no one could understand what he meant when he said that he "turned into a tree," he made a myth—a work of art that is—an impersonal or objective story woven out of his own emotion, as the nearest equation that he was capable of putting into words. That story, perhaps, then gave rise to a weaker copy of his emotion in others, until there arose a cult, a company of people who could understand each other's nonsense about the gods.

Similar speculations led to the writing of an uncollected poem called "Masks," which begins:

> These tales of old disguisings, are they not
> Strange myths of souls that found themselves among
> Unwonted folk that spake an hostile tongue . . . ?

A Lume Spento (1908), p. 40. Pound's interest in the origin of myth is contemporary with the researches of Frazer and Freud. See the note to A GIRL.

3. Daphne's metamorphosis into a laurel when pursued by Apollo (Ovid, *Metamorphoses*, I, 452–567) supplies images in HUGH SELWYN MAUBERLEY (ll. 192–193) and A GIRL.

[4. olde *1*; old 8+]

4. *that . . . couple:* Baucis and Philemon were metamorphosed into trees after unwittingly entertaining the gods (*Metamorphoses*, VIII, 624–724). They reappear in Canto 90 as an emblem of unity:

> Beatific spirits welding together
> as in one ash-tree in Ygdrasail.
> Baucis, Philemon. . . .

5. *elm-oak:* The trees in Ovid's account are *quercus* ("oak") and *tilia* ("linden, lime").

10. *I . . . tree:* Cf. Yeats's phrase, "I have been a hazel-tree" ("He Thinks of His Past Greatness When a Part of the Constellations of Heaven"). The ending of THE TREE is reminiscent of the early Yeats.

[11–12. many new things ——— That were *1*; many a new thing ——— That was 8+]

TS'AI CHI'H
[NO. 99. PRINTINGS: 21, 39, 40, 42, 43, 55]

Ts'ai Chi'h: Unidentified. "The name resembles Ts'ao Chih . . . as well as T'ao Ch'ien" (Fang).

There are curious parallels in imagery and phrasing between this poem and one of Pound's remarks on Remy de Gourmont's "sense of beauty": "The mist clings to the lacquer. His spirit was the spirit of Omakitsu; his *pays natal* was near to the peach-blossom-fountain of the untranslatable poem" (*Little Review* [Feb.–March 1919], 5).

VILLANELLE: THE PSYCHOLOGICAL HOUR
[NO. 154. PRINTINGS: 33, 39, 40, 42, 43, 55]

This is a villanelle in name only. That Pound appreciated the uses of this form is shown by his comments on Ernest Dowson's villanelles, in which, he says, "the refrains are an emotional fact, which the intellect, in the various gyrations of the poem, tries in vain and in vain to escape" (*Poetical Works of*

Lionel Johnson [1915], p. xvii). On the revival of such forms, see the note to A VILLONAUD: BALLAD OF THE GIBBET.

3. *middle-ageing care:* Cf. MIDDLE-AGED.

[5. I almost ——— the right pages 33; I had almost ——— the pages 39+]

[11. rain, wandering 33; the rain, the wandering 39+]

12. *little cosmos is shaken:* Quotation unidentified.

[16–19. [*lacking*] 33]

[22. drink at 33; drink of 39+]

27. *Between . . . morning:* In "The People" Yeats complains of

> The daily spite of this unmannerly town,
> Where who has served the most is most defamed,
> The reputation of his lifetime lost
> Between the night and morning.

"The People" was written in January 1915 and first published in the February 1916 issue of *Poetry;* in other words, VILLANELLE: THE PSYCHOLOGICAL HOUR originally contained an allusion to an unpublished poem by Yeats.

[30*a.* Youth would hear speech of beauty. 33; [*lacking*] 39+]

VILLONAUD: BALLAD OF THE GIBBET, A
[NO. 13. PRINTINGS: *1, 3, 8, 53, 55*]

In his "History of Imagism" F. S. Flint says that Pound "used to boast in those days that he was *Nil praeter 'Villon' et doctus cantare Catullum*" (*Egoist* [May 1, 1915], 71). Pound's admiration for the French poet François Villon (b. 1431) is recorded at length in the seventh chapter of *The Spirit of Romance* (1910), where Villon ("the only poet without illusions") is praised for his "unvarnished, intimate speech" and displayed as a suitable model for any young writer interested in bringing literature close to life. Exactly contemporary with Synge's translations, A VILLONAUD: BALLAD OF THE GIBBET and VILLONAUD FOR THIS YULE are belated contributions to the late nineteenth-century vogue for Villon (described by Omans) as manifested in the writings of Swinburne, Rossetti, Henley, Stevenson, and many others. Pound felt that "translations of Villon revived our poetry in the midst of the mid-Victorian dessication" (*New Age* [Aug. 1917], 308). As a bookish poet, he was fascinated by the illusion of originality in Villon: "all bards are thieves save Villon, master thief," he wrote in "Piazza San Marco" (a poem rejected from *A Quinzaine for This Yule* [1908] and first published in *A Lume Spento and Other Early Poems* [1965], p. 120). As Bornstein and Witemeyer point out, Pound's Villon is a *naiv* poet (in Schiller's sense of the word), and it is odd that Pound never suspected that the "I" of Villon's poems might be fictive and not autobiographical—the "I" of a persona, in fact.

Besides the quotation from Villon in HUGH SELWYN MAUBERLEY (l. 18*n*), there is an uncollected poem in *Blast* (1915) viz. "Et Faim Sallir Le Loup Des Boys" (cf. *Testament*, l. 168), and an unpublished one-act opera called "Le Testament" which is based on the life of Villon and was written 1920–1921. The word "villonaud" was coined by Pound to describe the blend of pastiche and translation by which he hoped to evoke the unique atmosphere of Villon's poems. "The Villonauds," he told W. C. Williams in October 1908, "are . . . what I conceive after a good deal of study to be an expression akin to, if not of, the spirit breathed in Villon's own poeting" (*Letters*, p. 36). Some of the names in the present poem are drawn from Villon (Culdou, François, Jehan, Margot, Marienne Ydole); others are coined in a Villonesque manner: Thomas Larron (French *larron*, "thief"), Jacques d'Allmain (French *Allemagne*, "Germany"), and Michault le Borgne (French *borgne*, "one-eyed"). ,

Technically the poem is something of a virtuoso piece: it rhymes throughout, but only three rhyme-sounds are used in forty-three lines of verse.

[*Epigraph:* En cest bourdel ou Tenoms nostr estat *1–8;* En ce ——— où tenons nostre ——— 53+]

The first quotation in the epigraph is the refrain from Villon's "Ballade de la Grosse Margot" (*Testament*, l. 1600); the second is the opening line of "L'Epitaphe Villon" (*Poésies Diverses*, XIV). Both are quoted in *The Spirit of Romance* (1910, pp. 187, 189).

1. *skoal:* The drinking toast is "Till then."

   gallows tree: Montfauçon, the Paris gibbet (cf. BALLAD OF THE GOODLY FERE, l. 2*n*).

2. *Francois:* François Villon.

   Margot: La Grosse Margot (*Testament*, ll. 1591–1627).

[4. That said *1, 3, 53+;* Who said 8]

7. *armouress:* La Belle Heaulmière (*Testament*, ll. 453–624).

9. *pinning:* Stabbing.

   Guise: A soldier of the duc de Guise.

[10. Hault *1;* Haulte *3+*]

10. *Haulte Noblesse:* Villonesque slang: the "high nobility" are men strung up high on the gallows. Henley's "Villon's Straight Tip to All Cross Coves" is a more ambitious experiment in the poetry of *argot.*

10–11. The bilingual rhyme is intended to give the reader the illusion that he is reading Medieval French rather than English (cf. ll. 39–40, 42–43; and VILLONAUD FOR THIS YULE, ll. 1 and 3).

11. *ill-address:* La Belle Heaulmière says she was ill-treated by her husband (*Testament,* l. 475).

12. *drue:* Loved one.

15. *Marienne Ydole:* Marion l'Idolle (*Testament,* l. 1628).

16. *brenn:* Burn.

18. *black:* The first of Villon's poems in slang begins by describing how corpses on the gallows are blackened (*noirciz*) by exposure.

27. *Jehan:* Jehan le Lou (*Testament,* l. 1110).

[29. Guillaulme *1;* Guillaume *3+*]

30. *Culdou:* Michault Cul d'Oue (*Testament,* l. 1338).

32. *St Hubert:* Patron saint of hunters.

[40. alway *1–53;* always *55*
faibleness *1, 3, 53+;* feebleness *8*]

40. *faibleness:* Partially anglicized from the French *faiblesse* ("weakness").

Footnote: Victor Hugo describes a gibbeted corpse in *L'Homme Qui Rit* (1869), part one, book one, chapter five ("L'Arbre d'Invention Humaine").

VILLONAUD FOR THIS YULE
[NO. 14. PRINTINGS: *1, 3, 8, 53, 55*]

See the introductory note to A VILLONAUD: BALLAD OF THE GIBBET. The form of VILLONAUD FOR THIS YULE is a ballade in which Pound has restricted himself to two rhyme sounds instead of using the customary three or four. Interest in the metrical forms of Old French poetry had been revived in the 1870s by Théodore de Banville, and the fashion was not long in reaching England. Gosse, Henley, Dobson, Dowson, and others all experimented with such forms as ballades, rondeaux, triolets, and villanelles, the aim being originally to counter what were felt to be the excesses of the "spasmodic" school.

[1. mort *1*;   morte   *3+*]

1–4. Adapted from Villon's *Le Lais*, 10–11:

> Sur le Noel, morte saison,
> Que les loups se vivent de vent. . . .

Bilingualism is a feature of A VILLONAUD: BALLAD OF THE GIBBET (ll. 10–11*n*).

5. *gueredon:* Guerdon, reward.

[6. makyth   *1, 3, 53+*;   maketh   *8*]

7. *Skoal:* Drinking toast.

8. *yester-year:* Borrowed from D. G. Rossetti, who translated Villon's line "Mais ou sont les neiges d'antan" (*Testament*, l. 336) as "But where are the snows of yester-year?" (*Works* [1911], p. 541).

10. *scented:* The Magi brought "frankincense, and myrrh" (Matt. 2:11)

13. *foison:* Abundant.

18. *Saturn . . . Mars . . . Zeus:* The star of Bethlehem has been identified as a major conjunction of Jupiter and Saturn, visible in 7 B.C. It was more usual to equate Zeus with God the Father than with God the Son.

20. *feat:* Neat.

22. Grey eyes inspire love in CINO (l. 40), and Christ's eyes are grey in BALLAD OF THE GOODLY FERE.

27. *But:* Unless.

Footnote: The Latin phrase means "a sign of the Nativity."

VIRGINAL, A
[NO. 65. PRINTINGS: *15, 42, 43, 53, 55*]

Pound may have intended this love sonnet to be set to music for the virginal he bought from Arnold Dolmetsch.

1. *Go from me:* An uncollected early poem called "L'Invitation" begins:

> Go from me. I am one of those who spoil
> And leave fair souls less fair for knowing them;
> Go from me. . . .

Poetry Review (Feb. 1912), 78. One of Elizabeth Barrett Browning's *Sonnets from the Portuguese* (1850) opens with the same three words, but Pound's source seems to have been Lionel Johnson's "Mystic and Cavalier," a poem which he printed in his edition of the *Poetical Works of Lionel Johnson* (1915), and which opens with the words: "Go from me: I am one of those, who fall" (p. 35). There seems to be another allusion to Johnson's poem in HUGH SELWYN MAUBERLEY (l. 126n).

[3. has 15–43; hath 53+]

4. *slight . . . arms:* The "slight" girl reappears in APPARUIT.

[6. with a subtle 15–53; with subtle 55]

WHITE STAG, THE
[NO. 19. PRINTINGS: 3, 8, 53, 55]

The image of the "white stag" derives from Malory's *The Tale of King Arthur* (III, 5), where guests at the wedding feast of Arthur and Guinevere see "a whyght herte . . . and a whyght brachet" pursued by "thirty couple of blacke rennynge houndis." Gawayne is given the task of capturing the white hart.

Pound included THE WHITE STAG in the book of poems that seemed to bring him the fame he was hunting. *Personæ* was published on April 16, 1909, and five days later he wrote to W. C. Williams: "I have been praised by the greatest living poet [W. B. Yeats]. I am, after eight years' hammering against impenetrable adamant, become suddenly somewhat of a success" (*Letters*, pp. 41–42).

WOMEN BEFORE A SHOP
[NO. 118. PRINTINGS: 23, 39, 40, 42, 43, 55]

A similar response to color is shown in L'ART, 1910.

2. The phrasing is repeated in Canto 83:

> The infant has descended,
> from mud on the tent roof to Tellus,
> like to like colour he goes amid grass-blades. . . .

agglutinous: Agglutinate. The whole line originally read: "Like to like nature. Damn your rhetoric" (Chicago MSS).

APPENDIX "A"

ADDITIONAL POEMS IN PERSONÆ (*1949*).

The New Directions *Personæ* (1949) collects in a couple of appendixes a number of poems not to be found in *Personæ* (1926). Those in "Appendix II" were published between 1934 and 1938, and lie outside the scope of this book; but five of the six pieces in "Appendix I" were printed in periodicals between 1912 and 1917, and belong chronologically with the poems in *Personæ* (1926). They can be placed on my Chronological List as follows:

15a. *Poetry,* I, 1 (October 1912), 7–8.
      65*a.* Middle-Aged
      65*b.* To Whistler, American

24. *Poetry,* IV, 5 (August 1914), 169.
      118*a.* Abu Salammamm—a Song of Empire

40a. *Little Review,* IV, 1 (May 1917), 11–12.
      169*a.* Pierrots

41a. *Little Review,* IV, 5 (September 1917), 8–16.
      169*b.* L'Homme Moyen Sensuel

45a. *Pavannes and Divisions* (New York, June 29, 1918).
      Reprints 169*a,* 169*b.*

55a. *Personæ* (New York, May 1949).
      As 55 but with additional reprints: 65*a,* 65*b,* 118*a,* 169*a,* 169*b.*

Pound's motives in belatedly salvaging poems written over thirty years previously can only be guessed at. PIERROTS is technically superior to much that was included in the 1926 *Personæ,* and merits inclusion for this reason alone; moreover, it draws attention to Pound's early interest in Laforgue and helps document his literary relationship with T. S. Eliot. MIDDLE-AGED and TO WHISTLER, AMERICAN are similarly of historical interest in establishing Pound's connection with the very first number of the most famous of modern poetry magazines. As for the other two items, L'HOMME MOYEN SENSUEL summarizes Pound's objections to the American way of life, and ABU SALAMMAMM—A SONG OF EMPIRE is a *jeu* that happens to trespass on his later interests.

ABU SALAMMAMM—A SONG OF EMPIRE
[NO. 118*a*. PRINTINGS: 24, 55*a*]

The epigraph alludes to what Pound calls "a tale from the southern Pacific," which tells how the "sultan of Zammbuk or some such place," when asked to comment on the state of the arts in his country, complains that "the arts have gone to pot":

> In my father's time . . . it was different. Then if we found any man who could carve beautifully he was caught at once and brought to the palace yard and kept there. He was chained, but he was given all the food and all the good drink that he wanted and all the women. And he would sit there with his tools beside him, idle. And after a time he would take up his tools and make something beautiful. . . . But now the English are come there. And they tell us that this is slavery. And they have forbidden the custom. The arts have gone to pot.

Patria Mia (1950 [1913]), pp. 94–95. The theme here treated frivolously was later to be conflated with the Confucian principle quoted as an epigraph to *Gaudier-Brzeska* (1916) and repeated in Canto 16:

> And Kung said . . .
> "When the prince has gathered about him
> "All the savants and artists, his riches will be fully employed."

Pound considered at one stage the idea of adding to this poem "a dedication to 'Kipling as was'" (Chicago MSS, July 8, 1914). When war broke out he asked Harriet Monroe to publish a note in *Poetry* to the effect that his poem "was written in April, was supposed to appear in July and has no bearing, contains no possible allusion to present outbreak" (Chicago MSS, Aug. 29, 1914). Pound's dislike of imperialism was later to find a creative outlet in HOMAGE TO SEXTUS PROPERTIUS. He undoubtedly shared W. S. Blunt's contempt for "the tyrannies and swindles of the Empire, 'a Semitic invention of Disraeli's'" (*Poetry* [March 1914], 222).

Bonga-Bonga: Victor Plarr had published poems by the fictitious aborigine Bonga Bonga (satires on colonialism and contemporary poetry) in the September 1913 issue of *Poetry and Drama*. Plarr seems to have been Pound's main source of information on the reputed activities of savages (cf. *New Age* [Oct. 9, 1913], 694).

1. George V was king of England 1910–1936.

8–9. *Dragon . . . Andromeda:* The allusion implies that George is Perseus.

23 f. Queen Victoria (d. 1901) was the *grand*mother of George V.

L'HOMME MOYEN SENSUEL
[NO. 169*b*. PRINTINGS: *41a, 45a, 55a*]

John Cournos tells in his *Autobiography* (1935) of how he once caught Pound "'doing a 240-line poem to show that it can't be done'" (p. 236). This poem was probably L'HOMME MOYEN SENSUEL, which is 242 lines in length and represents Pound's first attempt at avoiding the *impasse* of imagism (the second was NEAR PERIGORD). Perhaps the ambition grew out of conversations with Ford Madox Ford, whose "On Heaven" (printed in the June 1914 issue of *Poetry*) Pound was shortly to describe as "the first successful long poem in English vers libre, after Whitman" (*Little Review* [Oct. 1917], 20). Anyway, in April 1915 he sent his Byronic satire on the American way of life to H. L. Mencken (1880–1956), who was at that time editing the *Smart Set* (*Letters*, p. 101). Mencken rejected the poem, evidently on the grounds that it was unworthy of Pound; but his main reason for rejecting it must have been that the poem simply repeated many of the criticisms that Mencken himself had already made in essays published in the same periodical (*Smart Set* [Oct. 1913], 81–88; *ibid.* [Feb. 1914], 87–94). The poem was sent next to W. C. Williams, who was at that time on the editorial board of *Others*. "Perhaps you too will reject it as unworthy of my higher self," he wrote (Lockwood MSS, undated). His guess was right; and in fact the only person who expressed admiration for the poem was a man famous for his indifference to the higher self, Frank Harris: he was enchanted, and thought the rhymes worthy of Byron (*Little Review* [Oct. 1917], 40). The difficulty Pound experienced in finding a publisher for L'HOMME MOYEN SENSUEL was to be paralleled in the case of HOMAGE TO SEXTUS PROPERTIUS, where there was again a time lag of two years between the writing and publishing of the poem.

Title: Levin points out (p. 297) that the phrase *homme sensuel moyen* was coined by Matthew Arnold in an essay on George Sand (*Mixed Essays*, 1879). The epigraph is from Byron's *Don Juan* (I, lxi).

Footnote: The two "old gentlemen" were Comstock (d. September 1915) and Mabie (d. December 1916). "Two of the great" were Remy de Gourmont (d. September 1915) and Henry James (d. February 1916). The "anonymous compatriot" is Fitz-Greene Halleck, who in December 1819 published under the title of "Fanny" a Byronic satire of the New York society of his day (mentioned by Pound in the *Little Review* [Aug. 1918], 13).

1, 3. *my country . . . My country:* Imitated from the opening lines of Browning's *Sordello:* "Who will, may hear Sordello's story told: / His story?" The trick is repeated in lines 39–41.

11. Quotation unidentified.

14. *editor:* Ellery Sedgwick had been editing the *Atlantic Monthly* since 1908.

15. *Comstock:* Anthony Comstock (1844–1915) founded the Society for Suppression of Vice and was the leader of Boston's Watch & Ward Society. Pound later described him as being "dung-minded" (Chicago MSS, Sept. 16, 1916).

16. *president:* Woodrow Wilson, president of the U.S.A. 1913–1921. In *ABC of Economics* (1933) Pound writes that "all American and republican principles were lost during the damnable reign of the infamous Woodrow" (p. 53).

17. *ambassadors:* It was a common criticism that Wilson offered diplomatic appointments to minor men of letters.

18. *novelist:* T. N. Page (1853–1922), author of several novels including the popular *Red Rock* (1898), was made ambassador to Italy in 1913.

publisher: W. H. Page (1855–1918), a partner in the publishing house of Doubleday, Page & Co., was made ambassador to Great Britain in 1913.

preacher: Henry Van Dyke (1852–1933), appointed by Wilson in 1913 as minister of the Netherlands and Luxembourg. He is called the " 'sweet singer of a diabetic day' " in the last issue of *Exile* (1928).

[22. diliquescent   *41a+*;   deliquescent   *Faber and Faber*]

[25. a taste   *41a+*;   a state   *Faber and Faber*]

26. The Philadelphia Centennial Exposition was an educational and industrial exhibition held in 1876 to celebrate the centenary of the Declaration of Independence. See lines 54–55.

28. *Mabie:* Hamilton Wright Mabie (1845–1916), New York critic and editor associated with the *Outlook*. Mabie is called "Maybe" in Pound's correspondence (Chicago MSS).

Abbot: Lyman Abbott (1835–1922), editor of the *Outlook.*

Woodberry: George Edward Woodberry (1855–1930), poet, teacher, and editor who contributed to the *Atlantic Monthly* and the *Nation.*

29. *minds . . . quotations:* An odd complaint to have come from an allusive writer. The criticism was first broached in the *New Age* ([Sept. 5, 1912], 445):

> Nine out of every ten Americans have sold their souls for a quotation. They have wrapped themselves about a formula of words instead of about their own centres.
> They will judge nothing a priori. They will refer it to Emerson, or Mrs. Eddy, or whomsoever you will, but they will not a priori judge it for themselves.

31. *Dulness:* Cf. Pope, *The Dunciad.*

33–34. *cracks 'em . . . Maxim:* In *Don Juan* (II, cciii) Byron rhymes "maxim" with "tax 'em."

34. *Maxim:* Probably Hudson Maxim (1853–1927), author of *The Science of Poetry and the Philosophy of Language* (1910), rather than the inventor of the Maxim machine gun, Hiram Maxim (1840–1916).

39, 41. *Radway . . . Radway:* A Browningesque repetition (see ll. 1, 3*n*).

39. *pantosocracy:* Pantisocracy was the name given to Coleridge's and Southey's abortive plan to establish an ideal community along the banks of the Susquehanna. Byron alludes to it in *Don Juan* (III, xciii).

40. *gynocracy:* Gynaecocracy, government by women. Pound copies Byron's spelling (*Don Juan,* XII, lxvi).

45. *Parkhurst:* Charles Henry Parkhurst (1842–1933), minister of Madison Square Presbyterian Church, New York.

Journal: Mott says that in 1914 the New York *Evening Journal,* with nearly 800,000, had the largest daily circulation in the U.S.A. (*American Journalism* [1950], p. 715).

50. *Noyes:* The poet Alfred Noyes (1880–1958): "Noise is a Noyes-some pestilence. . . . Good God! he's the sort of thing that does death's of Captain Scot and 'Orpheus in the Underground' comic libretti" (Chicago MSS, Feb. 8, 1913).

51–52. *unyielding . . . Fielding:* Cf. Byron, *Don Juan* (IV, xcviii):

> I'm fond of yielding,
> And therefore leave them to the purer page
> Of Smollett, Prior, Ariosto, Fielding. . . .

"With Rabelais, Brantôme, Fielding, Sterne, we begin to find prose recording states of consciousness that their verse-writing contemporaries scamp. . . . I believe no man can write really good verse unless he knows Stendhal and Flaubert. . . . The main expression of nineteenth century consciousness is in prose. The art continues in Maupassant, who slicked up the Flaubertian mode" (*New York Herald Tribune Books* [Jan. 27, 1929], 1).

53. *set . . . mind:* A complaint made earlier in "PHASELLUS ILLE."

54–55. See line 26n.

57. *Gilder:* Richard Watson Gilder (1844–1909), editor of the *Century.* "It was truly a great day for American letters when the saintly and gentle and in every way model Gilder turned [R. L.] Stevenson out of his office. It was the symbolical act of his generation" (*Little Review* [April 1918], 27).

58. The Latin phrase is adapted from the proverb "de mortuis nil nisi bonum" ("of the dead speak kindly or not at all"). Pound substitutes "truthfully" for "kindly" before working in the allusion to Ibsen's play *The Master Builder* (1892).

59. *Poe:* Pound's opinion of Edgar Allen Poe (1809–1849) has generally been unfavorable, and in this case he ignores the fact that Poe's work was well known in America even before the French symbolists took an interest in it.

Whitman: The poems of Walt Whitman (1819–1892) were first published in England in 1868: "It is cheering to reflect that America accepted Whitman when he was properly introduced by William Michael Rossetti, and not before then" (*New Age* [Oct. 3, 1912], 539). On Pound's attitude to Whitman, see A PACT.

Whistler: James Abbott McNeill Whistler (1834–1903) went to Paris at the age of twenty-one and never returned to America. TO WHISTLER—AMERICAN is Pound's homage to the painter.

62. *James:* Pound once said that in the novels of Henry James (1843–1916) "the maximum sensibility compatible with efficient writing was present" (*Egoist* [Jan. 1918], 2). Pound's numerous essays on James were first collected in *Instigations* (1920).

65–66. *satire or . . . flatterer:* In *Don Juan* Byron rhymes "flattery" with "satire, he" (IX, v).

66. *Bennett:* The novelist Arnold Bennett (1867–1931). Pound's scorn for "nickle cash-register Bennett" (*Letters,* p. 389) is thought to have resulted in the Nixon portrait in HUGH SELWYN MAUBERLEY. A retractation, following on a reading of *The Old Wives' Tale,* appears in *Literary Essays* (1954, p. 429n).

67. *Red Bloods:* See THE CONDOLENCE.

71. *tariff:* "A protective tariff on books is an obstacle to the free circulation of thought and *must* be done away with" (*Poetry* [March 1917], 312). The complaint is repeated at line 218.

[72. other facts   *41a, 45a;*   other tracts   *55a*]

73. *Garcia:* Elbert Hubberd's *A Message to Garcia* (1899) describes the heroism of a courier in the Spanish-American War.

 Mosher: Thomas Bird Mosher (1852–1923), "the celebrated aesthetic publisher and book-pirate" (*Little Review* [Feb.–March 1919], 45). Mosher's failure to reprint *A Lume Spento* (*Letters,* p. 36) probably accounts for the inclusion of his name here among those of the damned.

74. *botts:* Parasitical worms or maggots. *Collicks* must be colics; *glanders* is a glandular swelling in the neck (*O. E. D.*).

75. *Sumner:* Probably Charles Sumner (1811–1874), who urged the abolition of slavery, and whose feats are celebrated in a poem by Longfellow.

76. *Freud:* See THE ENCOUNTER (l. 1n).

 Jung: C. G. Jung (1875–1961) seems to have been at this time simply a name that Pound associated with the "new psychology."

 sink: "America . . . is the sort of sink where a Comstock is possible" (*Egoist* [Oct. 1916], 159).

[82. add to   *41a, 45a;*   and to   *55a*]

86. *Vogue:* In 1914 Edna Woolman Chase became the editor of this fashion magazine (founded 1892). Pound contributed an article in October 1916.

88. *sans song:* In Shakespeare's *As You Like It* (II, vii, 165–166) Jaques describes the progress of man from infancy to

 second childishness and mere oblivion,
Sans teeth, sans eyes, sans taste, sans everything.

89–90. These lines parody the opening of Longfellow's "A Psalm of Life":

> Tell me not, in mournful numbers,
> Life is but an empty dream!

Pound thought Longfellow (to whom he is distantly related) "the ideal poet for a prohibitionist state" (*Little Review* [Dec. 1917], 55).

92. *Waldorf:* Upper-class goings-on in luxury hotels.

98. *Everybody's Magazine* had been founded in 1899.

100. *Ch . . . J:* Mockingly advertising the decency of his poem, Pound asked Mencken to "observe that 'whore' and 'Jesus' are left blank" (*Letters*, p. 102; cf. l. 210).

102. *Christian Endeavour:* The Young People's Society for Christian Endeavor. Pound himself attended such conventions "at [a] precocious age" (*New Age* [June 3, 1920], 77).

105. *pure Platonic grapple:* Byron's hero was at sixteen the victim of "a pure Platonic squeeze" (*Don Juan*, I, cxi).

111. *The Hudson Sail:* Unidentified.

122. *calor:* Warmth, passion, "not a misprint for color" (*Letters*, p. 103).

123. *fair Greek:* Here and in Canto 74 Pound alludes to a poem by Sappho, a poetess of the 7th century B.C., which describes the emotional turmoil of the lover as a "Petrarchan" series of contradictory states (II).

127–128. *aesthetic . . . emetic:* In *Don Juan* (II, xxi) Byron rhymes "pathetic" with "emetic."

129. *Masefield:* Believing that poetry should avoid archaisms, Pound had little sympathy for the poetry of John Masefield (1878–1967). He did, however, prefer Masefield's lyrics to his "God blast your dash blank 'alyards narrative" (Chicago MSS, Feb. 8, 1913).

137. *Century:* This is a favorite anecdote. "The 'Century Magazine' wants to bring its fiction 'as near to truth, and make it as interpretive of life, as conditions allow' ('Century Magazine' for September, 1913, page 791, col. 2, lines 29 and 30). . . . 'As conditions allow'!!!!!!" (*New Age* [April 23, 1914], 780; cf. *Egoist* [Oct. 15, 1914], 390). According to Edwards (p. 49), Pound had in 1908 sent poems to the *Century* (and to *Harper's Monthly, Scribner's*, and

the *American Magazine*) under the pseudonym of John Vore. All were rejected.

153. *date:* Presumably a misprint for "data," though all printings have "date."

154. *this . . . land:* England.

159. *whereby they got in:* Cf. Pope on grubs in amber ("Epistle to Dr. Arbuthnot," ll. 171–172):

> The things, we know, are neither rich nor rare,
> But wonder how the devil they got there.

165. *fifty grunts:* Gourmont's dictum supplies the epigraph to an essay by Pound in the *New Age* ([July 26, 1917], 288): "Fifty graduated grunts and as many representative signs will serve all needful communication between all thoroughly socialized men." Pound goes on to comment that "De Gourmont's jibe sums up the intellectual opposition to socialism." On the importance of Remy de Gourmont (1858–1915), see Pound's essay in *Instigations* (1920).

169. *mobs . . . kings:* In *Don Juan* Byron writes: "I wish men to be free / As much from mobs as kings—from you as me" (IX, xxv).

[182. "Know what they think, and just what books they've read, *41a+*; *[lacking]* Faber and Faber]

189. *flood of limbs:* Pound noted "the surging crowd on Seventh Avenue . . . pagan as ever Imperial Rome was" (*New Age* [Sept. 12, 1912], 466).

190. *Moscow . . . Mussqu:* The distortion is probably Byronic. In *Don Juan* Byron rhymes "ladies" with "Cadiz" (I, cxc), "ablutions" with "Russians" (VI, xcii), etc. On the other hand, Pound's "Mussqu" corresponds to the Russian pronunciation of the word "Moscow" in the accusative case [mʌskvʊ:].

199. *potationist:* Drinker. The word is Pound's coinage, probably invented as an antonym to "prohibitionist."

200. *Great White Way:* Broadway, New York.

210. *'em . . . house:* For the suppressed word, see line 100*n*.

217–218. *freedom . . . need 'em:* The rhyme occurs in Butler's *Hudibras* (II, iii).

218. *cheap books:* I.e., because of the tariff (l. 71*n*).

225. *Rodyheaver:* Unidentified. In one of Pound's "Imaginary Letters" there is a reference to "the Rodyheaver, or potential Xtn convert" (*Little Review* [Nov. 1918], 10).

230. *organization . . . sin:* Presumably the New York Society for the Suppression of Vice. In the inferno of Canto 14 one encounters

> the vice-crusaders, fahrting through silk,
> waving the Christian symbols. . . .

235. *Franklin:* Pound alludes to the eloquent opening paragraph of the *Autobiography* of Benjamin Franklin (1706–1790), in which Franklin ascribes his affluence to the blessing of God.

240. *Broadway Temple:* The very name is anomalous: "broad is the way, that leadeth to destruction" (Matthew 7:13).

MIDDLE-AGED
[NO. 65*a*. PRINTINGS: *15a, 55a*]

[*Subtitle:* A Study in an Emotion   *15a*;   [*lacking*]   *55a*]

For Pound, who was barely twenty-seven at the time of writing this poem, the age of thirty was a major turning point in life. "Any man whose youth has been worth anything," he wrote in his thirty-first year, "any man who has lived his life at all in the sun, knows that he has seen the best of it when he finds thirty approaching; knows that he is entering a quieter realm, a place with a different psychology" (*Gaudier-Brzeska* [1916], p. 47). The theme recurs in various forms in HUGH SELWYN MAUBERLEY (l. 17*n*), SALUTATION THE THIRD, THE TEA SHOP, and VILLANELLE: THE PSYCHOLOGICAL HOUR.

Sending MIDDLE-AGED to Harriet Monroe in August 1912 for publication in the first number of *Poetry*, Pound described his poem as "an over-elaborate post-Browning 'Imagiste' affair" (*Letters*, p. 44). This seems to be the earliest recorded usage of the word "Imagiste" in the history of imagist poetry. MIDDLE-AGED is much more discursive than later imagist poems, and shows that at this stage Pound had still to write the poems that would justify his poetic theories.

3, 13. *As . . . So:* Heroic similes are parodied in THE BATH TUB.

PIERROTS
[NO. 169*a*. PRINTINGS: *40a, 45a, 55a*]

[*Subtitle:* Scene Courte Mais Typique / (After the "Pierrots" of Jules Laforgue.) / John Hall   *40a*;   From the French of Jules Laforgue / (Scene Courte Mais Typique) *45a+*]

A translation of "Pierrots (Scène Courte Mais Typique)" by Jules Laforgue (1860–1887), from *L'Imitation de Notre-Dame la Lune* (1885):

Il me faut, vos yeux! Dès que je perds leur étoile,
Le mal des calmes plats s'engouffre dans ma voile,
Le frisson du *Væ soli!* gargouille en mes moelles . . .

Vous auriez dû me voir après cette querelle!
J'errais dans l'agitation la plus cruelle,
Criant aux murs: Mon Dieu! mon Dieu! Que dira-t-elle?

Mais aussi, vrai, vous me blessâtes aux antennes
De l'âme, avec les mensonges de votre traîne.
Et votre tas de complications mondaines.

Je voyais que vos yeux me lançaient sur des pistes,
Je songeais: Oui, divins, ces yeux! mais rien n'existe
Derrière! Son âme est affaire d'oculiste.

Moi, je suis laminé d'esthétiques loyales!
Je hais les trémolos, les phrases nationales;
Bref, le violet gros deuil est ma couleur locale.

Je ne suis point «ce gaillard-là!» ni Le Superbe!
Mais mon âme, qu'un cri un peu cru exacerbe,
Est au fond distinguée et franchè comme une herbe.

J'ai des nerfs encor sensibles au son des cloches,
Et je vais en plein air sans peur et sans reproche,
Sans jamais me sourire en un miroir de poche.

C'est vrai, j'ai bien roulé! j'ai râlé dans des gîtes
Peu vous; mais, n'en ai-je pas plus de mérite
A en avoir sauvé la foi en vos yeux? dites . . .

—Allons, faisons la paix, Venez, que je vous berce,
Enfant. Eh bien?
　　　　　　　—C'est que, votre pardon me verse
Un mélange (confus) d'impressions . . . diverses . . .

　　　　　　　　　　　　　　　　　　　(*Exit.*)

Pound owes his interest in Laforgue initially to T. S. Eliot, who had written poems in imitation of Laforgue some three or four years before meeting Pound in September 1914. Unlike Eliot, Pound did not attempt to create a persona out of the Laforguian Pierrot. Instead, he concentrated on the more purely verbal effects of Laforgue's poetry, particularly on that "dance of the intelligence among words" which he defined as *logopœia* (see p. 11 above). One aspect of Laforguian *logopœia* is the invention of portmanteau words like *éternullité* and *ennuiversel*, which are of limited scope in English because we tend to associate them with Lewis Carroll; more fruitful from Pound's point of view was Laforgue's trick of using Latinate polysyllables to create a tone of ironic impersonality. So in prose we have the experimental "divagation from Jules Laforgue" published in the *Little Review* as "Our Tetrarchal Précieuse" ([July 1918], 3–12); and in verse the equally experimental PIERROTS, which is far more polysyllabic than the original French. The polysyllabic technique is used in L'HOMME MOYEN SENSUEL and most famously in HUGH SELWYN MAUBERLEY; earlier examples occur in AU SALON and TRANSLATIONS AND ADAPTATIONS FROM HEINE.

Pound contributed an essay on Laforgue to the November 1917 issue of *Poetry*. PIERROTS was first published in the *Little Review* under the pseudonym of John Hall (other pseudonyms are listed on p. 142 above).

3. An allusion to the Vulgate Ecclesiastes (4:10): "Vae soli, quia cum ceciderit, non habet sublevantem se" ("but woe to him that is alone when he falleth; for he hath not another to help him up"—A. V.). The Latin is quoted in Canto 74.

7. *antennæ:* The image was first used in TAME CAT (l. 6n).

7–9. *perturbations-situations-complications:* A triplet from which Pound developed the unmistakable sound of the latter part of HUGH SELWYN MAUBERLEY. The sequence in the later poem reads: "application-graduations-exacerbation-invitation-invitation-isolation-examination-elimination-consternation-undulation-emendation-conservation-elimination-concentration." Gourmont, on the other hand, considered such words unsuitable for poetry (*Esthétique de la Langue Française* [1899], p. 21).

[16. I am 40a+; I a *Faber and Faber*]

[28a. (*Exit.*) 40a; [*lacking*] 45a+]

TO WHISTLER, AMERICAN
[NO. 65b. PRINTINGS: 15a, 55a]

The Whistler Exhibition at the Tate Gallery lasted from July to October 1912. Pound's poem on what the achievement of James Abbott McNeill Whistler (1834–1903) meant to other American artists was sent to Harriet Monroe for publication in the first number of *Poetry*, and it was clearly intended to be more than a mere eulogy. "I count him our only great artist," he wrote, "and even this informal salute, drastic as it is, may not be out of place at the threshold of what I hope is an endeavor to carry into our American poetry the same sort of life and intensity which he infused into modern painting" (*Letters*, p. 44). English readers who might have missed the poem were given a paraphrase of it in one of the articles Pound was writing for the *New Age* at about the same time:

> I have gathered from the loan exhibit of Whistler's paintings now at the Tate (September, 1912), more courage for living than I have gathered from the Canal Bill or from any other manifestation of American energy whatsoever.
>
> And thereanent I have written some bad poetry and burst into several incoherent conversations, endeavouring to explain what the exhibit means to the American artist.
>
> The man's life struggle is set before one. He had tried all means, he had spared himself nothing, he had struggled in one direction until he had either achieved or found it inadequate for his expression. After he had achieved a thing, he never repeated. There were many struggles for the ultimate nocturnes.
>
> . . . Dürer could not have outdone the two faces, "Grenat et Or" and "Brown and Gold—de Race." . . . These two pictures have in them a whole Shakespearean drama. . . . But what Whistler has proved once and for all is that being born an American does not eternally damn a man or prevent him from the ultimate and highest achievement in the arts. . . . He is, with Abraham Lincoln, the beginning of our Great Tradition.

New Age (Oct. 24, 1912), 612. Whistler is one of the heroes in L'HOMME MOYEN SENSUEL (l. 59). See also the introductory note to A PACT.

[5. is a part *15a+*; is part *Faber and Faber*]

5. *gone wrong:* Pound was to comment later on the way in which "all artists who discover anything . . . push certain experiments beyond the right curve of their art. . . . One does not know, simply does not know, the true curve until one has pushed one's method beyond it" (*Little Review* [Aug. 1918], 30).

7. The name of Albrecht Dürer (1471–1528) is usually invoked in Pound's writings as a symbol of inimitable precision.

15. *symphonies:* Whistler's synaesthetic term for pictures painted in one predominant color. ALBATRE is a verbal approximation to the Whistlerian symphony.

16–17. *tried . . . media:* Arthur Symons observed that Whistler "mastered, in his own art, medium after medium, and his work, in each medium, is conspicuous for . . . its precise knowledge of exactly what can be done with all the substances and materials of art" (*Studies in Seven Arts* [1906], p. 128).

18. Abraham Lincoln, president of the U.S.A. 1861–1865, is (rather surprisingly) not one of the heroes in the *Cantos*.

APPENDIX "B"

ILLUSTRATIONS, EPIGRAPHS, DEDICATIONS, ETC.

Page references in this section are to the Boni and Liveright and New Directions *Personæ*.

(a) *Illustrations*

Three of the four illustrations in *Personæ* (1926) are by Henri Gaudier-Brzeska (1891–1915). The frontispiece, done in charcoal and india ink, is a brush drawing for sculpture and was made by Gaudier-Brzeska about 1913.[1] The cover design following page 58 was made by Dorothy Shakespear Pound for a 1915 reprint of *Ripostes*.[2]

As for the drawings following pages 60 and 72, both were done in Gaudier-Brzeska's own copy of *Ripostes* [3] and this explains the presence of printed inscriptions on them. In the 1912 *Ripostes*, the poem called "The Tomb at Akr Çaar" comes to an end at the top of page 16, and it was here that Gaudier-Brzeska drew what Pound called a "fine design" for this piece.[4] The drawing now following page 72 of *Personæ* (1926) must have been made on page 34 of the first edition of *Ripostes* and underneath a short lyric called "An Immorality," in which Pound expresses his disinclination to "do high deeds in Hungary / To pass all men's believing." This drawing is a study for the "Hieratic Head of Ezra Pound" that Gaudier-Brzeska sculpted in 1915 (see MŒURS CONTEMPORAINES, V, 13*n*).

(b) *Epigraphs*

(i) Page 57: "Quos ego Persephonae maxima dona feram" ("that I may bear them [i.e., 'my three books'] to Persephone as my most precious offering"—Loeb). The quotation is from Propertius (*Elegies*, II, xiii*A*, 26). Pound first used it as the epigraph to *Canzoni* (1911)—his fifth book of poems, if one discounts *Provença* (1910)—and then again in 1912 as the epigraph to *Ripostes*. In HOMAGE TO SEXTUS PROPERTIUS the

---

[1] *Pound Newsletter*, no. 9 (Jan. 1956), 19.
[2] Donald Gallup, *A Bibliography of Ezra Pound* (London, 1963), p. 63.
[3] Now in Pound's possession (Gallup, *ibid.*).
[4] *Gaudier-Brzeska: A Memoir* (London, 1916), p. 47.

Latin is rendered: "Which I take, my not unworthy gift, to Persephone" (VI, 21).

(ii) Page 79: "Cui dono lepidum novum libellum" ("To whom am I to present my pretty new book?"—Loeb). This is the opening line of the dedication to Catullus' poems.

(iii) Page 80: "And the days are not full enough. . . ." These four lines are presumably by Pound.

(c) Dedications

(i) Page v. The dedication to Mary Moore first appeared in *Personæ* (1909) and was repeated in *Provença* (1910) and *Umbra* (1920). Nothing is known about her. She is not Marianne Moore.[5]

(ii) Page 57. Pound first met the American poet William Carlos Williams (1883–1963) in October 1902[6] when they were both students at the University of Pennsylvania. Their published correspondence shows what interests they had in common before the publication of *Ripostes*.

(iii) Page 79. "Vail de Lencour" is Mrs. Brigit Patmore,[7] whom Pound thought "one of the most charming people on this planet."[8] She married the grandson of Coventry Patmore and frequented the literary circle associated with the *English Review* when Ford Madox Ford was the editor. The pseudonym Pound gave her recalls the names of Saîl de Claustra (the Provençal poetess mentioned in THE ALCHEMIST) and Ninon de Lenclos, who organized a famous *salon* in the eighteenth century. "Vail de Lencour"'s beauty is celebrated in D. H. Lawrence's *Aaron's Rod* (1922: Clariss Browning) and also in Aldington's *Death of a Hero* (1929: Fanny; Pound is lightly disguised as Frank Upjohn).

(d) Miscellaneous

(i) Page vii: "Edition . . . of all . . . poems." *Personæ* (1926) is merely a selection of Pound's early work.

(ii) Page 1: "Personæ . . . 1908, 1909, 1910." Some of the personæ were not published until 1911 (see the Chronological List).

(iii) Page 55: *Ripostes*. This fencing term draws attention to the "modern," epigrammatic element in the collection. In a

---

[5] J. H. Edwards, "A Critical Biography of Ezra Pound, 1885–1922." Unpublished Ph.D. dissertation (California, 1952), p. 113.

[6] Edwards, *op. cit.*, p. 23.

[7] Derek Patmore, *Private History: an Autobiography* (London, 1960), p. 28.

[8] *The Collected Letters of D. H. Lawrence*, ed. Harry T. Moore, vol. 1 (London, 1962), xlix. Derek Patmore reproduces a photograph of Mrs. Patmore (*op. cit.*, p. 81), whose memoir of Pound was published in the *Texas Quarterly* in autumn 1964.

poem rejected from *Canzoni* (1911) Pound speaks of himself as singing "the swift delight / Of the clear thrust and riposte in fencing" (*Poetry Australia* [April 1967], 8).

(iv) Page 78. The definition adapted from Lewis' *An Elementary Latin Dictionary* (1891) was supposed to deter malicious reviewers from pointing out that the word *lustrum* means a bog (Pound himself used the word in this sense when recalling that Harold Monro "had gone through the two darkest *lustra* . . . 1902 to 1908, 1920 to 1930").[9] In actual fact, of course, it encouraged people to search the dictionaries for alternative meanings. One reader complained that "Ezra Pound is too absolutely degraded to offer sacrifices, much less expiatory ones; therefore we must be content to consider the book a collection of morasses, quicksands" (*Little Review* [Jan. 1918], 56). This method of ridicule is common in the journalism of the period, and *Blast* was another title that provided rich opportunities: an anonymous reviewer described the first *Blast* as "blastodermic" (*Athenæum* [July 1914], 26); and J. C. Squire was delighted to discover that "blast" can mean "a flatulent disease of sheep" (*London Mercury*, I [1920], 387).

(v) Page 126. Rihaku is the Chinese poet Li Po (A.D. 701–762). His name is given in Japanese because Mori and Ariga were Japanese. On Pound's indebtedness to Ernest Fenollosa (1853–1908), see the note to SONG OF THE BOWMEN OF SHU and page 14 above. The Fenollosa manuscripts are among Pound's papers at Brunnenburg.

Fenollosa studied Chinese poetry under Kainan Mori (1863–1911) and considered him "probably the greatest living authority" on this subject.[10] Pound says it was "Mori who taught Fenollosa to find more in the ideograph than is to be found in the dictionary."[11] Nagao Ariga (1860–1925) was another Japanese scholar of Fenollosa's acquaintance.

(vi) Page 143: "Poems from Blast." The typography is that of the original *Blast*, and was first used by the futurists.

(vii) Page 149: "Poems from Lustra (1915)." English editions of *Lustra* appeared in 1916, American editions in 1917. "1915" must be a misprint.

(viii) Page 234: "Poems . . . Added . . . in 1949." Pound transferred *Personæ* (1926) to New Directions in 1946.[12] An augmented edition of *Personæ* (an offset reprint of the 1926 text, together with a couple of appendixes) was put out by New Directions in May 1949. Of the poems printed in these

[9] "Harold Monro," *Criterion*, XI, 45 (July 1932), 585.
[10] "The Chinese Written Character as a Medium for Poetry [I]," *Little Review*, VI, 5 (September 1919), 64.
[11] "Mr. Pound and His Poetry [letter]," *Athenæum*, no. 4670 (October 31, 1919), 1132.
[12] Gallup, *op. cit.*, p. 64.

appendixes, "Donna Mi Prega" and the poems in "Appendix II" were first published after 1926 and so fall outside the scope of this study. Those published before 1926 are commented on in "Appendix 'A' " above. As for the poems of T. E. Hulme, these have been collected and edited by Alun R. Jones.[13]

[13] Alun R. Jones, *The Life and Opinions of T. E. Hulme* (London, 1960), pp. 155–182.

APPENDIX "C"

ADDITIONAL POEMS IN COLLECTED SHORTER POEMS (1968).

Several months after the present *Guide* was completed, Faber and Faber published *Collected Shorter Poems by Ezra Pound* (1968), "a slightly enlarged edition of the volume previously entitled *Personæ* [1952]." In this new edition, two poems are deleted from the 1952 text, but only one of them (OUR CONTEMPORARIES) appeared in the original 1926 *Personæ*. Among numerous additions to the 1968 text, only five poems were eligible by date if not by quality for inclusion in *Personæ* (1926). One of these ("Epilogue") was written in 1912 and has not been published previously; the other four can be placed on my Chronological List as follows:

12. *Poetry Review*, I, 2 (February 1912), 77–81.
    48a. Immorality, An [Oboes, III]

15. *The Ripostes of Ezra Pound* (London, October 1912).
    Reprints 48a.

16. *Poetry*, II, 1 (April 1913), 1–12.
    76a. Reflection and Advice [Pax Saturni]

20. *Smart Set*, XLI, 4 (December 1913), 47–48.
    95a. Rapture, The [Zenia, V]

28. *Blast*, no. 2 (July 1915), 19–22.
    146a. Our Respectful Homages to M. Laurent Tailhade

42. *Lustra of Ezra Pound with Earlier Poems* (New York, September 19, 1917) [unabridged].
    Reprints 48a.

43. *Lustra of Ezra Pound with Earlier Poems* (New York, October 16, 1917) [abridged].
    Reprints 48a.

53. *Umbra* (London, June 1920).
    Reprints 48a.

EPILOGUE [2]

The "five books" referred to are *The Spirit of Romance* (1910), *Canzoni* (1911), *The Sonnets and Ballate of Guido Cavalcanti* (1912), *Ripostes* (1912), and *The Canzoni of Arnaut Daniel* (projected as a book, but the material was published later in 1920 in *Umbra* and *Instigations*). "It has been my hope," Pound explained to Harriet Monroe in October 1912, "that this work will help to break the surface of convention and that the raw matter, and analysis of primitive systems may be of use in building the new art of metrics and of words" (*Letters*, p. 46).

EPILOGUE [2] was never published, although the original typescript is still to be seen among the Chicago MSS. Pound was later to write another EPILOGUE for *Lustra* (1916).

2. *exile:* Cf. THE REST.

IMMORALITY, AN
[NO. 48*a*. PRINTINGS: *12, 15, 42, 43, 53*]

The pragmatic Pound of the 1920s could hardly have been sympathetic toward the sentiment expressed in this poem (which curiously anticipates Yeats's "Politics"), and this is perhaps why "An Immorality" was excluded from the 1926 canon. See also page 261 above.

OUR RESPECTFUL HOMAGES TO M. LAURENT TAILHADE
[NO. 146*a*. PRINTING: 28]

Laurent Tailhade (1854–1919) collected his satirically invective verses in *Poèmes Aristophanesques* (1904). Pound writes admiringly of Tailhade in one of his articles on "The Approach to Paris" (*New Age* [Oct. 1913], 662) and quotes five of Tailhade's poems in "A Study in French Poets" (*Little Review* [Feb. 1918], 38–41). One of these ("Rus") is translated in *Listen* ([Spring 1960], 24).

[1. OM MANI PADME HUM / LET US ERECT A COLUMN, an epicene column / To Monsieur Laurent   28;   Come let us erect a phallic column to Laurent   *Faber and Faber*]

[5. of Monsieur Laurent   28;   of Laurent   *Faber and Faber*]

[9. Kordax   28;   Cordax   *Faber and Faber*]

9. *Zarabondilla . . . Cordax:* The traditional Spanish *zarabanda* has nothing in common with the notorious indecen-

cies of the κόρδαξ, which Aristophanes alludes to in *The Clouds* and which Pound calls "the dance of the phallus" in SALUTATION THE SECOND (l. 28).

11. Léon Bakst (1866–1924) designed costumes and decor for various productions by the Russian Ballet, among them *Cléopâtre*, which Pound recalls in LES MILLWIN.

13. The Latin *Et Dominus tecum* means "and the Lord be with thee."

RAPTURE, THE
[NO. 95*a*. PRINTING: 20]

This poem was originally the untitled fifth section of a sequence of epigrams called "Zenia." The title chosen for the Faber and Faber reprint glances ironically at a superbly erotic poem by Thomas Carew called "A Rapture."

[5. long as her head was averted.   20; long as she looked away.   *Faber and Faber*]

REFLECTION AND ADVICE
[NO. 76*a*. PRINTING: *16*]

This poem is written in the same manner as COMMISSION. Its original title seems to have been REFLECTION AND ADVICE (*Letters*, p. 53), but the text published in *Poetry* is called "Pax Saturni" ("The Peace of Saturn," i.e., the Golden Age) and carries the following verse epigraph from an unidentified "Contemporary," John Reed, who complained afterwards that Pound had cut the lines in such a way as to conceal their ironical intent (*Poetry* [June 1913], 112):

> Once . . . the round world brimmed with hate,
> and the strong
> Harried the weak. Long past, long past, praise God
> In these fair, peaceful, happy days.

14. *traitor:* Pound was charged with treason in 1943 for broadcasting on the Italian radio. Here, as in Canto I (where Odysseus/Pound is warned that he will "lose all companions" on his return to Ithaca/America), an early work is made to seem uncannily proleptic because of subsequent events in Pound's life. See also in this respect THE ALCHEMIST (l. 3*n*).

20–23. Pound managed to reassure Harriet Monroe that her squeamishness about these lines was quite unnecessary (*Letters*, p. 53).

[27*a*–*f*. In 16 *the following additional lines appear:*

Speak of the profundity of the reviewers,
Speak of the accuracy of reporters,
Speak of the unbiased press,
Speak of the square deal as if it always occurred.
Do all this and refrain from ironic touches:
    You will not lack your reward.]

BIBLIOGRAPHY

A comprehensive list of Pound's publications is provided by Donald Gallup, *A Bibliography of Ezra Pound* (1963). What follows is simply a list of the books and articles I have drawn on in compiling this *Guide:* those by Pound are listed chronologically; the rest are listed alphabetically. The place of publication of all books is London unless otherwise stated. Dates in square brackets are those of first editions in cases where only later editions were available.

BOOKS AND PERIODICAL ARTICLES BY POUND

Books

A Lume Spento (Venice, 1908).
A Quinzaine for This Yule (1908).
Personæ of Ezra Pound (1909).
Exultations of Ezra Pound (1909).
Miss Florence Schmidt . . . Book of Words (1910).
The Spirit of Romance (1910).
Provença (Boston, 1910).
Canzoni of Ezra Pound (1911).
The Sonnets and Ballate of Guido Cavalcanti (1912).
Des Imagistes [anthology; identical with item 21 on the Chronological List] (1914).
Poetical Works of Lionel Johnson (1915).
Gaudier-Brzeska: A Memoir (1916).
Pavannes and Divisions (New York, 1918).
Instigations of Ezra Pound (New York, 1920).
Umbra (1920).
The Natural Philosophy of Love (1957 [New York, 1922]).
Personæ (New York, 1926).
Selected Poems, ed. and intro. T. S. Eliot (1928).
ABC of Economics (1933).
ABC of Reading (1934).
Make It New (1934).
Jefferson and/or Mussolini (1935).
Polite Essays (1937).
Guide to Kulchur (1938).
Patria Mia (Chicago, 1950 [written 1913]).
The Letters of Ezra Pound, 1907–1941, ed. D. D. Paige (1951).
The Classic Anthology Defined by Confucius (Cambridge, Mass., 1954).

Literary Essays of Ezra Pound, ed. and intro. T. S. Eliot (1954).
The Cantos of Ezra Pound [1–71, 74–84] (1954).
Section: Rock-Drill 85–95 de los Cantares (1957 [Milano, 1955]).
Thrones 96–109 de los Cantares (1960).
Love Poems of Ancient Egypt (New York, 1962).
EP to LU, ed. J. A. Robbins (Indiana, 1963).
A Lume Spento and Other Early Poems (1965).

Periodical Articles

"Belangal Alba [poem]," *Hamilton Literary Magazine*, XXXIX, 9
(May 1905), 324.
"Canzon: The Yearly Slain [poem]," *English Review*, IV, 2 (Jan.
1910), 193–194.
"The Fault of It [poem]," *Forum*, XLVI, 1 (July 1911), 107.
"I Gather the Limbs of Osiris [V]," *New Age*, X, 9 (Dec. 28, 1911),
201–202.
"Echoes: I (Trecento) Guido Orlando, Singing [poem]," *North
American Review*, CXCV, 674 (Jan. 1912), 75.
"Prolegomena," *Poetry Review*, I, 2 (Feb. 1912), 72–76.
"L'Invitation [poem]," *Poetry Review*, I, 2 (Feb. 1912), 78.
"Salve Pontifex [poem]," *Poetry Review*, I, 2 (Feb. 1912), 78–80.
"I Gather the Limbs of Osiris [XI]," *New Age*, X, 16 (Feb. 15,
1912), 369–370.
"Patria Mia [I]," *New Age*, XI, 19 (Sept. 5, 1912), 445.
"Patria Mia [II]," *New Age*, XI, 20 (Sept. 12, 1912), 466.
"Patria Mia [III]," *New Age*, XI, 21 (Sept. 19, 1912), 491–492.
"Patria Mia [IV]," *New Age*, XI, 22 (Sept. 26, 1912), 515–516.
"Psychology and Troubadours," *Quest*, IV, 1 (Oct. 1912), 37–53.
"Patria Mia [V]," *New Age*, XI, 23 (Oct. 3, 1912), 539–540.
"Patria Mia [VIII]," *New Age*, XI, 26 (Oct. 24, 1912), 611–612.
"Patria Mia [IX]," *New Age*, XI, 27 (Oct. 31, 1912), 635–636.
"Patria Mia [XI]," *New Age*, XII, 2 (Nov. 14, 1912), 33–34.
"Through Alien Eyes [III]," *New Age*, XII, 13 (Jan. 30, 1913), 300–
301.
"A Few Don'ts by an Imagiste," *Poetry*, I, 6 (March 1913), 200–
206.
"America: Chances and Remedies [II]," *New Age*, XIII, 6 (May 8,
1913), 34.
"How I Began," *T. P.'s Weekly*, XXI, 552 (June 6, 1913), 707.
"[Review of] *Love Poems and Others*, by D. H. Lawrence," *Poetry*,
II, 4 (July 1913), 149–151.
"Troubadours: Their Sorts and Conditions," *Quarterly Review*,
CCXIX, 437 (Oct. 1913), 426–440.
"The Approach to Paris [V]," *New Age*, XIII, 23 (Oct. 2, 1913),
662–664.
"The Approach to Paris [VII]," *New Age*, XIII, 25 (Oct. 16, 1913),
726–728.
"The Serious Artist [III]," *New Freewoman*, I, 10 (Nov. 1, 1913),
194–195.
"Peals of Iron," *Poetry*, III, 3 (Dec. 1913), 111–113.
"The Tradition," *Poetry*, III, 4 (Jan. 1914), 137–141.
"John Synge and the Habits of Criticism," *Egoist*, I, 3 (Feb. 2,
1914), 53–54 [signed: "Bastien von Helmholtz"].

"Homage to Wilfred Blunt," *Poetry*, III, 6 (March 1914), 220–223.

"Allen Upward Serious," *New Age*, XIV, 25 (April 23, 1914), 779–780.

"The Later Yeats," *Poetry*, IV, 2 (May 1914), 64–69.

"Mr. Hueffer and the Prose Tradition in English Verse," *Poetry*, IV, 3 (June 1914), 111–120.

"Vorticism," *Fortnightly Review*, n.s., XCVI, 578 (Sept. 1, 1914), 461–471.

"Those American Publications," *Egoist*, I, 20 (Oct. 15, 1914), 390 [signed: "Baptiste von Helmholtz"].

"Webster Ford," *Egoist*, II, 1 (Jan. 1, 1915), 11–12.

"Affirmations [I]," *New Age*, XVI, 10 (Jan. 7, 1915), 246–247.

"The Renaissance [I]," *Poetry*, V, 5 (Feb. 1915), 227–233.

"Imagisme and England. A Vindication and an Anthology," *T. P.'s Weekly*, XXV, 641 (Feb. 20, 1915), 185.

"[Review of] *Ernest Dowson*, by Victor Plarr," *Poetry*, VI, 1 (April 1915), 43–45.

"Hark to Sturge Moore," *Poetry*, VI, 3 (June 1915), 139–145.

"A Rejoinder [letter]," *Poetry*, VI, 3 (June 1915), 157–158.

"Our Respectful Homages to M. Laurent Tailhade [poem]," *Blast*, no. 2 (July 1915), 21.

"Et Faim Sallir le Loup des Boys [poem]," *Blast*, no. 2 (July 1915), 22.

"American Chaos [II]," *New Age*, XVII, 20 (Sept. 16, 1915), 471.

"On 'Near Perigord,'" *Poetry*, VII, 3 (Dec. 1915), 143–146.

"Remy de Gourmont," *Poetry*, VII, 4 (Jan. 1916), 197–202.

"Thomas MacDonagh as Critic," *Poetry*, VIII, 6 (Sept. 1916), 309–312.

"The War and Divers Impressions. Mr. [C. R. W.] Nevinson Thinks that the Public Is More Interested in the War than It Is in Art," *Vogue*, XLVIII, 7 (Oct. 1, 1916), 74–75 [unsigned].

"Dreiser Protest," *Egoist*, III, 10 (Oct. 1916), 159.

"Things to Be Done," *Poetry*, IX, 6 (March 1917), 312–314.

"Dialogues of Fontenelle [XII]," *Egoist*, IV, 5 (June 1917), 70–71.

"Three Cantos [II]," *Poetry*, X, 4 (July 1917), 180–188.

"Provincialism the Enemy [III]," *New Age*, XXI, 13 (July 26, 1917), 288–289.

"Provincialism the Enemy [IV]," *New Age*, XXI, 14 (Aug. 2, 1917), 308–309.

"T. S. Eliot," *Poetry*, X, 5 (Aug. 1917), 264–271.

"Elizabethan Classicists [I]," *Egoist*, IV, 8 (Sept. 1917), 120–122.

"Studies in Contemporary Mentality [IV]," *New Age*, XXI, 19 (Sept. 6, 1917), 406–407.

"Editorial on Solicitous Doubt," *Little Review*, IV, 6 (Oct. 1917), 20–22.

"Elizabethan Classicists [III]," *Egoist*, IV, 10 (Nov. 1917), 154–156.

"Landor: 1775–1865. A Note," *Future*, II, 1 (Nov. 1917), 10–12.

"Irony, Laforgue, and Some Satire," *Poetry*, XI, 2 (Nov. 1917), 93–98.

"The Reader Critic," *Little Review*, IV, 8 (Dec. 1917), 55–56.

"Studies in Contemporary Mentality [XVIII]," *New Age*, XXII, 9 (Dec. 27, 1917), 167–170.

"The Middle Years," *Egoist*, V, 1 (Jan. 1918), 2–3.

"A Study of French Modern Poets," *Little Review*, IV, 10 (Feb. 1918), 3–61.

"The Hard and Soft in French Poetry," *Poetry*, XI, 5 (Feb. 1918), 264–271.

"The Classics 'Escape,'" *Little Review*, IV, 11 (March 1918), 32–34.

"A List of Books," *Little Review*, IV, 11 (March 1918), 54–58.

"Swinburne versus His Biographers," *Poetry*, XI, 6 (March 1918), 322–329.

"Music," *New Age*, XII, 19 (March 7, 1918), 377–378 [signed: "William Atheling"].

"Unanimism," *Little Review*, IV, 12 (April 1918), 26–32.

"Chinese Poetry [I]," *To-Day*, III, 14 (April 1918), 54–57.

"Chinese Poetry [II]," *To-Day*, III, 15 (May 1918), 93–95.

"Our Tetrarchal Précieuse," *Little Review*, V, 3 (July 1918), 3–12 [signed: "Thayer Exton"].

"In Explanation," *Little Review*, V, 4 (Aug. 1918), 5–6.

"Brief Note," *Little Review*, V, 4 (Aug. 1918), 6–9.

"A Shake Down," *Little Review*, V, 4 (Aug. 1918), 9–39.

"Art Notes," *New Age*, XXIII, 22 (26 Sept. 1918), 352 [signed: "B. H. Dias"]

"Breviora," *Little Review*, V, 6 (Oct. 1918), 23–24.

"Albert Mockel and 'La Wallonie,'" *Little Review*, V, 6 (Oct. 1918), 51–64.

"Mr. Villerant's Morning Outburst," *Little Review*, V, 7 (Nov. 1918), 7–12.

"Genesis, or, the First Book in the Bible ('Subject to Authority')," *Little Review*, V, 7 (Nov. 1918), 50–64 [unsigned].

"De Gourmont: A Distinction (Followed by Notes)," *Little Review*, V, 10–11 (Feb.–March 1919), 1–19.

"The Death of Vorticism," *Little Review*, V, 10–11 (Feb.–March 1919), 45–49.

"Mr. Pound and His Poetry [letter]," *Athenæum*, XCIII, 4670 (Oct. 31, 1919), 1132.

"'Homage to Sextus Propertius' [letter]," *New Age*, XXVI, 5 (Dec. 4, 1919), 82–83.

"Pavlova," *Athenæum*, XCIV, 4695 (April 23, 1920), 553 [signed: "T. J. V."].

"Indiscretions; or, Une Revue de Deux Mondes [II]," *New Age*, XXVII, 5 (June 3, 1920), 76–77.

"Indiscretions; or, Une Revue de Deux Mondes [VIII]," *New Age*, XXVII, 11 (July 15, 1920), 172–173.

"Indiscretions; or, Une Revue de Deux Mondes [XI]," *New Age*, XXVII, 14 (Aug. 5, 1920), 221–222.

"[Review of] Jean Cocteau, *Poésies 1917–1920*," *Dial*, LXX, 1 (Jan. 1921), 110.

"On Criticism in General," *Criterion*, I, 2 (Jan. 1923), 143–156.

"Donna Mi Prega," *Dial*, LXXXV, 1 (July 1928), 1–20.

"Wanted," *Exile*, no. 4 (Autumn 1928), 9 [signed: "Benjamin Peret"]

"How to Read [III]," *New York Herald Tribune Books*, V, 19 (Jan. 27, 1929), 1.

"Horace," *Criterion*, IX, 35 (Jan. 1930), 217–227.

"Harold Monro," XI, 45 (July 1932), 581–592.

"Teacher's Mission," *English Journal*, XXIII, 8 (Oct. 1934), 630–635.

"Five Poems," *Furioso*, I, 2 (New Year Issue, 1940), 5.

"Five French Poems," *Listen*, III, 3–4 (Spring 1960), 22–26.

"Four Translations [from Montanari (1) and Horace (3)]," *Agenda*, III, 5 (Sept. 1964), 1–3.

"Redondillas, or Something of That Sort [poem rejected from *Canzoni* (1911), intro. by Noel Stock]," *Poetry Australia*, no. 15 (April 1967), 4–11.

Unpublished Letters

Letters from Ezra Pound to Harriet Monroe in the University of Chicago Library (Harriet Monroe Modern Poetry Collection).

Letters from Ezra Pound to William Carlos Williams in the Lockwood Memorial Library, University of Buffalo.

GENERAL

Acker, W. *T'ao the Hermit* (1952).

Ackerman, R. W. *An Index to Arthurian Names in Middle English* (1952).

Agathias. [Poem in] *The Greek Anthology*, ed. and trans. W. R. Paton (Loeb Classical Library, 1925 [1915]), vol. 3, pp. 78–79.

Aldington, R. "Penultimate Poetry. Xenophilometropolitania," *Egoist*, I, 2 (Jan. 15, 1914), 36.

———. "Modern Poetry and the Imagists," *Egoist*, I, 11 (June 1, 1914), 201–203.

Aldington, R., trans. "The Poems of Anyte of Tegea," *Egoist*, II, 9 (Sept. 1, 1915), 139.

Amdur, A. S. *The Poetry of Ezra Pound* (Cambridge, Mass., 1936).

Anon. "Fine Art Gossip," *Athenæum*, no. 4523 (July 4, 1914), 26.

Anyte. [Poem in] *The Greek Anthology*, ed. and trans. W. R. Paton (Loeb Classical Library, 1925 [1915]), vol. 3, pp. 74–75.

Apuleius, L. *The Golden Ass*, trans. W. Adlington, rev. S. Gaselee (Loeb Classical Library, 1928 [1915]).

Aristotle. *The Politics*, ed. and trans. H. Rackham (Loeb Classical Library, 1932).

Arnaut. *Les Poésies Lyriques du Troubadour Arnaut de Mareuil*, ed. R. C. Johnson (Paris, 1935).

Asclepiades. [Poem in] *The Greek Anthology*, ed. and trans. W. R. Paton (Loeb Classical Library, 1920 [1916]), vol. 1, pp. 168–169.

Augurello, G. A. [Poem in] *Carmina Illustrium Poetarum Italorum* (Florence, 1719), I, 408.

Bantock, G. [Musical settings to] "South Folk in Cold Country," "Song of the Bowmen of Shu," "Lament of the Frontier Guard" (1923).

Barnes, B. *Parthenophil and Parthenophe* (1593), repr. in *Elizabethan Sonnets*, intro. S. Lee (1904), vol. 1.

Barry, I. "The Ezra Pound Period," *Bookman*, LXXIV, 2 (Oct. 1931), 159–171.

Baudelaire, C. *Les Fleurs du Mal*, ed. M. J. Crépet (Paris, 1930).

Beerbohm, M. *The Incomparable Max,* intro. S. C. Roberts (1962).

Benton, R. P. "A Gloss on Pound's 'Four Poems of Departure,'" *Literature East and West,* X (Sept. 1966), 292–301.

Bergman, H. "Ezra Pound and Walt Whitman," *American Literature,* XXVII, 1 (March 1955), 56–61.

Berry, A., ed. *Florilège des Troubadours* (Paris, 1930).

Bertran. *Poésies Complètes de Bertran de Born,* ed. A. Thomas (Toulouse, 1888).

Bion. [Poems in] *The Greek Bucolic Poets,* ed. and trans. J. M. Edmonds (Loeb Classical Library, 1923 [1912]).

Bornstein, G. J., and H. H. Witemeyer. "From *Villain* to Visionary: Pound and Yeats on Villon," *Comparative Literature,* XIX, 4 (Fall 1967), 308–320.

Boutière, J., and A.-H. Schutz. *Biographies des Troubadours* (Toulouse and Paris, 1950).

Bowen, S. *Drawn from Life* (1941).

Brooke. *The Collected Poems of Rupert Brooke, with a Memoir,* ed. E. Marsh (1918).

Browning, R., *The Poetical Works* (1897).

Buchanan, R. W. "The Fleshly School of Poetry: Mr. D. G. Rossetti [review of Rossetti's *Poems,* 5th ed.]," *Contemporary Review,* XVIII, 3 (Oct. 1871), 334–350 [signed: "Thomas Maitland"].

Buckle, H. T. *History of Civilization in England* (1857–1861). 2 vols.

Butler, S. *Hudibras,* ed. A. R. Waller (Cambridge, 1905).

Byron. *The Works of Lord Byron,* ed. E. H. Coleridge (1903), vol. 6 [*Don Juan*].

Callicter. [Poem in] *The Greek Anthology,* ed. and trans. W. R. Paton (Loeb Classical Library, 1948 [1918]), vol. 4, pp. 126–127.

Callimachus. *Callimachus and Lycophron,* ed. and trans. A. W. Mair (Loeb Classical Library, 1921).

Carne-Ross, D. S. "New Metres for Old: a Note on Pound's Metric," *Arion,* VI, 2 (Summer 1967), 216–232.

Catullus. *Catullus, Tibullus and Pervigilium Veneris,* ed. and trans. F. W. Cornish, J. P. Postgate, and J. W. Mackail (Loeb Classical Library, 1939 [1913]).

Chisolm, L. W. *Fenollosa: The Far East and American Culture* (1963).

Cicero. *The Speeches,* ed. and trans. N. H. Watts (Loeb Classical Library, 1935 [1923]).

———. *The Speeches,* ed. and trans. L. E. Lord (Loeb Classical Library, 1946 [1937]).

Cino. *Poesie di Messer Cino da Pistoia,* ed. S. Ciampi (Pistoia, 1826).

Coleridge, S. T. *Biographia Literaria,* ed. J. Shawcross (Oxford, 1907), vol. 2.

———. *The Poetical Works of Samuel Taylor Coleridge,* ed. J. D. Campbell (1893).

Collinge, N. E. "Gongyla and Mr. Pound," *Notes and Queries,* n.s., V, 6 (June 1958), 265–266.

Connolly, T. E. "Ezra Pound's 'Near Perigord': The Background of a Poem," *Comparative Literature,* VIII, 2 (Spring 1956), 110–121.

Cournos, J. *Autobiography* (New York, 1935).

Cowley, M. *Exile's Return* (New York, 1951 [1934]).

Cull, A. T. *Poems to Pavlova* (1912).

Dante. *The Divine Comedy,* trans. J. D. Sinclair (1939–1946). 3 vols.

————. *The Odes,* trans. H. S. Vere-Hodge (Oxford, 1963).

Davie, D. "Ezra Pound's *Hugh Selwyn Mauberley,*" in *The Modern Age,* ed. B. Ford (Penguin Books, 1961), pp. 315–329.

————. *Ezra Pound: Poet as Sculptor* (New York, 1964).

Dejeanne, J. M. L. "Le Troubadour Cercamon," *Annales du Midi,* XVI, 65 (Jan. 1905), 27–62.

Demetz, P. "Ezra Pound's German Studies," *Germanic Review,* XXXI, 4 (Dec. 1956), 279–292.

De Vega, L. *Poesías Líricas* (Madrid, 1914), vol. 2.

Dickens, B., and R. M. Wilson, eds. *Early Middle English Texts* (Cambridge, 1951).

Dobson, A. " 'Sat Est Scripsisse' [poem]," *Yellow Book,* II (July 1894), 142–143.

D'Orléans, C. *Poésies,* ed. P. Champion (Paris, 1923), vol. 1.

Dostoevsky, F. *The Brothers Karamazov,* trans. C. Garnett (1945 [1912]).

Doughty, O. *A Victorian Romantic: Dante Gabriel Rossetti* (1949).

Dowson. *The Poems of Ernest Dowson,* ed. M. Longaker (Philadelphia, 1962).

————. *The Stories of Ernest Dowson,* ed. M. Longaker (New York, 1960).

Drew-Bear, T. "Ezra Pound's 'Homage to Sextus Propertius,' " *American Literature,* XXXVII, 2 (May 1965), 204–210.

Du Bellay, J. *Œuvres Poétiques,* ed. H. Chamard (Paris, 1910), vol. 2.

Ede, H. S. *A Life of Gaudier-Brzeska* (1930).

Edel, L., ed. *Selected Letters of Henry James* (1956).

Edwards, J. H. "A Critical Biography of Ezra Pound, 1885–1922," unpublished Ph.D. dissertation, University of California, Berkeley, 1952.

Edwards, J. H., and W. W. Vasse. *Annotated Index to the Cantos of Ezra Pound, Cantos I–LXXXIV* (Berkeley and Los Angeles, 1957).

Elias de Barjols. *Le Troubadour Elias de Barjols,* ed. S. Stroński (Toulouse, 1906).

Eliot, T. S. *Collected Poems 1909–1935* (1936).

Eliot, T. S., ed. *Ezra Pound: Selected Poems* (1928).

Ellmann, R. "Ez and Old Billyum," *Kenyon Review,* XXVIII, 4 (Sept. 1966), 470–495.

Emslie, M. "Pound's 'Hugh Selwyn Mauberley,' I, iii, 13–16," *Explicator,* XIV, 4 (Jan. 1956), item 26.

Espey, J. J. *Ezra Pound's 'Mauberley': a Study in Composition* (1955).

————. "Vers Propertius," *Les Cahiers de l'Herne,* ed. D. de Roux (Paris, 1965), vol. 2, pp. 502–507.

Fang, A. "A Note on Pound's 'Papyrus,' " *Modern Language Notes,* LXVII, 3 (March 1952), 188–190.

————. "Fenollosa and Pound," *Harvard Journal of Asiatic Studies,* XX, 1–2 (June 1957), 213–238.

Farnell, I. *The Lives of the Troubadours* (1896).

Fitzgerald, E. *Selected Works*, ed. J. Richardson (1962).

Flint, F. S. "Verse," *New Age*, VI (Dec. 9, 1909), 137–138.

——. "[Review of] *Ripostes*," *Poetry and Drama*, I, 1 (March 1913), 60–62.

——. "The History of Imagism," *Egoist*, II, 5 (May 1, 1915), 70–71.

Forbes, C. A. "Ezra Pound and Sextus Propertius," *Classical Journal*, XLII, 3 (Dec. 1946), 177–179.

Ford, F. M. "The Poet's Eye [I–II]," *New Freewoman*, I, 6 (Sept. 1, 1913), 107–110.

——. "On Heaven," *Poetry*, IV, 3 (June 1914), 75–94.

——. *Thus to Revisit* (1921).

——. *Return to Yesterday* (1931).

Franklin, B. *Autobiography*, ed. W. Macdonald (1948).

Fraser, G. S. *Ezra Pound* (1960).

Frean, R. G. "Walter Pater's *Marius the Epicurean:* Notes and Commentary Preliminary to a Critical Edition," unpublished Ph.D. dissertation, University of Toronto, 1961.

French, A. L. " 'Olympian Apathein': Pound's *Hugh Selwyn Mauberley* and Modern Poetry," *Essays in Criticism*, XV, 4 (Oct. 1965), 428–445; cf. "Critical Forum," *ibid.*, XVI, 3 (July 1966), 351–359.

Friar, K., and J. M. Brinnin, eds. *Modern Poetry* (New York, 1951).

Gadan, F., and R. Maillard. *A Dictionary of Modern Ballet* (1959).

Gallup, D. *A Bibliography of Ezra Pound* (1963).

Gatti, C. *Verdi: The Man and His Music*, trans. E. Abbott (1955).

Gautier, T. *Émaux et Camées: Edition Définitive avec une Eau-Forte par J. Jacquemart* (Paris, 1881).

Giles, H. A. *A History of Chinese Literature* (1901).

——. *Chinese Poetry in English Verse* (1898).

Goldring, D. *The Last Pre-Raphaelite: A Record of the Life and Writings of Ford Madox Ford* (1948).

Goodwin, K. L. *The Influence of Ezra Pound* (Oxford, 1966).

Gosse, E. *The Life of Algernon Charles Swinburne* (1917).

Gourmont, R. de. *Esthétique de la Langue Française* (Paris, 1899).

——. *Le Problème du Style* (Paris, 1902).

——. *Lettres à l'Amazone* (Paris, 1925 [1914]).

Grant, J. *Harold Monro and the Poetry Bookshop* (1967).

Grierson, H. J. C., and G. Bullough, eds. *The Oxford Book of Seventeenth Century Verse* (Oxford, 1934).

Griffiths, J. C. [Letter in] *Times Literary Supplement*, no. 3372 (Oct. 13, 1966), 939.

Guttery, D. R. "Pastiche," *New Age*, XVII, 25 (Oct. 21, 1915), 603.

Hadrian. [Poem in] *The Scriptores Historiae Augustae*, ed. and trans. D. Magie (Loeb Classical Library, 1930), vol. 1.

Hagedorn, H. "The Cabaret Dancer," *Poetry*, VII, 3 (Dec. 1915), 125.

Hale, W. G. "Pegasus Impounded," *Poetry*, XIV, 1 (April 1919), 52–55.

Halleck. *The Poetical Writings of Fitz-Greene Halleck*, ed. J. R. Drake (New York, 1869).

Harris, F. [Letter in] *Little Review*, IV, 6 (Oct. 1917), 40.

Hassall, C. *Edward Marsh: Patron of the Arts* (1959).

Hatto, A. T., ed. *Eos: an Enquiry into the Theme of Lovers' Meetings and Partings at Dawn* (The Hague, 1965).

Heine. *Heinrich Heines Buch der Lieder*, ed. E. Elster (Stuttgart, 1887); ed. J. Lees (Manchester, 1920).

Henley, W. E. *Poems* (1898).

Holbrooke, J. C. *Op. 77, nos. 1 and 2* [accompaniments on oboe, viola, and piano for "Salutation" and "The Garret"] (1922).

——. *Op. 77 nos. 4 and 5* [clarinet obligatos for "The Tea-Shop Girl" and "Tame Cat"] (1923).

Holder, A. "The Lesson of the Master: Ezra Pound and Henry James," *American Literature*, XXXV, 1 (March 1963), 71–79.

Holly, H. *Creation: Post-Impressionist Poems* (1914).

Hombitzer, E. "Ezra Pound: *Phanopœia*. Hinweise zu einer Interpretation," *Neueren Sprachen*, XIV, 7 (July 1965), 568–578.

Homer. *The Iliad*, ed. and trans. A. T. Murray (Loeb Classical Library, 1924–1925). 2 vols.

——. *The Odyssey*, ed. and trans. A. T. Murray (Loeb Classical Library, 1924 [1919]. 2 vols.

Horace. *The Odes and Epodes*, ed. and trans. C. E. Bennett (Loeb Classical Library, 1929 [1914]).

——. *Satires, Epistles and Ars Poetica*, ed. and trans. H. R. Fairclough (Loeb Classical Library, 1932 [1926]).

Housman. *The Collected Poems of A. E. Housman* (1939).

Hueffer, F. *The Troubadours* (1878).

Hughes, G. *Imagism and the Imagists* (Stanford, 1931).

Hugo, V. *Œuvres Complètes* (Paris, 1907), vol. 8.

Hulme, T. E. *Speculations*, ed. H. Read (1924).

Hurwitz, H. M. "Ezra Pound and Rabindranath Tagore," *American Literature*, XXXVI, 1 (March 1964), 53–63.

Hutchins, P. *Ezra Pound's Kensington: An Exploration, 1885–1913* (1965).

——. "Ezra Pound and Thomas Hardy," *Southern Review*, IV, 1 (Jan. 1968), 90–104.

Ibycus. [Poem in] *Lyra Graeca*, ed. and trans. J. M. Edmonds (Loeb Classical Library, 1958 [1924]), vol. 2.

Irwin, W. R. "The Survival of Pan," *PMLA*, LXXVI, 3 (June 1961), 159–167.

Jackson, H. *The Eighteen Nineties* (1927 [1913]).

James, H. *The Ambassadors*, intro. F. Swinnerton (1948).

Jeanroy, A., ed. *Les Chansons de Guillaume IX, Duc d'Aquitaine* (Paris, 1913).

Jenyns, S. *Selections from Chinese Verse* (1899).

Johnson, L. *The Complete Poems*, ed. I. Fletcher (1953).

Jones, A. R. *The Life and Opinions of T. E. Hulme* (1960).

Julianus. [Poem in] *The Greek Anthology*, ed. and trans. W. R. Paton (Loeb Classical Library, 1919 [1917]), vol. 2, pp. 22–23.

Kandinsky, W. "Inner Necessity," trans. E. Wadsworth, *Blast*, no. 1 (June 20, 1914), 119–125.

Keats. *Letters*, ed. F. Page (Oxford, 1954).

Kenner, H. *The Poetry of Ezra Pound* (1951).

Laforgue, J. *Poésies* (Paris, n.d.), vol. 2.

Leavis, F. R. *New Bearings in English Poetry* (1954 [1932]).

Lee, P. and D. Murray. "The Quality of *Cathay*: Ezra Pound's Early Translations of Chinese Poems," *Literature East and West,* X (Sept. 1966), 264–277.

Legge, J., trans. *The Chinese Classics* (1871), vol. 4, pt. 2.

Leopardi, G. *Selected Prose and Poetry,* ed. and trans. I. Origo and J. Heath-Stubbs (Oxford, 1966).

Leslie, R. F. "An Edition of the Old English Elegiac Poems 'The Wanderer' and 'The Seafarer,' with a Study of Old English Elegiac Poetry," unpublished Ph.D. dissertation, University of Manchester, 1955.

Levin, H. *Refractions: Essays in Comparative Literature* (New York, 1966).

Lewis, C. T., and C. Short. *A Latin Dictionary* (Oxford, 1955 [1879]).

Lewis, W. "Inferior Religions," *Little Review,* IV, 5 (Sept. 1917). 3–8.

———. *Time and Western Man* (1927).

———. *Men without Art* (1934).

———. *Blasting and Bombardiering* (1937).

———. *The Letters of Wyndham Lewis,* ed. W. K. Rose (1963).

Longfellow. *The Writings of Henry Wadsworth Longfellow* (1886). 11 vols.

Lovelace. *The Poems of Richard Lovelace,* ed. C. H. Wilkinson (Oxford, 1930).

Lowell, A. *Six French Poets* (New York, 1915).

———. *The Complete Poetical Works,* ed. and intro. L. Untermeyer (Boston, 1955).

Machiavelli, N. *Florentine History,* trans. W. K. Marriott (1909).

Malory. *The Works of Sir Thomas Malory,* ed. E. Vinaver (Oxford, 1948 [1947]), vol. 1.

Marlowe, C. *Poems,* ed. L. C. Martin (1931).

Marsh, E. *A Number of People* (1939).

Martial. *Epigrams,* ed. and trans. W. C. A. Ker (Loeb Classical Library, 1919), vol. 1.

Martin, W. D. "Freud and Imagism," *Notes and Queries,* n.s., VIII, 12 (Dec. 1961), 470–471, 474.

———. "The Literary Significance of *The New Age* under the Editorship of A. R. Orage, 1907–1922," unpublished Ph.D. dissertation, University of London, 1961.

Merivale, P. "The Pan Figure in Victorian Poetry: Landor to Meredith," *Philological Quarterly,* XLIV, 2 (April 1965), 258–277.

Miner, E. *The Japanese Tradition in British and American Literature* (Princeton, 1958).

Monroe, H. *A Poet's Life* (New York, 1938).

Mott, F. L. *American Journalism: A History of American Newspapers in the United States through 260 Years: 1690 to 1950* (rev. ed.; New York, 1950).

Nagy, N. C. de. *The Poetry of Ezra Pound: The Pre-Imagist Stage* (Bern, 1960).

———. *Ezra Pound's Poetics and Literary Tradition: The Critical Decade* (Bern, 1966).

Navagero, A. [Poem in] *Carmina Illustrium Poetarum Italorum* (Florence, 1720), vol. 6.

Nelli, R., and R. Lavaud, eds. *Les Troubadours* (Paris, 1966), vol. 2.

Nemesianus. [Poem in] *Minor Latin Poets*, ed. and trans. J. W. Duff and A. M. Duff (Loeb Classical Library, 1935 [1934]).

Nicarchus. *See* Callicter.

Norman, C. *Ezra Pound* (New York, 1960).

Obata, S., trans. *The Works of Li Po* (1923).

Omans, G. "The Villon Cult in England," *Comparative Literature*, XVII, 1 (Winter 1966), 16–35.

Opie, I., and P. Opie. *The Oxford Dictionary of Nursery Rhymes* (Oxford, 1951).

Orage, A. R. "Readers and Writers," *New Age*, XVI, 3 (Nov. 19, 1914), 69 [signed: "R. H. C."].

Ovid. *The Art of Love, and Other Poems*, ed. and trans. J. H. Mozley (Loeb Classical Library, 1947 [1929]).

――――. *Metamorphoses*, ed. and trans. F. J. Miller (Loeb Classical Library, 1951 [1916]). 2 vols.

Owen. *The Poems of Wilfred Owen*, ed. E. Blunden (1955).

Palladas. [Poems in] *The Greek Anthology*, ed. and trans. W. R. Paton (Loeb Classical Library, 1948 [1918]), vol. 4, pp. 32–33, 252–253.

Parrhasius. [Poem in] *Elegy and Iambus . . . with the Anacreontea*, ed. and trans. J. M. Edmonds (Loeb Classical Library, 1931), vol. 2, p. 20.

Pater, W. *The Renaissance* (1888 [1873]).

――――. *Marius the Epicurean* (1892 [1885]). 2 vols.

Patmore, B. "Ezra Pound in England," *Texas Quarterly*, VII, 3 (Fall 1964), 69–81.

Pervigilium Veneris. *See* Catullus.

Petrarch. *Rime e Trionfi di Francesco Petrarca*, ed. F. Neri (Torino, 1963).

Pindar. *The Odes*, ed. and trans. J. Sandys (Loeb Classical Library, 1919 [1915]).

Plarr, V. "The Art of Lionel Johnson," *Poetry Review*, I, 6 (June 1912), 252–263.

――――. "A Note on a Savage Poet [Bonga Bonga]," *Poetry and Drama*, I, 3 (Sept. 1913), 344–347.

――――. *Ernest Dowson, 1888–1897* (1914).

――――. "Strasbourg [poem]," *Times*, no. 41,976 (Dec. 18, 1918), 11.

Plutarch. *Moralia*, ed. and trans. F. C. Babbitt (Loeb Classical Library, 1936), vol. 5.

Propertius. *Catulli Tibulli Propertii Carmina*, ed. L. Mueller (Lipsiae, 1874).

Propertius. Ed. and trans. H. E. Butler (Loeb Classical Library, 1922 [1912]).

Quinn, M. B. "The Metamorphoses of Ezra Pound," in *Motive and Method in* The Cantos *of Ezra Pound*, ed. L. Leary (New York, 1954), pp. 60–100.

Ramsey, W. *Jules Laforgue and the Ironic Inheritance* (New York, 1953).

Randall, A. E. "Neo-Nietzsche [poem]," *New Age*, VI (Feb. 3, 1910), 317.

Read, H. *A Concise History of Modern Painting* (1959).

Reed, J. "A Word to Mr. Pound," *Poetry*, II, 3 (June 1913), 112–113.

Reinach, S. *Apollo*, trans. F. Simmonds (New York, 1924 [1904]).

Richardson, L. "Ezra Pound's 'Homage to Sextus Propertius,'" *Yale Poetry Review*, VI (1947), 21–29.

Rimbaud, A. *Œuvres*, ed. M. Raymond (Lausanne, 1957).

Ronsard, P. de. *Œuvres Complètes*, ed. P. Laumonier (Paris, 1914), vol. 2.

Rose, W. K. "Ezra Pound and Wyndham Lewis: The Crucial Years," *Southern Review*, IV, 1 (Jan. 1968), 72–89.

Rosenthal, M. L. *The Modern Poets* (New York, 1960).

Ross, R. H. *The Georgian Revolt* (1967).

Rossetti. *The Works of Dante Gabriel Rossetti*, ed. W. M. Rossetti (1911).

Rummel, W. M. *Songs of Ezra Pound: For a Voice with Instrumental Accompaniment* (1913).

Russell, P. "The Youth of Ezra Pound," *Southern Review*, II, 2 (Spring 1966), 443–452.

Ruthven, K. K. "The Composite Mistress," *AUMLA*, no. 26 (Nov. 1966), 198–214.

Sackville, C. [Poems in] *The Poems of Sir George Etherege*, ed. J. Thorpe (Princeton, 1963).

Sackville-West, V. *Pepita* (1937).

Sappho. [Poems in] *Lyra Graeca*, ed. and trans. J. M. Edmonds (Loeb Classical Library, 1922), vol. 1.

Saul, G. B. *Prolegomena to the Study of Yeats's Poems* (Philadelphia, 1957).

Schmutzler, R. *Art Nouveau* (1964).

Shakespeare. *The Complete Works of William Shakespeare* (Oxford, 1955).

Shelley. *The Complete Works of Percy Bysshe Shelley*, ed. T. Hutchinson (1934).

Sidgwick, F. *Some Verse* (1915).

Simonides. [Poem in] *The Greek Anthology*, ed. and trans. W. R. Paton (Loeb Classical Library, 1948 [1918]), vol. 4.

Simpson, H. "The Poets' Club Revue [poem]," *Poetry and Drama*, I, 2 (June 1913), 168–170.

Sisam, K. "Mr. Pound and 'The Seafarer' [letter]," *Times Literary Supplement*, no. 2734 (June 25, 1954), 409.

Slatin, M. "A History of Pound's *Cantos* I–XVI, 1915–1925," *American Literature*, XXXV, 2 (May 1963), 183–195.

Smith, J. H. *The Troubadours at Home* (1899). 2 vols.

Smythe, B. *Trobador Poets* (1911).

Spenser, E. *Spenser's Minor Poems*, ed. E. de Sélincourt (Oxford, 1910).

Stead, C. K. *The New Poetic* (1964).

Steadman, P. "Colour Music and the Art of Lumia," *Image* (1964), 17–22 [the issue carries no serial number, but is subtitled "Kinetic Art: Concrete Poetry"].

Stock, N. *Poet in Exile* (Manchester, 1964).

———, ed. *Perspectives* (Chicago, 1965).

Storer, E., trans. "Poems and Fragments of Sappho," *Egoist*, II, 10 (Oct. 1, 1915), 153–155.

Stroński, S. *La Légende Amoureuse de Bertran de Born* (Paris, 1914).

Sullivan, J. P. *Ezra Pound and Sextus Propertius: A Study in Creative Translation* (1965).

Sweet's Anglo-Saxon Reader in Prose and Verse, ed. C. T. Onions (rev. ed.; Oxford, 1946).

Swinburne, A. C. *Poetical Works* (1904). 6 vols.

Symons, A. *Days and Nights* (1889).

———. *Silhouettes* (1896).

———. *Images of Good and Evil* (1899).

———. *Studies in Seven Arts* (1906).

Tanselle, G. T. "Two Early Letters of Ezra Pound," *American Literature*, XXXIV, 1 (March 1962), 114–119.

Taupin, R. *L'Influence du Symbolisme Français sur la Poésie Américaine de 1910 à 1920* (Paris, 1929).

Teele, R. E. *Through a Glass Darkly: A Study of English Translations of Chinese Poetry* (Ann Arbor, 1949).

———. "Translations of Noh Plays," *Comparative Literature*, IX, 4 (Fall 1957), 345–368.

Tennyson. *The Early Poems of Alfred Lord Tennyson*, ed. J. C. Collins (1900).

Terhune, A. McK. *The Life of Edward Fitzgerald* (1947).

Thompson. *The Works of Francis Thompson* (1913), vol. 1.

Thorley, W. "To Madame Lullin," *New Age*, XVI, 26 (April 29, 1915), 702.

Thornton, R. K. R. "The Poets of the Rhymers' Club," unpublished M.A. thesis, University of Manchester, 1961.

Tibullus. *See* Catullus.

Vallas, L. *Claude Debussy* (1933).

Vidal. *Les Poésies de Peire Vidal*, ed. J. Anglade (Paris, 1913).

Villon, F. *Œuvres*, ed. A. Longnon, rev. L. Foulet (Paris, 1932).

Virgil. Ed. and trans. H. R. Fairclough (Loeb Classical Library, 1934–1935 [1916, 1918]). 2 vols.

Voltaire. *Œuvres Choisies*, ed. G. Bengesco (Paris, 1889), vol. 6.

Wagner, G. *Wyndham Lewis: A Portrait of the Artist as the Enemy* (1957).

Waley, A. *A Hundred and Seventy Chinese Poems* (1918).

———. *The Book of Songs* (Boston and New York, 1937).

———. *The Poetry and Career of Li Po, 701–762 A.D.* (1950).

West, T. W. "D. G. Rossetti and Ezra Pound," *Review of English Studies*, n.s., IV, 13 (Jan. 1953), 63–67.

Williams, W. C. *Kora in Hell* (New York, 1920).

Witemeyer, H. H. "Ezra Pound's Poetry, 1908–1916," unpublished Ph.D. dissertation, University of Princeton, 1966.

Yeats. *The Variorum Edition of the Poems of W. B. Yeats*, ed. P. Allt and R. K. Alspach (New York, 1957).

———. "William Butler Yeats to American Poets," *Little Review*, I, 2 (April 1914), 47–48.

———. *Autobiographies* (1955).